THE CIA IN ECUADOR

AMERICAN ENCOUNTERS/GLOBAL INTERACTIONS

A series edited by

Gilbert M. Joseph and Penny Von Eschen

The series aims to stimulate critical perspectives and fresh interpretive frameworks for scholarship on the history of the imposing global presence of the United States. Its primary concerns include the deployment and contestation of power, the construction and deconstruction of cultural and political borders, the fluid meaning of intercultural encounters, and the complex interplay between the global and the local. American Encounters seeks to strengthen dialogue and collaboration between historians of U.S. international relations and area studies specialists.

The series encourages scholarship based on multi-archive historical research. At the same time, it supports a recognition of the representational character of all stories about the past and promotes critical inquiry into issues of subjectivity and narrative. In the process, American Encounters strives to understand the context in which meanings related to nations, cultures, and political economy are continually produced, challenged, and reshaped.

The CIA in Ecuador

Marc Becker

DUKE UNIVERSITY PRESS

DURHAM AND LONDON

2020

Typeset in Garamond Premier Pro by PageMajik

Library of Congress Cataloging-in-Publication Data
Names: Becker, Marc (Professor of history), author.
Title: The CIA in Ecuador / Marc Becker.
Other titles: American encounters/global interactions.
Description: Durham: Duke University Press, 2021. |
Series: American encounters/global interactions |
Includes bibliographical references and index.
Identifiers: LCCN 2020021175 (print)
LCCN 2020021176 (ebook)
ISBN 9781478010357 (hardcover)
ISBN 9781478011385 (paperback)
ISBN 9781478012993 (ebook)
Subjects: LCSH: United States. Central Intelligence Agency—Ecuador. |
Ecuador—Politics and government—20th century. |
Ecuador—Relations—United States. | United States—Relations—Ecuador.
Classification: LCC JL3029.16 B435 2021 (print) | LCC JL3029.16 (ebook) |
DDC 327.1273/086609045—dc23
LC record available at https://lccn.loc.gov/2020021175
LC ebook record available at https://lccn.loc.gov/2020021176

Cover illustration by Skillet Gilmore.

S|H
M|P

The Sustainable History Monograph Pilot

Opening up the Past, Publishing for the Future

This book is published as part of the Sustainable History Monograph Pilot. With the generous support of the Andrew W. Mellon Foundation, the Pilot uses cutting-edge publishing technology to produce open access digital editions of high-quality, peer-reviewed monographs from leading university presses. Free digital editions can be downloaded from: Books at JSTOR, EBSCO, Hathi Trust, Internet Archive, OAPEN, Project MUSE, and many other open repositories.

When you cite the book, please include the following URL for its Digital Object Identifier (DOI): https://doi.org/10.1215/9781478012993

We are eager to learn more about how you discovered this title and how you are using it. We hope you will spend a few minutes answering a couple of questions at this url: **https://www.longleafservices.org/shmp-survey/**

More information about the Sustainable History Monograph Pilot can be found at https://www.longleafservices.org.

COLOMBIA
CARCHI
ESMERALDAS
Pacific
Ocean
IMBABURA
Otavalo
Cayambe
SUCUMBIOS
PICHINCHA
Quito
NAPO
Tigua
Latacunga
ORELLANA
MANABI
COTOPAXI
Guaranda
TUNGURAHUA
LOS
RIOS
BOLIVAR
Riobamba
PASTAZA
GUAYAS
CHIMBORAZO
Milagro
Guayaquil
CAÑAR
MORONA-SANTIAGO
Cuenca
AZUAY
EL ORO
ECUADOR
SOUTH
AMERICA
LOJA
ZAMORA-
CHINCHIPE
PERU

CONTENTS

Abbreviations ix

Introduction
War of the Worlds 1

CHAPTER 1
Postwar Left 10

CHAPTER 2
CIA 26

CHAPTER 3
Coups 39

CHAPTER 4
Moscow Gold 54

CHAPTER 5
Divisions 69

CHAPTER 6
Transitions 93

CHAPTER 7
Populism 110

CHAPTER 8
Dissension 129

CHAPTER 9
Everyday Forms of Organization 160

CHAPTER 10
Communist Threats 184

CHAPTER 11
Resurgent Left 207

Conclusion
1959 233

Notes 251

Bibliography 295

Index 305

ABBREVIATIONS

ADN	Alianza Democrática Nacional (National Democratic Alliance)
AFE	Alianza Femenina Ecuatoriana (Ecuadorian Women's Alliance)
AFL	American Federation of Labor
ARNE	Acción Revolucionaria Nacionalista Ecuatoriana (Ecuadorian Nationalist Revolutionary Action)
CAS	Controlled American Source
CFP	Concentración de Fuerzas Populares (Concentration of Popular Forces)
CIA	Central Intelligence Agency
CIC	Counter Intelligence Corps
CIG	Central Intelligence Group
COB	Chief of Base
COS	Chief of Station
Cominform	Communist Information Bureau
CPSU	Communist Party of the Soviet Union
CPUSA	Communist Party of the United States of America
CREST	CIA Records Search Tool
CTAL	Confederación de Trabajadores de América Latina (Confederation of Latin American Workers)
CTE	Confederación de Trabajadores del Ecuador (Confederation of Ecuadorian Workers)
DCI	Director of Central Intelligence
FAS	Foreign Agricultural Service
FBI	Federal Bureau of Investigation
FDN	Frente Democrático Nacional (National Democratic Front)
FEI	Federación Ecuatoriana de Indios (Ecuadorian Federation of Indians)
FEUE	Federación de Estudiantes Universitarios del Ecuador (Federation of Ecuadorian University Students)

FEV	Frente Electoral Velasquista (Velasquist Electoral Front)
FOIA	Freedom of Information Act
FPTG	Federación Provincial de Trabajadores del Guayas (Provincial Federation of Workers of Guayas)
FTP	Federación de Trabajadores de Pichincha (Pichincha Workers Federation)
ICA	International Cooperation Administration
IMF	International Monetary Fund
IUS	International Union of Students
JCE	Juventud Comunista del Ecuador (Young Communists of Ecuador)
JCF	Juventud Comunista Femenina (Young Communist Women)
MCDN	Movimiento Cívico Democrático Nacional (National Democratic Civic Movement)
MIR	Movimiento de Izquierda Revolucionaria (Movement of the Revolutionary Left)
MNR	Movimiento Nacionalista Revolucionario (Revolutionary Nationalist Movement)
MSC	Movimiento Social Cristiano (Social Christian Movement)
NARA	US National Archives and Records Administration
NATO	North Atlantic Treaty Organization
OAS	Organization of American States
OIR	Office of Intelligence Research
OSA	Office of South American Affairs
OSS	Office of Strategic Services
PAO	Public Affairs Officer
PC	Partido Conservador (Conservative Party)
PCC	Partido Comunista de Colombia (Communist Party of Colombia)
PCE	Partido Comunista del Ecuador (Communist Party of Ecuador)
PCMLE	Partido Comunista Marxista Leninista del Ecuador (Marxist–Leninist Communist Party of Ecuador)
PLR	Partido Liberal Radical (Radical Liberal Party)
PSE	Partido Socialista Ecuatoriano (Ecuadorian Socialist Party)
PSRE	Partido Socialista Revolucionario del Ecuador (Socialist Revolutionary Party of Ecuador)

SAIIC	South and Meso American Indian Rights Center
UDE	Unión Democrática Universitaria (University Democratic Union)
UDNA	Unión Democrática Nacional Anti-Conservadora (National Democratic Anti-Conservative Union)
UPR	Unión Popular Republicana (Republican Popular Union—renamed CFP)
URJE	Unión Revolucionaria de la Juventud Ecuatoriana (Revolutionary Union of the Ecuadorian Youth)
URME	Unión Revolucionaria de Mujeres del Ecuador (Revolutionary Union of Ecuadorian Women)
USAID	US Agency for International Development
USD	United States Dollar
USIA	United States Information Agency
USIE	United States Information and Educational Exchange
USIS	United States Information Service
USOM	United States Operations Mission
VM	Vencer o Morir (Win or Die)
VRSE	Vanguardia Revolucionaria del Socialismo Ecuatoriano (Ecuadorian Revolutionary Socialist Vanguard)
WFDY	World Federation of Democratic Youth
WFTU	World Federation of Trade Unions
WPC	World Peace Council

Introduction

War of the Worlds

At 9 p.m. on Saturday, February 12, 1949, a breathless announcer interrupted a popular musical program on Radio Quito with the urgent breaking news of a Martian landing at Cotocallao on the northern edge of the Ecuadorian city. A reporter on the scene provided a terrifying description of the death and destruction that aliens were leaving in their wake as they advanced on the capital. The minister of government came on the air to urge calm in order to facilitate the evacuation of the city. The mayor told women and children to flee to the surrounding mountains, and called on the men to defend the city. Church bells tolled in warning, and listeners could hear a priest begging for divine intervention. Frightened citizens, some only in their pajamas, rushed into the streets in panic thinking that the world was coming to an end. A stream of police cars with their sirens blaring and lights flashing rushed north to Cotocallao to battle the Martian invasion.

If this narrative sounds familiar, it is because local producers adapted this radio depiction of H. G. Wells's classic novel *The War of the Worlds* from Orson Welles's broadcast of October 30, 1938, that claimed that aliens from Mars had invaded New Jersey. That airing terrified thousands in the United States, but the outcome in Ecuador was far worse.

Welles had informed his listeners that the broadcast was radio theater, but his Ecuadorian counterparts did not bother with those niceties. The radio station only belatedly explained that the broadcast was a hoax. Officials pleaded for people to remain calm, but watched helplessly as the crowd's fear turn to rage with the realization that they had been duped. The mob descended on the radio station and set it ablaze. Because the police had gone to Cotocallao, the government called in the military to restore order. The army responded with tanks and tear gas to disperse the crowd, but not before the station was reduced to rubble with the besieged staff of one hundred still inside. Some managed to escape out of a rear exit, but others were trapped on upper floors. As many as fifteen charred bodies lay in the wreckage. The daily newspaper *El Comercio*, Quito's oldest newspaper, owned the radio station and was located in the same building. The fire destroyed the newspaper's presses and files, and for three days it was not able to publish. When the paper resumed distribution, it was thanks only to the generosity of their competitor *El Día* who lent them their printing press.[1]

The communists had nothing to do with the broadcast or the resulting riot and ruin, but that did not stop the Central Intelligence Agency (CIA) from assuming that radicals must have been behind the mayhem. After all, the events matched the agency's preconceived notions of how communists operated. Rather than engaging in a serious political program to build a better world, US government officials charged that the communists were subversives bent on death and destruction designed to disrupt the smooth functioning of society. For that reason, the CIA was on the lookout for communist inspiration or instigation of violent events. In this case, however, the agency concluded that the riot had no political undertones, nor did any evidence emerge that it was communist-inspired. From an investigation into "sources inside the higher echelon of the National Headquarters of the Ecuadoran Communist Party in Quito," the CIA concluded that the communists were not aware in advance of the broadcast, nor did they have plans to exploit the carnage left in its wake. In fact, according to the CIA's sources, two communists lost their lives in the fire.[2]

Few people today remember or know about the broadcast of "The War of the Worlds" in Quito, but the CIA report speaks volumes on both the pervasiveness of US surveillance operations as well as the potential possibilities, boundaries, and obstacles to their knowledge and understanding of leftist movements in Latin America. United States officials were determined to implicate the communists in coup plots as they repeatedly pointed to external support for subversive movements. This included the fabled search for "Moscow gold" even as they were never able to find any concrete evidence to support their charges. Their investigations were ultimately misguided as they failed to comprehend the domestic roots of radical critiques of society. At the same time, CIA surveillance offers glimpses into internal debates within the communist party, and presents an opportunity to gain unique insights into the actions and thoughts of those involved in leftist, labor, and other social movements that challenged US hegemony in the region. The resolutions and platforms that emerged out of their congresses and other meetings illustrate the presence of intense discussion and a deep commitment to advancing a political agenda. Communists sought to empower marginalized workers and peasants to enable them to assume control over society—and this posed a threat to the economic interests of United States corporations, as well as those of the domestic ruling class in Latin America.

Disempowered people imagined another world without racial discrimination, sexual violence, and economic exploitation, one in which they democratically made decisions as to how they would run their lives. Examining the actions and motivations of communists who supported these struggles and the challenges that they confronted provides an opportunity to analyze the emergence of mass popular movements dedicated to the creation of a more just and equal society.

The artistic directors of the "The War of the Worlds" did not intend for the radio play to be an allegory on the cold war, but it was broadcast in that environment. The events of that Saturday night soon disappeared from the pages of the newspapers, but they reflected a much larger clash, as the socialist economist Manuel Agustín Aguirre would put it later that year, between two worlds and two different types of economies. On one hand was the current liberal, capitalist, laisse faire economy with all of its problems, and on the other hand the promises of a centrally planned socialist one. Capitalism had abandoned people to the blind forces of the market, whereas socialism promised to introduce a rational economic system that would lead to the liberation of humanity. "Slavery and freedom: two opposed and opposite worlds," Aguirre concluded. "It does not seem difficult to choose between them." The conflict would lead to a confrontation between two different worldviews, but Aguirre was optimistic that ultimately the future was bright.[3]

That the United States government would intervene in the internal affairs of a Latin American country to undermine the realization of such lofty goals comes as no surprise to scholars and even casual observers of the region. In 1950, the State Department readily admitted that it sought "to combat this Communist threat" in the region. It did so even as it claimed that the United States government adhered to a policy of nonintervention in the internal affairs of other countries.[4] Such high-minded declarations were obviously rhetorical and self-serving, as the long history of United States involvement in Latin America immediately makes apparent. Only four years later, Dwight Eisenhower's administration supported a military coup in Guatemala to overthrow the popularly elected Jacobo Arbenz government, followed by attempts to assassinate Rafael Trujillo in the Dominican Republic and Fidel Castro in Cuba.[5]

The goal of this book is not to document or analyze these interventions, nor to parse out the semantic differences between what an advocate might present as international solidarity versus what an opponent would denounce as imperial endeavors. Rather, as with my previous book on the Federal Bureau of Investigation (FBI) in Latin America during the Second World War, my intent is to use information that the CIA and other United States agencies gathered in the postwar period to document progressive movements for social change in a context where few other sources exist.[6] Even with all of the inherent limitations of foreign agencies, their extensive surveillance networks provided effective coverage of internal developments in Latin America. While one might question the wisdom or rationale behind those investigations, they do leave historians with a remarkable documentary record through which scholars can reconstruct the history of the left.

Surveillance

The postwar left in Latin America has been the subject of relatively little academic study. In comparison to the size of protest movements in the 1940s and 1960s, leftist mobilizations during the 1950s can appear small and insignificant. Even participants largely ignore those years in their memoirs, preferring to skip from the excitement of the mid-1940s antidictatorial battles to the intensity of the 1960s guerrilla insurrections.[7] Organizational capacity declined during these years, particularly from its height during a postwar democratic spring. This was due to a variety of factors, including cold war paranoia of communist subversion that led to a suppression of popular organizing efforts. The external ideological and economic interests of United States capitalists intermingled with those of the domestic ruling class in Latin America and reinforced a common agenda of repressing leftist aspirations. Furthermore, the emphasis that orthodox communist parties placed on peaceful paths to power contributed to the disappearance of 1950s activism from scholarly treatments and hence from popular memory as well. A result, as the scholar of social movements Hernán Ibarra observes, is a decade that has received little academic or popular attention.[8]

Despite this lack of study, making sense of organizational developments between the Second World War and the Cuban Revolution (what I term here as "the 1950s") is critical to gaining a better appreciation for the heightened level of militant mobilizations in the 1960s. The sociologist Floresmilo Simbaña has called the 1970s and 1980s the "worst" studied decades in Ecuador, not in the sense of a lack of studies but because the investigations that scholars have undertaken do not adequately account for the degree of social movement organizing during those years that influenced subsequent and much more visible political developments in the 1990s. His argument is that to understand contemporary Indigenous mobilizations properly, we need a better comprehension of the organizing activities that laid the groundwork for them.[9] Indigenous activists celebrate the 1990s as a "gained decade" in terms of large protests, but those participants could not have realized those achievements were it not for advances in grassroots organizing efforts during the 1980s, even though those years are remembered as a "lost decade."[10] Similarly, political activism in the 1960s can only be properly understood if we have a clear analysis of what preceded it during the 1950s. Intense and continual organizing efforts in the years after the Second World War laid the groundwork for subsequent militant mobilizations that would not have happened were it not for those earlier, less visible actions. Political strength does not emerge out of a vacuum, but is built on much longer organizational trajectories.[11]

Even though the 1950s represents a void in studies of Ecuador's social mobilizations, it is not objectively speaking a decade during which nothing happened. Militant leftists remained actively involved in a wide range of political movements and engaged in intense debates over how to transform their society. Much as the neoliberal 1980s provide an important context for understanding heightened levels of Indigenous protest in the 1990s and the advances of the pink tide in the 2000s, the conservative 1950s are key for a proper interpretation of the radical and turbulent 1960s. Without an appreciation for the context that a longer trajectory of social movement organizing provides, subsequent militant actions can appear to be an aberration rather than the result of sustained political engagement.

One explanation for a lack of adequate studies of the 1950s is a paucity of sources that chronicle social movement activities. As a reflection of this absence, Ibarra only includes one document from the 1950s in his impressive anthology on the communist left from 1928 to 1961.[12] This lack of written material is part of a broader phenomenon among progressive activists. Brad Duncan sought to chronicle the printed legacy of the US radical left in the 1970s in his book *Finally Got the News*. In an interview, Duncan comments:

> Most participants never kept any of those flyers, because ultimately they were organizing tools meant to mobilize people for specific events. So they're by definition ephemeral, which is why almost no one keeps them, which makes studying the history of radical movements more difficult. We know that our enemies want to erase this history. So do your part for people's history and don't throw away a damn thing.[13]

As I note in my previous book on the FBI, activists rarely took the time, or had the inclination, to record their actions. This is particularly the case when repressive governments could use that information to prosecute them. Militants sometimes destroyed their own archival records rather than being caught red-handed with incriminating evidence. Military regimes, furthermore, routinely burned subversive material because they feared its contents. As a result, little communist party material from the 1950s survived in Ecuador.

In the absence of other sources of information, police surveillance can provide an important opportunity to reconstruct the history of popular movements. They allow scholars to see and understand aspects of this history that government agencies were not looking for or did not find particularly important or interesting. As such, these records have remained underutilized and undertheorized as a window through which to critique social movement challenges to exclusionary government structures.[14] In my previous book, I drew on FBI counterintelligence documents that I serendipitously discovered among State Department records to write a history of the political left in Ecuador during the 1940s. Long before the cold war, FBI director J. Edgar Hoover famously maintained a paranoid and irrational fear of communism and that fixation carried over when Franklin D. Roosevelt extended the bureau's mandate to include Latin America. With the signing of the National Security Act of 1947, those surveillance operations moved from the purview of the FBI to the newly created CIA. Unsurprisingly, intelligence gathering continued without a break under the new agency, seemingly utilizing the same tactics, drawing on the same sources, and perhaps even employing the same agents. The CIA perpetuated Hoover's anticommunist agenda without pause, even though, as with the FBI, its officers reported on the presence of weak and small parties that provided little threat to United States security concerns.[15]

While governments typically establish agencies such as the CIA for the collection and analysis of intelligence, they tend to drift into covert operations instead.[16] Much has been written about the CIA's attempts to subvert democracy in pursuit of the US government's imperial agenda, and little need exists to revisit that history here.[17] Nor is that the purpose of this study. Rather, another aspect of the agency's work provides scholars with a rich fount of information on the social and political history of other countries. Whereas anticommunist operatives might plant fraudulent documents and advance derogatory narratives to undermine their opponents, if functioning properly those who gathered intelligence would seek to create an accurate and unfiltered record of political events, especially since these documents would be only for internal use rather than public dissemination as propaganda tools.[18] A review of CIA documentation before it drifted into covert regime change operations reveals a preponderance of items about Latin American from the late 1940s and early 1950s that contain a wealth of information on domestic developments. This book mines the massive archive that the CIA and other agencies created, not for what it can tell us about those agencies or United States policy objectives and decisions, but rather what we can learn from the activities that government officials investigated.

In 2000, the CIA released some of their declassified intelligence documents in redacted form in the CIA Records Search Tool (CREST) database at the US National Archives and Records Administration (NARA) at College Park, Maryland. Although advertised as a publicly accessible repository of CIA records, in reality the material was available only on a limited basis on a stand-alone workstation that was not always operational. In January 2017, the CIA published the records of the CREST collection online in their Freedom of Information Act (FOIA) Electronic Reading Room that provides for their easier and wider dissemination. The release of these and other CIA surveillance documents fill in gaps in a context where few other sources exist, and as such offer scholars an excellent opportunity to explore the history of the Latin American left in more depth than was previously possible. This study turns to these artifacts to chart social movement organizing efforts during a "lost decade" of political activism during the 1950s.[19]

My training is as a social historian, and this book does not purport to be a diplomatic study, nor is it particularly concerned with national security issues, United States policies, or the intricacies of intelligence gathering (although, of course, by necessity it is framed by those investigations).[20] The diplomatic historian Alan McPherson has quipped, "The more historians find out about the Cold War in the hemisphere, the more that Cold War itself fades to the background."[21] That paradox holds true for this work. It is not specifically about the cold war per se, except that chronologically the period it covers corresponds with the first decade of what historians have traditionally understood to be the cold war. My concern is not US-USSR relations, but instead how activists in Latin America advanced an alternative vision of how to organize the world. It shares with the historian Greg Grandin an understanding of this epoch as a sociological process and historical experience that is best interpreted through the lens of intellectual history and bottom-up mobilizations.[22] And, in that fashion, it does directly engage issues of a capitalist versus socialist mode of production that was at the heart of the cold war. The cold war was peripheral to the events chronicled in this book even as that larger political context profoundly informed and prescribed the world in which militants operated.

Toward a Deeper Study

CIA documentation provides an especially important opportunity to explore a variety of issues that communists as well as the broader left faced in the early postwar period, with ramifications that extend well beyond both that time frame and the borders of Latin America. While both United States and Latin American government officials could be blinded by their own anticommunist assumptions and attitudes, the information that they assembled offers a unique opportunity to delve deeply into the internal workings of communist parties. While the communist party in Ecuador was never particularly large or strong, its members struggled with universal issues of organization, strategy, and tactics as they sought to advance their political agenda. In the process these militants created the conditions for heightened levels of political activism in the 1960s. Advances during the 1950s were very much part of a longer trajectory of active engagement that has either been lost or largely forgotten. Although politically antagonistic to communism and the left in general, CIA surveillance provides convincing documentation of the persistence of social movement organizing during that decade. The data that CIA officers generated allows us to push at the edges of our knowledge and understanding of how communists operated, in Ecuador and elsewhere.

The opening of the Third or Communist International (Comintern) archives in the aftermath of the collapse of the Soviet Union contributed to an explosion of studies of local communist parties. As the historian Barry Carr aptly notes, most of these studies examine the period from the creation of the Comintern in 1919 to its formal closing in 1943. Access to available sources inform and constrain many of these studies, particularly with an abundance of material in the Comintern archive from the 1920s through the first half of the 1930s, after which the volume drops off noticeably. Carr observes, "As a result of this imbalance we know much more about the development of Latin American communism during its first two decades than over the last four or five decades of its evolution." He calls for studies that explore local parties in the aftermath of the closure of the Comintern, particularly during the onset of the cold war.[23]

Not only do we need better examinations of the postwar period, but we also need to understand variations both between parties in different countries and among disparate political tendencies within a single country. Despite being organized as national parties of a centralized movement, communists never functioned in a univocal fashion. Carr states, "We have to distinguish between the policies and prescriptions elaborated by the directorates of political parties ('the policy of the Central Committee') and the actions of the members and cadres in the local cells and committees." Carr urges us to think of *communisms*—in the plural—to understand better how these ideologies and strategies were debated, and the influences that peripheral actors had on the formation of centralized policies. This approach also acknowledges and incorporates expressions that were not part of the pro-Soviet communist party, including other leftist tendencies such as anarchist, socialist, Trotskyist, Maoist, social democratic, and left-liberal parties.[24]

My work takes up Carr's call by delving into crucial events in Ecuador. Both politically and historiographically this country existed on the periphery of CIA operations and US-Latin American relations and the cold war itself. Even so, significant and broader issues of political strategies and strategic alliances that have long plagued the left played out during the postwar period in Ecuador, and are worthy of a deep and penetrating study.

By no means is the CIA documentation perfect. CIA history staff member Woodrow Kuhns excuses the intelligence agency's failures. "Dramatic, sweeping events, such as wars and revolutions, are far too complex to predict or analyze perfectly," he states.[25] A more fundamental problem is the underlying political agenda that drove its intelligence collection efforts and colored its perspectives and analyses. A large part of the dissident CIA officer Ralph McGehee's complaint about the agency with which he worked for a quarter century was the disinformation campaigns that attempted to mold public opinion, and the manufacture of false intelligence to justify policies and advance institutional or personal interests.[26] These shortcomings, however, are the limitations of any historical documentation. Even with all of their inherent deficiencies, these surveillance records present scholars with penetrating insights into the struggles and difficulties that the Latin American left confronted in the postwar period. Inadvertently, they highlight how activists responded to the challenges and opportunities that they encountered. More sources are better than no sources, and as historians we work with the sources we have rather than the ones we wish we had. It is in this context that the opening of long-closed archives and the release of declassified documentation have led to calls to reexamine the cold war, as "not only a possibility but a necessity."[27] This book contributes to that larger historiographic project.

CHAPTER 1

Postwar Left

THE LATIN AMERICAN LEFT should have emerged from the Second World War in a strengthened position. Objectively, many factors played to their advantage. The left's archenemy, fascism, had been resoundingly defeated in the war. The Soviet Union momentarily enjoyed warm relations with the other Allied powers, thanks in large part to the leadership role it had taken in defeating the Nazis in Germany. Many hoped that a United States-Soviet Union alliance could bring peace to a war-weary world. The international political environment had decisively shifted against dictatorship, leading to unprecedented political openings in Latin America that provided the left with more breathing room than it had ever previously enjoyed. A brief period of calm between the Second World War and the onset of the cold war allowed for the flourishing of democracy in Latin America as elected civilian governments replaced authoritarian dictatorships.[1] In this environment, leftists across the Americas participated in governments, including joining cabinets in Chile, Cuba, and Ecuador. An embrace of a peaceful and electoral path to power seemed to be bearing fruit.

Neither the CIA nor the communists operated in a political vacuum. In order to comprehend fully how Ecuadorian communists and the left in general fared in this environment, including the types of programs they advanced and the obstacles they faced in doing so, we must first step back and look at the broader context in which they operated. This includes an overview of the different political parties and social forces that existed in the country, and how the left responded to a rather unique (both for Ecuador in general as well as for Latin America at the time) succession of elected civilian governments.

This chapter provides an empirical grounding on which to build an understanding of how communists rose to the challenges they encountered, and how their actions allowed them to build a base for subsequent triumphs and advances. A primary concern was the construction of electoral alliances to gain a larger voice in the midst of shifting political landscapes. A countervailing tendency insisted that their struggle should be rooted in peasant and working-class organizations. Electoral versus social movement strategies (in addition to an option for armed struggle) have long divided the left, and Ecuador in the 1950s was no exception—nor were the debates that surrounded these issues extraordinary. Rather, Ecuadorian communists faced many of the same threats and opportunities that activists around the world have long confronted as they fought to end economic exploitation, racial discrimination, and social injustice.

Cold War

The anticommunist cold war historian and State Department analyst Rollie Poppino observes, "The acceptance and respectability of communism in Latin America reached a peak in the years between 1944 and 1947." He continues, "Communist parties generally were in a stronger position than they had ever enjoyed, and their over-all membership soared to heights they have since been unable to equal." Communists gained adherents and sympathizers "because their programs seemed to promise fulfillment in Latin America of the popular aspirations for a better life and personal and political liberties that figured so prominently among the war aims of the Allies." The control they exercised in labor movements reflected the level of support for their political and economic programs both locally and internationally.[2]

The liberal political scientist Robert Alexander who collaborated closely with State Department and labor officials in the United States on their anticommunist campaigns expressed a similar analysis. During 1945 and 1946, he acknowledges, "Latin American Communists were at the zenith of their power and influence." Not only did they operate legally in most countries, they also had elected members to local governments as well as federal legislatures in about half of the countries in the hemisphere. With their participation in the Chilean cabinet, they "seemed well on the way to achieving the first Communist government of the hemisphere." With that victory, others were sure to follow.[3]

Despite all of these advantages, communists soon became marginalized. A period that should have represented a shift to the political left, unprecedented labor militancy, and a consolidation of democratic governance instead ended with suppression of communist parties, repression of labor movements, the exclusion of the left from politics, and a dramatic swing to the right with the installation of military juntas and heightened levels of political violence.

Poppino notes that "tactical blunders and embarrassing revelations" alone do not account for the dramatic fall in prestige. He points as well to "the actions of political adversaries and hostile governments which destroyed the respectability of the party, cut into the sources of Communist strength, and appeared to eliminate Communist political influence in most of Latin America." This included successful attempts to wrest control of labor and student organizations from the communists. Conservatives removed communists from office, outlawed their parties, and closed their newspapers. In this repressive environment, party strength declined precipitously along with a rise in military and authoritarian dictatorships. These regimes championed their anticommunist credentials in part "to win favor or to forestall criticism from the United States," but also to eliminate domestic opposition to their hold on power. In short, according to Poppino, "Communist fortunes declined as rapidly as they had risen."[4] As the cold war reached deeper into Latin America, these conflicts became ever more intense.

Political Parties and Social Movements

A traditional interpretation of Latin American political structures presents them as built on a triad of forces that include the *latifundia* or land-holding system, the military, and the Catholic Church. British ambassador Norman Mayers expanded on that definition to identify the principle power players in Ecuador in the 1950s as the military, the church, bankers, certain families, labor organizations, universities, and the cultural center known as the Casa de la Cultura (House of Culture). Governments were ultimately beholden to the will of the armed forces, the ambassador noted. The Catholic Church remained "the main supporter and organizer of conservatism," and held "considerable control" over that political party. Bankers exercised particular influence on the coast. Families were either conservative or liberal, and Mayers listed the most important names (as will become apparent in this book) as Plaza, Jijón, Chiriboga, Estrada, and Ycaza. "Religion, nationalism and family are still strong conceptions and values in this old-fashioned country," the ambassador commented, even with an ever-present undercurrent of nineteenth-century liberal anticlericalism. The traditional powerbrokers were all of European heritage. "The Indians are apart and their values unknown," the ambassador reported.[5] Those of African descent did not even warrant a mention, and only men registered in his calculations.

As with the rest of Latin America, battles between conservative and liberal parties defined the nineteenth-century political landscape. Scholars generally recognize Gabriel García Moreno, who embraced a fanatical adherence to Catholic doctrine and was president from 1861 to 1865 and again from 1869 to 1875, as the initiator of modern conservatism in Ecuador. He founded the Partido

Conservador (PC, Conservative Party) in 1869 and attempted to install a theocratic though modernizing state that included massive road and railway-building projects.[6] Eloy Alfaro, who seized power in an 1895 revolution, was the principal figure behind Ecuadorian liberalism. That same year he founded the Partido Liberal Radical (PLR, Radical Liberal Party). Alfaro stripped the Catholic Church of the powers and privileges it had enjoyed under García Moreno, and implemented a wide variety of social reforms. Liberals subsequently held dominance over Ecuador's politics for the next half-century.[7]

Socialists established Ecuador's third traditional party (after the liberals and conservatives), the Partido Socialista Ecuatoriano (PSE, Ecuadorian Socialist Party), in 1926 in the aftermath of a military coup on July 9, 1925, known as the *revolución juliana* or July revolution. A cadre of young progressive military officers—who had become disillusioned with what they condemned as a corrupt and opportunistic coastal liberal oligarchy who were unable to bring about any real change—led that revolt. In power, they introduced a series of modernizing social reforms.[8] The socialist left soon fractured, particularly over the issue of whether to affiliate with the Moscow-based Comintern that Vladimir Lenin had created to lead a global revolution. At its second congress in 1931, party leader Ricardo Paredes who favored such affiliation formally transitioned the PSE into the Partido Comunista del Ecuador (PCE, Communist Party of Ecuador). Socialists who opposed subjecting party policies to external control regrouped in 1933 to launch a new socialist party with the previous name PSE. A third group comprised primarily of progressive military officials constituted the Vanguardia Revolucionaria del Socialismo Ecuatoriano (VRSE, Ecuadorian Revolutionary Socialist Vanguard).[9] These rival leftist groups sometimes collaborated with one another, and at times fought for the allegiance of their peasant and working-class base. Often they formed alliances with liberals, most commonly as the Frente Democrático Nacional (FDN, National Democratic Front) or a variation thereof.

In the 1950s, the political landscape became more complicated than the traditional tripartite division into conservative, liberal, and socialist parties, particularly with the rise of personalist and populist movements.[10] Expanded literacy rates brought new voters into the electoral process, which should have expanded the left's base of support, but instead these new political groupings gained their allegiance. At the time, political scientists identified populists running personalist campaigns as the primary characteristic of the country's political system.[11] The most significant and long lasting of these was the *Velasquista* movement that backed the perennial populist José María Velasco Ibarra in his various campaigns for the presidency. Velasco Ibarra was a political chameleon who made a career out of campaigning on promises to govern on behalf of the poor. Once in office, however, he betrayed their interests and ruled instead in favor of the oligarchy. As a result, he managed to finish only the third (1952–56) of his five terms in office. He assumed the presidency for the first time in 1934 with conservative support, but failed to complete a full year before popular opposition to his policies led to his removal. He returned the second time in the aftermath of a May 1944 revolution. Optimistic hopes for the creation of a more inclusive and just society fell under his sway, but his conservative populism and authoritarian style so alienated the population that his defense minister Carlos Mancheno removed and exiled him in an August 1947 coup. Velasco Ibarra's last two times in office (1960–61 and 1968–72) similarly resulted in military governments. As with Peronism in Argentina, Velasco Ibarra's coalition was not ideologically coherent and found itself divided into various wings with competing interests.[12]

Galo Plaza Lasso formed the Movimiento Cívico Democrático Nacional (MCDN, National Democratic Civic Movement) in 1948 as a vehicle for his electoral aspirations. The MCDN, and the Plaza family in general, had an uneasy relationship with the liberals with whom they competed for votes. On an opposing pole of the political spectrum, in 1951 Camilo Ponce Enríquez and Sixto Durán Ballén founded the Movimiento Social Cristiano (MSC, Social Christian Movement) that quickly displaced the PC as the main right wing force in the country—and the only grouping from this period to survive as a potent political force into the twenty-first century. Although conservatives in whatever form comprised the largest single political party in the 1950s, with their roots in narrow aristocratic interests they never managed to poll a majority of the vote.

In 1942, Jorge Luna Yepes founded the Acción Revolucionaria Nacionalista Ecuatoriana (ARNE, Ecuadorian Nationalist Revolutionary Action) as a "third way" movement that opposed both "Yankee imperialist capitalism" and "Bolshevik Marxist imperialism," as well as both the conservative and liberal parties. Spanish falangist and Italian fascist movements strongly influenced its ideology. It drew support from conservative Catholics; embraced "hispanismo," a celebration of Hispanic culture; and assumed extremely nationalist, authoritarian, hierarchical, and doctrinaire positions.[13] Opponents denounced the organization as comprised of thugs who formed shock troops to attack student activists, labor unions, and the press. The British consul James McAdam Clark described the ARNE as a small, nationalist organization that was "falangist in origin" with a tendency "to xenophobia and paramilitary training." The ARNE "seems to be quite well organized," Clark remarked, particularly in terms of its ability to infiltrate its members into positions of influence.[14] Although it was "weak in numbers," it was "loud in self-assertion."[15] The German-Ecuadorian writer Lilo Linke similarly described the group as a small but "aggressive and vociferous" force who embraced a militaristic style of organization.[16] Both the left and more established political parties feared the ARNE as a threat because of its extremist ideology and inflammatory tactics. The populist politician Velasco Ibarra, however, courted the support of the ARNE both in his 1952 presidential campaign and subsequently while in office, including naming its leader Nicolás Valdano Raffo as secretary-general of his administration. The British ambassador found the party to be "strange company for a President who claims to be liberal in his politics and lay in his convictions."[17] While naturally ARNE members would be attracted to Velasco Ibarra's caudillo style of leadership and could only gain from his popularity, his acceptance of their backing was a blatantly opportunistic move.

A populist party known as the Concentración de Fuerzas Populares (CFP, Concentration of Popular Forces) briefly threatened to become the dominant political force in Ecuador during the 1950s. Its leader Carlos Guevara Moreno initially joined the Unión Popular Republicana (UPR, Republican Popular Union) that Rafael Mendoza Avilés had created to campaign for mayor of Guayaquil in 1947. Mendoza lost that race, and two years later Guevara Moreno assumed control of the party and renamed it the CFP. Guevara Moreno supported Velasco Ibarra during both his second time in office in 1944 and again during his third term in 1952, but he tangled so badly with the president during both of those mandates that he end up exiled from the country. In between those two terms, Plaza imprisoned Guevara Moreno for a year after he led a failed coup attempt against his government. Despite Guevara Moreno's popularity in Guayaquil, his ambitious attempt to become Ecuador's leading caudillo eventually failed.

In 1931, Guevara Moreno together with Rafael Coello Serrano formed a group in Guayaquil that they called the Communist Party, Section of the Communist International. Guevara Moreno later joined an international brigade on the side of the Republicans in the Spanish Civil War, providing him with unmistakable leftist credentials. In 1945, as minister of government in Velasco Ibarra's administration, Guevara Moreno turned against his former comrades on the left and willingly resorted to violence and shock tactics to squelch all opposition. The *New York Times* aptly described Guevara Moreno as "a former Communist who turned against Moscow but is expert in the use of Communist techniques to sway the masses."[18] He used demagoguery and antisystemic rhetoric against persistent social and economic problems to appeal to the working class. At the same time, breaking with the communists led his former comrades to condemn him as an opportunist and traitor. PCE secretary general Paredes denounced the CFP as being financed by reactionary bankers and exporters who were closely associated with Yankee imperialism.[19] The competition for the same base of support led to the CFP becoming a principle opponent of the communists. No love was lost between the two forces.

In addition to these parties, several social movements played significant roles in shaping the political landscape in the 1950s. Most significant was the powerful leftist trade union federation Confederación de Trabajadores del Ecuador (CTE, Confederation of Ecuadorian Workers). The CTE sought to establish regional federations in each province, as well as connections with continental and global labor movements. The two most important provincial organizations were the Federación de Trabajadores de Pichincha (FTP, Pichincha Workers Federation) centered in the capital city of Quito in the highlands, and the Federación Provincial de Trabajadores del Guayas (FPTG, Provincial Federation of Workers of Guayas) based in the commercial center of Guayaquil on the coast. Under the leadership of socialists and communists, these federations assumed intensely nationalist and radical positions. The CTE also affiliated with the Mexico-based Confederación de Trabajadores de América Latina (CTAL, Confederation of Latin American Workers) as well as the World Federation of Trade Unions (WFTU).[20] A persistent goal of United States government officials was to break Ecuador's labor movements away from communist control.

In the rural highlands, the Federación Ecuatoriana de Indios (FEI, Ecuadorian Federation of Indians) became a dominant political force. Although in subsequent decades new organizations surpassed it in size and significance, the FEI was the first successful attempt in Ecuador, and indeed one of the first in the Americas, to establish a pan-ethnic federation for and by Indigenous peoples. The Alianza Femenina Ecuatoriana (AFE, Ecuadorian Women's Alliance) promoted the incorporation of women into political movements, supported the cause of world peace, and lent solidarity to victims of war. The militant Federación de Estudiantes Universitarios del Ecuador (FEUE, Federation of Ecuadorian University Students) provided the most important voice for students. The FEUE allied with the Prague-based International Union of Students (IUS). As with the labor federations, the United States Embassy and CIA engaged in a long campaign to sever student ties with communist-affiliated organizations.

Labor unions (in particular the CTE), universities, and the Casa de Cultura all tended to the left, with some members associated with the communist party. In May 1947, assistant military attaché Adelbert Boggs drafted a detailed thirteen-page report on the organization and operation of the PCE that summarizes the functioning of the party. Party headquarters were in Quito with an executive committee that oversaw daily operations. Regional committees operated on both the coast and in the highlands with six provincial committees under them. The base of the party was comprised of about sixty cells with a total estimated registered membership of five thousand (out of the country's population of three million). Cells ranged from 20 to 150 members, with an average of 40 to 50 in each. About half the cells (and about half the members) were located in Guayaquil, with Quito representing another sizable proportion. A bi-annual congress was the party's main decision-making body, with national and regional conferences meeting in the interim. Boggs estimated that 80 percent of the members were not active, but if sympathizers in labor unions, student groups, and among government employees were included the total could reach 20,000. Those numbers varied based on the whims of political opportunism and the current popularity of party leadership. The party sought to implement its program through the organization of labor unions that would contribute to the fostering of a Marxist class consciousness and the spreading of a communist ideology among workers and others in its base. Its primary objective was to gain power through legal means, specifically via engagement with the electoral process.[21] This emphasis on peaceful and gradual paths to power is what eventually led a radical wing to break from the party in the 1960s.

Intelligence estimates consistently repeated this figure of communist party strength at five thousand, a number that other operatives may have lifted from Boggs's report. In 1952, the State Department's Office of Intelligence Research (OIR) dropped that number to 2,500, noting that the main base of support still remained in Guayaquil and Quito. The significance of the change in numbers is not immediately apparent, if indeed those numbers represented anything more than rough guesses. A larger membership base would have allowed the PCE to register their party with electoral authorities, but that was not necessarily desirable because doing so would expose their members to government surveillance. Instead, a significant base of supporters favored dedicating their energies toward the mobilization of labor and other grassroots movements. According to the OIR, communists were "influential, but not dominant" in the CTE, and also exercised importance in transport and other industrial unions. Similarly, communists were influential but not dominant in student and teacher groups. The OIR also claimed that the PCE drew support from socialists through their front organizations, particularly in labor, student, cultural, and political activities.[22] The report presents an image of communist strength in Ecuador that was not necessarily out of line with what was the case in other Latin American countries.

While publicly United States officials and the Latin American ruling class exaggerated their fear of communism as they engaged in propaganda campaigns against the party's political agenda, in private correspondence individual diplomats sometimes painted a quite different picture. Henry Dearborn at the Ecuador desk in the State Department astutely observed in April 1947, "We have known that the Communist Party in Ecuador has been weak and futile for over a year." He noted that the party "shows little indication of recovering the relatively strong position which it had in 1944 and 1945."[23] In 1949, the embassy's labor attaché Benjamin Sowell similarly conceded in an internal memo that few communists were present in the country and that their actions did not justify close surveillance.[24] This phenomenon was not unique to Ecuador nor to Latin America. Around the world, communist parties faced struggles over leadership and conflicts over strategy, particularly between peaceful paths to power versus revolutionary violence and tension between submission to a Soviet political line and autonomous processes.[25]

In contrast, the British ambassador Mayers noted that even though the PCE was legal and only had about five thousand members, "these small numbers do not reflect its real strength and influence, which is greater than they would lead one to suppose."[26] Linke similarly stated that the PCE had survived "for many years mainly because of the perseverance of half a dozen persons who succeeded in obtaining the scanty backing of small workers' groups just sufficient to keep the party alive."[27] The ability for the PCE to punch above its weight is in part what makes it an important topic of study.

Popular Fronts

Coalition building has long been key to winning elections, but how and with whom to build alliances can be highly controversial. The 1928 sixth Comintern congress launched its "ultraleft" phase that advocated a "class against class" organizing strategy instead of working with other progressive forces. At the Comintern's seventh congress in 1935 and with a fascist threat looming on the horizon, Soviet leaders reversed course and returned to a previous policy of building coalitions with other sympathetic forces. In March 1934 and in anticipation of this policy change, communists in Ecuador began to appeal for a united front with vanguardists, socialists, and liberals to keep the conservatives out of power. Subsequently, the political center and left would periodically coordinate activities. Competing interests, however, frequently led to divisions on the left that opened up the way for conservative victories. The formation of anticonservative alliances remained an intensely contested and complicated undertaking, with significant trade-offs no matter how they were formed.

The Chilean left had more experience with popular front experiments than anyone else in Latin America, which led Alexander to observe that although small in numbers the Ecuadorian Communist Party was, along with the Chilean Communist Party, "one of the two best manipulators of fellow-travelers in the whole continent."[28] In 1946, Gabriel González Videla won election with communist party support and he initially rewarded several of its members with cabinet positions. This triumph launched a period of intense social mobilizations. But this democratic opening quickly came to an end in what scholars term the "Chilean cold war." After a year in office, González Videla swung abruptly to the right and repressed labor movements that challenged his economic policies. Communists quit his government rather than acquiesce to his conservative policies. A significant turn to the left within the communist party hindered the continuation of the alliance and contributed to ruling class fears in the face of growing working-class politicization. González Videla, in turn, outlawed the communist party and severed diplomatic ties with the Soviet Union. A leftist goal of achieving positive policy reforms through collaboration with a moderate government had reached a dead end.[29]

Similarly, the Ecuadorian left continually debated what position to take in elections, including who to run as candidates and whether to form coalitions with other parties. As in Chile, these coalitions were not without a great deal of controversies and complications. At the time, Alexander faulted the Ecuadorian socialists for being too eager to work with the communists in a broad progressive electoral front. He complained that socialists too easily fell victim to fears of a conservative victory as an excuse to collaborate with the communists, both in electoral alliances and in the labor movement. As a result, the socialists, even though they outnumbered the communists, "generally followed policies dictated by the Communists," a common complaint that United States officials also made.[30] Decades later and in retrospect, the historian Enrique Ayala Mora had a somewhat different interpretation of the ultimate outcome of these alliances. He observes that during the 1950s the communists "did not undergo any significant growth and increasingly diluted its revolutionary strategy in order to permit alliances with Liberalism and a degree of participation."[31] Unlike what Alexander feared, this strategy did not appear to leave the communists in a stronger position.

The communists would run their own slate of candidates when they failed to build a popular front with other progressive forces, but alone they never polled particularly well. Furthermore, often the left performed better in local races than they did in presidential contests, but that did not deter activists from dedicating most of their attention to the race at the top of the ticket. The CIA observed that their total of five thousand votes in the June 1950 midterm congressional election was "a considerable increase" over their previous tally of about three thousand. Nevertheless, "Communists continue to occupy a position of minor political importance in the country." The agency did not foresee "any significant gains in the coming months."[32] But that did not dissuade the CIA from its continued surveillance of the left. If it admitted that the communists did not present a threat they would lose their raison d'état, and by extension historians would have lost an important source of documentation on the left.

Even with these admissions of weakness, the CIA continually monitored communist party participation in elections, a rather paradoxical concern for an agency that assumed that communists would only engage in illegal and violent activities. Analysts never bothered to comment on that contradiction. Furthermore, a certain amount of irony exists in the PCE's insistence on being included in electoral coalitions because, as Karl Marx famously noted, elections are little more than a mechanism by which the oppressed are allowed once every few years to decide which particular members of the ruling class would misrepresent and repress them in parliament.[33] What does emerge from the surveillance, however, are insights into internal party debates. One intelligence report, for example, concerned a closed party meeting in Quito to decide whom to support in the upcoming November 1948 municipal elections. The party instructed cell leaders to tell members to campaign for a selected list of candidates.[34] These compromises meant that opponents exaggerated the level of a communist threat and at the same time the left had no clear path forward by which to gain power. Inherent contractions throve on all sides. This embrace of an accommodationist position eventually led a left wing of the party to break away in the aftermath of the Cuban Revolution.

The communist party consistently realized more success as a social movement that engaged with labor and other social issues than as an electoral or armed force. In part this was the result of both tactical and ideological choices.

According to the dominant mode of communist thinking, unindustrialized and economically dependent countries such as Ecuador were not ready for a socialist revolution. Orthodox interpretations of Marxist theory stipulated that a more fully developed capitalist economy needed to emerge before a transition to socialism could begin. In part, that perception is what led communists to engage in popular front alliances with more moderate groups. But that did not stop activists from pressing militant political agendas, particularly in the realm of labor organizations.

Democratic Parentheses

The 1950s are known as an extraordinary (for Ecuador) twelve-year "democratic parentheses" during which a series of three presidents were elected in what critics generally recognized as free and fair elections and were able to finish their terms in office and hand power to an elected successor from an opposing party.[35] It had been a quarter century since a duly elected president, José Luis Tamayo (1920–24), had successfully completed his four-year term of office. The July 1925 revolution introduced an exceptionally chaotic period with frequent and extraconstitutional changes in power. Twenty-one chief executives held office between 1931 and 1948 and not one managed to complete a term. Now, even as military regimes took hold in the postwar period elsewhere in Latin America, Ecuador faithfully held presidential elections every four years, even though literacy requirements excluded a majority of the country's population from voting. In addition, voters participated in midterm congressional elections and yearly municipal and provincial contests. This sequence of electoral campaigns provides the context in which the left pressed their political demands.

This democratic parenthesis emerged in the aftermath of the May 28, 1944, *revolución gloriosa* or "glorious revolution" that opened up political spaces and allowed for the flourishing of subaltern mobilizations that ushered in a period of progressive reforms. A general strike on that day culminated with the removal of the unpopular president Carlos Alberto Arroyo del Río.[36] The *gloriosa* was part of a broader "democratic spring" that spread across Latin America in the midst of the Second World War. Residents became conscious of the irony of fighting fascist dictatorships in Europe while suffering under authoritarian regimes at home. These contradictions led activists to revolt against their local governments. A hemispheric movement began in May 1944 with a general strike that removed the military dictator Maximiliano Hernández Martínez in El Salvador. His fall on May 9 had repercussions throughout the region, with protests in one country encouraged uprisings in others. Revolts in Honduras, Nicaragua, Costa Rica, and Ecuador soon followed. Student strikes in Nicaragua attempted but ultimately failed to remove Anastasio Somoza García from power. The most significant and longest-lasting of these protests was in Guatemala that led to the resignation of Jorge Ubico on July 1 and introduced a ten-year period of progressive reforms. That democratic experiment ended with a 1954 CIA-backed military coup followed by decades of genocidal violence. The brief postwar democratic spring of which the communists had taken advantage was an anomaly rather than the new normal.

Ecuador's democratic parentheses began with the election in 1948 of the modernizing landowner and pro-United States politician Plaza. The future president had been born in New York City where his father Leónidas Plaza Gutiérrez was stationed as a minister to the United States. Plaza had a long history of political involvement. Velasco Ibarra appointed him as ambassador to the United States in 1944, and later in 1968 he was elected secretary general of the Organization of American States (OAS). In all of these positions he maintained close relations with the United States, which gave him a reputation as an agent of imperialism. Plaza also owned the extensive Zuleta hacienda in northern Ecuador where he acted as a modernizing landowner. Both in and out of government he was committed to a capitalist mode of production.[37]

Plaza's election appeared to introduce a remarkable period of political stability and economic growth, but that development represented more superficial form than substance. Booming banana production led to a quickly expanding export economy, with Ecuador providing up to 25 percent of the global market. Not everyone shared equally in this economic growth. While profits soared for plantation owners, workers' wages declined, which led to rising rates of inequality. With government policies swinging ever more rightward during the 1950s, workers and peasants protested their marginalization from economic growth, which contributed to the strengthening of the left.[38]

After four years in office, Plaza handed power to the populist leader Velasco Ibarra for his third of five terms, the only one he was able to complete successfully. Velasco Ibarra, in turn, handed power over to his minister of government Camilo Ponce Enríquez, the first conservative elected as president of Ecuador since the 1895 liberal revolution more than sixty years previous. Ponce, in fact, was only one of three conservatives who won a presidential election in Ecuador in the twentieth century.[39] Hernán Ibarra aptly notes that Plaza was associated with imperialism, Velasco Ibarra with the oligarchy, and Ponce with feudalism.[40]

None of these politicians represented popular aspirations for a more just and inclusive social order.

In 1960, Velasco Ibarra returned to the presidency for his fourth of five times in office. As with all except the immediately preceding mandate, his governance quickly degenerated into a military regime, bringing an end to a succession of elected civilian administrations. Caught between an unwillingness to promulgate agrarian reform legislation and an inability to contain rural protest, the military forced the populist president out in November 1961 after only fourteen months in office. His vice president Carlos Julio Arosemena Monroy assumed control until he too was removed in a July 1963 military coup. Ecuador had returned to its status quo ante of frequent and extraconstitutional changes of power.[41] At the same time, the triumph of the Cuban Revolution in 1959 had triggered a period of intense protest across Latin America that in Ecuador fostered the drafting of a 1964 agrarian reform law and opened up possibilities for participation for previously excluded populations.

Despite an apparent rightward shift in politics, electoral support for conservatives steadily declined during the 1950s. In 1948, the conservative candidate Manuel Elicio Flor Torres won 40 percent of the vote in the presidential election, which turned out to be a high point of their strength. That dropped to 33 percent for Ruperto Alarcón Falconí in 1952 and to the low of 29 percent with Ponce's election in 1956. A variety of demographic and sociological factors explain this loss of electoral support. One was population shifts from the highlands to the coast and from rural to urban areas, in both cases from places where conservatives traditionally held dominance to those of liberal control. A modernizing capitalist economy also swung the country away from a feudal mode of production that, together with the backing of the Catholic Church, had provided the conservatives with their base of support.[42] Paradoxically, Ayala Mora observes, "the loss of control over the electoral majority allowed the Conservative Party to increase its share of power, especially at the local and congressional levels." This was due in large part to a change in social forces, particularly with the old landholding oligarchy becoming a new agricultural bourgeoisie, and a fracturing of traditional alliances.[43]

Rising literacy rates accompanied these demographic shifts, which brought new voters into the political system who had risen out of the working class and had little reason to support the aristocratic liberal and conservative parties. Restrictions on suffrage rights meant that before the 1940s only 3 percent of the population partook in contests that selected what were purportedly popular and democratic governments. Participation rates began to rise with the 1948 election, the same year in which (literate) women first participated in significant numbers, but literacy requirements meant that less than 15 percent of the population was even eligible to vote. Over the course of the next decade, the percentage of voters slowly grew to almost 20 percent. Rather than opting for liberals or leftists, however, these new voters provided populist politicians with their margins of victory. Although leftists might see conservatives as their biggest enemies, it was populists who denied them electoral victories.

ALTHOUGH FEW RECOGNIZED IT at the time, Plaza's election in 1948 had ushered in an unusually politically stable decade for Ecuador. This period of apparent tranquility should have offered the left a golden opportunity for growth. The communist party did not face the legal or physical repression that its counterparts did in many other countries. Furthermore, a functioning electoral system was consistent with the peaceful and parliamentary path to socialism that many of the communist leaders advocated. Yet, the communists had difficulties in turning this situation to their advantage. Instead, growing cold war tensions led to a rising tide of anticommunist sentiments. Domestic and international factors intertwined and reinforced each other to create the hostile environment in which the left operated. In comparison to the 1940s democratic spring and 1960s guerrilla insurrections, a combination of repressive local governments and international cold war policies seemed to circumscribe the possibilities for advancing social change in the 1950s. Overcoming those challenges would require a long and uphill struggle.

During the 1950s, even as the political center in Ecuador *appeared* to shift rightward, a remarkable period of constitutional continuity settled over the country. While the left seemed to lose space to an ascendant right, the conservative share of the popular vote actually declined during those years. Conservatives may have been the largest single electoral force, but they never enjoyed majority backing, particularly among the large, disenfranchised population. Although the entire left lost electoral support at the top of their tickets during this decade, it was also a time of advances on a local level, particularly in terms of articulating party platforms, building labor movements, and finding other ways to advance progressive ideas. Electoral contests as well as the popular fronts and labor and student organizations that the left fashioned to press their agenda formed an organizational base for the much more militant actions that emerged in the 1960s.

An analysis of political developments in the 1950s demonstrates that the communist party never disappeared, but rather continued to play a significant role across the decade and beyond. In a fractured political environment, if the left were to emerge victorious it would have to build coalitions with sympathetic forces. Deep political divisions, however, complicated that process. In particular, rising anticommunist sentiments marginalized what was a small but well-organized segment of the left. Realizing organizational success proved to be immensely difficult to achieve. The left momentarily lost some political space, but, as Greg Grandin notes, in the process it transformed "power relations that allowed broader participation in politics, culture, and society."[44] Those transformations laid the groundwork for dramatic developments that were to come. Throughout all of these twists and turns, CIA surveillance provides insights into the strengths, weaknesses, opportunities, and threats that the party confronted. Our understanding of the past is richer for the documentary record they left behind.

CHAPTER 2

CIA

THE CENTRAL INTELLIGENCE AGENCY justifiably has gained a reputation as the covert action arm of the United States government, particularly as a result of its involvement in subverting progressive democratic governments in places such as Guatemala in 1954 and Chile in 1973 and replacing them with brutal, right-wing military dictatorships. Covert actions including interventions in the internal affairs of other countries is the most controversial of the CIA's clandestine functions, but that is not the agency's only or even original purpose. The National Security Act of 1947 that President Harry Truman signed instructed the CIA to correlate, evaluate, and disseminate intelligence, as well as to perform other duties related to intelligence gathering on national security issues. The agency quickly expanded from that rather limited mandate to other, often less savory, tasks.[1]

Broadly speaking, intelligence agencies such as the CIA engage in three different types of activities. First is the collection of raw data through surveillance of targeted sources; second is research and analysis of that information combined with other secret, official, and public sources to create finished intelligence to guide policy makers in their decision-making processes; and third are the covert operations designed to act on that intelligence to alter political landscapes. Critics have long complained that the CIA's primary task has not been to coordinate the collection of information or to analyze that data, but to conduct covert foreign policy.[2] Those operations have garnered extensive attention. In addition, most published memoirs and studies of the CIA retain a top-down perspective that emphasizes the roles of CIA directors, Washington-based politicians, and other policy makers.[3] Their actions and the intelligence that analysts (known colloquially as the "wise men") produced at agency headquarters tells us more about United States policy objectives than it does about the subjects they analyzed.

Rarely studied are the raw data that CIA officers collected from their agents in the field. Even with its inherent limitations, the information that these officers compiled based on human intelligence can provide useful and sometimes even fascinating empirical data that scholars can parse for their unique insights into local developments. This surveillance sometimes revealed valuable details that are difficult or impossible to find anywhere else. As with any historical documentation, both the field reports and finished intelligence produced in Washington must be read carefully and critically for the gaps and perspectives that they contain. When correlated with other sources, this material can lead to a fuller and more robust picture of how the left responded to challenges that it faced.

Before delving into the details of the CIA's surveillance of the Ecuadorian left, it is first worth considering how and why the agency collected this information, and who did the collecting. The more we know about a source, the better we can critique it and the more we can extract from it. Understanding the strengths and weaknesses of the material assists us in gaining a deeper appreciation for the light it sheds on historical events.

Albert Haney

A strict code of secrecy complicates the process of identifying the authors of CIA reports or even the names of individual officers or analysts. Allegedly for national security purposes, government agencies redact names of operatives and methods of investigation or withhold entire documents that might assist with the identification of those involved in clandestine activities or the specific nature of their operations. The suppression of the identities of officers makes it exceedingly difficult to know how information was acquired or the qualifications of those who drafted agency reports.

Anything related to the CIA or spy operations in general inherently elicit a good deal of popular interest. Former CIA deputy director Ray Cline complains that the public's fascination with espionage and covert actions overshadows the agency's principal responsibility of "analytical research to reduce raw data to meaningful ideas."[4] As Donald Daughters, a former FBI agent during World War II in Chile, noted in an oral history interview with his grandson and anthropologist Anton Daughters, "It's always the Americans who are most interested in gossiping about anything that smells of secret intelligence. It really gets people excited, gets the blood flowing, and they can't wait to talk about things that relate to secret intelligence."[5] That is not the intent of this work, but rather a reliance on the CIA is part of an attempt to locate information and exploit its value in a situation where few other sources exist. In fact, the specific origins of the raw data—whether it came from diplomatic officials, CIA officers, or military attachés—is of less interest in this work than the insights that the documentation can shed on domestic developments in Latin America. Identifying authorship, whether individual or collective, and methods of collection is primarily of interest for its value in parsing out assumptions and perspectives that help evaluate the validity of the data and, more importantly, provide a mechanism for analyzing the information that it contains. Author and context are key for gaining a fuller understanding of a source.

As is often the case, a censor's pen is not always complete and the withholding of information can be partial and uneven. Sometimes two different inspectors will review the same document at different times resulting in two different sets of redactions, leaving an uninitiated outsider a bit confused and bewildered about what exactly was objectionable with the information that was withheld.[6] In those cases, one has to wonder, as did former CIA consultant Chalmers Johnson, whether the redactions simply hide the potential embarrassment "to have it known that such conventional journalism passed for strategic thought."[7] As Sherman Kent, who pioneered many of the methods of intelligence analysis for the CIA, determined in 1951, 95 percent of the material in CIA estimates was available from publicly available sources.[8] On rare occasions, internal correspondence mentions a name in passing that allows not only for confirmation of the CIA as the source of information but also points to a specific individual as a CIA officer. Sometimes corroborating material, including from other government agencies, inadvertently allows for the identification of a source.[9] It is at those times that researchers begin to gain a better understanding of the resultant documentation.

The inconsistent nature of redactions allowed for the identification of Army Colonel Albert Richard Haney as the first CIA officer stationed in Ecuador. Haney arrived in Quito in February 1947, before the CIA formally began operations in September of that year, with the designation of "attaché" in the embassy. The FBI at that point was wrapping up its counterintelligence efforts in Latin America and passing its operations off to the Central Intelligence Group (CIG), the immediate forerunner of the CIA. According to former FBI agent and historian Raymond Batvinis, the agency's director J. Edgar Hoover gave his personnel the option of either returning to conventional FBI work or joining the CIA. "Many chose the CIA," Batvinis claims, "and by 1950, three years after it came into existence, every CIA station chief in Latin America had previously served" with the FBI in Latin America.[10] Haney painted a somewhat different picture of the transfer of authority. "Hoover didn't like losing the responsibility," Haney later commented, "and in most countries of Latin America the FBI burned its files and dismissed its agents rather than turn them over to us." Haney claimed that when he arrived in Quito the only thing that the bureau had left behind "was a row of empty safes and a pair of rubber gloves in what had been an FBI darkroom." He hired the ex-FBI chief's driver and through that person contacted most of the bureau's sources and reconstructed their spy network. "I have a feeling J. Edgar is never going to forgive us for taking over this territory," Haney concluded.[11] Richard Bissell, who was later in charge of covert actions at the CIA, similarly stated that he did not "believe the FBI ever got over its Western Hemisphere operation's being turned over to the agency."[12] The legendary tensions between the different agencies ran deep.

Ecuador was not Haney's first—nor his last—post in Latin America. Before coming to Ecuador as a major in the army, he was assigned in July 1945 as an assistant military attaché to Colombia, a post he held for about a year.[13] In January 1947, the department appointed him to Quito as a level six Foreign Service staff officer (FSS-6) with an annual salary of $5,940. A month later, the department designated him as an "attaché" to the Quito Embassy, apparently his diplomatic cover for his work with the nascent agency.[14] After two years in Quito, in mid-1949 he moved to Santiago, Chile with a promotion to a level four Foreign Service staff officer (FSS-4) although he still held the title of "attaché" and continued with the CIA.[15] Haney remained in Chile through 1951 when the agency promoted him to Chief of Station (COS) in South Korea.

Scholars have described Haney as "a handsome, rugged six-footer who had left a Chicago business career . . . to enlist in army counterintelligence" during World War II. He headed up the US Army's Counter Intelligence Corps (CIC) in Panama rounding up German immigrants whom the government feared might be potential Nazi agents.[16] Bissell described Haney as "young, bold, and enthusiastic about the possibilities for covert action," which made him an ideal candidate for such work.[17] Haney had a "pugnacious personality," with one co-worker claiming, "I didn't know anyone who liked Haney."[18] In his history of the CIA, the journalist Tim Weiner describes Haney "as garrulous and ambitious" who some thought "a dangerous fool" who tended to fabricate evidence or, worse, employed informers who were "controlled by the other side."[19] Despite—or maybe because—of these character flaws, Haney enjoyed a lengthy career in the CIA.

Haney had decided to join the CIA against the wishes of his wealthy spouse Irene Budlong Haney who wanted him to return to his business career in the United States. In Ecuador and Chile, the couple lived "rather expensively in accordance with Mrs. Haney's tastes." In 1951, she divorced him rather than accompany him to Korea.[20] It was particularly in Korea where Haney ran into trouble for fabricating evidence in the United States-led war against the north. Despite the "human wreckage" he had left behind in Korea, CIA director Allen Dulles tapped him in 1953 to lead Operation PBSUCCESS, the CIA's plot to overthrow Guatemalan president Jacobo Arbenz. Consistent with his previous track record in Korea, Weiner describes Haney's plans for the Guatemalan coup as "one of the loosest cannons in the CIA's arsenal."[21] Despite his incompetence, six months later the CIA-engineered military coup removed the democratically elected Arbenz from office.

It is unlikely that Haney was alone in his initial post with the CIA in Ecuador. At a minimum, he would have had the assistance of one or two office support staff to type correspondence and perform other clerical duties. He may have also had one or two case officers under his command, even though it is difficult to verify the identities of his assistants and collaborators. Even so, by all appearances, the CIA's initial footprint in Ecuador was significantly smaller than that of its predecessor the FBI. At the height of its operations in October 1943, the FBI had twenty-one people in Ecuador with five in its Legal Attaché Office in Quito, four clerical officers, four undercover agents, two radio operators, a police liaison officer, and a police security officer. Two agents were at the consulate in Guayaquil, in addition to undercover agents in both Guayaquil and Cuenca.[22] The CIA never approached that extent. Station size varied from two (as in Chad) to several hundred (as in Saigon during the Vietnam War), but most had twenty-five to thirty people.[23] The agency's Ecuador station would have been on the small size.

CIA stations operated with the approval of the State Department and generally under the cover of an embassy or consulate.[24] In order to maintain that appearance, CIA officers needed to transfer stations every two to four years, as was the practice in the diplomatic service. That created a problem for the agency, as it was not always easy to hand over sources and agents from one officer to the next.[25] The head of CIA operations in each country was called the Chief of Station (COS), and reported to the ambassador.[26] The reality could be—and often was—quite different. Case officers habitually lied, including to State Department colleagues and ambassadors, especially about controversial operations.[27] Ambassadors often recognized and accommodated themselves to these contradictions. Although as part of the career foreign service Maurice Bernbaum had his share of dealings with the CIA—including during previous stints in Ecuador and at the Ecuador desk at the State Department in Washington—when he returned to Ecuador as ambassador in 1960 he pretended not to know anything about CIA operations even though he theoretically oversaw them.[28]

The COS typically worked out of the political section of the embassy, and was responsible for coordinating CIA influence with political parties, civic associations, student groups, labor unions, the media, and the military. Under the COS were Chiefs of Base (COB) who often worked out of consulates in different regions of the country. Philip Agee, a dissident agent who gained fame for "naming names" in his memoir *Inside the Company,* arrived in Ecuador at the end of 1960 after the Cuban Revolution and in the context of the agency significantly ramping up its activities to prevent another such catastrophe in the hemisphere. He described the CIA's Ecuador operation as "small," even though it had a budget of more than half a million dollars. In addition to Agee's post as operations officer, the Quito station consisted of the COS James Noland, reports officer John Bacon, operations officer Robert Weatherwax, a communications officer, an administrative assistant, and a secretary-typist. The post of deputy chief was vacant when he arrived, but was filled the following year. The Guayaquil operation consisted of the COB Richard Wheeler (his predecessor in Quito), an operations officer, an administrative assistant, and a secretary-typist.[29] Presumably, the CIA station was much smaller during the late 1940s when Haney first launched its operations.

Agee does not name the station's assistants, who were generally young women and hence tend to become invisible in the historical record. In a subsequent memoir, he recounts meeting the deputy chief of mission's secretary Sharon Hurley in Germany in the 1970s after he left the agency. He "hardly noticed" her even though her "desk had been a minute's walk down the hall" from his in Quito.[30] Because they typed the outgoing cables and dispatches, read incoming traffic from headquarters, and maintained financial records, the dissident CIA officer John Stockwell describes an assistant as one of a very small handful of people "who knows everything the CIA is doing."[31] Seemingly no memoirs, studies, or extended discussions exist of their role in the agency's operations. Researchers have ignored their activities to the detriment of gaining a fuller understanding of history.

Both the FBI and CIA placed some of their personnel under commercial cover in which they purportedly worked for an amenable United States firm. One example of commercial cover was David Atlee Phillips who published an English-language newspaper in Chile in 1950 when Haney recruited him into the CIA. That cover was effective because the business provided a justification for his presence in Chile and a reason for him to move around and meet people. The newspaper also furnished the agency with convenient access to a press that they could use to print their propaganda.[32] Sometimes personnel would go under "deep" cover, which meant cutting all ties to the government and blending into the local landscape until the agency needed them for an operation.

The most common was "official" cover in which spies ostensibly became State Department employees, including receiving State Department passports and full diplomatic protection.[33] In the case of the FBI during the war, the secretary of state would cable ahead to the embassy that a legal attaché was arriving and that "his salary and expenses will be paid by another Government agency."[34] Even so, none of the FBI agents were included in the State Department's foreign service lists that provided the rank and salary of all diplomatic officials, whereas each CIA officer is listed the same as other personnel (except that undercover agents would not show up in diplomatic records). In both cases their absence or inclusion makes it difficult for subsequent scholars to identify individuals who worked for their respective agencies. Unless an operative went on to a distinguished (or notorious) career in the CIA, that person could fade into the historical background with little trace—which presumably was the agency's intent. The tendency to refer to CIA stations euphemistically as a "controlled American source" (CAS) further complicates identification of agency personnel.[35] Even so, in essence, the State Department provided diplomatic cover for political police engaged in illegal spying in other countries.

The size of the staff of the United States diplomatic mission in Ecuador expanded dramatically during the 1950s, but when Haney arrived in 1947 it was still quite small. At that time, the embassy staff in Quito had fourteen members including consuls, attachés, and other officers, plus six more at the Guayaquil Consulate and two military attachés.[36] By 1960, the embassy employed eighteen officials divided into executive, political, economic, consular, and administrative sections. In addition, the diplomatic mission included four military attachés; fifty-eight with the International Cooperation Administration (ICA), the predecessor of the present-day US Agency for International Development (USAID); seven at the United States Information Agency (USIA); one with the Department of Agriculture's Foreign Agricultural Service (FAS); plus six more officials in the Guayaquil Consulate.[37] The CIA had many places in the embassy where it could hide its officers.

CIA operatives were often but not always located in the political section of the embassy or consulate. In the case of Ecuador in the early 1960s, Agee states that the CIA's base operation in Guayaquil "forms the entire small political section of the Consulate." In contrast, Weatherwax was "under Public Safety cover in USOM," the United States Operations Mission in the Quito Embassy.[38] Furthermore, political attachés were not necessarily CIA officers. For example,

George Jones entered the Foreign Service in 1956 when he was twenty-one years old. His first international post was to Quito in November 1958 as a political officer, but he was never part of the CIA. Jones left Ecuador in November 1960 just before Agee arrived and went on to a long career in the Foreign Service. All of these factors complicate a fuller understanding of the data that the different agencies generated. Even so, the distinctions between the different agencies becomes more academic if the interest is not in critiquing United States policy but rather reading the documentation their personnel generated for what it can tell us about local conditions in Latin America.

Information Reports

George Jones, the political attaché in the Quito Embassy in the late 1950s, categorized CIA officers as "professional intelligence officers" who "were very dedicated to their career, very hard working" and the information they generated "was certainly useful." Much of the data they produced, "too much of it" really, "covered the same areas that the embassy political officers were working on" and that created "a constant source of irritation." Jones complained that the CIA officers did not tell "Washington that much more about normal, overt politics that was of any tremendous interest." At the same time, "The same point could be made about much of our reporting, was there really any need for Washington to know who was in and who was out, and what the inner machinations were of party X compared with party Y." He said that officials in Washington had

> an insatiable demand for information . . . which drove both the embassy and the CIA, and yet one wonders what Washington ever did with the mountains of information that it got. Other than to fill up the files and demonstrate how well informed they were. I always thought that by far, we were the best informed government in the world. We produced the best information of any foreign service in the world. I had much more doubt about our knowing what to do with the information that we got. At times I think there was a lot of information for information's sake, rather than relating it to things that we really needed to know.

In particular, Jones applauded the CIA's reporting on the communist party. While the quality and level of information would vary between countries and at different times, "there were times and places where they had really good penetration into the leadership of the extreme left and were able to give us some really useful information about what the left were up to."[39] Even though Jones thought the amount and detail of information that the agency collected was excessive and perhaps even meaningless, it does provide historians with a valuable source for a study of communism in Latin America.

As Jones notes, CIA officers drafted a surprisingly large volume of intelligence (later called information) reports that detailed local developments in their country of surveillance. Patrick McGarvey, a CIA officer who left the agency after fourteen years in a state of disillusionment, relates the "tremendous pressure" to produce reports, because come promotion time officers were judged based on the number of cables sent to Washington. "Quality doesn't count, just quantity," McGarvey complains.[40] As a result, the reports were often only a page or two in length and sometimes a sequence of memos summarizes different topics from the same informer. Agee states that the reports were a pain to produce because of the specific format and model that the CIA required their officers to follow.[41] The reports typically feature factual narrative summaries of political developments, presumably drawn from raw data that their contracted agents had collected and on other inside knowledge extracted from their sources. Before declassifying these reports, the CIA redacted all indication of who (or what) their sources might have been and how their officers acquired the information, which makes it difficult to draw definite conclusions regarding their provenance and validity. Sometimes the reports concluded with brief editorial or evaluative comments, although the CIA also redacted any identifying marks as to who those commentators might have been. Occasionally case officers would transcribe information from an organization they had placed under surveillance or enclose a copy of a proclamation that the group had distributed. These documents provide valuable details that are difficult or impossible to find anywhere else.

The first intelligence report on Ecuador in the CREST database is dated May 1947 and concerns the visit of an Italian economic commission to Ecuador.[42] That topic is a historical anomaly, and not a common subject in the agency's records. Before the war Italian military missions provided training in many Latin American countries, and their governments were as loath to give up the Italian's expertise and access to hardware as the United States was eager to displace them. The defeat of Benito Mussolini solved that problem, and Italy was no longer a competitor for imperial control over Latin America.

The second intelligence report (see figure 2.1) is more representative of where the CIA dedicated its efforts. That one is dated two days after the first, and concerns communist party activities. It is one-page long and includes three topics of examination. The first is a report on an Indigenous conference in Quito, the second notes that party leader Pedro Saad had recruited one hundred new

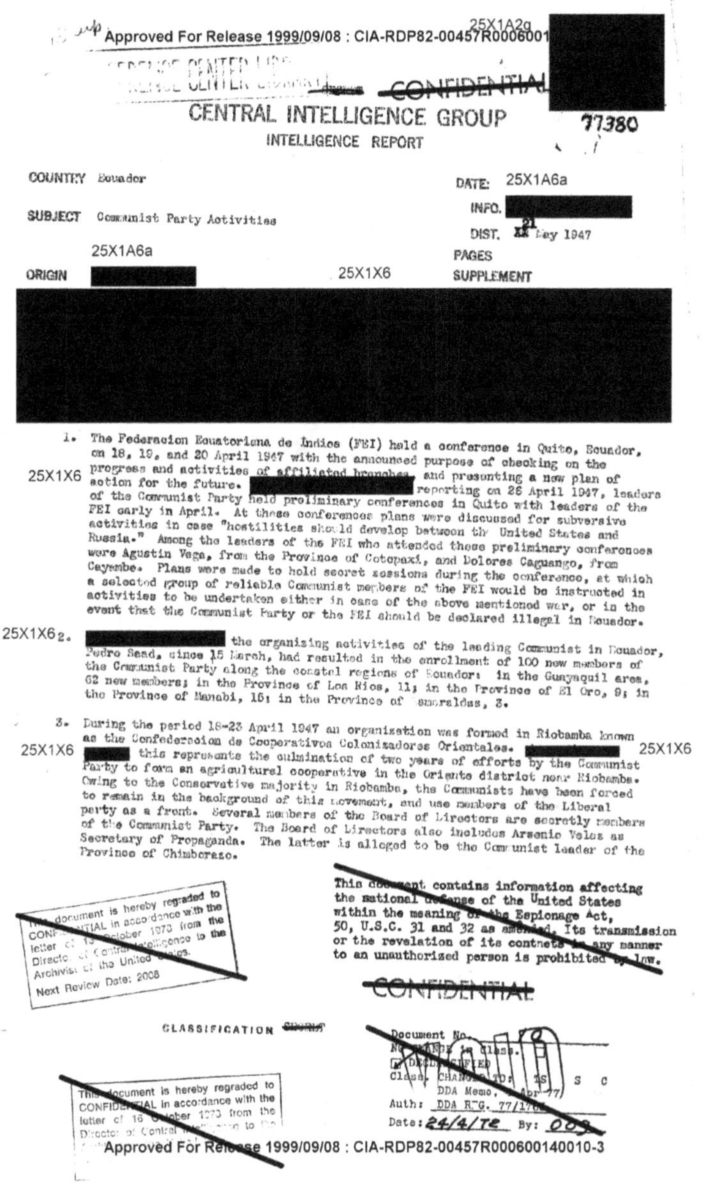

Approved For Release 1999/09/08 : CIA-RDP82-00457R000600140010-3

25X1A2g

CONFIDENTIAL

CENTRAL INTELLIGENCE GROUP

INTELLIGENCE REPORT

77380

COUNTRY Ecuador

SUBJECT Communist Party Activities

25X1A6a

ORIGIN

DATE: 25X1A6a

INFO.

DIST. 21 May 1947

PAGES

SUPPLEMENT

25X1X6

1. The Federacion Ecuatoriana de Indios (FEI) held a conference in Quito, Ecuador, on 18, 19, and 20 April 1947 with the announced purpose of checking on the progress and activities of affiliated branches, and presenting a new plan of action for the future. 25X1X6 reporting on 26 April 1947, leaders of the Communist Party held preliminary conferences in Quito with leaders of the FEI early in April. At these conferences plans were discussed for subversive activities in case "hostilities should develop between the United States and Russia." Among the leaders of the FEI who attended these preliminary conferences were Agustin Vega, from the Province of Cotopaxi, and Dolores Caguango, from Cayambe. Plans were made to hold secret sessions during the conference, at which a selected group of reliable Communist members of the FEI would be instructed in activities to be undertaken either in case of the above mentioned war, or in the event that the Communist Party or the FEI should be declared illegal in Ecuador.

25X1X6 2. the organizing activities of the leading Communist in Ecuador, Pedro Saad, since 15 March, had resulted in the enrollment of 100 new members of the Communist Party along the coastal regions of Ecuador: in the Guayaquil area, 62 new members; in the Province of Los Rios, 11; in the Province of El Oro, 9; in the Province of Manabi, 15; in the Province of Esmeraldas, 3.

3. During the period 18-23 April 1947 an organization was formed in Riobamba known as the Confederacion de Cooperativos Colonizadores Orientales. 25X1X6 this represents the culmination of two years of efforts by the Communist Party to form an agricultural cooperative in the Oriente district near Riobamba. Owing to the Conservative majority in Riobamba, the Communists have been forced to remain in the background of this movement, and use members of the Liberal party as a front. Several members of the Board of Directors are secretly members of the Commnist Party. The Board of Directors also includes Arsenio Velez as Secretary of Propaganda. The latter is alleged to be the Communist leader of the Province of Chimborazo. 25X1X6

This document contains information affecting the national defense of the United States within the meaning of the Espionage Act, 50, U.S.C. 31 and 32 as amended. Its transmission or the revelation of its contnets in any manner to an unauthorized person is prohibited by law.

This document is hereby regraded to CONFIDENTIAL in accordance with the letter of 16 October 1978 from the Director of Central Intelligence to the Archivist of the United States.

Next Review Date: 2008

CONFIDENTIAL

CLASSIFICATION

Document No. ___
NO CHANGE in Class.
DECLASSIFIED
Class. CHANGED TO: TS S C
DDA Memo, 4 Apr 77
Auth: DDA REG. 77/1763
Date: 24/4/78 By: 009

Approved For Release 1999/09/08 : CIA-RDP82-00457R000600140010-3

FIGURE 2.1. The second intelligence report from the CIG on Ecuador that includes information on an Indigenous conference and communist efforts to organize an agricultural cooperative. Source: Central Intelligence Group (CIG), "Communist Party Activities," May 21, 1947, CIA Electronic Reading Room, https://www.cia.gov/library/readingroom/document/cia-rdp82-00457r000600140010-3.

members on the coast, and the third relays information on communist efforts to organize an agricultural cooperative in Riobamba.[43] These reports subsequently came at a fast and furious pace, and largely maintained this emphasis on communist activities. The memos often appear in batches—sometimes as many as five a day—and number in the hundreds, and this is just for Ecuador. Although identifying details in the declassified versions of these documents are redacted, it is reasonable to assume that many if not most of these initial ones represent Haney's work.

In addition to the information reports sent to Washington, Haney also submitted secret memos—typically related to communist activities—to the embassy staff in Quito. The first (or at least the first that has come to light) is also from May 1947 and concerns a cable that he had received warning that communist parties throughout Latin America were seeking to infiltrate United States embassies through domestic servants and locally hired personnel. Their goal was to identify staff who were working on anticommunist campaigns.[44] Coming as he did in the midst of the departure of the FBI in March 1947 and before the formal creation of the CIA in September 1947, Haney conducted his investigations under the auspices of the CIA's precursor Central Intelligence Group (CIG). He signed his work as "civil attaché," a variation on the FBI's "legal attaché" and a moniker that the bureau's agents sometimes also used. This pattern continued even after the creation of the CIA. For example, in December 1947, chargé d'affaires George Shaw provided a copy of a memo to the civil attaché—presumably Haney—that concerned Saad's application for a visa to visit his father Kalil who was undergoing treatment for cancer in the United States. Saad's request for a visa triggered quite a diplomatic scramble, including questions as to how his father had acquired a visa. Ultimately the consulate denied the communist leader the visa because of his political affiliation.[45]

Haney's investigations resulted in detailed records of labor and communist party activity. A July 1947 memo concerned a trip of Mexican labor leader Vicente Lombardo Toledano's associate Francisco Arechandieta Ortega through South America to organize a congress of petroleum workers. Along the way Arechandieta contacted both labor and communist leaders. Haney stated that Arechandieta was "reportedly carrying plans for the coordination of sabotage for all oil pipelines in Latin America."[46] A week later, Haney provided Shaw with a detailed, seven-page memo on Arechandieta's activities while in Ecuador. The document closed with an editorial comment that Ecuadorian security agents had botched their surveillance of Arechandieta, and despite their efforts the labor leader had managed to establish contact with local communists and successfully completed his mission.[47]

A certain amount of duplication was involved in communicating this information to Washington. Shaw dutifully forwarded Haney's first memo on Arechandieta to the State Department, identifying the source only as "a reliable informant, which is graded B-3," a pattern that became standard practice.[48] Rather than forwarding the second report, Shaw indicated that it would reach the department "through other channels," presumably directly from the CIG in Washington. Without naming Haney, Shaw indicated that the CIG officer had done his work well, with a careful observation of the movement and actions of the international labor leader.[49]

The next memo concerned communist affiliations of student representatives to a forthcoming congress in neighboring Lima, Peru. In this case, Shaw handwrote a note on the memo to "file" it rather than report it to the State Department.[50] The embassy may have grown weary of the flood of information from an overeager operative. Conceivably, the return of Ambassador John Simmons to his post resulted in more judicious communications with Washington. Or, perhaps, the embassy staff simply determined that this specific bit of information was not of sufficient value to communicate to Washington. Another possibility is that in reality the extant documentation may just be skimming the surface of the depth of collaboration between the newly formed CIA and diplomatic personnel in the embassy. Other memos detailing the sharing of information may have been lost, destroyed, or not yet released to the public. Ultimately, the precise provenance of specific pieces of information are of secondary concern if the interest is to uncover the history of the left.

The handful of surviving memos from Haney are either signed personally by him or appear anonymously from a "controlled American source," the euphemism for the CIA station. Initially embassy officials stated that the information, which they quoted verbatim in their dispatches to the State Department, came from "a reliable source," while later missives simply indicated that it came from a "controlled American source." Often the same information also appears in information reports that an officer sent to CIA Headquarters, though in an edited format and sometimes with a similar or identical subject line. Haney, as well as other CIA officers, likely provided the same information in different formats according to the needs and desires of a specific audience.

A curiosity is that the CIA information reports carry a distribution date about a month after the events they describe—and a month after embassy personnel communicated the same information to the State Department. Reading the archival documentation as it appears to have been received in Washington would seem to indicate that the State Department was constantly scooping the CIA on information from its own personnel, which given the nature of inter-agency disputes would hardly seem likely. Embassy dispatches and CIA intelligence reports that communicated similar if not redundant information to their respective agencies in Washington could alternatively point to a sharing of information, a reliance on the same informers, or even a certain amount of competition to be the premier source of intelligence. More likely, the variance may just reflect a difference between sending and reception dates that could merely denote the length of time it took for a diplomatic pouch to arrive in Washington. The released versions of the CIA reports typically have the date of information redacted as well as the first paragraph of the report, which presumably would shed light on the delay.[51] The redundancies between different government agencies, including repetition in the submission of data to Washington reflects, as Jones complained, a push for more, though not necessarily better, information.

THE DOCUMENTATION THE CIA left behind on its investigations of subversive movements in Ecuador reflects exaggerated fears, misplaced concerns, and bureaucratic attempts to justify the agency's existence. While the surveillance inadvertently provides a rich source of documentation on domestic affairs in Latin America, CIA officers interpreted those developments through a cold war lens that colored their understanding of the events they observed. This distortion emerges particularly apparent in the constant attacks that Galo Plaza Lasso faced on his administration. Rather than recognizing the communists' commitment to a peaceful transformation of society, a prevalent assumption among United States policy makers was of the presence of an international conspiracy that sought to sow chaos across the region. What their narrative ignored was that the communist party was opposed to involvement in military coups and instead advocated working within the confines of the established political system to achieve political change. Despite these shortcomings, the agency's written record provides a rich archival source for understanding communist organizing efforts. Although partial and often problematic, it allows insights into how political activists shaped their struggles and advanced their concerns. The types of issues they confronted transcend time and space, and permit a better understanding of the world they inhabited.

CHAPTER 3

Coups

A disconnect often appears between the CIA's reporting on internal political developments and local realities, and nowhere does this emerge more plainly than in the United States fears that communists would disrupt the smooth functioning of society. Despite the PCE's orthodox adherence to a peaceful transition to socialism, the CIA constantly sought to implicate the party in extraconstitutional challenges to power. This contradiction is particularly evident in its treatment of repeated coup attempts against Galo Plaza Lasso's government as well as the destruction that came in the wake of "The War of the Worlds" radio broadcast. Even though communists were not involved in either, agency officials tried hard to tie them to the unrest. In such cases, CIA reports say more about Washington's policy objectives than they do about local realities. Nevertheless, a careful parsing of the surveillance data lends insights into the communist party's electoral strategies and other mechanisms they used to advance their political agendas.

Galo Plaza Lasso

Leftists have long debated what position to take in electoral contests, and the 1948 presidential campaign in Ecuador was no exception. After intense discussions and negotiations, a coalition of liberals, socialists, and other leftists nominated the populist and former dictator General Alberto Enríquez Gallo for the presidency. Enríquez Gallo's candidacy led to contentious arguments within the communist party over whether or not to ally with liberals in support of a moderately progressive politician. From their perspective, an Enríquez Gallo presidency would definitely be preferable to the alternatives: the independent Plaza who was the candidate of a reactionary bourgeoisie and would deliver the country to the Yankees, or the conservative Manuel Elicio Flor Torres who threatened to return Ecuador to the oppression of its feudal past. The communists criticized Flor for his "defense of the interests of large landholders who oppress the Indians." The PCE presented an alternative platform that included agrarian reform and the development of cooperatives to "protect Indians and peasants" and abolish "exploitative feudal vestiges." They called on "workers, peasants, Indians, servants, teachers, artisans, etc., to defend their conquests, the Labor Code and social laws, to not permit their destruction."[1] To this end, the communists urged the importance of organizing a broad, progressive coalition that would block the election of conservative, pro-imperialist, and feudal candidates. The socialist and liberal parties, however, excluded the communists from their coalition, which led to no small amount of consternation among party members. In the end, the party urged their members to cast blank ballots in the presidential election. Enríquez Gallo proved to be a relatively colorless and weak candidate, and Plaza narrowly defeated Flor, although he crushed Enríquez Gallo by a wide margin.[2]

Communists approached Plaza's election with a good deal of wariness. A CIA officer (presumably Albert Haney) reported that coastal party leader Enrique Gil Gilbert had stated that the PCE "would probably be forced to operate clandestinely after Galo Plaza assumed office." Gil Gilbert informed cell leaders that the party had developed a plan for "the exact dates, times, and places of future secret Communist meetings in Guayaquil" in case the party were to be outlawed.[3] Shortly after Plaza took power, Haney reported that the communists welcomed his opposition because they thought that outlawing their party would backfire and make the PCE more popular, even though little evidence exists that this idea would work out so well in practice. Nevertheless, some leaders pondered whether the party could work more efficiently if it were forced underground. This included acting "in ways which are presently denied to it"—apparently a vague reference to members who advocated more militant action that eventually led to a left-wing breakaway in the 1960s. Some members proposed distributing handbills that would provoke the government into action. While Gustavo Becerra was preparing a handbill in his bookstore that called for a leftist coalition to oppose Plaza, the police arrived and seized the entire lot. Party leaders were incensed and at first planned to respond with a public statement, but then thought better of it. Becerra, who was head of the party's intelligence activities, investigated how police knew about the handbills and who ordered them to confiscate their propaganda.[4] Unfortunately, the available documentation does not indicate the outcome of his inquiry, though of course it is notable that the CIA had access to this information. It may be an indication of an infiltrator in the party or collaboration between United States and local government officials. At least dating to the FBI in the 1940s, the United States had significant police training missions that facilitated the sharing of information, although covert activities that involved direct intervention in the internal affairs of another country did not escalate until the Eisenhower administration.[5]

After barely a month in office, the CIA reported that opposition to Plaza's government had increased appreciably. This opposition ranged from the extreme right to the extreme left, but these contestations for power came from competing elements of the political class rather than leftist militants who sought a fundamental structural transformation of society. Although various military and civilian conspiracies repeatedly threatened the president, the inability of these opponents to unify their forces assured his continuance in office. Even so, a political context in which it appeared that Plaza would not be able to hang on for the full four years of his term provided ready gist for such a narrative.[6]

"The Communists are reported to have decided to take advantage of Plaza's statement that he would not declare the Party illegal," an officer related. "They are accordingly endeavoring to organize all political opposition to Plaza into a solid coalition, and to organize a series of paralyzing labor strikes." The communists were engaged in "strenuous efforts" to form a coalition with other socialist and leftist parties, and took steps to plant discontent toward the government in these other groups. To this end, they held numerous meetings with other parties. "The Communists have also stated boldly that the Plaza administration could not be expected to remain in office for more than six months," the officer asserted.[7] Misstatements of fact in this unusually lengthy and detailed information report could call any and all of these hyperbolic assertions into question, although given that it was a quarter century since any elected president had successfully completed a four-year term in office it would have been a fair assumption that Plaza would not be able to finish his either.

Press reports, both in the United States and in Ecuador, were full of news of repeated coup attempts throughout Plaza's presidency. Intelligence operatives were continually on the lookout for communist involvement in these challenges, even though thoughtful reflection should have revealed that such actions were not consistent with the party's current political line. Instead, communist leaders advocated for achieving change through peaceful and parliamentary means. Nevertheless, in November 1948 the US military attaché in Quito reported that Plaza was "thoroughly aware" of potential coup threats, and was "doing everything possible to offset any revolutionary action or attempt of violence." While it would be possible to avoid a successful coup, doing so "seems very difficult." According to the attaché, complicating the president's task was both a strong, presumably conservative, pro-Argentine element in the country and "a small well-knit Communist Party" that "assisted and encouraged" the unrest.[8] Such statements conflated reactionary anti-United States sentiments in Argentina with the communists' much more ideologically driven anti-imperialist positions. The exaggeration of anticommunist fear mongering should have been obvious, especially since ten days later the same attaché opined that while a military coup was likely, the result would not necessarily be "a Leftist regime" since the best organized opposition came from other quarters.[9] Even so, the next report a week later claimed communists were "actively attempting [to] organize opposition groups into [a] revolutionary movement."[10] Despite their best attempts, United States officials were never able to prove communist complicity in repeated coup attempts against Plaza's government, even as it should have been readily apparent that those endeavors typically came from the right rather than the left.

To further its ideological agenda, the CIA maintained its surveillance of the communists whom they considered to be an "active and a potential source of trouble in an emergency." Even though the communists were not an effective threat to the stability of Plaza's government, they were "taking advantage of the present economic crisis by agitation among the workers and by actively participating in strikes." The biggest threat came from their presence in organized labor rather than as an illegal and subversive force. Nevertheless, the Plaza government was adroitly coping with the situation, and at present it was "under control." The communists appeared to be harassing the government with the goal of discrediting it, but stopping short of precipitating its overthrow for fear that such an action would bring the conservatives to power. In fact, a common apprehension that Plaza's fall would only benefit a political opponent halted much of the opposition to his government. Similarly, rival factions in the military balanced one another out, even though opportunistic elements could act in an unpredictable fashion. In this environment, the communist party sought to increase "its organizational activity in order to revitalize and strengthen its position with labor and with members of the armed forces."[11] CIA analysts were at least partially right in that regard.

CIA case officers willingly stretched the available evidence to implicate communists in these potential military coups, even when they were obviously of rightist rather than leftist inspiration. In one example, an officer reported "Guayaquil Communists are planning to cut communications with Quito in the event of trouble," as if including this comment would sully the communists' name.[12] One particularly long memo attempted to clarify the "confusion as to the true identity of the organization behind the leftist, subversive troop movement" through a review of previous coup threats. Despite his best attempts to lay blame at the feet of the communists, the CIA officer (presumably Haney) had to concede no evidence existed of communist inspiration or control of the coup attempts despite the government's tendency to label all movements as such.[13]

Communist steadfast opposition to coup plotting did not mean that other sectors did not try to garner their support. In at least one case, Colonel César Alfaro, deputy chief of the armed forces, and the populist Carlos Guevara Moreno sought out communist support for their coup attempts. Rather than pledging support, the communists agreed "to promote a campaign of national unrest." Comments that Pedro Saad had made at an open meeting, however, contradicted that information. "Despite the grave errors made by the Plaza administration," a CIA report summarized him as stating, "the Communists would continue to support Plaza for the time being rather than give aid to a military-arranged coup." The report followed this with an editorial comment: "This statement may have been made for Plaza's consumption."[14] Further straining the credulity of an alliance between Guevara Moreno and the communists was what the CIA itself reported several weeks later—that Guevara Moreno had claimed that if he seized power he would immediately ban the PCE. Even if his statement was an opportunist gesture to gain the support of the United States government (which it probably was), it also won him the backing of the falangist group ARNE.[15] The communists had little to gain from such shenanigans.

A CIA officer also attempted to implicate the communists in "revolutionary actions" that the VRSE leaders General Luis Larrea Alba and Dr. Eduardo Ludeña were coordinating between Quito and Guayaquil. The VRSE's history and military roots made it more likely that its members would engage in a military coup than those of the PCE, but distinctions between various leftist groups often escaped the agency. What their "intelligence" mostly reflected was a lack of understanding of deep divisions on the left. This report describes the VRSE as "a radical socialist party closely affiliated with the Communist Party," and Ludeña was "generally regarded as a Communist" who "handles VRSE matters of a clandestine nature."[16] In an eagerness to blame all troubles on the communists, the report collapses the entire left together into an undistinguishable and homogeneous whole, and exaggerates the close connections between the two leftist parties. Several weeks later, a case officer once again reported that Larrea Alba and Ludeña were preparing to lead an army revolt. According to the informer, the situation was serious.[17] Several days later, this same information appeared in a weekly summary published at CIA Headquarters in Washington. Given the general dissatisfaction with the Plaza administration, the CIA analyst ranked the threat to the stability of his government as serious.[18] The agency suffered from a feedback loop in which listening to its own rhetoric reinforced its anticommunist assumptions.

The socialists were also more likely to support a coup attempt than were the communists, something that emerges numerous times in CIA reports. According to a case officer, the communist preference for the status quo "irritates the Socialists who claim that the Communists are holding back from a leftist demand for revolution by the people and accordingly are obstructing their chances of ultimate success." At one point the socialists turned to their 1948 presidential candidate Enríquez Gallo to see whether he would lead a "revolution."[19] Lingering distrust between the general and the communists meant that the latter were less than excited about supporting the general. As long as the Plaza government did not persecute the communists, they were content to leave things alone. Even so, the CIA maintained a paranoid and seemingly irrational fear of the PCE.

Communist leaders publicly and repeatedly reiterated their moderate position. For example, the FEUE invited Saad to give a talk to a packed auditorium at the Central University in Quito in commemoration of the third anniversary of José María Velasco Ibarra's March 30, 1946, self-coup that represented a definite blow for the left. In his opening comments, FEUE president Juan Manosalvas noted that both the socialists and communists were in favor of peace and opposed imperialist forces that were attempting to provoke a new world war. In his speech "The Process of Democracy in Ecuador," Saad declared that Marxists were against an immediate alteration in the constitutional order because of the danger of a right-wing military junta taking power as had happened recently in Venezuela and Peru. Rather, at present, he saw the Plaza government as the lesser of two evils. He counseled patience and predicted that soon Ecuador would achieve a proletarian democracy through a democratic-bourgeois revolution. In the meantime, he advocated for a revision of the conservative 1946 Constitution in order to confiscate foreign oil companies, break up large landholdings, provide women with equal rights, and introduce universal suffrage.[20] A week after the speech, the embassy's first secretary Maurice Bernbaum forwarded the CIA's summary of the speech that was largely extracted from media accounts to the State Department. Bernbaum added his own editorial comment on the PCE's hesitancy to advocate for the overthrow of Plaza's government due to a fear that the party might lose its "liberal privileges" under an inevitable resulting right-wing military dictatorship. Both Bernbaum and Haney noted the leftist criticism that Saad faced for his cautious position, from radical communist party members as well as the socialists who were much more vocal in their condemnation of the Plaza government.[21]

Military officials and perennial coup plotters César Alfaro and Carlos Mancheno, the military officer who removed Velasco Ibarra from office in August 1947, were more deeply involved in these plots than the communists ever were, but those facts did not conveniently fit an anticommunist narrative. This was the case even though the CIA and other US government agencies had access to ample information that implicated military officials in subversive maneuvering.[22] In one case, a CIA officer claimed that the communists had followed a threatened coup attempt in January 1949 "with great interest" and afterward "received a full report" on the events. According to this report, the communists "frequently invoke the name of Colonel Carlos Mancheno" even though their conspiratorial efforts were not related.[23] In March 1949 as part of an effort to score a political comeback, Mancheno managed to negotiate his election as president of the local liberal party council in Quito. His appointment triggered a strong opposition from some other liberal party members who feared that he was attempting a return to power.[24] CIA analysts concluded that he represented the radical wing of the liberal party. That wing did not have substantial strength, but his election was noteworthy because of his links with subversive activity in the military.[25]

On July 26, 1949, Mancheno launched yet another failed coup attempt against the Plaza administration. That action led Plaza to quip, "I am witnessing a demonstration of the national sport."[26] CIA analysts described this attack as a "fiasco" that indicated to both Mancheno's friends and enemies "that the armed forces were by no means inevitable collaborators in any revolutionary movement." Military leaders quickly repudiated Mancheno's action and pledged loyalty to the president, while those liberals and socialists who had supported the putsch "were quickly and unequivocally disowned by their parties." Significantly, now the CIA observed that the communists had "been notably inactive and extremely careful to avoid giving any appearance of participation" in Mancheno's repeated coup attempts. According to the CIA's analysis, their absence was motivated by an understanding that the coup had little hope of success, and that those who led the uprising were not sympathetic to the communist party or its goals. The outcome of the coup would not have likely been in their favor.[27] Notably, rather than instigating the coup attempt, it was the liberals who approached the communists and asked for their support with the latter responding in a noncommittal fashion rather than the communists leading the charge.[28]

On the eve of the coup, according to "information from a controlled American source," the party was in the process of reassessing its policy toward the current government. Since the communists were "making such progress under the favorable atmosphere of the Plaza Government," they had decided to adopt "a policy of non-opposition." According to the CIA officer, the PCE was afraid of the potential ramifications of either a military coup or the assumption of a conservative government to power, and therefore had opted to work peacefully and wait for "der tag," a more conducive time to press their agenda. At the same time, the CIA's source cautioned of plans for a strike in the Ancon oil fields "to promote new disturbances" since with the resolution of other strikes "the labor horizon apparently appeared too calm."[29] Even so, Haney was determined to present the PCE's policy of nonopposition to Plaza as opportunistic rather than principled in nature. According to his memo, communist leaders had taken this position only after they received assurance from the Plaza administration that the government would not seek to circumscribe the party's political freedoms as long as they refrained from engaging in revolutionary action. While the PCE was critical of Plaza's pro-United States policies, they avoided involvement in coup plotting "primarily because they did not wish to have the PCE outlawed by the government in retaliation."[30] Haney made no mention or acknowledgement that perhaps this political position emerged out of an ideological assumption that Ecuador did not meet the basic objective conditions necessary for a revolutionary transformation of society. Interpreting the decision in transactional terms highlights how his anticommunism hindered his ability to understand communist motivations.

But that was not the end of the story. Based on information from sources in both Quito and Guayaquil, Haney claimed that party leaders had decided on a change in policy toward the Plaza government. Allegedly at a July 14, 1949, meeting at Saad's house in Guayaquil, Alfredo Vera and Ana Moreno had agreed to join in efforts to "guide the Party's political efforts to the overthrow of the Plaza administration." Reportedly the communists would join socialists and liberals in their conspiracy, and were attempting to collaborate with leftist army officials such as Larrea Alba, Enríquez Gallo, and a Colonel Quintana. The hope was that these officials "would create a military government that would be friendly to the Communist Party." In return for their support, the communists were to receive a share of cabinet posts in the new coalition government, specifically the ministries of education and economy. The alleged targeting of those two ministries was to reduce the United States influence in the country and provide jobs to party members that would strengthen the party's financial situation and enable stronger support for worker strikes. According to these informers, liberals were more interested in the collaboration of the communists than were the socialists, but both recognized that the communists were the only group that was sufficiently disciplined and organized to carry through on a revolutionary conspiracy. The plan was to have the communists organize a series of labor strikes during the installation of congress on August 10 that would target United States companies. The goal was that the strikes would so disrupt the country and its economy that it would force leftist military officials to step in and restore order. Saad had abandoned all other party activities to dedicate himself to organizing this opposition to the government.[31]

Other, competing narratives emerged out of the CIA's reporting on these coup attempts. According to another memo, communist leaders were gathered in Quito on the eve of the revolt to plan their upcoming congress in Guayaquil. Unlike the liberals and socialists, they "had no knowledge of the revolution."[32] After its collapse, according to Haney, the coastal regional committee of the PCE declared that although the party was in favor of "a revolution which would bring a true Liberal into power, the Party could not support an oligarchic government such as Mancheno, allied with Arroyo del Río and Carlos Guevara Morena [*sic*]." Mancheno's coup attempt demonstrated the level of popular discontent with the Plaza government due to the interventions of "the Yankee imperialists, the Church and the rich factory and hacienda owners." The memo continued, "When the time was ripe, the PCE would advise its members when to strike against these forces." The statement closed with a list of party goals, and a declaration that the only path to a genuine revolution would "be one in which the true leaders of the masses would be brought into power and the pueblo liberated from their imperialistic masters."[33]

Bernbaum faithfully forwarded this information from Haney to the State Department, but added his own caveats and qualifying comments. He rightfully observed, as he had noted in previous correspondence, that the PCE had little to gain from engaging in coup plotting. In fact, earlier in July liberal leaders whom the CIA now accused of cavorting with the communists in conspiring against Plaza had been arrested—much to the consternation and condemnation both of the party and the general public—in an alleged plot against the government, but there were no whispers of communist involvement in that activity.[34] To underscore this point, Bernbaum noted that the communists had no knowledge or involvement with Mancheno's July 26 attempt. What Bernbaum should have recognized, and perhaps did, was that the conspiracy that the CIA officer laid out was most unlikely, both in terms of the people involved and how it did not match with the party's current line. Vera, for example, came from a conservative wing of the party that made it improbable that he would engage in such insurrectionary tactics. Moreno was one of the party's most militant members and constantly tangled with Saad, and was therefore unlikely to collaborate with him in as sensitive of an operation as this would be. Bernbaum seemingly acknowledged the problematic content of this "intelligence" with his equivocal concluding comment that perhaps the nature of such an alliance would emerge during the forthcoming session of congress.[35] A week later, the embassy once again cited what it considered to be reliable reports of communist intentions to instigate strikes that would correspond with the opening session of the federal congress on August 10.[36] Rather than crediting the PCE with pursuing a serious political agenda, United States officials had trouble seeing beyond an alleged desire to disrupt the smooth functioning of society.

Of all the different forces at play, the communists acted in the most rational and least opportunistic fashion. In retrospect, their abstinence from coup plotting played to their benefit because, as a CIA analyst in Washington remarked, "no one, in or out of the government, has tried to make a whipping-boy of the Communists." This observation contributed to the CIA's conclusion that "Nothing in the current Ecuadoran situation is causing or immediately portends noticeable change in status of US security interests in the area."[37] Had the communists lent their support to the coup, inevitably the CIA would have used it as a justification to ramp up their anticommunist rhetoric. Ambassador John Simmons expressed a dissenting view to that which the intelligence agency advanced. From his perspective, Plaza faced more of a threat from a military coup or a right-wing opponent like Guevara Moreno than from the communists.[38] Blinded by their own anticommunist assumptions, the CIA continually exaggerated the threat that the PCE actually presented to the country's political stability.

After a year in office, Plaza passed a milestone by surviving two more coup plots. Near Loja, in southern Ecuador, authorities arrested Quito city council member and FEUE president Bolívar Gálvez and liberal leader Julio Moreno for alleged involvement, but again the coup attempt was not of communist inspiration.[39] Plaza credited the army with suppressing these attacks on his administration. The *Hispanic World Report*, a monthly summary of news from the Hispanic American Studies program at Stanford University, thought that ironic since the military typically took the lead in such attempts.[40] On November 4, 1949, assailants damaged a bridge in Cuenca with a bomb blast just after Plaza had crossed it. Some again accused the communists of being the author of the attack, but no evidence emerged of their involvement.[41] It seemed as if these attacks would never cease. None of these putsches had managed to advance a leftist agenda.

A careful study reveals a mixed record on the ability of various United States agencies and individuals to understand repeated coup plotting in Ecuador. Haney's strong anticommunist sentiments in particular colored his ability to present an objective and accurate assessment of communist attitudes. His track record helps explain a marked disconnect between State Department reports that featured a more measured analysis and those of CIA officers who tended toward exaggerated and conspiratorial statements. A result is that United States diplomats articulated somewhat more accurate understandings of the communist party's tactical positions than did CIA officers and analysts, even when the embassy staff relied on CIA investigations as their source of information.

War of the Worlds

It was in the midst of this coup plotting and challenges to Plaza's hold on power that Radio Quito broadcast its version of the "The War of the Worlds." The CIA engaged in a deep investigation of the incident, desperate to determine whether a communist conspiracy underlay the events. In retrospect, it is not odd that the agency would do so. Several years later, Welles's original transmission of "The War of the Worlds" provided a model for a "panic broadcast" designed to undermine Jacobo Arbenz's progressive government in Guatemala.[42] In Ecuador, the socialist lawyer Juan Isaac Lovato provided a legal defense for those who had staged the play, which in the minds of some further implicated the left in the violence. In the end, and with a good deal of stereotyping and racist disdain, analysts at CIA Headquarters in Washington looked to the event as "another dramatic incident showing the emotional instability of Latin American crowds and their potential for violent reaction to chance events."[43] At a different time and in another place, analysts would have immediately recognized the events for what they were—an innocent prank gone terribly awry.

Looking for scapegoats, the police detained Radio Quito's dramatic director Eduardo Alcarás and art director Leonardo Páez who had staged the broadcast. The station owners refused to take responsibility for the chaos, claiming that Alcarás and Páez had prepared the broadcast without their knowledge.[44] A CIA officer discovered that Alcarás had signed a monthlong contract with Paéz and Carlos Mantilla Ortega, the general manager of the radio station and director of *El Comercio*, to produce two radio dramas, including "The War of the Worlds." Despite claims of innocence, Mantilla had been complicit in a series of planted stories leading up to the broadcast, including one sensationalist report the day of the broadcast that alleged unidentified flying object (UFO) sightings around

Quito.[45] Alcarás brought the script from Chile where he had previously been involved in its production, and local performers rehearsed the script in the studio. According to a CIA report, the radio production itself only lasted for fifteen minutes, from 9:15 p.m. when it broke into a regularly scheduled music program to 9:30 when Alcarás announced that it had been a dramatization and was not true. Apparently in that short amount of time news spread quickly across Quito leading to panic and destruction. Within half an hour people had broken into the *El Comercio* building and began to destroy it and its contents. According to the CIA, the police had not headed out to Cotocollao as the press had reported but instead had retreated to their police stations where lacking proper leadership they were "utterly confused and disorganized." Fearing a coup attempt, minister of defense Manuel Díaz Granados mobilized military troops who descended on the station with their tanks and dispersed the crowd. With the army having cleared the way, the firefighters were finally able to approach the building and put out the flames.[46]

Despite this narrative, the CIA was not content to let the communists off so easily. In an attempt to connect the communists with the unrest, an officer noted that *El Comercio* and Radio Quito supported president Plaza whereas the left opposed him. In fact, the officer claimed, the communist party had "prohibited all Party members from reading the *El Comercio*, charging it with being a capitalistic, anti-Communist newspaper." Furthermore, allegedly leftist university students cut fire hoses, broke fire hydrants, and otherwise interfered with the efforts of the firefighters to put out the fire. Meanwhile, the paper's owners Carlos and Jorge Mantilla Ortega met with the president and emphatically denied that they knew anything about the broadcast, and declared that the fire was the work of the communists and must have been premeditated in order to cause so much damage. Furthermore, they asserted that they had not been aware that they had been harboring communist agitators in the radio station. Defense Minister Díaz Granados concurred that communists had planned the entire event.[47]

Almost a year earlier, on April 9, 1948, the assassination of the popular liberal leader and presidential candidate Jorge Eliécer Gaitán in neighboring Colombia led to massive protests known colloquially as the *Bogotazo*. At the time, both the mainstream media and the newly formed CIA looked to the communists as a convenient scapegoat. It did not matter that the communist party, neither in Colombia nor in Ecuador, had anything to gain from engaging in such illegal activities. Now, a year later, events appeared to be repeating themselves with some pointing to the communists as attempting to turn Quito into a "second Bogotá." Particularly in Guayaquil, a series of arson attempts fueled speculation that political agitators were seeking a repeat of those events.[48] This perceived threat and fear became a common theme in both embassy and CIA reports. "The actual strength of the communists," an informer told vice consul Walter Houk, "was a difficult thing to gauge." From Houk's perspective, the communists "did not have much of a political organization, but that they had agitators who would be ready to take advantage of any unrest or upheaval, and might produce great damage with the volatile populace in their spell, similar to the Bogotá riots of last year."[49] The CIA freely quoted sources that reinforced this narrative. For example, the Mexican youth leader Manuel Popoca Estrada was in Ecuador at the time and allegedly joined student activists in the storming of the radio station. According to the agency, "Popoca wrote a letter to a prominent Communist leader in Guayaquil, stating that the local Communists had nothing to do with the radio broadcast but in his opinion the entire incident was a good thing as it showed the people how much power they had once they were organized into a mob."[50]

Despite these conspiracy theories, the CIA "ascertained from reliable sources that the Communist Party Headquarters knew nothing whatever in advance of the broadcast and were as frightened by it as were the majority of the people of Quito." For several days, party leaders remained "very apprehensive over the public charges and rumors that they were responsible for the broadcast and fire." The party debated publishing a handbill proclaiming their innocence and denouncing the authorities for their failure to prevent the broadcast and resulting death and destruction. In the end, they decided that it would not be politically expedient to do so.

While the responsible (and some would say conservative) party leaders sought to distance themselves from the disturbances, the CIA emphasized that "as individuals, certain members participated in both phases of the incident." Furthermore, the CIA was adamant that when news of the chaos reached Guayaquil some members there "were elated over the incident and were only awaiting an opportunity to take similar action." According to this narrative, Ecuador was on the verge of a social explosion and the communists should take advantage of the situation. Fostering this paranoia were media reports of attempts to start fires in Guayaquil that because of its wooden construction could be consumed in a conflagration. The CIA, of course, linked those anonymous arson attacks to communist conspiracies.[51]

"In a very confidential conversation," party leader Saad blamed the riot and destruction on Ecuador's distressed state of affairs. He feared that the communists, as well as other leftist parties, were losing control. He acknowledged that some in Guayaquil wanted to burn and sack the city in a repeat of what had happened at Bogotá a year earlier, and that the party was attempting to avoid such actions. A problem, as could be observed in Bogotá, was that when a crowd lacked a proper political orientation it would go its own way. The party sought to "guide the people but economic misery is driving them now to wild ideas." Saad confessed that he hoped that "the worst can be avoided although the danger is great."[52] His statements are not reflective of a party that advocated for violent and extraconstitutional changes in power.

Most of those the police had arrested in connection with either having participated in the broadcast or the assault on the radio station were not communists and had no record of involvement in political activities. The exceptions were Gustavo Ramírez Gutiérrez, a Nicaraguan communist who was deported from the country; the French communist Raymond Mériguet who claimed he was not in Quito at the time; and a communist university student named Romo Leroux (presumably Ketty Romo-Leroux). The CIA contended that Raúl Molestina, the pianist for Radio Quito and one of those who died in the fire, "was an ardent Communist and the leader of the Communist Party Cell 'San Blas' in Quito." The officer also identified violinist Corsino Durán Carrión, another employee of the station, as a communist, and possibly Luis Cevallos as well.[53] None of these people played visible roles in the annals of the party's history. Nevertheless, if indeed the communists were behind the violence, they suffered from it as much as anyone.

THROUGHOUT ALL OF these coup threats and other political disturbances, what US government officials did not generally recognize, or did not want to admit, was the communist party's opposition to extraconstitutional alterations in power. As the labor historian Jon Kofas testifies, "the Ecuadorean Communist party was not revolutionary and presented no threat to the oligarchic-dominated institutions. Not only were the communist party's links to Moscow insignificant, but the party preached reformism and European-style social welfare programs within the parliamentary system."[54] No evidence exists that the PCE seriously pursued plans for sabotage, which raises questions as to the validity of the CIA's intelligence.

Decades later, the agency finally seemed to recognize that reality. "The country has no significant subversion or terrorism problem that immediately threatens its neighbors," its 1970 handbook on the region stated.[55] "The PCE has never attempted guerrilla warfare or terrorism as a means to overthrow the government," an analyst wrote three years later in a national security estimate.

"It has publicly denounced such tactics and indicated its support for the *vía pacífica* or nonviolent approach to revolution."[56] This conservative tendency within pro-Soviet parties was, of course, what led Fidel Castro to break from the communist party in Cuba. Similar tensions also tore at communist unity in Ecuador. In the meantime, the CIA sought to undermine the legitimacy of the PCE by forwarding a narrative that rather than responding to domestic conditions it relied on foreign support to advance its radical agenda.

CHAPTER 4

Moscow Gold

UNITED STATES OFFICIALS AND members of the domestic ruling class have long claimed that outside agitators rather than unequal and exploitative class structures are to blame for political unrest in Latin America. Both pointed to foreign support to explain the rise of militant movements. This included a fabled search for "Moscow gold," even though neither was ever able to provide any concrete evidence to prove their charges. These investigations were ultimately misguided as they failed to comprehend the domestic roots of radical critiques of society. Even so, stereotypes of communists as stooges of a foreign power persisted and served as an effective tool to undermine the left's efforts to propagate its message.

The Ecuadorian communist party grappled with a variety of problems in advancing its political agenda, and confronting charges of foreign funding was only the beginning. The party faced continual obstacles with the publication of its newspaper *El Pueblo*, including convincing party members to take the distribution of the paper seriously and to pay for copies that they received. The party also encountered difficulties in maintaining its bookstores and newsstands where it could distribute its propaganda. Despite these challenges, the PCE engaged in a variety of other endeavors including promoting the projection of movies from the Soviet Union in local theaters. In order to move forward, the party would have to overcome many barriers to its success.

Funding Sources

An almost pathological urge to uncover external sources of funding for subversive activities runs throughout United States surveillance of the left. These notions persisted for decades, and were even prevalent among what would otherwise be considered a well-informed population. In his book on communism in Latin America, Robert Alexander states, "The Communists never have lacked for money." He claimed that they had fifteen to twenty full-time workers in Guayaquil in the 1940s, an obviously inflated number. He similarly reported bloated figures for party expenditures on labor congresses and elections.[1] Thirty years later, the renowned political scientist (and former career Foreign Service officer) Cole Blasier asks how small and impoverished communist parties in Latin America could "have continued to function all these years without Soviet help?"[2] Rumors of "Moscow gold" would never die.

In line with attempts to undermine legitimate political activism, CIA officers regularly included unsubstantiated or unconfirmed information on external backing in their reports. Further complicating efforts to corroborate these details is the agency's practice of redacting the names of their informers. In one case, the CIA reported without comment the opinion of one person who was "usually very well informed on Communist activities . . . that at the present time Pedro Saad ranks third among the leading Communists in America." Saad traveled frequently, and intended to "attend an important Communist meeting in Montevideo." Since Saad had returned from a meeting in Warsaw, Ecuador had become the center of communist activities in Latin America and instructions for other parties emanated out of Guayaquil. The officer expected Saad to receive European visitors with instructions and propaganda on a regular basis, including the possibility of "a Russian expert in Communist tactics." Revealing the persistent but never verified gossip of "Moscow gold," Saad allegedly returned from Europe with "a considerable sum of money" to advance the communist cause in Ecuador.[3] A continual problem with surveillance sources was overeager informers or even government officials who were willing to exaggerate or manufacture information in order to justify their activities (as well as the payments they would receive for passing on the information).

On the other hand, and seemingly in contrast to this narrative, CIA officers and other United States officials reported on the party's continual struggle to raise funds, which included resorting to benefit dances, raffles, and parties.[4] A military attaché in 1947, for example, painted a dismal picture of the party's finances. The attaché noted that funding came from individual dues, voluntary contributions, party enterprises, and fundraisers. Those with government jobs were expected to make additional contributions. The party did not pay salaries for any of its officers, and its principle expenses were rent for party headquarters, travel expenses, meeting costs, publication expenses, and medical and legal assistance for those in need. Nevertheless, a large number of members were chronically in arrears with their dues, which hurt the party's finances. The report closed with the admission that it had been "some time" since the local party had received funds from Moscow. Party leaders were hopeful that Moscow would provide "direct financial support," but no evidence ever emerged that those wishes were realized.[5]

As the attaché had observed, according to party statutes the PCE was self-financed with member dues that were supplemented with donations from sympathizers and fundraisers. Members were expected to pay 1 percent of their income into the party coffers, although those who were unemployed or physically ill could be temporarily exempted. Those with government positions would be charged dues at a higher rate. The payments were to be split evenly between the local cell and higher-level party organs.[6] But the party faced continual difficulties in actually collecting these funds. One CIA report indicated "that the financial condition of the party is critical, and that at every cell meeting leaders plead for more contributions." A report from 1949 indicated that only about half the cells had contributed funds in recent months as party statutes dictated.[7] Another memo a couple of months later bluntly stated, "The Party is urgently in need of funds." The collection of monthly dues had fallen off sharply, with only one-third of the members in Pichincha up to date with their payments.[8]

Financial considerations appeared at all levels of the party in all parts of the country, including at a weekly meeting of the party's Pedro Saad cell that gathered in Quito at a small cafe operated by a person named Oña. Jorge Arellano Gallegos presided over the meeting of about thirty members that lasted for only half an hour. The main topic was the need to raise 5,000 sucres (about $285 USD) to establish a cafe to generate revenue for the cell. The cell would raise the money through the sale of one hundred shares at fifty sucres each, and Arellano had already sold twenty shares. Arellano closed the short meeting with a request that all cell members attend a gathering at the party's headquarters the following day to hear a call for political action.[9] While the party faced continual financial pressure, militants never lost sight of their larger political objectives.

The issue of fundraising was a common topic not only at local party meetings but also at national congresses. At the PCE's fifth party congress in 1952, the finance commission characterized the present status of party finances as "disastrous," primarily because of a failure to collect dues. The party's principal sources of income were interest payments from investments with an agrarian cooperative at Tigua and with the Rumiñahui press in Quito. The commission presented a short report that pledged to educate party members about their financial responsibilities; establish provincial controls for party finances; develop new sources of income from the sale of publications, social functions, bookstores, and collection of funds from friends and sympathizers; and initiate a broader fundraising campaign.[10] The party's financial difficulties presented fundamental and seemingly unsurmountable obstacles to the growth of the party.

The problem of dues collection never went away. A congress of the Guayas provincial committee in August 1953 dedicated an entire session to party finances. Most comrades fell perpetually behind in their dues payments, which continued to place the party in financial distress. Only the Joaquín Gallegos Lara and Pedro Saad cells emerged from the inquisition with clean records.[11] After the party's sixth congress in 1957, the CIA pointed to a chronic lack of funds as one of the key factors that contributed to the decline of the party.[12] Those factors hardly provided evidence for the presence of Moscow gold.

One of the CIG's first intelligence reports from 1947 discussed the PCE's collection of funds for the purchase of a printing press to publish a daily newspaper. Militants sold bonds for the project, which essentially represented a donation to the party. The officer alleged that the bonds were "a 'cover-up' for the receipt of funds from abroad." But the intelligence report hardly served to support this accusation. The party had only collected 25,000 of the necessary 70,000 sucres, and so looked to other fundraising strategies such as holding dances and other social events. The first dance only netted 1,075 sucres, but still the party hoped to raise sufficient funds to purchase the press by the end of the year.[13] This is not a reflection of a party flush with funds or with access to generous external revenue flows. The CIA inadvertently documented that reality as it repeatedly reported on the party's "severe financial situation."[14]

Months later, a CIA officer reported yet again on the party's ongoing efforts to secure the necessary financing to purchase a printing press that would allow it to publish their propaganda. At present the communists had a small, manual press that could only be used for occasional handbills. Allegedly the party now had 60,000 sucres at its disposal, though the author of the intelligence report questioned this amount. Either it was exaggerated, he concluded, or it was an indication that the party had received money from outside of the country because "local contributions and other normal sources would not account for it."[15] As always, the officer did not provide any evidence to support that claim. Another CIA report outlined the amount of funds (8,000 sucres) it needed for propaganda and organizational work at an upcoming CTE congress and noted its inability to raise that amount. Party treasurer María Luisa Gómez de la Torre planned to initiate a program of voluntary donations from the general public to meet that shortfall.[16] Instead of external funding sources, what emerges evident in these reports was that the lack of funds compromised the party's ability to act.

In April 1950, CIA analysts in Washington concluded, "Communist leaders have ambitious plans for a general strike, but given the present lack of funds and the declining enthusiasm of rank-and-file party members, such plans have little chance of realization without considerable financial support from abroad." After a redacted sentence, the report continues, "As yet there is no clear evidence that the PCE has received financial help from any other foreign source."[17] CIA officers believed that if it were able to document external sources of funding they could challenge the party's legitimacy, but clear-headed analysts removed from the immediate pressure of fabricating evidence were not able to do so.

Even with these limitations, CIA officers were often all too willing to entertain rumors of funding flows even when they lacked any documented basis in facts. The militantly anticommunist minister of government Eduardo Salazar Gómez, for example, alleged that various agents had brought "large sums of money" from Russia into Ecuador, possibly through the Mexican and Uruguayan embassies. He surmised that the money was intended to launch a leftist coup against the government. Albert Haney passed this information on to Ambassador John Simmons even though he readily admitted that he lacked confirmation of its veracity.[18] United States government officials repeated these types of rumors and suppositions ad nauseam even as they implicitly acknowledged the absence of such funds. "Although it has been reported that American dollars reach the hands of local Communists," the public affairs officer (PAO) Reginald Bragonier in the Quito Embassy commented in response to a questionnaire on Soviet propaganda, "there is no evidence that such funds are used to support any publication other than perhaps *El Pueblo*, Communist sheet, which has appeared irregularly in the past." Based on nothing more than what would amount to legal hearsay, Bragonier proceeded to note that "it has been reported, but not confirmed, however, that a sum of money was received recently from Moscow to establish a publishing plant in Ecuador."[19] Even the most remote rumor of foreign funding warranted repeating.

Another alleged plan involved raising funds by blackmailing small merchants in Quito and Guayaquil with "riot insurance" to protect their shops.[20] Even though criminal endeavors were not consistent with the party's operating procedures, CIA officers continued to report on similar types of actions. According to one informer, the party collected funds from business owners in Guayaquil to subsidize their next electoral campaign. This source declared that the payments were in cash rather than check to avoid leaving any record of the transactions.[21] These statements could either be ideologically motivated to denounce a party to which an informer was opposed, or they may have been designed to curry favor with a US government agency by telling officials what they thought they might want to hear.

A curiosity in a confidential CIA information report on PCE finances is the redaction of what would appear to be the name of the treasurer of the central committee for the province of Pichincha (see figure 4.1). This person reported to Gómez de la Torre that payment of monthly dues from party members and sympathizers had fallen off sharply. Typically, the CIA only redacts the names of its officers and informers before releasing documents, which raises the possibility that the treasurer was on the CIA payroll. It was standard FBI practice in the United States to place its infiltrators in positions of control over a targeted group's finances because of the information and possibilities for disruption it could generate. A leftist distaste for dealing with money facilitated such activities, and similar factors may have been at play here. If this were the case, the report that "only about one-third of the 400 quota payers have paid up to date and many of the remainder are as much as three months in arrears" could be evidence of active attempts to embezzle money with a goal of disrupting party activities, though of course that information could have come from a local police operative rather than a CIA agent. If indeed a party treasurer were either on the CIA or police payroll, surely the agency would have been aware that its accusations of external funding sources were simply not true (or, alternatively, provided concrete incriminating evidence of such payments that are notably absent from the historical record).[22]

Echoing these persistent searches for "Moscow gold," an OIR report sought evidence for the source of funding for a massive mobilization of Latin American students to the Berlin Youth Festival in August 1951. The report noted that the Ecuadorian party "receives a small amount of outside direction and financial assistance," though it failed to provide any specific details.[23] CIA analysts in Washington expressed similar concern with how communists had funded the attendance of nine communist and left-wing socialist delegates from Ecuador at the festival. According to their intelligence, the Quito and Guayaquil city councils, the ministry of education, the Casa de la Cultura, and the government's development fund Corporación de Fomento all had contributed funds. The report included a comment (author redacted) that the donation from the Guayaquil city council was "not surprising since Communists have recently been able to obtain influential positions in Guayaquil municipal affairs." Quito's mayor had made the contribution "on a cultural basis," but the CIA analyst found that explanation less than convincing "since the Quito city council is predominantly Conservative and the Mayor is allied with a violently anti-Communist group,"

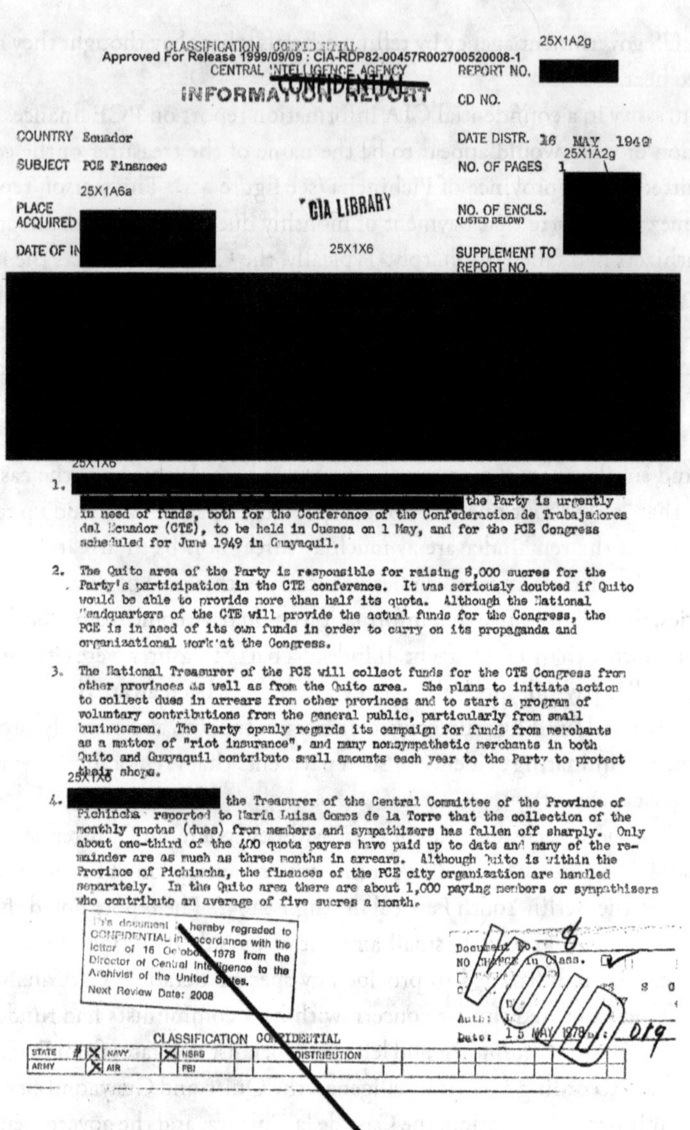

CLASSIFICATION CONFIDENTIAL

Approved For Release 1999/09/09 : CIA-RDP82-00457R002700520008-1

25X1A2g

CENTRAL INTELLIGENCE AGENCY

CONFIDENTIAL

INFORMATION REPORT

REPORT NO.

CD NO.

COUNTRY Ecuador

SUBJECT PCE Finances

25X1A6a

PLACE ACQUIRED

DATE OF IN

CIA LIBRARY

25X1X6

DATE DISTR. 16 MAY 1949

25X1A2g

NO. OF PAGES 1

NO. OF ENCLS. (LISTED BELOW)

SUPPLEMENT TO REPORT NO.

25X1X6

1. the Party is urgently in need of funds, both for the Conference of the Confederacion de Trabajadores del Ecuador (CTE), to be held in Cuenca on 1 May, and for the PCE Congress scheduled for June 1949 in Guayaquil.

2. The Quito area of the Party is responsible for raising 8,000 sucres for the Party's participation in the CTE conference. It was seriously doubted if Quito would be able to provide more than half its quota. Although the National Headquarters of the CTE will provide the actual funds for the Congress, the PCE is in need of its own funds in order to carry on its propaganda and organizational work at the Congress.

3. The National Treasurer of the PCE will collect funds for the CTE Congress from other provinces as well as from the Quito area. She plans to initiate action to collect dues in arrears from other provinces and to start a program of voluntary contributions from the general public, particularly from small businessmen. The Party openly regards its campaign for funds from merchants as a matter of "riot insurance", and many nonsympathetic merchants in both Quito and Guayaquil contribute small amounts each year to the Party to protect their shops.

25X1X6

4. the Treasurer of the Central Committee of the Province of Pichincha reported to Maria Luisa Gomez de la Torre that the collection of the monthly quotas (dues) from members and sympathizers has fallen off sharply. Only about one-third of the 400 quota payers have paid up to date and many of the remainder are as much as three months in arrears. Although Quito is within the Province of Pichincha, the finances of the PCE city organization are handled separately. In the Quito area there are about 1,000 paying members or sympathizers who contribute an average of five sucres a month.

This document is hereby regraded to CONFIDENTIAL in accordance with the letter of 16 October 1978 from the Director of Central Intelligence to the Archivist of the United States.

Next Review Date: 2008

Document No. 8

NO CHANGE in Class.

VOID

Auth:

Date: 15 MAY 1978 By: 019

CLASSIFICATION CONFIDENTIAL

STATE	X	NAVY	X	NSRB		DISTRIBUTION
ARMY	X	AIR		FBI		

CONFIDENTIAL

Approved For Release 1999/09/09 : CIA-RDP82-00457R002700520008-1

FIGURE 4.1. A CIA information report on PCE finances with the name of the treasurer of the central committee of the province of Pichincha redacted. Source: Central Intelligence Agency (CIA), "PCE Finances," May 16, 1949, CIA Electronic Reading Room, https://www.cia.gov/library/readingroom/document/cia-rdp82-00457r002700520008-1.

the CFP. Rather, the report concluded that the "Communist-dominated" FEUE had misrepresented the nature of donations from the ministry of education and the Casa de la Cultura. The conniving students had drawn on the council's naiveté to hide the communist nature of the festival. Finally, while acknowledging that "some money was evidently raised locally," the CIA claimed without providing any documentary evidence that "little doubt" existed "that the larger part of the delegates' expenses is being financed from abroad."[24] The obvious intent was to delegitimize the validity of progressive mobilizations.

These (failed) attempts to document external sources of subversive activity continued for decades. In a 1956 State Department report on communism in Latin America, an estimation of Soviet control over Latin American communist affairs remained more an issue of supposition than one of documented evidence. The department maintained that external support was "essential to the maintenance of the Communist apparatus in Latin America" even though it lacked concrete evidence to prove that point.[25] A 1973 CIA national security estimate persisted in these allegations, without ever presenting any documentation to back up its claims, that "The PCE continues to be dependent on the Soviet Union for financial aid." The agency proceeded to point to "other kinds of aid" such as "payment of passage for PCE leaders attending meetings in the East European Communist countries and scholarships for students to study in the Soviet Union."[26] If this were the extent of "the known Soviet financial support," it is not that different from academic associations providing assistance for scholars from the Global South to attend international congresses when they could not otherwise afford to do so, or governments and foundations providing scholarships to students for university degrees. The gestures could be seen in turn as propagandistic, manipulative, altruistic, or simply self-serving in terms of raising the level of discourse and debate by bringing diverse perspectives into meetings.

El Pueblo

Complicating the party's financial situation was the fact that members owed the party a significant amount of money for copies of the party newspaper *El Pueblo*. The distribution of *El Pueblo* was a persistent problem for the party, and one that leaders sought to address by urging members to distribute unsold copies.[27] The Guayas provincial committee was responsible for about half of this debt. In 1952, leaders decided to require payment of all of these debts within a month of the party's fifth congress or they would impose sanctions on the laggards. Rather than buying on credit, the congress recommended that local parties purchase copies of the paper and retain any profits from their sale. That way the cost of the paper and impetus for making effective use of limited party resources would be shifted from the central committee to local organizations and cells. Furthermore, the congress urged members to use the paper as an opportunity to engage in political education as that would ensure future sales as more people became interested in the communist message. The newspaper administrator Pedro Ortiz Aldas claimed that the newspaper would be forced to suspend publication if the problem of payments was not promptly solved.[28] Lack of secure funding for the party's newspaper was a persistent problem that never went away.

The historian Hernán Ibarra postulates that often copies of the paper remained in party offices or private houses, which limited its ability to advance a political agenda.[29] This theme emerged repeatedly in the paper's pages. One editorial commented on the weekly's long tradition of struggle and its importance in pressing working-class demands, but expressed concern that the party had not dedicated sufficient resources to assure that issues were sold and that the money was collected. Financial difficulties frequently required that the paper suspend publication. The newspaper was critical to the party's anticonservative and antifascist struggles, and party leaders pleaded with their members to work to assure its success.[30]

A preoccupation with finances was an ever-present matter in party gatherings. The primary topic of discussion at a February 11, 1953, meeting of the PCE's propaganda committee held at the office of Alfonso Quijano Cobos in Guayaquil concerned this issue of raising funds for *El Pueblo*. One tactic was to offer free subscriptions for various communist publications as a prize to the individual and cell who sold the most copies. The committee held a second meeting the following night at the home of Franklin Pérez Castro to schedule future meetings for local cells. At that meeting, Pérez Castro distributed bonds to raise funds for *El Pueblo*.[31] Similar points appear in a circular that the propaganda committee distributed later in the year. Party leaders urged cell members to sell the paper because otherwise the publication would be forced to close, and members needed to take their duty to distribute the party organ seriously. The circular also highlighted the need to promote a pamphlet that denounced the granting of contracts to pave Guayaquil streets to private contractors.[32]

Half a year later, CIA officers continued to report that the paper was "in imminent danger of being discontinued for lack of funds." Its closure "would be a very serious setback for the Party."[33] In 1957, the embassy's public affairs office claimed that "a PCE sympathizer" had bequeathed a house to the party in his will that was sold for 300,000 sucres, about $16,000 USD. Paredes had refused to turn the money over to current "leaders for fear that it will be uselessly dissipated." Instead, he advocated investing the money in real estate and using those profits to fund projects. "The Party is badly in need of the money to finance *El Pueblo*," the information officer Clifford Adams related, "but all efforts to convince Paredes of this need have to date been unsuccessful."[34] Assuring the survival of *El Pueblo* was a long-term concern for the PCE, and something that would not have been an issue if it had access to a secure revenue stream.

Although the economic realities of publishing a newspaper were always foremost in the agency's recounting of these discussions, party leaders never lost track of the importance of having an organ in which they could advance their political agenda. CIA surveillance helps document both the party's attention to internal study as well as efforts to propagate their ideology. The party urged a fight for freedom of the press and victory for the demands of workers at San Carlos, Servitransa, and Hacienda Bola de Oro. Cells were to prepare wall posters featuring slogans advancing their struggles.[35] The party needed money to operate, but generating revenue was not the purpose of the party. Notwithstanding financial difficulties and internal conflicts, the fight would go on.

Newsstand

Despite a persistent belief that "Moscow gold" funded communist activities in Ecuador, the CIA continued to report on the PCE's "acute financial situation" and the party's efforts to raise money. The Guayas provincial committee decided to sponsor several raffles in which the winning numbers would be the same as those of the Guayaquil city lottery. One of the raffles was for an "elegant and authentic Chinese robe, completely embroidered by hand" that the Guayas committee had on display at the newsstand that it maintained at the main post office in Guayaquil. The party was selling 250 tickets for 5 sucres each, which would net the committee 1,250 sucres, or about $75 USD. PCE leaders asked party members in the Guayaquil area for more suggestions about the most effective method to raise funds for the party.[36] Franklin Pérez Castro convinced his brother Ismael, the manager of *El Universo*, to post 3,000 sucres as a guarantee to the Guayaquil lottery for use of their numbers. When Ismael discovered that he was liable for the entire amount and that the raffle was to benefit the PCE, he became "extremely angry with his brother."[37] Such subterfuge would not have been necessary if the party had access to a reliable stream of funding.

On the night of July 1, 1953, someone attempted to burn down the PCE's newsstand. The attack destroyed some of the party's propaganda material stored at the stand and damaged the stall's walls and floor. The PCE blamed their right-wing opponents in the ARNE for the attack, and the CIA admitted knowledge of its involvement. ARNE members, whom the communists derogatorily labeled as "gallinazos" or buzzards, had printed counterfeit tickets for the PCE raffle. The communists notified the police commissioner of the falsification, and Pérez Castro denounced the fraud in his family's newspaper *El Universo*. The agency noted that "the counterfeit tickets was a topic of the day in Quito," but gave no indication whether the CIA was implicated in this subversion.[38] In any case, the ARNE appeared to be quite capable of acting on its own and possessed the motivation to do so without external encouragement.

The attack on the newsstand was part of a larger pattern of politically motivated assaults on the party. One example was a 1951 robbery at PCE Headquarters in Guayaquil. According to Saad, at 10:30 a.m. on Tuesday, June 26, 1951, six unknown individuals carrying knives and guns broke into the party headquarters. At the time, the only people in the building were the young communists Carlos and César Muñoz. The assailants locked the two up in the party's bookstore. The attackers proceeded to ruffle through papers on Saad's desk and took several documents. Saad declared that the assault was not one of common crime because they did not take anything of value, even though typewriters, bicycles, and other items were present in the office. The communist leader charged that it was a political attack carried out by either Ecuadorian or international reactionary elements who sought to appropriate party documents. The party leadership planned to meet and release a formal statement on the attack.[39] That occurrence highlights the constant threats under which the party operated. CIA surveillance often provides effective documentation of the nature of these attacks and the conditions under which the communists operated.

During the end of June and beginning of July 1953, the newsstand sold between 20 to 200 sucres worth of material a day. The most popular publications included those sent from abroad (*Unión Soviética*; *Por una paz duradera, Por una democracia popular*; *La Mujer Soviética*; *Tiempos Nuevos*; *Historia del Partido Comunista de la URSS*), as well as the party's newspaper *El Pueblo*. The CIA reported that after July 9 newsstand sales had fallen off significantly, and currently did not exceed 1.60 sucres a day. "This sudden and sharp drop in sales was caused by the shortage of propaganda material," the agency noted, "and was interpreted by the PCE as a sign that the government interception of propaganda in the Guayaquil post office was becoming even more effective."[40] A year later, the foreign minister Luis Antonio Peñaherrera proudly told Ambassador Sheldon Mills that while previously serving as minister of government he had ordered the burning of communist material and that now very little was reaching those to whom it was addressed.[41] The CIA report provides no indication as to whether the agency may have been complicit in the interdiction of that material, but given the agency's turn toward covert action under the Eisenhower administration this might have been the beginning of direct intervention in Ecuador's internal affairs. Communists blamed a similar disruption in the delivery of printed materials in Quito not on the CIA but on the conservative and famously anticommunist minister of government Camilo Ponce Enríquez who had his own motivations for taking such actions. In light of Peñaherrera's comment, they were probably not entirely wrong in their identification of the domestic roots of their troubles.

The problems facing the newsstand were not easily solved. In late February 1954, the PCE decided to suspend operation of the newsstand as well that of its bookstore. According to the CIA, "The newsstand would be turned over to any comrade who desired to assume the business and could pay the rent, with the understanding that he would continue to sell the PCE newspaper *El Pueblo* there, as well as bits of Communist literature remaining in stock." Meanwhile, the party took steps to assure that its endeavors would be more commercially successful. Rafael Echeverría's wife Ana Bartonova de Echeverría reportedly stated that the party's executive committee decided that the style of the humor magazine *Don Pepe* that party member Mentor Mera published was "too markedly pro-Communist and that an effort will be made in future issues to soften the tone of the 'satire' so that the magazine will have a more general appeal." *El Pueblo*, however, would maintain its explicitly communist political line.[42] A declining base of support was a growing problem for the communists and contributed to their mounting financial difficulties even as members sought to expand the party's influence.

Movies

As CIA surveillance effectively demonstrates, some subversive activities that in the heat of the moment might seem prescient could appear in retrospect to be a tactical error, and party leaders would quickly attempt to distance themselves from such enterprises. In one case, students disrupted a Saturday-night showing of the anticommunist movie *Iron Curtain* with the release of foul-smelling chemicals. According to press reports, "A shameful and outrageous event happened yesterday to a large audience that attended the special function at the Bolivar Theater shortly after the movie 'Iron Curtain' started." The articles described a situation in which "Unknown elements threw lunette substances at the public that gave off an unbearable smell of asafetida and hydrogen sulfide, forcing most spectators, especially the ladies, to leave the theater." This mention of the threat to women appears designed to appeal to traditional gendered norms and how communist actions jeopardized the stability of society. The police detained three students for their actions.[43]

Curiously, US vice consul Benjamin Sowell was present at the opening night of the film, perhaps because the State Department had already advised its embassies to be on watch for such acts of sabotage. Sowell observed the absence of an adequate police presence for a film that might be expected to face political opposition. On the other hand, he also noted the lack of street demonstrations or efforts to block the sale of tickets. Rather than police, Sowell maintained, it was the minister of defense Manuel Díaz Granados who was present at the showing who personally arrested the three students. That a similar disruption took place at the film's opening in Guayaquil left Ambassador Simmons convinced that the vials with the offending substance had come from outside the country. He believed that the communist party was following orders it had received, but party leaders did not make an issue out of the disruption because they did not want to precipitate a break with Galo Plaza Lasso's government.[44]

According to the CIA, the central committee of the PCE had instructed six students to disrupt the showing of the movie by making catcalls and releasing the chemical substances into the theater. Only three students were able to follow through on the instructions because a theater usher prevented the others from acting. Guillermo Lasso (whom the agency described as a "Communist lawyer") managed to gain the students' release through his personal connections with a friend in the ministry of government. The CIA officer reported, "Later the same evening at a meeting at Communist Party headquarters it was decided to refrain from further action against the showing of this movie in order to avoid reprisals from the authorities."[45] Seemingly that should have been the end of the story.

The CIA presents the students as operating under the instructions of the party's central committee, but it is equally possible that the students acted on their own and that party leaders reprimanded them for their irresponsible behavior. After all, their actions garnered very negative press coverage. *El Comercio* denounced the students in an editorial. "By their fruits you will know them," the editorial read. It proceeded to declare that the world had been divided in two: "those who are with democracy, that is, with America, and those who are with communism, that is, with Russia." In the newspaper's mind, actions such as that in the movie theater demonstrated that the communists "cannot really be reconciled with the republican and democratic duties imposed by our institutions." The editorial proceeded to ask if the communists were acting independently or as agents of a foreign power. In a dig seemingly designed to hurt party leaders the most, the paper declared that the communists had behaved no better than the falangists who were the archenemies of the left.[46]

Another possibility is that the entire event may have been staged to harm the party. Ambassador Simmons admitted as much when he acknowledged that press reports had not identified the troublemakers as communists. Simmons quoted the socialist newspaper *La Tierra* that those whom the police arrested had not done anything, and the stink came from the film itself. In fact, vice consul Sowell complained about the presence of a rowdy Saturday-night crowd in the cheap seats in the balcony, and the entire commotion may have been an attempt to regain control over the theater.[47] In any case, releasing the chemicals did not gain the party any adherents, or raise its profile or reputation—much less advance communist policies or ideologies.

If anything, the negative fallout from the incident in the theater pushed the communists away from pursuing extraconstitutional actions to achieve their political objectives. But it did not lead them to shy away from using movies to advance a progressive agenda. Several months later, the CIA reported that the party had purchased a projector and planned to bring in Soviet films for propaganda purposes in small coastal communities.[48] Several years later, the PCE sought to acquire distribution rights for Soviet films, and Saad planned to discuss the matter personally with Soviet officials on an upcoming trip to Moscow. Not incidentally, the films could also provide the party with a much-needed revenue stream.[49]

In contrast to the protests against *Iron Curtain*, when party leaders learned that the Soviet film *El Gran Concierto* would be projected at the Central Theater in Guayaquil they urged party members to attend. The party contrasted the "healthy, artistic spectacle" of this film with "morbid Yankee movies." The party hoped for the film's success, "so that more Soviet pictures will be shown, thus breaking the imperialist encirclement" of cultural activities in Latin America. In communicating this news to CIA Headquarters, a case officer added the comment that "Guayaquil newspapers have carried sensational advertisements for the film," and that the price for orchestra seats for this film had been raised from the normal price of 7.80 sucres to 10.80 sucres.[50] Soviet films continued to realize commercial success. They were particularly popular in poor neighborhoods and some theater owners preferred them over Hollywood movies.[51] The Soviet Union also sponsored film festivals, including a well-publicized one in Ecuador with high-caliber productions that "were well attended and received favorable reviews."[52] The agency feared that it was losing a battle for the hearts and minds of the Ecuadorian people.

WHAT EMERGES IN the examination of these various examples is that the United States government's fixation on "Moscow gold" was overblown. The accusations emerged from a paranoia fear of external intervention in the region, a paternalistic notion that disadvantaged peoples could never mobilize on their own behalf and therefore the stimulus for actions must come from elsewhere, an attempt to undermine legitimate political activities, and a direct counterattack to leftist challenges to United States hegemonic control over the rest of the hemisphere. Government officials rarely if ever reflected on their motivations in the extant documentation, and these different factors are not necessarily contradictory or mutually exclusive. Nevertheless, the discussions of Moscow gold indicate the types of impediments that leftists confronted in their struggles for a more just and equitable world.

Communists faced endless challenges as they sought to advance their agendas, and ultimately finances were the least of their worries. Communists operated in an antagonistic environment, both domestically and internationally, as they sought to promote their visions for building a new and different world. Anticommunist sentiments flourished in a variety of political and cultural environments and were expressed through various venues. Financial challenges were often just an external manifestation of these larger dynamics. Documentation from an assortment of public and confidential sources indicates the depth of opposition that the left needed to tackle. As if that were not enough, divisions within the PCE continually frustrated the party's attempts to present a united front against persistent problems of exploitation and marginalization.

CHAPTER 5

Divisions

In August 1949, the PCE held its fourth party congress, the first of three that it would convene over the next decade. These meetings were part pageantry and part internal debate, and provide scholars with opportunities to examine the public and private faces of what otherwise could be a secretive party. Throughout this entire time, the CIA monitored communist party activities, at times leaving us with the only records to which we have access of internal discussions and party congresses. A result is the ability to observe how a party responds when powerful forces rise against it. Those challenges exacerbated already existing divisions within the party.

The communists held their congress in the midst of a shift in CIA surveillance tactics. After more than two years in Ecuador, the CIA case officer Albert Haney left in mid-1949 for a new post in Chile and it is unclear who replaced him. A continued flow of information does indicate the presence of the agency's personnel, even though the quantity of material slowed and the quality deteriorated. As with all interpretations extrapolated out of the available records, it is difficult to know whether a complete image of communist party activity emerges and how much lost or withheld material distorts our understandings of internal debates and tactics. As an indication of these competing narratives, an examination of the resolutions that came out of the congress and the party's response to a powerful earthquake that tore through central Ecuador during the course of their meeting provide a dramatically different depiction of the PCE's message and priorities from that which the CIA advanced.

What does become evident from the available documentation on the congress are the roots of a conflict between moderate and militant wings of the party that led to a split in the 1960s. Examining in detail each of the party congresses and the forces present in them, beginning with the fourth congress in 1949, permits a deeper analysis of these complicated issues that contributed to this eventual division.

Internal Party Workings

By the late 1940s, longtime communist leader Ricardo Paredes had made apparent his desire to resign his position as secretary general of the party and return to his medical practice in Manta on the coast. That decision brought difficulties and tensions within the party to a head, particularly between the two wings as represented by Paredes and his counterpart Pedro Saad. Paredes's departure necessitated a party congress to select a new leader, and those elections threatened to trigger the exodus of his followers from the central committee. But that outcome was by no means certain. The US assistant military attaché Adelbert Boggs surmised that Paredes's withdrawal might strengthen the party since it would remove a source of internal friction.[1]

Paredes was born in 1898 in the central highland town of Riobamba and trained to be a physician at the Central University in Quito. He founded the socialist party in 1926 and two years later was a delegate to the sixth Comintern congress in Moscow. In 1931 he converted the PSE into a communist party and served as its secretary general on multiple occasions over the next several decades. Paredes worked closely with Indigenous communities, including assisting them with organizing rural syndicates and cooperatives. He helped found the FEI in 1944, and that federation selected him as their representative to the 1944–45 Constituent Assembly that drafted a new and progressive constitution. Through those activities, he gained a reputation as a dedicated and sincere activist.[2]

In June 1948, United States consul Perry Ellis visited Manabí to check on communist activity in the region. He reported little action and few members among the agricultural workers who comprised the majority of the local population. Since moving there, Paredes had not made many public appearances, and most of his political participation was limited to contacts with other doctors and lawyers.[3] If Paredes was inactive at first, he did not remain that way for long. In November 1949, he was the featured speaker at a celebration of the thirty-second anniversary of the triumph of the Bolshevik Revolution.[4] At the end of the 1950s, William Moreland, Ellis's successor as consul in Guayaquil, reported that Paredes was an active political organizer in the city. Under his guidance, "the Communist movement had acquired alarming proportions." Manta was "being converted into the principal Communist agitation center in Ecuador."[5] Whether or not he was in the leadership of the party, Paredes would continue to fight to advance his communist beliefs.

Saad emerged out of a quite different trajectory. He was born in Guayaquil in 1909, a decade after Paredes. He was the son of Lebanese immigrant parents who ran a moderately successful textile and clothing business. He worked as an accountant with the family business, and hence was financially independent. Saad studied at the prestigious Vicente Rocafuerte High School and then for a law degree at the University of Guayaquil. Saad honed his speaking and debating skills at the university, which subsequently served him well both with mobilizing workers as well as petitioning for their rights as labor representative in the federal congress. Saad did not submit his thesis for his law degree because apparently he thought establishing himself as a lawyer would hamper his work with the labor movement. Instead, he dedicated his life to advocating for the rights of impoverished and marginalized peoples. When his father died in 1953 Saad closed the family's clothing store and devoted all of his energy to fighting for social reforms as the secretary general of the communist party. Although Paredes had founded the party, Saad spent more years in leadership positions and ultimately had a larger influence in defining its character and priorities.[6]

As with many disputes, the divide between Paredes and Saad was in part personal and in part ideological. The two leaders represented two different generations, two different parts of the country, and two different political orientations. Paredes was from the highlands and rooted his conception of the struggle in the demands of rural Indigenous communities, whereas Saad came from the coast and was much more closely attuned to the needs of the urban working class. Tactically, Saad was more likely to engage in elections and political negotiations in congress, whereas Paredes preferred to root his struggles in grassroots social movements. As the historian Hernán Ibarra notes, the ascendancy of "Saad represented a generational shift," in part due to "his leading role in the 1944 revolution, along with his career as a labor leader and senator for coastal workers in congress." While acknowledging that "the role of 'personality' is always problematic" as a mechanism of historical interpretation, Ibarra observes that Saad possessed "open expressive features and effective management of oratory" that was very unlike "Paredes who had a reserved personal nature."[7] In fact, an FBI informer had earlier said that Paredes "rarely appears in public demonstrations because he is a poor speaker, lacking in personality and force" even though he was one of the "better educated Communists in Ecuador."[8] These leaders had different strengths and weaknesses.

Party statutes required that the secretary general reside in Quito, and an open question lingered as to whether Paredes would return to the capital or whether someone would replace him. In his absence, Saad assumed designation as acting secretary general, even though he remained in Guayaquil and would not formally adopt that title until the 1952 party congress. With Saad's emphasis on labor struggles, his ascendancy would require a different kind of party. These changes led to a struggle for succession in the party, with Paredes hesitant or perhaps unwilling to give up his leadership role.

Some party members supported Saad as the new party leader because they did not think that the alternative, Primitivo Barreto, was "forceful enough to direct Communist activities," even though just several days earlier a CIA officer had reported growing support for Barreto because he would be more representative of workers than Saad. Because he was not a manual laborer, Saad always faced a certain amount of resistance to the high positions in the PCE and CTE that he held. Some of Saad's supporters in Guayaquil were concerned that the promotion from regional to national leader would provide him with "more prestige but less authority." Despite insistence that as secretary general of the PCE he relocate to Quito, Saad resisted doing so. He did not believe that anything of importance would happen in the capital that necessitated his presence there.[9] Rather, as a labor leader maintaining his presence in the commercial center of Guayaquil was more important to him. Regionalism was a strong political, economic, and cultural force in Ecuador, and it was present as much inside the party as outside.

Part of Saad's resistance to moving to Quito was that if he did so Enrique Gil Gilbert, the secretary general of the coastal region, would gain more strength locally. The two had their disagreements, and Saad could emerge from the move in a weakened position.[10] Gil Gilbert was a novelist best known for his 1940 book *Nuestro pan*, which critiqued problems that the working class faced, especially rice growers in Milagro. The book won several prizes, including honorable mention in a literary contest that led to its publication in English in 1943 as *Our Daily Bread*.[11] Gil Gilbert worked actively with labor unions and on antifascist committees. He won election to the 1944–45 Constituent Assembly as a representative of the province of Guayas, and subsequently served as a member of the *tribunal de garantías constitucionales* (tribunal of constitutional guarantees), a provision of the 1945 Constitution designed to place a check on executive power. During the war he collaborated with US government officials on antifascist campaigns, but afterward both the CIA and State Department actively trailed him and reported on his activities.[12] In November 1948, Secretary of State George Marshall asked the US Embassy in Caracas to verify that Gil Gilbert was traveling through Venezuela en route to Mexico and to report on his activities.[13] On the way to Venezuela he stopped for a week in Colombia where both the local police and the CIA kept tabs on his activities. Gil Gilbert claimed that his travel was under the auspices of the Ecuadorian Casa de la Cultura, but US ambassador to Colombia Willard Beaulac reported (drawing on material from a "controlled American source") that he spent little time visiting with cultural institutions—or with communists either, for that matter.[14] A CIA information report—probably the source for Beaulac's telegram—provides more details on Gil Gilbert's time in Colombia, including his complaints to the police about surveillance of his activities.[15] In Venezuela, Ambassador Walter Donnelly indicated that Gil Gilbert's publicized activities also only involved meetings with intellectuals and writers, including the renowned author Waldo Frank. As in Colombia, Gil Gilbert claimed that he represented the Casa de la Cultura and was in Venezuela to prepare for the forthcoming Congress for Peace and Democracy. Rather than continuing on to Mexico, Gil Gilbert returned to Quito at the conclusion of his visit.[16] The following year CIA agents similarly trailed Gil Gilbert during a trip to Peru and an officer filed a lengthy and detailed report on his activities.[17] Investigations of communist activists never stopped at a country's borders. Notwithstanding Gil Gilbert's conflicts with Saad, he was an important party leader and apparently warranted the investment of significant resources into investigating his activities.

In response to challenges to his authority, Saad informed the PCE central committee that he would remain in Guayaquil because the party was more active and numerous there than in Quito.[18] CIA information reports reveal intimate knowledge of the communist party's inner workings and highlight the presence of disputes and conflicts that led to Saad's resistance to make the move to Quito. The PCE had received a directive (the reports do not say from where) to restructure its activities, and the agency summarized the resulting changes in the Guayaquil branch of the party. The directive had called for "a reorganization and purification of labor syndicates," which "practically assures the elevation to power of Gil Gilbert's followers and the demotion of Saad." This led to a discussion within the party of sanctioning incompetent leaders. According to a CIA informer, "Saad admitted that he had made errors, but at the time they had been made in good faith." He claimed that he had not personally gained from his actions, nor had that ever been his intent.

In contrast, Gil Gilbert's faction criticized Saad for emphasizing labor organization "without imposing Party adherence on labor members," which had resulted in a weakened party. "If he had obliged all syndicate members to join the Party," the criticism went, "these organizations would now be valuable auxiliaries." Instead, the party was smaller than it should or could have been. The conflict created a good deal of unrest in the party, and provided an example of comrades pointing fingers and looking for culprits to explain their shortcomings.[19] A month later, a CIA officer reported that "Elías Muñoz, an ardent young

Communist and intimate friend of Enrique Gil Gilbert, has been appointed Secretary General of the Guayaquil Local Committee."[20] Muñoz was a rising star in the party, and Gil Gilbert's wing was in ascendancy.

Part of the tension in the party concerned how aggressive communists should be in advancing their political agenda. The CIA reported that Saad allegedly received a mimeographed circular from the Latin American section of the French communist party that suggested that for the time being Latin Americans "adopt a policy of 'passive resistance.'" Engaging in aggressive activities "would not produce desired benefits and could only result in affecting their long-range interests and the interests of the world cause." The CIA operative (presumably Haney) noted that local party leaders had followed this policy of passive resistance for the past two months. "They are satisfied with the incumbent political administration as they are not being molested and are comparatively free to carry on their penetration activities among labor and the military classes."[21] This moderate approach to political action is what eventually would lead to a split in the party, with younger and more militant members pressing their cautious leaders to engage in more aggressive actions.

In March 1949, United States consul Ellis reported that he had gained access to the local communist party's work program. He summarized the document's main points, which included strengthening the FPTG, maintaining the Popular Alliance coalition that had performed well in the previous November's local elections, creating new party cells, fortifying existing ones, expanding the distribution of the party's newspaper *El Pueblo*, and increasing attendance at party meetings. Ellis's concluding remark was that "interest had fallen so low that attendance was poor and even cell leaders were not showing up for regular meetings." Party leaders recognized their shortcomings and were working hard to address them.[22] This was hardly the description of a party worthy of surveillance, but that did not slow down US government infiltration efforts.

The following day, a CIA case officer submitted a report to his superiors in Washington that drew on the same information as that from the consulate. Since (as with all declassified reports) the agency redacted details on the provenance of the information, it is difficult to ascertain whether it originated with a source in the consulate or CIA, or whether it represented a collaborative effort. Although both communiqués summarized the same document, the CIA report includes data not contained in the dispatch from the consulate. The CIA officer stated that the present work program was not as extensive as a previous one from November 1948, and furthermore repeated parts of that plan. A "close check" revealed that recruitment goals in the previous directive had failed. Among other details, the CIA officer reported plans to continue discussion groups (the current reading was the *Communist Manifesto*) and expand propaganda campaigns, including the distribution of literature.[23]

With this growth of communist activities in Guayaquil, the CIA increased its surveillance activities in that part of the country. The CIA case officer Haney purportedly was based in Quito, and that is the origin of most of the information he initially collected. With Saad assuming more control over the party, most of the material now came from Guayaquil. In the absence of better documentation, it remains unclear whether Haney moved his base of operations to the coast or whether another officer joined him in the agency's surveillance of the Ecuadorian left. In any case, whomever it was, a CIA case officer maintained access to good sources of information on the party in Guayaquil.

A report on the work plan for the first part of the year was followed with the next one for March 21 to June 20, 1949. Unfortunately, an enclosed photostatic copy of the report is missing from the declassified documentation, although another CIA memo from several days later summarizes its contents in English. According to the case officer, the main points of the plan included the recruitment of five hundred new members, the monthly collection of 3,500 sucres ($220 USD), the establishment of a library, the purchase of a mimeograph machine and other equipment for spreading propaganda, the expansion of labor activities, support for the Popular Alliance electoral coalition, publication of a confidential weekly bulletin for party cells, and the organization of public assemblies and other educational activities to advance communist objectives. The case officer indicated that when party leader Franklin Pérez Castro presented the current goals he "made no reference to the success or failure of the [previous] work plan," even though "the fact that many of the same objectives are cited in the new work plan would indicate that little success had been achieved toward increasing the Party strength." Furthermore, at this secret meeting Pérez Castro emphasized the importance of boosting party membership. At the same time, he complained that too many members were opportunists rather than loyal adherents, and that too many of the party cells had ceased to function.[24] Despite enjoying conditions that seemingly would contribute to its growth, the party faced continual challenges in realizing its objectives.

Although by 1949 most of the CIA surveillance concentrated on communist activities in the coastal city of Guayaquil, they occasionally ventured beyond that narrow locus. One information report, for example, concerned the reorganization of party cells in the central highlands. The evaluation noted that "the cells were in a very poor state of organization and that their activities amounted to practically nothing." The party's executive committee received the report, but delayed action until Saad would have an opportunity to comment on it.[25] Saad had gained de facto control over the party, not just its coastal affiliate but its organizational apparatus across the country.

If the party in Quito was poorly organized, that was not reflected in its ability to generate propaganda statements. Or perhaps the reorganization of local cells had reinvigorated party activity. In either case, in March 1949 the PCE's central committee distributed two thousand copies of a handbill denouncing the current economic crisis in the country (see figure 5.1). According to the case officer who forwarded a copy of the leaflet to CIA Headquarters in Washington, Nela Martínez, María Luisa Gómez de la Torre, Gustavo Becerra, César Endara, and Bernardino Andrade, "all prominent members of the Communist Party," drafted the text that reflected current party thinking.[26] Surveillance efforts dedicated to the defeat of communism at the same time served to document their ideas and organizational efforts; a copy of this document likely would not have survived were it not for this intelligence agency.

The handbill began with the declaration "Ecuador is going through a crisis that is the result of the global situation of capitalism, which is already facing a deep depression." The party denounced the country's ruling class as unable to solve serious problems of unemployment, closed factories, workers thrown out into the street, and bankrupt businesses. In the countryside, peasants faced an even more severe crisis of low prices for their commodities. Wealthy landholders maintained their antiquated forms of production, and technical "experts" from the United States imposed policies that handicapped domestic development. The result was that farmers were not able to supply local markets, and the country had to import potatoes even though this was a product originally domesticated in the Andes. These shortcomings highlighted the failures of capitalism. In the face of this crisis, the party proposed a series of measures to stem the suffering of the people and launch a process of national reconstruction. These included an agrarian reform program to distribute land to peasants, the halting of debt payments for farm workers, guaranteed fair prices for agricultural produce, credit for the development of domestic industrialization, blocking the importation of products that displaced domestic production, outlawing speculation, and taxing wealthy landowners and industrialists. "We do not think that these measures mean a definitive solution for all national problems," the party admitted. Those resolutions would only emerge "with a revolutionary transformation of our national life" that included a move to socialism. But applying these limited measures, the party promised, would provide immediate relief for the present

POR LA DEFENSA DE LA VIDA DEL PUEBLO

Manifiesto del Comité Central del Partido Comunista

El Ecuador se encuentra atravesando una grave situación, resultado de la situación mundial del capitalismo, que se enfrenta ya a una depresión profunda, anunciadora de la crisis, que será mucho más grave que el año 1929, y resultado también de la incapacidad de las clases dominantes ecuatorianas para resolver los problemas del pueblo.

Se ha iniciado la desocupación; fábricas que cierran, echando a la calle a sus obreros; negocios que quiebran; depresión comercial son los síntomas en las ciudades.

Y en los campos, la más grave amenaza sobre él campesino. Como si fuese poco el peso del recargo cambiario de cinco sucres, que en definitiva lo paga el campesino, obligado a vender sus productos a $ 13 por dólar y a cubrir su vida a $ 20 por dólar, una caída catastrófica de los precios de esa producción campesina; el cacao que baja de $ 500 a $ 150 el quintal; baja del precio del algodón; amenazas de baja del banano. El espectro de la miseria paseándose por los campos ecuatorianos.

Ante este cuadro, sigue la desastroza política del Gobierno y de los sectores dominantes de la economía.

El Gobierno, con su política tributaria injusta, que pesa íntegra sobre el pueblo, mientras los grandes terratenientes y capitalistas no pagan; con la carencia de todo plan financiero y económico; con el peligro de un déficit presupuestario que tratará de cubrir con nuevos impuestos.

El Instituto de Fomento de la Producción con una integración que no puede inspirar confianza en su actividad, lo que, de no remediarse sólo servirá para apoyar aún más a las argollas de terratenientes todopoderosos y a un pequeño grupo de capitalistas especuladores.

Los grandes terratenientes manteniendo sus viejas formas de producción, sometiéndose a las orientaciones, imperialistas en cuanto a las producciones a desarrollarse y siguiendo los consejos de los «técnicos» norteamericanos, interesados en impedir nuestro desarrollo, lo que ha producido la incapacidad de abastecer nuestro mercado habiendo tenido que importar hasta patatas.

Los industriales que han dilapidado sus gigantescas utilidades arrebatadas al pueblo. sin modernizar sus fábricas, sin ampliar su producción, sin crear reservas suficientes para la transformación progresiva de sus instalaciones.

Todas las clases dominantes dispuestas a echar sobre el pueblo el peso de la situación, planteando ya como salido la devaluación del sucre, a pesar de las condiciones monetarias ventajosas hoy existentes en el país.

La devaluación no significará otra cosa que una disminución del salario real del obrero, de los ingresos de los empleados y de todos los que viven de su trabajo ya que producirá inevitablemente un alza de precios, aumentada por la especulación sin control.

Frente a estos hechos, el PARTIDO COMUNISTA DEL ECUADOR, que siempre ha luchado y luchará por obtener un robustecimiento de la economía nacional en beneficio del pueblo y la mayor independencia posible de esta economía respecto al imperialismo extranjero, presenta un programa concreto y breve de medidas que, de aplicarse firmemente, evitarán el agravamiento de la miseria e iniciarán un proceso de reconstrucción nacional, destruyendo el semifeudalismo de nuestra economía agraria y robusteciendo nuestra industria.

1.— Oposición a la devaluación del sucre, en cualquier forma que se pretenda;

2.— Iniciación de la reforma agraria, repartiendo tierras a los campesinos, aumentando el crédito a ellos, apoyando su trabajo con implementos mecánicos, etc.;

3 — Moratoria de todas las deudas de los campesinos pobres y medios;

4.— Asegurar por el Instituto de Fomento, Bancos de Fomento, Banco Central, etc., un precio justo para los artículos producidos por el pequeño campesino;

5.— Orientación de la política del Instituto de Fomento hacia el desarrollo de los

FIGURE 5.1. A manifesto from the central committee of the Communist Party of Ecuador that defends the lives of the Ecuadorian people in the face of an economic crisis. Source: Partido Comunista del Ecuador (PCE), "Por la defensa de la vida del pueblo: Manifiesto del Comité Central del Partido Comunista," March 1, 1949, included in Central Intelligence Agency (CIA), "Handbill of Partido Comunista del Ecuador," April 8, 1949, https://www.cia.gov/library/readingroom/document/cia-rdp83-00415r002600040002-6.

situation. The party called for "a great mobilization of the people, of workers, peasants and popular masses" to implement this agenda. The party declared that it was ready to take the lead in this struggle.[27]

Despite the PCE's forceful statements, CIA analysts in Washington consistently noted the party's lack of "unity, effective leadership, and prestige," which prompted the agency to characterize the communists as "ineffective." The PCE had not managed to improve its situation, and it studiously avoided actions that might trigger government repression. As a result, "no serious problems at present disturb Ecuador's international relations," by which the agency meant perceived United States interests in the region. "The current Ecuadoran situation contains no elements which cause or immediately portend noticeable change in the status of US security interests in the area," was the CIA's evaluation.[28] The agency considered the communist party, and Ecuador in general, to be mostly harmless. That assessment, however, did not mean a halt in the agency's investigation of what it was convinced were subversive activities.

Fourth PCE Congress (Guayaquil, August 1–7, 1949)

In the first week of August 1949, communists gathered in Guayaquil for the PCE's fourth congress. Party statutes stipulated that it was to hold a congress every other year, but it never met that often. Its last meeting was in November 1946 in Quito, and it would not convene again until July 1952—the closest it ever came to its goal of a biannual meeting.[29] The CIA had reported on pending plans for a party congress ever since the agency's establishment two years earlier. An intelligence report from October 1947 had indicated the possibility for a congress in Guayaquil the following month. Among the agenda items were organizational details such as the naming of a secretary general, the selection of a new central committee, and finding new premises for party headquarters. A key issue was the attempt of the American Federation of Labor (AFL) to break the CTE away from the CTAL. Haney alleged, "These measures are being taken in an effort to strengthen the position of the Party and to advance plans for sabotage."[30] Mentioning the threat of violence may have been a lame attempt to justify the dedication of resources to surveillance of the party.

Half a year later, Haney once again reported on the intent to hold the congress in July 1948 to implement reorganization plans that Saad and Barreto had allegedly received at a CTAL meeting in Mexico.[31] Another six months passed, and Haney reported that the PCE central committee had met in January 1949 and scheduled the fourth party congress for June 6, 1949. "For two years attempts have been made to set the date for the Congress," the case officer commented, "but each time that a date had been decided it had to be postponed. The PCE needs to hold a Congress to revise its statutes, to legalize numerous changes in its administration, and to elect new officers."[32] Eventually the party would have to meet.

Nevertheless, as now seemed inevitable, the party once again missed their deadline. Instead, on June 13 a planning commission comprised of Pedro Saad, Ana Moreno, Enrique Barrezueta, and Fortunato Safadi met to discuss the pending congress. Now their target date was July or August, but insufficient funds threatened to result in further delays. Local leaders calculated that the congress would cost 30,000 sucres, mainly for the travel and hotel expenses for the delegates. A CIA informer reported that the party currently had 25,000 sucres in its coffers. Since party statutes stipulated that their bank balance should not fall below 10,000 sucres, the party needed to raise 15,000 sucres. Party leaders were optimistic that between fundraising campaigns and relying on those delegates who were able to cover their own expenses that they would be able to raise enough money for the congress. While 130 delegates had attended the last congress in 1946, because of the party's severe financial situation fewer members would come this time. Furthermore, the reason for meeting in Guayaquil was because the largest delegation of party members resided in that city and gathering there would hold down on expenses. In any case, the party's central committee proceeded to draw up a program of action for the congress to approve and sent out invitations to comrades in other Latin American countries. Nela Martínez, en route to a peace conference in Paris, carried an invitation to the Latin American branch of the French communist party. The tentative agenda included the presentation of reports from central and provincial committees on their activities since the 1946 congress, revision of party statutes, approval of a new political program appropriate for the current political situation, election of new members for the central committee, and the drafting of contingency plans in case the party were forced underground.[33]

In the middle of July, a CIA officer reported that the PCE had "tentatively set" the "definite date" for their congress for August, and if it did not meet then it would probably have to be delayed until November. The two main agenda items for the congress included analyzing international events and examining internal problems in the party. On the first point, the party tasked Pérez Castro with explaining the development of world communism and its effects on the PCE, including the role the party would play in case of war between the United States and the Soviet Union. Saad was to address internal issues as well as report on the activities of the central party. Saad planned to characterize Galo Plaza Lasso as "a rich landowner" who was "dominated by the oppressive Yankee." He would also warn Plaza that the communists expected to be able to continue to operate with complete freedom. The party also planned to incorporate more flexibility into party organization. In part this was to reflect reality, as local leaders often operated quite independently from central command structures anyway. On a related matter, the CIA had no evidence that the party had received any international support or instructions—an admission that conflicted quite directly with United States attempts to portray local militants as operating as part of a vast conspiracy emanating out of Moscow.[34] Five days later, the liberal *El Día* similarly announced that the PCE would inaugurate its congress on August 1 in Guayaquil. According to the newspaper, the party would address issues related to the current political situation and decide on what approach it should take to the Plaza administration. Naturally, the announcement made no mention of plans for sabotage.[35]

Only days before the congress was to convene, a CIA officer again reported that barring a last-minute inability to raise sufficient funds it would begin on August 1. Saad wanted to delay the meeting until later in the year, but some members had pressed him to hold the assembly before the federal congress met on August 10. Financial exigency meant that fewer delegates would attend than what the party had originally planned. Even so, the coastal regional committee issued a confidential bulletin to local cell leaders proclaiming that the congress would "be of extraordinary importance" for the "study of the conditions of the world and our country." The committee proceeded to lay out suggestions for how to organize discussions at the meeting. Each cell should discuss agenda items and proposed revisions to the party statutes in order to enhance the overall value of the meeting. The coastal committee included recommendations for which cells should prepare reports on a variety of topics, including land reform, worker organization, cooperatives, and colonization. The committee suggested that in their discussions of the party statutes, the cells pay particular attention to conditions for entrance into the party, the duties of members, dues payments, party discipline, and the youth movement. Finally, and rather ironically since this document made its way into the hands of the CIA, these discussions should not be made public.[36] The CIA had effectively penetrated the party.

The communist congress faced an almost complete media blackout. Quito's daily *El Comercio* did not carry a single article on the congress, and the socialist newspaper *La Tierra* only carried one short story. *La Tierra*'s piece was buried in the inside pages, and reported on the congress's opening session two days after it took place. According to *La Tierra*, "a large public attended the solemn act." Delegates elected Paredes as president of the congress and the audience warmly welcomed his comments. Saad presented an eloquent report on communist labors on the coast. The inaugural session ended with other speeches and a reading of statements.[37] That was the extent of the report, and the paper did not follow up on the discussions or conclusions from the congress. A powerful earthquake hit Ecuador in the middle of the meeting, which might explain a lack of media attention as everyone was absorbed with more immediate and urgent matters. Or, perhaps, the newspapers simply believed that the communists played a marginal role and concluded that the congress was not worthy of their attention.

A biography of party leader Paredes does not provide many more details on the congress, except to note that deep divisions ran through the central committee that eventually split the party between its pro-Soviet wing and a "Trotskyist and pro-China" group that became the Partido Comunista Marxista Leninista del Ecuador (PCMLE, Marxist–Leninist Communist Party of Ecuador) in the 1960s. At this point, however, those tensions were expressed as a rift between an orthodox Marxist wing grouped around Paredes, and Saad's tendency "that adhered to a conciliatory Browderist thesis."[38] Earl Browder had been the secretary general of the Communist Party of the United States of America (CPUSA) during the war and had called for a secession of attacks on capitalist countries and instead advocated support for bourgeois nationalist forces to prepare the ground for an eventual move to socialism in the distant future. Saad's embrace of Browder's class-collaborationist policies was very unpopular among dogmatic Marxists.[39] That split between a moderate and much more militant wing tore at the party and complicated attempts to realize common objectives. The congress was to select a new secretary general, but apparently Paredes retained that titular position with Saad assuming more responsibilities albeit in an acting role. Without access to internal debates, it is difficult to ascertain how those discussions played out.

United States officials similarly dedicated little attention to the congress, which is surprising considering how committed they were to monitoring communist activities, the frequency with which they repeated announcements of the imminent nature of the assembly, and the extent of the CIA's penetration of the party. It is apparent that they were not unaware of the meeting. A week before the congress, vice consul Walter Houk in Guayaquil cautioned that at the gathering the communists would exploit the country's current economic crisis to attack United States companies and to agitate for workers' demands including calling for wage increases.[40] A month later, a report on international communist travels indicated that Pompeyo Márquez, a member of the politburo of the Communist Party of Venezuela, had traveled to Guayaquil for the meeting.[41] But if Houk or any other US officials submitted any reports on the congress, they have not come to light.

The only US government report available on the congress is a short analysis drafted at CIA Headquarters in Washington almost three months later. As with all CIA intelligence summaries, the agency's analysts do not cite the sources of their information, which as always means that their conclusions should be taken with a grain of salt. The CIA report mistakenly refers to the congress as the party's sixth—rather than its fourth—and declared that the meeting was plagued by bitter personal disputes between party leaders. As a result, the assembly was significantly less successful than its previous one in 1946. The congress decided to change the PCE's organizational structures because rivalries were tearing the party apart. It abolished regional committees because they had assumed too much power and were acting too independently from central committee control. Instead, the congress assigned their functions to provincial committees. The CIA, however, contended that these organizational changes would not bear fruit unless "the present competition for leadership ceases and a widely acceptable group of leaders emerges." The CIA analysts did not think that such a development was likely. "The Communists evidently recognize the present low level of the party's prestige," the agency's analysts opined. They were too weak to be actively plotting against the government, and it was unlikely that they would play a significant role in any revolt. The agency's conclusion was that the communists were "biding their time until conditions are such that there will be greater certainty of an opportunity for unequivocal leadership."[42] If that was their evaluation, it might explain the general lack of attention to the congress.

In June as the communists were trying to pull together their assembly, socialists held an extraordinary congress to decide on what position the PSE should take toward the Plaza government as well as to select a new governing council. The US Embassy's chargé d'affaires Maurice Bernbaum characterized their meeting as "tense and stormy," which threatened to split the party in two.[43] The congress saw the resignation of Emilio Gangotena who represented a conservative tendency in the party. He had been reelected to that post at the last party congress only half a year earlier, which at the time the US military attaché in Quito had celebrated because he opposed cooperation with the communists.[44] Now the former student activist and FEUE leader Plutarco Naranjo assumed the leadership position. The assembly proclaimed its strong opposition to the

Plaza government, as well as its willingness to collaborate with other progressive forces in an electoral front.

While State Department personnel heavily covered socialist activities, the CIA dedicated little attention to the socialists, preferring instead to concentrate on the communists. The agency's main concern was with what it saw as communist success in its penetration of its sister party. It reported that of fourteen members (including alternates) who were elected to the new directorate, "eight are known Communists or Socialists sympathetic to Communist Party policies." Despite this alleged level of infiltration, the CIA's informer acknowledged that no close working relationship existed between the two parties "primarily because the leaders of the Communist Party do not wish to become entangled in any agreement which might bring about the outlawing of their party." While the communists "tacitly and morally support Socialist opposition to the government," they would "remain on the sidelines in matters of national politics." Clearly, the communists were taking a more conservative and cautious position than the socialists, but this did not stop the CIA from contending that the communists controlled the party through people they had allegedly placed on the directorate.

The CIA report proceeded to list the members of the directorate, together with their political affiliations (socialist, communist, or communist sympathizer). For those with an understanding of Ecuadorian politics, the results are quite laughable. The socialist lawyer Gonzalo Oleas, who a decade later would go on to lead a right-wing split off of the party, is listed as "Socialist, but Communist sympathizer." The labor leader Pablo Duque Arias who subsequently collaborated willingly with the embassy and on occasion butted heads with the communists was a "Communist sympathizer."[45] The designations were at best wishful thinking and more likely simply a reflection of paranoia, conspiratorial thinking, and red-baiting.

The fact that no embassy dispatches or CIA information reports on the communist congress have come to light does not, of course, mean that they do or did not exist. Such documents might have been lost, destroyed, misplaced, or simply not yet released to the public. Alternatively, if the mainstream media did not cover the congress those officials may not have had access to the publicly available information on which they relied for filing dispatches. Another possibility is that personnel changes may have created a gap in surveillance coverage, or other more pressing issues or policy changes distracted officials from dedicating attention to the congress. In May, only a couple months before the congress, a remarkably high volume of CIA information reports on the communist party in Guayaquil climaxed and then suddenly stopped. For whatever reason, the CIA field reports often came in batches. But this time it is as if a case officer quickly filed an entire backlog of reports over the course of a several days before leaving and the agency failed to assign another person to continue the surveillance of the party. What we do know is that it was around this time that Haney left his post in Quito for Chile. The State Department's Foreign Service list for July 1, 1949, still includes Haney as an attaché at the embassy in Quito, but the next quarterly installment indicates that he was appointed as an attaché (his cover as COS) to the US Embassy in Santiago on August 17 with a promotion from FSS-6 to FSS-4.[46] The available documentation does not indicate when he left Ecuador, but it would not be unusual for a CIA officer to return to the United States for a period of time before proceeding on to the next assignment.

The second curiosity is that even though Haney's post was in Quito almost all of the CIA's reporting during the first half of 1949 came from Guayaquil. On one hand, that is only logical as the coastal city was now the center of communist activities, and Haney may have moved to that city or cultivated contacts there. On the other hand, the uptick in reporting from Guayaquil might point to the arrival of another CIA operative (which would be highly likely). If that were the case, the Foreign Service list does not immediately shed light on who that person might be. That list includes five people at the Guayaquil Consulate, most of whom appear to be career foreign service officers. The one exception is assistant consular attaché Allen Lester who arrived on March 15, 1949, with the rank of FSS-8 and may have been a CIA officer.[47] Another possibility, of course, is that the CIA officer was not stationed with diplomatic cover in the consulate but operated undercover, perhaps ostensibly as an employee of a United States commercial firm.

Another peculiarity is how the CIA's reporting changed around this time. Originally in 1947 with the establishment of the agency, a "controlled American source" drafted memos that the embassy quoted verbatim in their dispatches to the State Department. Those memos soon disappeared from the available archival collection, but embassy dispatches continued to quote the memos in a similar fashion. In 1949, this pattern shifted to a new format. From February through August, a series of sequentially numbered memos from the embassy in Quito addressed for distribution to the Division of North and West Coast Affairs at the State Department largely mirror information reports that CIA officers submitted to their headquarters in Washington (though continuing with a month delay as before). No memos appear between May 20 and June 21, which might correspond with Haney's departure. But then the memos briefly resume. This sequence of extensive and fairly high-quality reporting on the PCE then once again inexplicably stops with a July 28, 1949, memo on the eve of the congress. With the unevenness of the release of CIA documentation, of course, those dates might mean nothing. Perhaps, alternatively, that was the date of Haney's departure. If that were the case, a simple lack of staffing provides a possible explanation for the absence of surveillance of the congress. In either case, a minimal amount of documentation on the fourth party congress has surfaced from any United States governmental source. It is difficult to ascertain whether this is due to a lack of personnel, a failure to release material, the loss or destruction of documents, or whether it reflects a change in policy priorities.

CIA reports continued throughout the second half of 1949, but they were not of the quantity or quality of the first half of the year. With Haney gone, the pace of reporting dropped off, though that might simply reflect a new person in the post and the accompanying delays with a novice coming up to speed on internal Ecuadorian politics and reporting responsibilities. The emphasis also shifts from documenting internal discussions within the Guayaquil branch of the communist party to larger political issues of military coups and border disputes with neighboring Peru and Colombia. The numbered sequence of memos addressed to the Division of North and West Coast Affairs continues through the PCE congress before coming to a final and definitive stop on August 19. But instead of discussing that meeting, the memos only relate information on Mancheno's coup plotting against the government and political intrigues within Plaza's government. The available documentation in the CREST database follows a similar trajectory. The CIA has redacted the location in Ecuador where officers acquired their information in the declassified information reports, but it would appear that after Haney's departure almost all of the information originated in Quito and therefore was concerned with political developments in the capital rather than leftist subversion on the coast. Ironically, the departure of one dogmatic and obnoxious CIA officer may have undercut potential insights into the 1949 communist party congress.

Intense CIA surveillance of the PCE resumes in December, once again with a particular emphasis on Guayaquil. One information report includes a mimeographed copy of the party's bulletin from months earlier that criticized Plaza's earthquake reconstruction plans.[48] In response to a State Department request for examples of communist propaganda, a CIA officer provided the embassy with samples of political handbills, a mimeographed throw sheet *Antorcha*, the party bulletin, and a handbill from the last municipal election—all from

Guayaquil—plus *Crisol*, a communist sheet from Loja and a communist publication called *Realidad* from Quito that apparently the embassy personnel collected earlier in the year.[49] After a break of several months, once again the agency resumed its role as a biographer for the party. Unfortunately, the transitions in staffing means that we are left with only a minimal amount of information on what transpired at the fourth party congress.

For Peace, Democracy, and Progress

The PCE published their political resolutions from the congress, and they paint a quite different picture of that from the brief conclusions of the CIA analysts in Washington.[50] The resolutions were a public statement, and available to anyone who might wish to know the party's current political orientation. Logically the declaration would seek to present a positive and empowering image, rather than the divisive one contained in the CIA report. As framed in the document's title "For Peace, Democracy, and Progress," the statement appealed for peaceful coexistence between capitalist and communist governments. This declaration was consistent with Saad's accommodationist position that reflected the continued influence of a Browderist line. At the same time, the resolutions were long on rhetoric that denounced imperialist penetration of peripheral economies and called for the implementation of policies that would favor the working class, peasants, and other poor and marginalized peoples. Those statements indicate the presence of more militant participants, likely grouped around Paredes, who influenced their contents. At the same time, the resolutions follow a standard (for the time) communist line of opposing palace coups and favoring peaceful opposition to the current Plaza government. Underlying the document is an orthodox Marxist interpretation of the need for a nationalist bourgeois revolution to establish the proper objective conditions before a move toward socialism could be contemplated as a step toward the final goal of communism. Although the statement does not provide specifics, it does acknowledge problems and shortcomings within the party, and appeals for the creation of a popular front to group socialists and other progressives together into an anticonservative alliance. It applauds those in Guayaquil for having made the most progress in this direction.

The lengthy statement begins with an optimistic portrayal of the communist world. Although the battle was hard, the forces in favor of democracy and freedom were overcoming imperialism. The statement celebrated economic advances in the Soviet Union, its struggle to free the oppressed, and movement toward the establishment of a just and permanent peace. The party extolled advances in Eastern Europe and Asia including the Chinese Revolution and ongoing struggles in Greece and Spain. "It is the victorious socialist society," the party declared, "that marches towards communism." A growing peace movement demonstrated that war was not inevitable, and communist parties had taken the lead in that process. Even with these advances, people could not relax in the face of imperialist aggression. With the recent formation of the North Atlantic Treaty Organization (NATO), Truman was heading back to war in violation of the United Nations charter. The spreading of foreign military bases around the world and the development of nuclear weapons were part of the shift in that direction. The Marshall Plan sought to enslave Europe through the destruction of domestic industries that could compete with those in the United States. The war had created a formable concentration of power in the hands of United States monopolies.

Latin America played a central role in this struggle. United States imperialist forces saw the region as a source for raw materials and a location for its military bases from which to launch its campaigns. This program had been advanced through agreements such as the 1947 Tratado Interamericano de Asistencia Recíproca (TIAR, Inter-American Treaty of Reciprocal Assistance, also known as the Rio Treaty or Rio Pact) that provided for mutual hemispheric defense and the formation the following year of the OAS in Bogotá, Colombia. Petroleum companies and other industries were attempting to colonize Latin America. The United States supported the repressive dictatorships of Anastasio Somoza in Nicaragua and Rafael Trujillo in the Dominican Republic. A rising tide of resistance, however, confronted these imperialist and repressive forces. Sustaining a movement in favor of peace, democracy, and progress would require a strong organization to coordinate the forces of resistance, and the communists contended that this is what they could contribute to the struggle.

The global situation of imperialism added to the economic crisis that Ecuador faced, with falling prices for its commodities and rising unemployment rates. Plaza's policies of attracting foreign investment only made the situation worse since they converted Ecuador into a producer of raw materials for export to the United States rather than bolstering internal economic development. The Plaza administration was incapable of solving these problems, and his pro-imperialist policies and alliances with reactionary forces presented a danger to Ecuador. The result would be ruin for the country's workers and peasants. The PCE called for a democratic bourgeois revolution under the leadership of the proletariat to confront these issues. People needed to organize and mobilize broad democratic, anticonservative, antifeudal coalitions. In Ecuador, this would take the form of an anti-imperialist agrarian revolution that would break up the current land-holding system with an agrarian reform program that would redistribute land to the rural masses and agricultural workers. At present the movement was weak, the party admitted, and needed to be strengthened. A goal was government control of the economy to encourage diversification and expansion of production through industrialization and nationalization of foreign companies. Only through the socialization of the means of production could the country solve its problems, end exploitation, overcome class divisions, and avoid ruin.

The communist party rejected palace coups as a solution to Ecuador's problems. Such activity would only result in more misery and reaction. Instead, the party called for a strengthening of democratic institutions. Achieving these goals would require the elimination of "feudal obstacles that weigh heavily on Indians and peasants" through the conversion of state-owned estates into experimental farms and cooperatives. Industrialization of the economy would be achieved through making better use of the country's natural resources with a goal of providing better products for the people. The communist program called for higher salaries, price controls, and an expansion of the social security system to agricultural workers. Education should be free and universal, and there should be an absolute separation of church and state. Ecuador's sovereignty needed to be defended, which required revisions to the Rio de Janeiro Protocol that in 1942 ceded half of the country's territory to Peru. The PCE also demanded the severing of diplomatic relations with Francisco Franco's falangist government in Spain, and the establishment of relations with the Soviet Union.

The PCE called for the formation of an anticonservative, antifeudal, and anti-imperialist coalition similar to that which led the May 1944 revolution. They appealed to socialists, vanguardists, and other progressives to collaborate with them in achieving these objectives. Of primary importance was the preservation of the unity of the labor movement, and in particular defense of the CTE from attacks that sought to divide and weaken it. A struggle for a better life, for democracy, progress, and peace should not be stopped but instead would deepen. The party placed importance on the mobilization of the "rural masses, Indians, *montuvios* [coastal peasants], salaried agricultural workers, and peasants, in a struggle for their lives and land." A strong worker-peasant alliance was necessary to achieve these goals, and the PCE saw itself as the lead organizer of this process. Only by strengthening the party, consolidating its ideology, and addressing its shortcomings would it achieve this task. The resolution concluded with an acknowledgment that too often such political statements were not put into action.

It called for the party to become "an authentic guide of all oppressed people of Ecuador," and to defend democracy and national sovereignty as it engaged in a struggle for "a society without classes, without exploitation, without oppression of any type."[51] It looked forward to an optimistic future.

As the PCE acknowledged, party resolutions are aspirational rather than a reflection of concrete, lived realities. As such, this document tells us more about communist hopes and dreams than their current struggles. It also provides a dramatically different perspective than that contained in the CIA records. Underlying this statement is an implicit acknowledgment of the party's roots in rural campaigns, and an awareness that the possibilities for a socialist revolution remained remote on the distant horizon. This cognizance contributed to the consolidation of Saad's moderate leadership in the party while at the same time frustrating more radical militants who would eventually break from the party. Those tensions were readily evident in the resolutions that emerged out of the fourth party congress.

Earthquake

On August 5, 1949, one of the most destructive earthquakes ever to strike Ecuador tore through the central highlands. Its epicenter was located to the southeast of Ambato, the capital of the province of Tungurahua. The violent quake, which killed more than five thousand people and left an additional one hundred thousand homeless, had a magnitude of 6.8 on the Richter seismological scale and originated at a depth of forty kilometers below the surface. The convergence of three tectonic plates causes frequent earthquakes on the Pacific Coast of South America. This earthquake was the second worst up to that time in Ecuador's modern history. It was only exceeded with a 1797 earthquake in Riobamba and subsequently surpassed by a catastrophic 7.8-magnitude earthquake in April 2016 near the small city of Pedernales on the coast. In South America, only the 1944 San Juan earthquake in Argentina that killed ten thousand people was deadlier.

The 1949 earthquake leveled the small towns of Guano, Patate, Pelileo, and Píllaro, though the city of Ambato because of its size suffering the most amount of damage. According to observers, Pelileo, which was constructed largely of adobe bricks, "simply disappeared." Only three hundred of its 3,500 inhabitants survived. Landslides changed the course of streams and blocked rivers, adding to the destruction and at points leaving the countryside unrecognizable. The diversion of the Patate River completely submerged Quero under a newly formed lake. Even the distant cities of Quito and Guayaquil experienced some damage. A lack of proper sanitation contributed to the spread of a typhus epidemic while the disruption of communication networks hindered recovery efforts.[52]

President Plaza personally traveled to Ambato to direct rescue and relief work. Aid flooded into the country, including provision of medical supplies and the arrival of a Red Cross team stationed at the United States military base in the Canal Zone in Panama. Calls came in from around the world and from all political corners in support of the victims. These included a statement signed by a range of leftist parties in the coastal province of Guayas.[53] The Cuban communist leader Blas Roca sent his condolences to PCE secretary general Paredes, and the World Peace Council sent their expressions of solidarity from France to Gómez de la Torre.[54]

The earthquake temporarily suspended direct attacks on the government as the country pulled together with recovery efforts, and Plaza was able to play this good will to his advantage. Nevertheless, as the immediate effects of the catastrophe retreated into the background, animosity to the government once again rose in intensity. According to the CIA, "Although the Communists continue their policy of watchful waiting, the Socialist and Liberal parties have resumed active opposition to the Plaza administration." The president's clumsiness in particular played "admirably into the hands of leftist agitators." The ministry of defense expressed doubt about the loyalty of several army units to the government, which contributed to the administration's weakened condition.[55] Adding to the difficulties, the British minister John Carvell observed, was that most of the immediate relief aid came from foreign missions and was largely squandered due to a lack of proper control. Little visible reconstruction actually took place.[56]

A month after the quake, the PCE released a statement denouncing the ineptness of the government's response to the tragedy and declaring that the party would "fight in defense of the lives of the popular masses."[57] The government had presented a proposal to congress for a 250 million sucre loan from the Central Bank to pay for reconstruction with a plan to pay it back over the course of twenty years with new taxes. Tobacco, liquor, and entertainment events would all require a "patriotic stamp" that would cost one sucre. Property taxes would increase 5 percent, and the government proposed a 2.5 percent income tax (though labor protests led to a reconsideration of that proposal). The communists Pedro Saad and Segundo Ramos, the representatives for workers in the federal congress, led the legislative opposition to this proposal. Together with other leftists and democrats, they gathered twenty votes against the proposal because of the undue burden it would place on workers. Saad argued that the Central Bank did not function as a commercial bank that could loan money, but instead its purpose was to set monetary policy. The only way it could raise these funds was through the printing of currency, and that would result in inflationary pressure on the economy that would increase the cost of living and lead to a devaluation in the local currency that would be disastrous for Ecuador's balance of payments.

Saad forwarded a counterproposal that earthquake relief be funded instead through taxes on private capital. Specifically, the communists proposed a 1 percent tax on wealthy landowners who, incidentally, currently paid nothing, as well as on commercial, industrial, and banking ventures; urban property; and foreign businesses. Saad claimed that those taxes would garner 10 billion sucres. According to Saad, the communist plan would fund reconstruction without causing injury to the livelihoods of the working class. In denouncing regressive taxation policies and pressing for progressive taxes instead, the PCE presented itself as the principle defender of working-class interests, and called on laborers to support the communist party.

Although the PCE failed in its legislative attempt to implement an alternative proposal for reconstruction, it exploited the natural disaster to advance the party's interests. The PCE closed its two-page statement on reconstruction efforts with a series of slogans that highlighted the program that it advocated: no taxes on workers' salaries, and taxation on the capital gains of wealthy landowners. Even though the oligarchy rejected their proposals, the PCE promised to continue to organize a mass struggle to force congress to roll back the new taxes that hurt the working class and to search for new solutions to the current economic crisis. In contrast to persistent US government claims that the communists were only interested in sabotage and violence, party leaders presented themselves as reasonable and rational actors who forwarded concrete and proactive policy proposals.

Communist exploitation of the failure of reconstruction efforts for their own political ends and their framing of the issues in terms of class struggle deeply bothered United States diplomatic officials. One communication complained that when USIE officers visited Pelileo they discovered "Commies taking advantage [of the] situation." As evidence of this interference, the officers brought back sample copies of communist publications, including some from Mexico.[58] In all honesty, US aid programs were hardly more altruistic, but the earthquake does highlight how disasters easily become avenues for advancing political agendas and how they reveal deep class cleavages in society.

DEBATES AT THE fourth party congress of the PCE highlight the inherent difficulties in transitions of leadership. In the case of those grouped around Ricardo Paredes and Pedro Saad, the scuffles also reflected different cultural orientations, personal styles, and political agendas. The party shifted from a concentration on rural highland Indigenous struggles to an emphasis on urban working-class organizations on the coast. Tensions that accompanied these changes emerged in the preparations for the congress, during the congress itself, and in the resolutions that came out of the congress.

Whether for opportunistic or ideological purposes, the communist party placed itself at the front of working-class struggles even as it faced deep divisions within its own ranks. It strove to remain relevant and visible as political sentiments appeared to drift away from socialist solutions to the pressing problems that the country faced. Despite difficulties and in the midst of many different transitions, the party continued fighting for a fairer and more just world. In doing so, and in the face of these challenges, activists laid the basis for political developments that were to come in the future.

CHAPTER 6

Transitions

THE 1950S WERE A period of continual transitions for the communist party in Ecuador. The new and upcoming head Pedro Saad took over the reins from the party's founder and longtime secretary general Ricardo Paredes. With a change in leadership, the party underwent a corresponding conversion from an emphasis on rural and Indigenous communities to urban labor issues. The party's organizational base also shifted from the capital Quito in the highlands to the commercial center of Guayaquil on the coast. According to the communist author and militant Elías Muñoz Vicuña, "The main characteristic of these years was the policy of unmasking imperialism and the action of organization and struggle of the masses for their immediate demands and rights."[1] Party members continued to fight for a more just and equal world, even when such possibilities appeared remote. In the process they laid the groundwork for future political advances.

Internal transitions in the party took place in the midst of larger political transformations. Most notable was the 1949 Chinese Revolution that brought Mao Zedong to power. Much as the 1917 Bolshevik Revolution in Russia had inspired militants to form socialist parties in their own countries, the Chinese Revolution similarly triggered heightened levels of activism in Latin America and elsewhere in the underdeveloped periphery of the global economy. These developments brought both opportunities and challenges. In the 1960s divisions between the Soviets and Chinese would break wide open with fractures that ran throughout communist parties around the world. The groundwork for these changes were laid during this time.

In addition to this global context, CIA surveillance of communist involvement in labor activities along with its other investigations shed light on the party's persistent presence and political actions. Women, with longtime activist Nela Martínez in the lead, defended the rights of striking workers and inevitably faced sanctions from government officials for their actions. Communists and socialists continued to tangle over what stance they should take toward the Galo

Plaza Lasso government, with socialists ultimately accepting positions in his administration while the communists retained their status of principled opposition. While the two left parties often disagreed over tactics—sometimes fiercely so—they shared similar goals of advancing the interests of the working class.

Although the communists faced constant obstacles, they also used whatever mechanisms they had at their disposal to press their political agenda. The party was particularly effective at supporting labor movements and encouraging strike activity. This ability to provide structure and leadership to working-class demands is what gained it the antagonism of both domestic and international opponents, and in turn resulted in the dedicated attention of surveillance agencies that ultimately chronicled the PCE's actions. With access to that information, we can begin to reconstruct histories that might otherwise have been lost or forgotten.

China

On October 1, 1949, Mao Zedong established the People's Republic of China. The Communist Party of China was founded in 1921 and initially allied with the Chinese Nationalist Party (the Kuomintang). In 1927, the alliance broke down when the conservative leader Chiang Kai-shek gained control of the Kuomintang. The communists retreated to the countryside to build up their local bases under Mao's guidance as head of the Red Army. In 1945 at the end of the Second World War and with the defeat of the Imperial Japanese Army, the communists and nationalists fought for control of China. By the end of 1948, the communists had gained the upper hand in the conflict and it became apparent that they would soon defeat the Kuomintang.

With victory imminent in China, the CIA reported that their Ecuadorian counterparts were realizing success in their penetration of the country's army. "They believe the advances in China have made a deep impression in the lower echelons of the Latin American armies," a CIA information report stated, "and claim to be in a position where they can now control the lower ranks of the Ecuadoran Army." Even so, the communists were hesitant to test the depth of their strength in case their attempts resulted in failure. "Their policy is to await coordinated revolutionary activity in Latin America which would be part of a world revolution," the agency declared.[2] Saad claimed that the party could depend on 60 percent of the noncommissioned officers in the army, although a CIA case officer thought that number to be inflated. According to that officer, it "probably includes many disgruntled persons who would balk at supporting a

Communist movement were it identified as such." Saad noted that if the minister of defense attempted to undermine the communist presence by moving members to another unit, they would just pick up where they had left off organizing their previous unit.[3]

At the same time, the coastal branch of the party convened several closed meetings to plan actions to take advantage of the political openings that communist victories in China provided. In particular, the party looked to increase activity among its existing cells, establish new cells among agricultural workers, and form a new communist-controlled cooperative in the Milagro area.[4] These measures underscored the communist desire to build a strong political movement rather than conspiring with meaningless palace coups that would leave existing exploitative structures intact. These reports also indicate continued aspirations for a global communist revolution that would abolish the entire capitalist system, rather than being content with much more limited nationalist and reformist movements.

CIA surveillance reinforces a perception that the organizational process was more advanced in Guayaquil than Quito. Seemingly drawing on information from informers in Ecuador (although source data is redacted in the declassified versions), one document reported on the active engagement of the PCE's Guayaquil branch "with both political and military revolutionary elements." Some central committee members allegedly advocated that the time was right "to form a revolutionary political front to cooperate with the military in overthrowing the government." According to the CIA case officer, the communists faced two obstacles in achieving their objective: "the apathy or inertia of the anti-government groups; and the reluctance of these groups to participate in any movement with the Communists."[5] Despite Saad's best efforts, rising anticommunist sentiments meant that the party faced increased difficulties in finding partners who would ally with them in common political struggles.

Another CIA information report indicated that Saad pointed to the situation in China as having a positive effect on growth in communist party membership. In 1948, the Guayaquil branch had received an average of thirty-five membership applications a month, but in the first twenty-four days of January 1949 (through the date of receipt of information for the report) they had received more than one hundred. Saad expected interest in the PCE to increase even more after the Chinese communists declared final victory. In anticipation of this development, the party was planning propaganda campaigns to promote the advantages of a communist system over a capitalist one. Even so, Saad indicated that the party was leery of expanding its membership too quickly. The party accepted new applicants only as sympathizers until they could demonstrate their sincerity to the communist cause. He remained alert to the possible presence of infiltrators who could open the party to disruptive forces.[6] The extent of CIA surveillance would make it appear that they were not careful enough.

Responses to the Chinese Revolution provide examples of the close collaboration between the CIA and other US agencies, particularly on the ground in South America. In February 1949, a "controlled American source," presumably Albert Haney, forwarded a handbill from the coastal communist party to the embassy as evidence of the local influence of communist victories in China (see figure 6.1).[7] Ambassador John Simmons, in turn, had the handbill translated in English and a week later forwarded that translation to the State Department in Washington. The flyer celebrated "the heroic Chinese people who are in a victorious campaign defeating the militarist Chinese bandits led by Chiang Kai Shek, servants of the Feudal Chinese masters and of Yankee Imperialism." The party called for a "popular assembly in favor of a democratic China," and proclaimed that their battles were "showing us the road of our own social liberation" over Ecuador's feudal masters and reactionary capitalists. The gains in China demonstrated that united the people could achieve national liberation, and that imperialism was not an invincible force. The leaflet concluded with a proclamation, "For the destruction of imperialism and the social and national liberation of Ecuador."[8] The communists expressed optimism that soon victory would be theirs as well.

Simmons commented that "such propaganda designed to make political capital of communist successes in China had been anticipated in reports reaching a controlled American source."[9] And, in fact, Haney had been providing Simmons with a continual flow of information, some of which survives in different formats at different points in the archives. In one report, Haney added that the impetus behind this increased activity was the receipt of a circular from France on the subject of communist victories in China.[10] A persistent assumption was that the party responded more readily to external stimuli and influences than to local factors. Such comments reflected both negative attitudes toward the organizational capacity of local communists, as well as a primary concern with external cold war tensions rather than the domestic roots of rebellion.

The Chinese Revolution continued to have a significant influence on the Ecuadorian left throughout the 1950s and eventually contributed to a split in the party in the 1960s. Throughout this time, the CIA tracked travel between the two regions. CIA analysts feared that communist leaders—particularly those in

GRAN ASAMBLEA POPULAR PRO CHINA DEMOCRATICA

LOCAL: Sociedad de Carpinteros DIA: Viernes 4 de Febrero

HORA: Ocho de la noche

El día 4 de Febrero próximo, en la Sociedad de Carpinteros se efectuará un gran homenaje del pueblo de Guayaquil al heroico pueblo chino que en victoriosa jornada está derrotando a los bandidos militaristas chinos encabezados por Chiang Kai Shek, sirvientes de los señores Feudales chinos y del Imperialismo Yanqui, que trataban de sojuzgar para siempre a la gran Nación China, para mantenerla en la miseria y la explotación.

La derrota de los señores Feudales y más fuerzas anti-democráticas chinas nos está enseñando el camino de nuestra propia liberación social; la unidad de nuestro pueblo, que encabezado por la clase trabajadora y las fuerzas democráticas tiene la obligación de combatir a muerte contra sus enemigos irreconciliables: los señores Feudales de la Sierra y los capitalistas antipatriotas y reaccionarios, antiprogresistas.

La derrota del imperialismo yanqui nos está demostrando, en este ejemplo, que la unidad del pueblo y su decisión por la lucha pueden conseguir la liberación nacional y que el Imperialismo, no es de ninguna manera, una fuerza invencible, sino al contrario, una fuerza decadente y corrupta, pronta a ser derrotada por las fuerzas de los pueblos del Orbe.

Junto al pueblo de Guayaquil, se encontrarán en esta magna Asamblea, las fuerzas democráticas, leales y consecuentes defensoras de los intereses del pueblo y de la Patria.

TODO GUAYAQUIL A LA ASAMBLEA DEL 4 DE FEBRERO, QUE SERA UNA GRAN FECHA EN LAS JORNADAS POLITICAS DE GUAYAQUIL!

LA CLASE TRABAJADORA, LOS PARTIDOS POLITICOS DE IZQUIERDA, LOS ESTUDIANTES, LAS INSTITUCIONES CULTURALES, TODOS LOS QUE AMEN LA LIBERACION DEL PUEBLO, CONCURRID A LA ASAMBLEA DEL 4 DE FEBRERO!

POR LA DESTRUCCION DEL IMPERIALISMO Y LA LIBERACION SOCIAL Y NACIONAL DEL ECUADOR.

Partido Comunista del Ecuador· C. R. L. y C. L. de Guayaquil

FIGURE 6.1. A flyer calling for a "popular assembly in support of a democratic China" in celebration of communist victories in China. Source: Partido Comunista del Ecuador (PCE), "Gran Asamblea Popular Pro China Democrática," 1949, BEAEP.

Ecuador, Chile, Colombia, and Costa Rica—looked to apply "the methods and activities of the Chinese Communist Party to Latin American conditions."[11] Beyond ideological affinity, party leaders pointed to parallels between the two regions that included foreign economic domination and their semi-colonial political status. Many members believed that China provided "a better model for agrarian Latin America than does the more industrialized USSR."[12] A definitive split between pro-Soviet and pro-Chinese wings of the communist parties did not occur until the 1960s, but preliminary indications of those fractures were present much earlier.

La Industrial

In 1950, a simmering conflict over wages and working conditions at the cotton textile factory La Industrial in Quito broke out into a strike. Workers accused their boss of abuses and a failure to comply with the stipulations of the 1938 Labor Code. They demanded that the factory's owner allow fired workers to return to their posts, stop revenge actions against labor organizers, and raise salaries by 35 percent.[13] As the strike dragged on, other factories joined solidarity actions with the laborers at La Industrial. Organizers began to talk about launching a general strike.[14] Workers took to the streets in protest. The police fired teargas on the demonstrators, even though the march was comprised primarily of women workers and their children. Three of the workers ended up in the hospital with injuries.[15] When the strikes and marches did not lead to the desired results, labor leaders at the factory launched a hunger strike. They vowed to continue the struggle until their demands were met.[16]

In the middle of this hunger strike, Mariana Carvajal, the ten-month old daughter of the factory worker Luz María Corral, died of malnutrition. Her mother had spent the last thirty-six days holed up in the plant in support of the industrial action, and both her parents were participating in the hunger strike. Workers took the baby's body to the labor union headquarters for a funeral wake.[17] The next afternoon, workers and their family members accompanied the body to the cemetery. Three workers carried the banner of La Industrial's labor union at the head of the procession. Following the banner were supporters who collected funds for the family of the deceased to pay for burial and other expenses. After parading through the city and across the central plaza, the mourners arrived at the San Diego Cemetery to bury the baby. At the cemetery, a series of labor leaders spoke, including communist militant Reinaldo Miño,

CTE president César Humberto Navarro, and FTP president César Florencio González.[18]

The leftist student federation FEUE published a poetic statement on Carvajal's death in its newspaper, together with a photo of Corral holding the child and the father by their side. The story began,

> One Saturday afternoon, we buried a girl, a brief tenant of life. Her fragile existence broke like a stem and the earth devoured it in its bottomless face.

The essay continued with the observation that the story of the dead child was "at once simple and terrible." She had been born into poverty to working-class parents who wanted to work and improve their lives, but the wealthy factory owners wanted to close the plant. This led to the long, drawn out walk out that ended with the hunger strike in order to move justice forward. The child was an innocent victim of that protest, and a sacrifice to save the lives of others. With her burial, the article concluded, the strikers planted justice. "And this dead girl is the diminutive seed of justice. And the seed will germinate someday. A very true and very clear day."[19] The students hoped their passionate statement would help advance the rights of the workers.

The death of the child had little effect on the factory owner, who called in the police to evict the striking workers from the plant—even though the government refused to follow through on his request.[20] Finally, after a forty-day strike, the workers peacefully left the factory after reaching an agreement with the owner on the payment of wages. The FTP was not content with the settlement—from their perspective it was a violation of Ecuador's labor code. The federation announced plans for a general strike in Pichincha in order to defend all of the country's workers from such abuses.[21] The struggle was intense, and communists were in the middle and actively involved with it.

Two days after Carvajal's funeral, the Quito police announced that they were looking for the communist militant Nela Martínez to question her about the amount of money she had collected for the child's family. Officers had searched for Martínez late into the night without being able to find her. Police Chief Jorge Quintana declared that the child's parents, Luis Carvajal Ruiz and Luz María Corral, had accused Martínez of not giving them all of the money she had collected from workers during the funeral procession. A woman named Hipatia Nicolalde had told them that 60 sucres and 55 cents could not be the total that Martínez had mustered from their fellow workers, and charged that she had pocketed the rest. Carvajal Ruiz and Corral denounced Martínez for profiting from their tragedy. They also denied that their child had died as a result of the strike. The police chief Quintana declared that as soon as they could find Martínez he would be able to establish the validity of the allegations against her, and that he had requested the collaboration of the provincial police to arrest those implicated in this issue.[22]

The FTP protested against the charges that the police had brought against Martínez. Workers gathered at the Casa del Obrero, the workers' center that was a standard gathering point in Quito, declared that the accusations were not true. They alleged that the police had distorted the events, and that the 60 sucres that Martínez had given the parents was the total amount that they had collected. The workers denied that Martínez was even present when organizers handed the collected funds over to Carvajal's parents. The feminist AFE also responded with a strongly worded statement that pledged their unequivocal support for Martínez, one of the founders of the organization. It called the charges slanderous, outrageous, and lacking any basis in fact. The AFE denounced those who advanced the indictment as dishonest, and declared their absolute support for Martínez who was well known for her honesty and integrity. The police chief Quintana responded to these statements with a defense of his actions, stating that in questioning Martínez he was simply following through with an investigation into the accusations that the parents had made based on Nicolalde's allegations.[23]

Martínez, who was not in hiding, went to the police station when she heard that they were looking for her. Together with her friend and comrade María Luisa Gómez de la Torre, she presented the police with a statement proclaiming her innocence. After a short interview with Quintana, Martínez turned to leave. Instead, two officers stopped her and placed her under arrest. When Martínez insisted on seeing the arrest warrant, the officers would only tell her that they were following "órdenes superiores," higher orders. Martínez protested angrily, contending that her detention was a violation of her rights and democratic principles. The police insisted that the summons she faced had nothing to do with political concerns, but rather a criminal charge that she had embezzled funds collected for the deceased child's family. Martínez pleaded her innocence, and claimed that she had yet to see the indictments that she was facing. Nevertheless, Quintana locked her in a holding cell until the accusations that Carvajal's parents had brought against her could be investigated. Quintana also stated that he wanted to confirm how Carvajal had died, whether it was due to asphyxiation from tear gas that the police had fired on the strikers, as some sources indicated, or whether the child died at home and not in the factory, as her parents claimed.[24]

The following day, the ministry of government that oversaw the police clarified that the arrest order against Martínez was still in effect, which is why she was imprisoned. Nevertheless, the ministry ordered her release, a directive with which the police immediately complied.[25] With that, the entire incident seemed to dissipate and be forgotten. Martínez does not even mention the incident in her autobiography.[26] Rather than an insignificant event, it was just one more episode in the long struggle of a committed communist who suffered repeated imprisonments and other repressive reprisals for her actions.

Intriguingly, the CIA archives document local police efforts to discredit Martínez's successful organizing efforts "by falsely accusing her of keeping money which was collected for the family of a baby who died during the recent *La Industrial* hunger strike." The CIA report summarizes the same narrative that appeared in the media, perhaps the source for their information. It recounts how Martínez and other activists solicited material and moral aid for the strikers. The women had collected money during the baby's funeral procession, and entrusted Martínez with delivering the collected funds to the family. Media reports indicated that she had kept a sizable amount of the funds for herself, and only gave 60 sucres to the family. Other witnesses, however, declared that they had collected a total of 60 sucres and that Martínez had delivered the entire amount to the family. None of these sources ever presented a convincing explanation for why Martínez might want to keep some of the money that the solidarity activists had collected. If anything, given her history, she was more likely to add funds to the pot from her own pocket if the amount collected was insufficient.

According to the CIA officer in Quito, Martínez and others had collected the money "in order to gain adherents to the Communist cause among the laboring classes," which led to the police attempts to discredit their activities.[27] The way the CIA reports the story that the charges were "announced in the press" would indicate a planted story and a concerted campaign against the communists. The officer states, "after the first accusations appeared in the press, Martínez publicly denounced the chief of police," even though such a statement does not appear in *El Comercio*. According to the CIA, the police chief used her public statements as a justification to draft a statement for the dead child's mother to sign that accused Martínez of absconding with the collected funds. Drawing on private information from the police, the case officer reported that the police chief paid the mother 50 sucres to sign the statement. With that "evidence" in hand, he then called in Martínez. The communist activist willingly presented herself to police headquarters convinced of her innocence, completely unaware of the fabricated charges that she would face. It was on that basis that the police detained Martínez overnight, but released her the following day when she promised to return if so ordered.

Some crucial parts of this story disappear from the historical record, particularly the actions and motivations of the parents, Corral and Carvajal Ruiz. From media reports, it would appear that the baby's mother Corral willingly participated in the hunger strike, but then turned against those who sought to gain political advantage from her child's death, but they give little indication why this might be. A reasonable assumption is that a mother's grief at losing a child was intense, and she may not have appreciated having a private event politicized. Media and intelligence reports do not indicate whether this was Corral's first or only child, but in the absence of mention of other children that probably was the case. Furthermore, given the demographics of textile factory workers Corral may have been a young mother. The picture of her that the FEUE printed in their newspaper would seem to confirm that fact. She may have felt embarrassed or feared moral or criminal sanction with accusations of being an irresponsible mother for letting a child die while engaged in a political action. The authorities could have easily taken advantage of her marginalized status to attack the communists. An attempt at denial of culpability, either from the parents who may have feared being cast as irresponsible for taking their child to a protest or the police who did not want to face charges of killing an innocent baby, may have played into the parents' statement that the baby was at home when she died. Finally, we do not know anything about Corral's political beliefs and attitudes. If she were politically antagonistic to the left, or simply apolitical, she may have been tempted to take both the 60 sucres from the march as well as the additional 50 sucres from the police. Presumably with a long drawn out strike in process she would be in a difficult financial situation, and the bribe from the police to pursue charges against Martínez may have been too tempting to pass up. Unfortunately, with the available documentation it is impossible to determine the thoughts and motivations that informed the actions of the two parents.

The CIA report includes other information that was not publicly available, which indicates collaboration with Ecuador's police forces. According to the agency, when Gómez de la Torre who had accompanied Martínez to the police station became nervous that the police would also detain her, she surreptitiously destroyed two letters in her purse. Apparently an informer was able to retrieve the correspondence, because the agency reported that one was a subscription to the *Revue Partisans de la Paix*, a publication of the World Peace Council in France, and the other was to PCE secretary general Paredes who was currently living in Manta. The CIA provided specific information on the contents of both letters. The first was addressed to the attention of R. Simon at 15 rue Feyseau in Paris and included $10 USD for the subscription. The second to Paredes related recent communist activities in Quito, including police efforts to break up communist demonstrations as well as the slander campaign against Martínez in the current La Industrial case. The CIA report does not reveal whether Gómez de la Torre had not been successful in hiding her communications and whether the police recovered their contents, or whether the information came from an infiltrator in the communist party to whom she may have later related the specifics of the encounter. The level of detail, including the specific address for the French periodical, would seem to indicate that police provided the particulars to the CIA from information that they had retrieved. If this were the case, it would amount to a police admission that they had arrested Martínez on trumped up charges, and perhaps the CIA was even complicit in attempts to discredit her political activities.[28]

A month later in a report on "subversive" activities in Ecuador, CIA analysts in Washington confirmed that the charges of absconding with funds had merely been a pretext to imprison Martínez. Its intent was to warn "the Communists that any great increase in their activities may henceforth be countered with stronger measures on the part of the government." Both the Ecuadorian government and the CIA were concerned with the leading roles that women played in communist activities. Martínez was a good organizer, and she had dedicated her efforts to assembling housewives in Quito into peace committees. Other prominent communist women were actively organizing in Guayaquil as well, which led to a strengthened left.[29] Surveillance provides evidence of the government's repressive actions, but more importantly chronicles strategies the left employed and the challenges they faced in advancing their political agenda.

The CIA's complicity with Martínez's arrest in Quito in the midst of the strike at La Industrial was part of its broader preoccupation with communist infiltration of labor groups. This was the case even though according to the agency's own internal intelligence estimates the communists held little power in the hemisphere. In a March 1950 assessment of communist capabilities in Latin America, CIA analysts concluded that parties remained small and activities "continued at about the same low level." Much of their emphasis was on maintaining their influence in labor organizations, even as they fought for their very existence.[30] At the same time, CIA analysts expressed a fear that even though communist strength and influence was minor, this trend of declining influence that had been evident since the closing of postwar democratic openings in 1947 might be coming to an end. On the one hand, governmental anticommunist actions had led to communist losses in Mexico, Argentina, and Colombia, and repressive actions had prevented gains in Brazil, Bolivia, and Chile. On the other hand, major political parties had accepted communist collaboration in Guatemala, El Salvador, and Cuba, which reduced their political isolation, made them appear more respectable, increased their ability to attract new recruits and collect funds, and in general strengthened their political position. While these recent advances were not large, the CIA feared that they might portend future communist gains. In addition, communists could exploit political and economic instability in Chile, Bolivia, Paraguay, and Ecuador.[31] The agency effectively capitalized on anxieties over potential communist advances to justify continued surveillance of their activities.

Socialist Ministers

In 1950 and approaching the halfway point in Plaza's mandate, coup threats began to drop off as the president consolidated his control over the country. In an annual review of Ecuadorian events, the British ambassador John Carvell summarized 1950 as a largely peaceful year with few significant events. He credited economic improvements and simple luck with Plaza's unprecedented ability to hold on to the presidency, because in his frank and quite derogatory assessment Ecuadorians "are as yet neither politically nor ethically fitted for the democratic way of life as we understand it."[32] Journalist Milton Bracker presented a somewhat more optimistic appraisal in an article in the *New York Times*. Together with Uruguay, Bracker saw Ecuador as a relative anomaly in the region in that it had largely been spared from the military governments and extraconstitutional changes in administration that had recently plagued other countries.[33] From his perspective, the future looked bright for Ecuador.

Following up on Bracker's analysis, in April 1951 veteran Latin American correspondent Herbert Matthews reported in the *New York Times* that Ecuador was "providing one of the most remarkable of all Latin American experiments in democracy." Under the leadership of a "tall, dark and handsome young athlete," Ecuador had achieved a certain amount of stability and prosperity. In glowing terms, Matthews described Plaza as having "imposed democracy and stability from above" and of maintaining "it by sheer force of personality." Despite repeated attempted coups, Matthews was optimistic that Plaza would manage to preserve order in the country. He recognized, however, that one of the president's largest liabilities was his close identification with the United States. Those imperial connections did not play well in a nationalistic environment.

From Matthews's perspective, the biggest danger to a continuance of democratic rule was not the socialist left, but conservatives who had been out of power for more than half a century and "at last see a good chance to come back, and their traditions are by no means democratic." Matthews describes Plaza as attempting to organize a progressive coalition for the upcoming 1952 presidential elections to prevent the right from returning to power. At the same time, he retained profoundly anticommunist sentiments. One of the difficulties Plaza faced in office was eliminating communists from his party. From his perspective, "democracy is the best answer to communism." Plaza contended that the "two are incompatible," and he was committed to their removal from positions of authority.[34] The cold war and red scare were becoming more readily apparent in Ecuador.

In an attempt to hold on to power in the face of constant threats, Plaza frequently rotated out cabinet ministers. Among the changes was the appointment of five different ministers of government. In May 1951, Plaza engaged in yet another cabinet shakeup, apparently to bring his government in line with plans to form a progressive coalition to contest the 1952 presidential elections. Plaza eliminated conservatives and added a liberal and two socialists, Carlos Cueva Tamariz at education and Colón Serrano at economy. Of the two, Cueva Tamariz was the more significant. He was born in Cuenca, and during his public life he alternated between academic and political careers. He founded a student federation while at the University of Cuenca in the 1920s. In the 1930s he began teaching history and law at the university, and in 1944 assumed the post of rector—a position he held on and off until the 1970s. Beginning in the 1920s, he served multiple terms on the city council of Cuenca and as a deputy in the federal congress. In the 1930s, he helped refound the socialist party. He also held the position of minister of the interior, and in 1938 was considered for the presidency of the republic. He had run for vice president on a liberal-socialist ticket with Alberto Enríquez Gallo in 1948, but lost that position to the conservative candidate Manuel Sotomayor y Luna. The British Embassy described Cueva Tamariz as "a Socialist with tendencies towards the Left of that Party, who was "considered one of the most qualified for office."[35] He remained politically active for the next several decades. Similarly, Serrano was one of the founders of the socialist party and also served in various educational, political, and diplomatic roles.

The appointments resulted from Plaza caving to pressure from the left to strengthen an anticonservative front. In exchange for the cabinet posts, Plaza gained socialist support that helped solidify his government's hold on power. At the same time, the nominations sowed discord between the socialist and communist parties. From the socialists' perspective, access to the cabinet posts was an opportunity to gain a seat at the table and have a say in the shaping of policy. The communists, however, condemned the selections as a meaningless gesture that did little to advance a leftist agenda. Underlying communist opposition was the recognition that Plaza was successfully marginalizing them as a political player.[36]

In the midst of this cabinet shakeup, the United States Embassy's chargé d'affaires John Hamlin sent a telegram to the State Department highlighting that the principal factor underlying the current political crisis was a fear that leftist disunity would result in a conservative victory in the 1952 election. Hamlin noted that appointment of a leftist minister of government might temporarily ease the situation, but he did not discount the possibility that a deteriorating political situation could still result in a coup.[37] *El Comercio* reported that conservatives responded to the shift to the left in the cabinet with the comment that "The government tries to deliver the country into the hands of a single party, which serves to open a path for the triumph of communism."[38] Hamlin relayed this statement to the State Department, adding his additional concern that a "Commie triumph . . . will place continental security in danger."[39] Despite all appearances and Plaza's claims to the contrary, the US Embassy feared that his policies exposed the country to a communist threat. United States officials had difficulties distinguishing between socialists and communists, with some embassy personnel contending that no meaningful difference existed between the two. That confusion was at play with Plaza's nomination of Cueva Tamariz and Serrano.

In a summary of the week's political events, Hamlin noted that Plaza first offered the portfolio of education to Benjamín Carrión, president of the Casa de la Cultura and editor of the new progressive newspaper *El Sol*, and the post at finance to Angel F. Rojas, a socialist from Guayaquil. Both declined the positions, favoring instead to continue their publishing and cultural activities. The posts then passed on to Cueva Tamariz and Serrano in exchange for a tacit agreement with the socialist party to stop its opposition to the government. Hamlin cautioned that as a result of this development, the socialist cabinet ministers would "promote [their] party policies within [the government] while Socialist Commie inclined newspapers and cultural org[anizations would] mold public opinion." From Hamlin's perspective, those negative influences included both *El Sol* and the Casa de la Cultura as well as the socialist party newspaper *La*

Tierra that often reported on communist party events and policy statements. Hamlin feared that these developments represented a growth in leftist strength in the country. As a reflection of this ascendancy, the VRSE, an "off shoot [of the] Socialist party, closer to Communism," that had been inactive for a long time had begun to reorganize its provincial committees.[40] He feared that leftist unity could challenge US interests in the region.

The advantages of having socialists in the cabinet to achieve broader leftist objectives were more apparent to outsiders than to the Ecuadorian communists. In June 1951, the United States Embassy in Quito reported on a comment that the Chilean communist Juan Esteban García Moreno had made at a communist assembly in Guayaquil that Ecuador was one of few countries where communists had complete freedom of action. García Moreno claimed that it would be easier for the communists to implement their plans with "so many Socialists in the cabinet and ministerial positions." Rather than opposing this development, García Moreno urged the communists to exploit the opportunities that socialist participation in government provided to them. He spoke of Chile's own experience with the collapse of their popular front government and of Gabriel González Videla subsequently outlawing the party, and he wanted his Ecuadorian counterparts to avoid the same fate.[41]

Although approaching the issue from an entirely different ideological perspective, the Office of Intelligence Research at the State Department echoed García Moreno's sentiments. The OIR complained that the socialist party contained "many pro-Communist elements," and that "Socialist labor and student groups continued to show a strong pro-Communist trend." Although conflicts between Plaza's MCDN and the PCE had complicated the process of building an anticonservative electoral front, the OIR cautioned of the potential for increased communist influence in the June 1952 presidential election. The socialist cabinet appointments had further ramifications that concerned the State Department. The appointment of a socialist as minister of education strengthened the position of "Communist youth-student groups," including providing official support for a delegation to the Third World Youth Festival for Peace in Berlin in August. Despite evidence to the contrary, the OIR feared a growing leftist presence in Ecuador.[42]

For their part, analysts at CIA Headquarters commented, "the recent appointment of Socialists (one of whom is reported to have had some connections with the Communist Party) to two of the eight cabinet posts during the recent cabinet reorganization was motivated by a desire to reduce some of the opposition to the Government and improve the present administration's chances of serving out its term until 1952." Ironically, the CIA expressed less concern than did the embassy or the OIR about this development since Plaza maintained a strongly pro-United States policy and did not delegate broad authority to his cabinet ministers. According to the CIA, "he would probably not hesitate to remove these men from the cabinet if convinced that they are at any time seeking to further Communist objectives." These factors "should serve as a sufficient check to prevent the Communist Party from gaining any notable advantage through any influence it may have with the two Socialist ministers." In this case, the CIA accurately viewed Plaza as friendly to United States interests, and contended that his actions should be embraced rather than feared.[43]

Socialists strongly defended the cabinet appointments from conservative attacks, in particular Cueva Tamariz at education who they saw as a bulwark against a return to conservative Catholic control. Maintaining free, secular, and universal access to education was key to the creation of the type of world that they envisioned. The PSE organized a meeting of workers, students, and teachers to demonstrate their solidarity and affirm their willingness to take to the streets in support of a secular education system if necessary.[44] Conservatives would not easily or readily give up their advantages, which heightened the potential conflict facing the country.

"NO PRIVILEGED CLASS voluntarily resigns any of its privileges," the journalist and labor organizer Albert Rhys Williams observed in the context of the 1917 Bolshevik Revolution. "No class steeped in tradition discards the old and gladly embraces the new."[45] This truism repeatedly emerged apparent in Ecuador during the 1950s as communist militants appealed to the model that the Chinese Revolution offered and as they sought to advance labor struggles. Meanwhile, party members continued their collaboration with working-class campaigns as dedicated activists who toiled to build a better world. The collection of donations for the parents of a recently deceased child, as Martínez and others had done in the midst of the strike at La Industrial, was hardly a radical action. Rather, it reflected a humane response to an exploitative situation—not entirely unlike the types of reforms that socialist leaders attempted to realize with their acceptance of ministerial posts in Plaza's government. The ruling class refused to make even these minor concessions.

Throughout all of these transitions, deep divisions ran through the PCE between those grouped around the labor organizer and coastal communist leader Pedro Saad who wanted to collaborate with progressive governments and others such as party founder and longtime leader Ricardo Paredes who advocated for a much more militant position of relying on grassroots social movement pressure.[46] According to the CIA, former Trotskyists who challenged "the advisability of blindly following orders from the USSR" contributed to further discord within the party. Bitter debates threatened a split within the communist ranks, but in the CIA's assessment the party could little afford divisions when it was "making every effort to expand and strengthen the organization."[47] Whether or not the party could navigate these conflicts would define its ability to survive and flourish. Even minor and gradual changes required a great deal of effort, and with the growth of external populist threats the much more profound transformations that many leftists desired appeared to recede ever more distantly on the horizon.

CHAPTER 7

Populism

POPULIST POLITICIANS PROVIDED AN equal if not greater threat to the political left than either domestic conservative opponents or external surveillance agents. Populists competed for the allegiance of the same working-class base as the socialists and communists, but with quite different ends in mind. Rather than advancing an ideological agenda of fighting for a more equal and just society, populists typically engaged in personalistic campaigns that advanced an individual leader who portended to embody the interests of society as a whole. Their emotional and nationalist appeals that superficially emulated a radical rhetoric of railing against the oligarchy proved to be effective at mobilizing working-class support, even if it ultimately worked against their own class interests.

Populist efficacy at launching successful electoral campaigns made it difficult for the left to counter their actions. In general, socialists and communists realized most success when organized as social movements that pressed their demands as part of a broader campaign for the rights of workers. Nevertheless, some communist leaders consistently pushed for the formation of an electoral popular front to defeat conservatives and remove populists from political power. Ironically, even as United States officials condemned leftists for their alleged subversive activities, it was these conservatives and right-wing populists who were much more willing and even eager to resort to military coups that would create a break in the constitutional order.

All of these issues played out across the 1950s, and were most visibly on display in Ecuador in the 1952 presidential campaign. To the surprise of pundits and many observers, the perennial populist candidate José María Velasco Ibarra won that election. Despite the left's best efforts to form a coalition to keep conservative and populist forces out of office, infighting over different personalities and political ideals thwarted efforts at progressive unity. Anticommunist sentiments also meant that liberals and socialists willingly turned against the PCE in order to shore up their own electoral prospects. All of these factors not only left the communists marginalized, but also assured that the left would remain out of power.

Communist Party Platform

By the time of the 1952 presidential election, the PCE's secretary general, Ricardo Paredes, was losing influence in the party even though he still occasionally issued strongly worded statements. In light of the serious problems that the country faced, in February 1951 Paredes penned a lengthy statement "full of love and emotion" that contended that the party was dedicated to a defense of the country's interests as it charted "the only way that leads to independence, progress and happiness."[1] The statement began with a discussion of financial and other problems that the country's social welfare institute and social security system faced. Paredes declared that the PCE was the first party to fight for the establishment of a social security system, was its strongest defender, and remained the strongest critic of the abuses within the system, including of government attempts to raid its funds for other purposes. "The Communist Party fights and will continue fighting so that the social security benefits be extended to agricultural workers and Indians," the statement asserted.

Paredes criticized abuses in the distribution of aid in the aftermath of the 1949 earthquake. He contrasted how that aid served to enrich a few individual capitalists with the reconstruction of the Polish capital of Warsaw that was destroyed in the Second World War. "The resurrection of Warsaw is the product of the magnificent work of the socialist government," Paredes wrote. He compared a socialist belief in social justice and the need to meet human needs with the crimes that the capitalist government in Ecuador committed in its reconstruction efforts. Paredes called for the punishment of officials who were responsible for the neglect, theft, and diversion in the distribution of the aid. Instead, worker and neighborhood committees should be placed in charge of rebuilding. Similar problems of fraud and abuse had occurred with an Export-Import Bank (Eximbank) loan for a water project in Quito that only ended up enriching the contractor Harold Smith. That disgrace followed in the footsteps of the humiliating experience with the US-based Ambursen Engineering Company that charged millions of dollars for the poorly constructed Quevedo-Manta Road. Furthermore, the loan conditions required that the Ecuadorian government contract with United States companies rather than local businesses, with the result that the development projects benefited the United States rather than Ecuador. The PCE called for the punishment of public officials who were implicated in the theft of public funds and "indemnification of damages from the imperialist companies that have harmed Ecuador." As US government officials never hesitated to point out, the communists exploited every opportunity to blast international corporations for extracting wealth from the country.

On top of these structural issues, other problems had increased hunger in Ecuador. Flooding had led to poor harvests in the Ecuadorian highlands. To alleviate the resulting misery, the PCE called for the implementation of government measures against speculation and the provision of basic necessities at affordable prices. While the cost of living continued to skyrocket, salaries remained low. The wages that workers received were not enough to cover their basic necessities, even as transnational companies recorded unprecedented profits. In this context, it was the responsibility of labor unions and leftist parties to fight for the rights of workers, because none of the other political parties would do so. Paredes pointed out that the conservative party collaborated with liberal governments to benefit from this situation, thereby highlighting that both represented bourgeois interests. Neither provided the type of true alternatives that Ecuador so desperately needed.

More objectionable than the traditional liberal and conservative parties were the "traitors" Carlos Guevara Moreno and Rafael Coello Serrano. They had defected from the communist party to form the reactionary group CFP that exploited popular discontent to impose a ferocious dictatorship. They engaged in an intense derogatory campaign that presented themselves as the saviors of the country through the organization of a military coup. The CFP was a "miserable fascist group in which there are some deceived people." That gang had a long, dark history of political crimes, theft of public funds, and collaboration with the Yankees in violations of national sovereignty. More than any other bourgeois-feudal political group in Ecuador, Paredes charged, the CFP was positioned to destroy the country. The communist leader announced that the PCE was on guard to counter whatever moves might be afoot to launch a coup against the Ecuadorian government and install a reactionary government that would aggravate an already bad economic situation.

It was in this situation that the PCE looked ahead to the 1952 presidential election, still more than a year away. The current president Galo Plaza Lasso had limited his statements to calls for free elections and attempts to unify disparate liberal forces in a campaign against a potential right-wing candidate. Nevertheless, according to Paredes, his government pursued policies that were paving the way for the election of a conservative government. Plaza had not implemented a democratic and progressive program, nor was he a person who was capable of doing so. This failure was to be expected, because as a wealthy landowner Plaza represented the concerns of a bourgeois-feudal sector of the Ecuadorian population. His government had advanced those class interests, including strengthening the position of imperialist companies and unconditionally subjugating Ecuador to United States businesses that wanted to dominate the world. These factors were leading to a third world war.

Following this compelling political analysis, the communist party statement concluded on a much more polemical note. In capital letters, the document screamed that the only way to avoid the ascension to power of a reactionary government was through the construction of a powerful national patriotic front comprised of authentic liberals, the socialist and communist parties, other leftists, and the broad popular masses. This coalition should draft a democratic and progressive platform that forwarded a program of national independence in peaceful collaboration with other countries. This electoral front should elect as their presidential candidate a patriotic, capable, and honest man who would be faithful to the fulfillment of such a program. In the communists' eyes, the nomination of Antonio Quevedo, who some had forwarded as a potential candidate, would be a serious mistake. Quevedo was a lawyer who had served in the Foreign Service in Great Britain and the United States. In his current position on the UN Security Council, he had faithfully followed the dictates of Yankee imperialism in support of war and against Ecuador's needs. Paredes warned that his actions disqualified him as a viable candidate for a unified left.[2]

According to Paredes, the communist party had consistently laid out a path toward liberation, progress, and happiness for the Ecuadorian people. Fundamental to their program was the construction of a democratic and progressive government free from foreign imperialist domination, an agrarian reform that redistributed land to those who worked it, increases in salaries for workers, guarantees for the rights of workers, development of national industries, improvements in education, enhancements in communication networks, extension of credit, and pressure on capitalist and foreign companies to adhere to the country's laws. Paredes argued that in the shadow of the threat of a new global war that would destroy the planet, the PCE "rises as the force most consciously defending national interests, as the firmest champion of the independence, progress and well-being of its people." The party "constitutes the firmest guarantee for us to achieve a large, free and prosperous homeland." Paredes invited all workers, peasants, Indians, students, artisans, and anyone else who desired a liberated country to join their party. He called on the PSE, the CTE, and liberals to unite in a Frente Patriótico de Liberación Social y Nacional (Patriotic Front for Social and National Liberation) to realize those goals.[3]

The communists remained committed to the formation of an electoral popular front, and throughout the 1950s advocated for a variously named "Frente de Liberación Social y Nacional" (Social and National Liberation Front) or "Frente Democrático de Liberación Nacional" (Democratic Front of National Liberation) to build a unified force to march toward a better future. Despite Paredes's earnest pleas for others to join the communists in such a coalition, his call went largely unheeded, as the left lost political space in the June 1952 presidential vote and succeeding elections. With a turn to the right, the left gained more clout as an organized social movement than an electoral force. Notwithstanding the statements in this party platform, that reality is something that Paredes had long understood.

José María Velasco Ibarra (1952)

The 1952 election returned José María Velasco Ibarra, who had been removed through military coups his two previous times in office, to the presidency. The vote count was the largest up to that point in Ecuador's history, even though it barely surpassed 10 percent of the population. Suffrage was limited to literate men over eighteen years old and optional for literate adult women. The 1950 census gave the illiteracy rate at 43.7 percent, although it was probably somewhat higher, which means that many of those who were eligible failed to participate. The electoral system was still highly exclusionary with literacy restrictions baring the majority of the country's population from voting, and in particular those whose class interests the left represented. The scholars Juan Maiguashca and Liisa North calculated that the percentage of the vote equaled the size of the urban middle class and concluded that the working class played no significant role in Velasco Ibarra's election. Unlike Argentina's populist president Juan Perón, Velasco Ibarra's electoral success was not predicated on the mobilization of a working-class base.[4]

Despite these limitations, for the most part the election was peaceful and that it happened at all was an accomplishment. Velasco Ibarra emerged with a significant margin (153,934 to 118,186) over his nearest competitor, which provided him with a clear mandate even though with 43 percent he did not win a majority of the total votes cast. The *Hispanic American Report* applauded outgoing president Plaza for managing to conduct the electoral process in a largely peaceful and democratic fashion, even as his supporters and preferred candidate faced defeat. That publication expressed more hesitation as to the future of Velasco Ibarra's presidency. They questioned whether the new president, "who has been denounced as a disciple of Perón, will cultivate Ecuador's *descamisados* [shirtless ones] or the employer class" as he had done in his previous terms in office.[5] Given Ecuador's tumultuous history, it was a fair assumption that he would probably not complete his term.

The Liberal Radical Party had selected the newly elected mayor of Quito José Ricardo Chiriboga Villagómez over the independent liberal Eduardo Salazar Gómez as their presidential candidate.[6] The British Embassy identified Chiriboga Villagómez as "a clever and ambitious man" who due to his intrigues was "not much favoured by 'respectable' Liberals." Those mainstream liberals backed instead the wealthy lawyer Salazar Gómez who had worked for the General Electric Company for the previous fifteen years and enjoyed Plaza's endorsement.[7] When he was passed over for this party's nomination, Salazar Gómez began to build an Alianza Democrática Nacional (ADN, National Democratic Alliance) that grouped Plaza's MCDN, the PSE, the VRSE, dissident liberals, and other groups into an electoral coalition.[8] Salazar Gómez chose Clodoveo Alcívar Zevallos, a recently resigned minister of social welfare and someone popular with the left, as his vice presidential running mate.[9] The conservatives nominated Ruperto Alarcón Falconí, but the British discounted his candidacy because he was "distrusted by many of his own party, being considered too rigid and extremist to stand any chance of obtaining any marginal support outside the fairly disciplined ranks of the Conservative Party."[10] As with most presidential contests in Ecuador, this was to be a multi-party race where no candidate would win majority support.

As political parties debated whom to support, the Pichincha provincial committee of the PCE claimed an obligation to bring to power men who held the people's confidence and who had supported a truly progressive and democratic program. They denounced all of the presidential candidates as "nothing other than lackeys of Yankee imperialism, who once in control of the presidency of the republic will tighten even more the chains of oppression." Instead, they called for others to join the communists in their Social and National Liberation Front to break the bonds of imperialism with a march toward progress and freedom.[11] Their pleas for the construction of a popular front never gained much traction, and for the most part were ignored.

In addition to the traditional mainstream candidates, to the cheers and jeers of supporters and opponents Velasco Ibarra announced his plans to campaign yet once again for the presidency. He had spent the last five years in exile in Argentina after being removed from office in a 1947 coup. According to CIA analysts in Washington, he had reached an agreement with the "neo-fascist revolutionary Guevara Moreno" of the CFP to launch a coup against Plaza. For his part, Plaza sought to counteract those plans, including looking for a pretext on which to arrest Velasco Ibarra. Meanwhile, Plaza's defense minister, Manual Díaz Granados, reportedly was planning his own coup, even though such an extraconstitutional move would run counter to the president's desire to preserve a process of democratic succession.[12] Despite ongoing concerns about communists disrupting the country's peace, such threats continued to come from the right rather than the left.

In this context, John Hamlin, counselor of the US Embassy, presented an assessment of which candidate would best serve United States interests. If the primary concern were control over communists, Velasco Ibarra would be preferable, followed by the conservative Alarcón Falconí and the liberals Chiriboga Villagómez and Salazar Gómez. If other political, economic, military, and cultural concerns were incorporated, Velasco Ibarra moved to the bottom of the list leaving Alarcón Falconí as their first choice. Embassy officials were particularly concerned with socialist and communist support for Salazar Gómez. Velasco Ibarra's "inconsistent and unpredictable nature" together with his populist and Peronist influences made him undesirable.[13] Whether weighing in on an election conflicted with the State Department's theoretical adherence to nonintervention in the internal affairs of another country apparently did not occur to Hamlin. Rather, his comments formed part of a much longer history of United States attempts to control electoral outcomes in the region.

In the months before the 1952 presidential election, CIA analysts and State Department officials reported repeatedly on political violence and threats of violence. Velasco Ibarra claimed that "a Communist minority of the University party which has no respect for the constitution" had sponsored a meeting on February 21 to oppose his candidacy. He accused those who wanted to exclude him from the campaign of acting in a dictatorial fashion.[14] On March 3, another failed coup took place in Guayaquil. Defense minister Díaz Granados announced the arrest of seven naval officers and ten civilians, most of whom were CFP members. Although both Velasco Ibarra and Guevara Moreno denied involvement, it appeared that the CFP had led the attempt. Sailors testified that the plan had been to capture the military barracks, arm civilians, and seize Guayaquil.[15] "Thanks to the clearly defined action of the Army, the situation created in Guayaquil has been totally controlled and there exists no danger of any kind," Díaz Granados stated.[16] Meanwhile, on March 10 a group of conservatives stoned the independent liberal candidate Salazar Gómez while he was campaigning in Tulcán. Two people were killed in the resulting chaos, while the candidate and others were injured.[17] Ten days later, another political battle in Quito killed one and injured several more.[18] Another fight on April 12 between the adherents of Salazar Gómez and Velasco Ibarra in Cuenca left one dead, many more injured, and a radio transmitter destroyed. The bloodshed led the United States Embassy to worry that this might be the forerunner of more serious disturbances.[19] It appeared increasingly unlikely that the election would take place.

The violence led Salazar Gómez to withdraw from the race, throwing the progressive Democratic Alliance coalition that grouped various socialist and dissident liberal groups into disarray. Salazar Gómez thought that his withdrawal would push the liberals to unite around the official Liberal Radical candidacy of Chiriboga Villagómez, but instead it drew a less popular candidate Modesto Larrea Jijón into the race. The British Embassy noted that Larrea Jijón was "not endowed with political talent, but is ambitious and self-seeking."[20] His candidacy split the progressive vote and doomed the liberal's chances of winning the election.

The PCE had previously sent an open letter to the PSE asking them to abandon the "false position" that the socialist party and the Democratic Alliance had adopted in backing the candidacy of Salazar Gómez. The communists proposed that instead they form an authentic democratic front to support a candidate who could defeat the reactionary forces.[21] The socialists rejected the communist overture, and instead, from the PCE's perspective, fostered divisions within the democratic movement.[22] The socialists retorted that their party was national in character, and therefore could never be confused with the PCE "whose directives of an international character are perfectly known."[23] Now, with Salazar Gómez's withdrawal, the PCE once again raised the issue of creating a popular front to confront a growing reactionary force, to defend national sovereignty, to fight for better living conditions, and to guarantee democracy. They called on the PSE, VRSE, liberals, and other democratic forces to join them.[24] Ultimately, their efforts were in vain.

As the June 1 election approached, the *New York Times* reported on the growing political tensions on an almost daily basis, as did CIA analysts in Washington. About six weeks out, the CIA noted a fraught political situation and persistent rumors of a pending "revolution." On April 18, university students burned Velasco Ibarra in effigy in Quito's main square.[25] Velasco Ibarra's entry into the contest had upset what had otherwise promised to be a "fairly normal" procedure as military and political leaders scrambled to realign themselves in light of the new political context. CIA analysts repeated rumors that communist leaders were organizing shock troops while leftist students actively engaged in propaganda campaigns against the caudillo. A persistent rumor was that the minister of defense Díaz Granados would engage in a coup to protect Ecuador from bloodshed and stop Velasco Ibarra's possible election.[26]

At the end of April, CIA analysts related that "the stormy Ecuadoran election campaign" may have reached a crisis point. The agency continued to convey rumors of Díaz Granados's coup plotting. In response, on April 23, Plaza once again sacked his cabinet in order to get rid of his defense minister who was best positioned to lead a coup, though CIA analysts cautioned that this action may not be sufficient to prevent a coup, countercoup, or other repressive actions.[27] Rather, the cabinet resignations together with Salazar Gómez's withdrawal from the race "increased the likelihood of serious disturbances."[28] Every day the political situation became more tense and polarized.

In an effort to calm political tensions, Plaza invited members of the opposition to participate in the cabinet but none would agree and the ploy failed.[29] When Plaza finally formed a new cabinet he retained the ministers of defense, foreign relations, and public works, but excluded the two socialist ministers who had joined the previous year. The PSE secretary general, Luis Maldonado Estrada, stated that the president had offered the socialists two portfolios, but they refused because the party formed part of the Democratic Alliance coalition that had decided to remain independent of the government.[30] Plaza, for his part, promised that the new cabinet would represent "absolute political neutrality" in order to oversee "the freest and cleanest election contest" in Ecuador's history.[31]

On April 26 and in the midst of all this chaos, Velasco Ibarra returned from his five-year exile in Argentina for the final month of campaigning for the presidency. A crowd of almost three thousand enthusiastic supporters welcomed the caudillo at the airport in Quito, but when they escorted him to his residency they clashed with his left-wing opponents. Two people were killed and eight were wounded in the melee, even though army and police forces held the city in an effective state of siege.[32] The following day those numbers were revised to one dead and twenty-four injured, with interior minister Enrique Coloma claiming that "complete normality" has been restored.[33] The embassy reported that the socialist leaders Gonzalo Karolys, Hugo Larrea Benalcazar, and Alberto Cabeza de Vaca had been imprisoned for the duration of Velasco Ibarra's visit to Quito in response to threatening statements that they had made at an anti-Velasco Ibarra assembly.[34] The embassy credited actions that the army and police had taken with preventing more serious disorders.[35]

With Ecuador swirling downward into a chaos from which it appeared unlikely to recover, Herbert Matthews published an essay in the *New York Times* that highlighted broader patterns of regional unrest. The article featured a map of thirteen coups across Latin America over the past five years, including the August 1947 removal of Velasco Ibarra in Ecuador. Among the more recent events were Fulgencio Batista's March 10 coup in Cuba, and the Movimiento Nacionalista Revolucionario (MNR, Revolutionary Nationalist Movement) coming to power in Bolivia through a popular revolt on April 11. Matthews labeled those events as "symptoms and examples, not aberrations" of the problems the continent faced, and he expected other similar outbreaks before the year was over. At the root of these problems was militarism, nationalism, populism, poverty, overpopulation, and disease. In addition, Matthews claimed, "Communism plays on the extremes of wealth and poverty and on economic distress, and it also often makes a close alliance with nationalism." Nevertheless, "thus far the Communists have failed to gain a secure foothold in any country in Latin America." Across the region, they did not have sufficient numbers "to take power anywhere, but they are enough to make trouble anywhere." As a result, "What they can do in almost every country is to stir up trouble, discontent, strife, uneasiness." Matthews proposed that more economic and technological assistance from the United States, as well as more leaders such as Plaza who were committed to democratic institutions, were key to solving these problems.[36]

Ironically or not, the day after Matthews's article appeared, CIA analysts in Washington released an intelligence memorandum on increased instability in Latin America. Similar to Matthews, and perhaps reflecting a sharing of information, the CIA noted the violent changes of government in Cuba and Bolivia, and warned that military coups were imminent in other countries. The analysts identified inflation and related economic problems as the source of the unrest in addition to populist currents that emanated out of Argentina under Perón's control. Notably, in the agency's internal intelligence evaluation, communism and anti-imperialism played lesser roles, once again indicating that political rhetoric often outpaced more measured and rational assessment. The memo proceeded to detail the internal situation in the principal Latin American countries. In Ecuador, the return "of the twice-deposed rightist demagogue Velasco Ibarra and . . . the withdrawal of the left-wing coalition candidate, Salazar Gómez" had thrown the contest into chaos. Those changes left open the possibility for "a bid for power from either the opportunistic Defense Minister, Díaz Granados, or the neo-fascist Mayor of Guayaquil, Guevara Moreno." Even if the election were successfully held, the loser might still launch a coup against the winner.[37]

Political stability and a peaceful transfer of power appeared to be a remote possibility.

With the election only a week away, CIA analysts reported on a gunrunning operation in the Caribbean. Among the possible destinations for the weapons was "Ecuador, where political conditions are highly unstable with the approach of the 1 June presidential elections."[38] Just days before the election, the CIA reported that a majority of voters in Guayaquil who would have supported Salazar Gómez "now favor a pre-election coup and a military dictatorship." Predictably, defense minister Díaz Granados also favored a military junta, but had failed to act because of a lack of popular support. Salazar Gómez's replacement candidate Larrea Jijón for the Democratic Alliance never gained much electoral backing or sufficient support to launch a successful coup. Nevertheless, the CIA cautioned that his adherents might attempt such a move if election results indicated that the conservatives would win.[39]

Fears of a military coup continued up until the election. Only days before the vote, Guayaquil's populist mayor Guevara Moreno went into hiding when the police issued a warrant for his arrest under charges of contempt for the government for remarks he had made in his newspaper *La Hora*. When news of his pending arrest spread, hundreds of CFP partisans converged on city hall. Two of Guevara Moreno's supporters were killed in the resulting skirmishes with the police.[40] Plaza said that he believed in freedom of speech, but that Guevara Moreno had offended so many people with his statements that public opinion forced him to act.[41] The government tried to dial back the tension by announcing that Guevara Moreno would not be arrested if he emerged from hiding to vote. If he did not vote, which in Ecuador was obligatory for literate adult males, he would lose his civil rights, including his right to retain office as mayor of Guayaquil.[42] Logically, Guevara Moreno feared efforts at entrapment or blackmail to flush him out of hiding.

By the time the election took place, it had been reduced to a contest between the conservative candidate Alarcón Falconí and the independent Velasco Ibarra. The liberal vote had been split between Chiriboga Villagómez who was from a section of the Liberal Radical Party nicknamed "Los Supremos" and Larrea Jijón who was from another faction called "Los Auténticos." Further confusing to observers was that everyone except Alarcón Falconí in the four-way race identified themselves as liberals, with even Velasco Ibarra claiming to be an independent liberal. A last-minute scramble to unify the splintered progressive vote failed, which meant that neither Chiriboga Villagómez nor Larrea Jijón stood a reasonable chance of winning.[43] According to the British Embassy, many liberals considered Larrea Jijón "too much of a Conservative" to suit their tastes.[44] Many observers assumed that in this fractured environment Alarcón Falconí would win the election, even though conservatives only had minority support. Conservatives looked forward to their best chance of winning an election and returning to office in the more than half a century since their defeat in Eloy Alfaro's 1895 liberal revolution.

Liberals were particularly upset at clerical interference in the electoral process. Priests threatened parishioners with purgatory and hell if they did not vote for the conservative party. Plaza's government lodged multiple diplomatic protests with the papal nuncio about the Catholic Church's activities, reminding the church hierarchy that under the terms of the Concordat clergy were not allowed to interfere in politics. His government threatened priests who engaged in electioneering with arrest and prosecution for their activities.[45] The papal nuncio agreed to issue orders for priests and religious orders to stop their interventions on behalf of the conservative candidate Alarcón Falconí, although it was not entirely clear that their activity had ceased.[46]

Sam Pope Brewer reported in the *New York Times* that the army traditionally had backed the liberal party in opposition to the conservatives, which heightened fears of a military coup if a candidate unacceptable to them won the contest.[47] Apprehension over a foreboding and seemingly inevitable coup increased when on the eve of the election a group of retired military personnel identifying themselves "defenders of the fatherland" published a statement calling on Ecuadorians to vote for the Liberal Radical candidate Chiriboga Villagómez. Their statement cautioned that a conservative resurgence would destroy gains in political, economic, and social liberties that Ecuador had made. The group warned that the army could not remain indifferent if fanaticism threatened to return to power. In response, Plaza called on the military to respect the constitutional order.[48] On the eve of the vote, the chief of staff and heads of the army, air force, and navy issued an official statement confirming that the military would abide by its oath and support the constitutional succession of power.[49] Even with these official assurances, tension remained at a high level.

During Velasco Ibarra's previous mandate as president in the aftermath of the 1944 glorious May revolution he had initially enjoyed the backing of liberals and leftists, including communists. Now, however, he was engaged in a "bitter feud" with those groups, and instead drew support from the "neo-fascist Guevara Moreno's Concentration of Popular Forces and from the militant right-wing National Ecuadoran Revolutionary Action."[50] Plaza had denounced both the CFP and ARNE for their lack of commitment to democracy and charged that they imitated "totalitarian systems such as international communism."[51] For his part, Velasco Ibarra declared that he represented "the people," and had no commitment to the CFP, the ARNE, or any other political party, although he admitted that the CFP supported his campaign.[52]

Despite expectations that the conservative Alarcón Falconí would win, with the support of the CFP Velasco Ibarra captured a plurality of 43 percent of the fewer than 360,000 votes cast (out of a total population of more than three million). Velasco Ibarra crushed his closest rival Alarcón Falconí by almost forty thousand votes. The liberals Chiriboga Villagómez and Larrea Jijón placed a distant third and fourth place.[53] Many voters in Quito supported Velasco Ibarra instead of the Democratic Alliance. Apparently when it became apparent that Larrea Jijón stood no chance of winning his supporters switched their votes to Velasco Ibarra to prevent Alarcón Falconí from emerging victorious, which assured the caudillo's return to office.[54] Most of Velasco Ibarra's support came from Guayaquil where, according to the British ambassador Norman Mayers, "dissatisfied elements from all political groups voted for him."[55] In large part, Velasco Ibarra drew his support away from progressive candidates.

Congressional elections held at the same time as the presidential race gave conservatives a slight legislative advantage. The senate would have sixteen conservatives, nine liberals, seven Velasquistas, and one independent. The house would have twenty-one Velasquistas, twenty conservatives, thirteen liberals, five socialists, and five independents. While Guevara Moreno was able to convince his supporters in Guayaquil to vote for Velasco Ibarra, that support did not carry over to his congressional slate. The new president would have to deal with an antagonistic congress.[56]

The election results threw Ecuador's political establishment into a period of deep reflection. Given the liberal's numerical advantage, the conservatives questioned whether they could regain office through electoral means. Liberals had to confront the fatal consequences of their divisions, and were left "pondering the charge that the people would not have deserted them if they had not deserted the people." Socialists faced frustration after entering the election with a coalition that registered at the bottom of the polls.[57] Since the communists had been excluded from the Democratic Alliance they advocated casting blank ballots in the presidential race, which left them even more isolated from the political landscape.[58]

As the British Embassy reported, the outcome "surprised everyone" because "on the eve of the polls the result was considered to be as good as decided and the Conservative candidate, Dr. Ruperto Alarcón, was already named as the first Conservative President of Ecuador since 1895." Instead, as had happened previously, the Ecuadorian electorate "voted not for a party but a personality." The embassy observed, "A clear majority of Ecuadorians want to give Velasco Ibarra another term of office; not the wisest heads, perhaps, but still the majority." Most people gave him a year, two at the most, before he would be once again removed from office.[59] While Velasco Ibarra's win prevented a return to reactionary conservative rule, it did not mean the ushering in of a period of tranquility or progressive governance.

Edgar McGinnis of the Office of South American Affairs (OSA) in the State Department feared that given the pattern of Velasco Ibarra's removal from power in 1935 and 1947, his election would contribute to political instability. While the caudillo repeatedly demonstrated that he could attract and win support at the ballot box, questions remained about whether he could retain a sufficient level of backing to govern effectively. Reflecting the analysis that the Quito Embassy had forwarded in March before the election, McGinnis commented that due to Velasco Ibarra's "inconsistent and unpredictable nature" his election was "less desirable from the standpoint of US policy than Alarcón's election would have been." On the other hand, McGinnis was relieved that Velasco Ibarra was "definitely anti-communist."[60] Echoing McGinnis's interpretation, the OIR also observed that the communists had failed in their attempts to forge effective coalitions with other progressives, and the elections had brought to office candidates whom the communists opposed. This development had increased their political isolation, and this pleased US officials.[61]

CIA analysts expressed a certain amount of relief when the election was held with a minimum amount of disruption. "The possibility of an army coup is now probably somewhat more unlikely than it has been for the past few weeks," a report stated. "Velasco is believed to have a fair chance of being inaugurated in September." Nevertheless, the agency was concerned with the ties he had developed with Perón's government during his years of exile in Argentina.[62] Pundits repeatedly accused Velasco Ibarra of betraying Peronist tendencies, something that the caudillo vehemently denied. Even so, fear of Perón's influence over Velasco Ibarra remained a preoccupation for US policy makers, although a larger concern should have been the president-elect's association with the proto-fascist CFP with its Mussolini influences and the ARNE with its inspiration from the Spanish falange.[63] International considerations blinded US officials to local dynamics.

The *New York Times* welcomed Velasco Ibarra's victory as "an example of democratic electoral procedure of which the whole inter-American community can be proud." By all indications, the vote was free and fair in so much as it reflected the will of literate males who by their very nature were overwhelmingly wealthy and urban in their residence. As indication of the election's fairness, the newspaper pointed to Plaza's opposition to Velasco Ibarra's candidacy and the fact that the outcome fooled pundits and reporters. The newspaper's support came even though the president-elect possessed "a record which is worrisome to contemplate" because in his previous two times in office "his impetuosity and ambitions led him to turn his regimes into dictatorships—and each time the army drove him from power." The paper feared Perón's potential influence on his government, as well as his "demagogic" nature. Nevertheless, if Getulio Vargas could rule democratically upon his return power in Brazil, perhaps there was hope for Velasco Ibarra's third time in office. Encouraging as well was the military's support for the constitutional process of succession. "This is how Governments ought to be changed in free countries," a *New York Times* editorial concluded, "and one must extend special congratulations to President Galo Plaza Lasso, for whom this peaceful and democratic election was a personal triumph."[64] In a postmortem on the electoral process, Brewer who had reported on the election for the *New York Times* congratulated Ecuador on what he characterized as the country's first free election. But he also expressed concern that even if Perón had no direct influence over Velasco Ibarra's government, worrying "signs that his regime may run to the same lines of demagogic appeal to the poorer classes" still existed.[65] For the socialist left, of course, a more disturbing tendency was that the working class responded better to the emotional appeals of a populist like Velasco Ibarra than to calls for a class struggle to transform society.

The *Hispanic American Report* similarly noted the significance of the election. Plaza was the first president in more than a quarter century (twenty-eight years, to be precise) to serve out the term to which he had been constitutionally elected.[66] A year earlier, Matthews commented that the country's current stability was "providing one of the most remarkable of all Latin American experiments in democracy." Matthews credited the New York-born and United States-educated president Plaza with the rapid shift from "comic opera revolutions—twenty-seven in twenty-five years" to "a genuinely democratic regime."[67] From the perspective of United States officials, Plaza was the type of politician whom they could embrace and who would advance their interests.

The journalist Lilo Linke pointed out that the socialists were torn between a defense of principles and practical politics. "The Socialists, once an influential party, have lost all their former significance," Linke stated, "in part because for years now they have been unable to make up their minds as to how far to the left they should go." Their opportunism and vacillating on whether or not to collaborate with Plaza's government cost them support. Much of the socialist backing came from university students, "and even there the suspicion seems justified that quite a number of so-called Socialist students are at heart Communists." As for the PCE, Linke said that after thirty years of existence the party had "made little headway." Previously they had held dominance in the CTE, but both the party and the trade union appeared to be "quietly fading away."[68] The political winds were shifting against the left, but not in a way that particularly favored another political party or ideology.

The United States Embassy reported on the negative repercussions that echoed through labor and the broader left as a result of the defeat of the Democratic Alliance. The embassy stated, "The Socialist-Communist dominated CTE and its affiliates hewed to the political line of the Socialist Party, which in turn increasingly reflected communist ideologies." Furthermore, the CTE's regional affiliates, including the FTP, publicly condemned the CTE for its role in the alliance. An economic attaché in the US Embassy noted that the FTP "identified itself more and more with the international communist line." In particular, the FTP opposed the bilateral military pact between the United States and Ecuador, and supported the formation of pro-peace committees. The embassy cautioned that the defeat in the June elections had triggered a radicalization and polarization in the labor movement along with a corresponding rise in the power of the left. The conservative wing of the socialist party was grouped under three-time secretary general Emilio Gangotena who denounced communist influence in the party and abruptly resigned his position in August. Manuel Agustín Aguirre, who represented the left wing of the socialist party, declared at the ninth FTP congress less than a month after the elections that Velasco Ibarra's victory signified a triumph for the dominant class, and that workers must mobilize to meet this challenge.[69]

The political left emerged both weakened and strengthened from the campaign. The socialists' political position was significantly marginalized as a result of losing their two cabinet posts in Plaza's government, and then backing the wrong horse in the presidential race. The PSE had trouble identifying a strong candidate, and then entered into an alliance with a weak contender who finished last in the polls. The socialists only held two seats in the house, and three in the senate. The only communist in congress would be Pedro Saad, the senator for coastal labor. At the same time, the OIR observed, similar to Bolivia with the recent ascension of the MNR to power and Chile with Carlos Ibáñez del Campo's election, the new government was sensitive to ultra-nationalist and leftist pressure, which provided the communists with more freedom of action.[70] For the left, that pressure came not as an electoral force but through grassroots mobilizations.

Despite all of these disturbances and the repeated coup attempts during his four years in office, Plaza successfully completed his term and on September 1 handed off power to his successor. Linke described Velasco Ibarra as "an educated but highly-strung President of the *caudillo* type," who faced a precarious and uncertain situation.[71] The British Embassy characterized his new cabinet "as a system of not too brilliant satellites which would not outshine their sun," with two possible exceptions: Luis Antonio Peñaherrera, previously ambassador in Washington, as minister of government, and the future president Carlos Julio Arosemena Monroy as minister of defense. Several of his ministers quickly left his government, starting with the minister of public works.[72] Few expected that Velasco Ibarra would remain long in office. It is a witness to the remarkable political changes in the country that ultimately he was able to survive the entire tenure of his term—the only one of five that he was able to complete.

Although Velasco Ibarra presented himself as a liberal secularist, once in office he quickly took a conservative turn which, as the British Embassy noted, meant "clerical and reactionary."[73] That decision led the Liberal Radical Party to instruct their members to resign their positions in his government.[74] Some refused, which led to the suspension of party stalwarts José Ricardo Chiriboga Villagómez, Jorge Villagómez Yepes, and José Vicente Trujillo who served respectively as Ecuador's ambassadors to the United States, the United Nations, and Mexico.[75] By the end of 1953, Velasco Ibarra only had one member in his cabinet with whom he started the year—the minister of education. Velasco Ibarra's continuance in office provided a superficial veneer of stability to a political situation that was unmistakably chaotic and transitory.

The most significant resignation was that of his minister of government Peñaherrera who held the most powerful appointive office. In his place, Velasco Ibarra named the conservative Camilo Ponce Enríquez. In its review of 1953, *El Comercio* defined Ponce's designation as the most decisive political event of the year.[76] Handing the post that defined the administration's political positions to a conservative represented a definitive and unmistakable turn to the right. Furthermore, naming a doctrinaire right-winger who would not hesitate to employ a heavy hand in dealing with the administration's opponents represented a significant political realignment.[77]

The conservative Ponce quickly became the left's most determined opponent. While the Catholic Church responded warmly and positively to the appointment, Gonzalo Villalba, the secretary general of the Pichincha provincial committee of the PCE, retorted with a burning statement that noted that the reactionary and pro-government forces organized into the ARNE and conservative party "feel popular rejection of their policies which are contrary to the interests of the great majorities, to the interests of the country." Wealthy commercial, financial, industrial, and landholding concerns were imposing policies that exploited the working class and led to hunger, unemployment, misery, and prisons. Villalba condemned Velasco Ibarra for his attempts "to disorient the Catholic people in order to pull them into a religious struggle and divert them from a daily combat for bread and freedom." In response to charges that communists were opposed to religion, Villalba appealed to a liberal heritage and declared that the PCE respected all religious beliefs, and considered freedom of religion to be an important democratic gain. He contended that charges that communists opposed religion were an attempt to halt a popular struggle for a better life. In the face of this threat, the communists called on its members to remain alert to fascist provocations that might disrupt their work. Instead, they called on people to join them in a democratic front for national liberation that would fight for higher salaries, lower prices, full employment, land for the peasants, and democratic freedoms.[78] Achieving these goals would require both theoretical reflections as well as direct political actions.

AS SIGNIFICANT AS WHAT CIA case officers targeted in their investigations is what they ignored. Although CIA analysts in Washington kept abreast of developments in the 1952 presidential election, no information reports from case officers stationed in Ecuador on these events have surfaced. It is as if the rise of populist candidates held no importance for them. Instead, those officers on the ground paid more attention to other issues such as communist involvement in the labor movement.[79] This was the state of affairs even as the PCE prioritized an orthodox line of pursuing a peaceful and parliamentary path to power, which is seemingly where the agency should have dedicated its energies were it truly interested in countering communist advances. It is as if the agency understood where the true potential for leftist subversion lay better than did party leaders—and that was not in electoral campaigns, but in mobilizing grassroots support for social change.

Velasco Ibarra's election and the rise of populism represented a setback for the left. As the new president assembled his cabinet, it became undeniable that his government represented a rightward alteration from Plaza's previous administration. With the closing of electoral spaces, the left turned to its reliance on social movement organizing strategies to advance its political agenda. Nevertheless, some communist leaders clung to their fantasies of forming an anticonservative alliance to compete for power through peaceful and parliamentary means. Contentious debates over strategy continued to fracture the party. How best to confront a populist challenge remained a persistent and perennial challenge for the political left. All of those issues and tensions would emerge on full display at the communist party's upcoming congress.

CHAPTER 8

Dissension

THE ELECTION OF JOSÉ María Velasco Ibarra to the presidency represented a shift in Ecuador toward more conservative policies and more populist and personalistic styles of governance than that of the previous Galo Plaza Lasso administration. Parallel to these political changes, the communist party experienced its own internal transitions in leadership styles and policy emphases as it sought to confront this rightward drift. As with politics on a federal level, disagreements within the PCE divided members over tactics and ideology. This sparing included debates over whether to pursue strategies that would appeal to broader audiences or to adhere to political lines that were more doctrinaire in nature.

Between Velasco Ibarra's election as president on June 1, 1952, and his inauguration on September 1 of that year political parties and various other groupings convoked assemblies to debate how to respond to the rise of populist candidates. One of those was the fifth communist party congress that met in Ambato at the end of July. The congress, which party statutes dictated should be held biannually, came on the heels of their long-delayed third congress in November 1946 in Quito, and the fourth congress in August 1949 in Guayaquil. Unlike the 1949 congress, thanks to CIA surveillance we have a detailed summary of what transpired at this meeting. Among the monumental resolutions was one to formalize Pedro Saad's designation as secretary general of the party, even as serious dissension ran through its ranks over that decision. Delegates also struggled with how to proceed in the context of a political system that favored populist politics. Decisions at this congress determined the direction that the party would take for the next several decades.

Fifth PCE Congress (Ambato, July 24–29, 1952)

The central committee of the communist party decided at a December 1951 meeting in Guayaquil to hold their next party congress in Ambato. The congress would "examine with greater responsibility the role played by our party in defense of national democracy," and would advocate "for the improvement of people's living conditions, for peace, and for the realization of social and national liberation from the grip of Yankee imperialism." The assembled delegates would assess party activities and regroup their forces in order to continue the struggle against wealthy landholders who exploited and oppressed the masses. The congress was intended to strengthen the party's internal democracy as well as impose communist discipline. "Collective responsibility does not exclude the individual," the central committee declared, "rather they complement and harmonize each other." Delegates would also address organizational problems, revise party statutes, and select a new central committee with a goal of elevating the most capable leaders who were loyal to the people and would stay true to communist ideologies. As part of its ongoing campaign to build a broad electoral coalition, the party called on its members to study their statement "Towards a Democratic Front for National Liberation" in preparation for the meeting. One intent of the assembly was to foster the formation of a party that would provide leadership to the working class in its struggle for a more just and equal society.[1]

The reason for the selection of Ambato as the venue is not immediately obvious. Quito, as the country's capital city and headquarters for the party, would be a more logical choice. As might be expected, Quito was a common location for most political party gatherings, as well as those of many other organizations and federations. Guayaquil was the de facto center of communist activism and the largest city in Ecuador as well as its commercial hub, and hence an equally likely option. Occasionally meetings would be held in Cuenca, Ecuador's third largest city, located in the southern highlands. As a provincial capital and at the time the country's fourth largest city, Ambato was a less typical location for a national meeting. The selection might have been a compromise between the two largest cities, a deliberate decision to search out a geographically central site, or a reflection of a desire to move the party away from an urban intellectual sphere in order to take the struggle to the masses.

In 1944, the FBI's legal attaché Charles Higdon had identified Quito, Guayaquil, Esmeraldas, Milagro, Chimborazo, and Cayambe as the principle centers of communist activities in Ecuador, but he made no mention of Ambato.[2] Perhaps that was now changing. In 1947, the military attaché Adelbert Boggs reported six party cells in Ambato with a total membership of four hundred.[3] That would have made it numerically speaking the third largest center of communist activity after Guayaquil and Quito. In an almost throwaway comment in the midst of strike activity at two textile mills in Ambato in October 1948,

US ambassador John Simmons similarly described the city as "the center of Communist influence in Ecuador."[4] Those developments would have provided the party with a local base of support for the congress. Ongoing reconstruction efforts in the aftermath of the devastating 1949 earthquake offered additional symbolic value. In 1951, the CTE (which otherwise confined their meetings to Guayaquil, Quito, and Cuenca) and the socialist youth had also held their national assemblies in Ambato for similar reasons, leading United States officials to observe that the destruction from the earthquake "affords [an] excellent site [for] Socialist Commie elements [to] exploit unrest and anti-govt sentiment."[5] In fact, the decision to hold these meetings in Ambato may have encouraged a political turn to the left in the city.

At the time of the PCE congress, the conservative José Arcadio Carrasco Miño was mayor of Ambato. The documentary record does not indicate what kind of reception party members received from local residents. Five years later, the conservative Quito city councilor José Antonio Baquero de la Calle strongly opposed communist use of that city's municipal theater for their inaugural session. Liberals who appealed to notions of freedom of assembly won the day in terms of allowing the communists access to that venue, and similar dynamics may have been at play in Ambato. What we do know is that before and after the congress the socialist Neptalí Sancho Jaramillo was mayor of the city. He had grown up surrounded with a feudalistic system in which wealthy landowners controlled social and political structures and Indigenous workers faced extreme discrimination and exploitation. Sancho first won office in 1947, and held that position during the 1949 earthquake. His election represented a break from traditional conservative power structures, and the advancement of policies that sought to empower poor and marginalized people.[6] In November 1949 he lost the mayoral race to a concerted conservative-liberal coalition that ran Carrasco Miño in an election fraught with controversies over the use of reconstruction aid. Sancho would subsequently go on to win additional terms as mayor in 1953 and 1959, as well as election as deputy to the federal congress in 1950 and again in 1956. His supporters spoke of him in glowing terms. "Seldom has a man incarnated the will of the people, of his people, like this simple and honorable Neptalí Sancho, a sincere man of great will and great heart," one commemoration read. For that reason, the people fervently and enthusiastically backed him, and his electoral victories represented not only a triumph for Ambato but also for all Ecuadorians.[7]

Sancho came from the left wing of the socialist party, and in the 1960s joined the faction that formed the Partido Socialista Revolucionario del Ecuador

(PSRE, Socialist Revolutionary Party of Ecuador). He was not opposed to collaborating with the communists, and in the years before the congress had worked closely with Saad on various occasions. In his role as a deputy in the federal congress, he joined Saad in September 1950 in an interpellation of the treasury minister over accusations of misappropriation of earthquake relief funds.[8] The following month, the two participated in an assembly that the FTP had organized at the Casa del Obrero in Quito to discuss legislative proposals concerning social services and bus fares.[9] After holding its congress in Ambato in 1951 the CTE once again gathered there in September 1961 during his last term in office, apparently to encourage political engagement among the local residents. That meeting attracted the CIA's attention and made the electoral defeat of the socialist mayor a priority for the agency.[10]

Although Sancho was a socialist rather than a communist, he may have invited and encouraged the communists to come to the city. Considering the general inability of United States officials to distinguish between socialists and communists, his election may have led Ambassador Simmons to consider the city to be the center of communist activity. That might also explain why at the time of the last party congress, a CIA operative reported

> It is known that the communist mayor of Ambato, Neptalí Sancho, has little regard for Saad, Gil, Barreto, or the rest of the communist leaders. Saad said that although he knows Sancho does not obey party instructions, and the communist organization in Ambato is primarily one of Sancho's personal development, the party should not abandon the syndicate movement there, since from an ideological point of view so much progress has been made.[11]

Obviously since Sancho was not a communist he would have little need to follow party dictates. On the other hand, the PCE probably would have liked to have brought a successful politician such as Sancho into its fold, and that would have inevitably caused a dance around competing political interests. Holding the congress in Ambato may have been an attempt to piggyback on other organizational developments already in process.

Quito's *El Comercio* newspaper, often treated as the paper of record in Ecuador, did not carry a single mention of the communist congress, although they published front-page articles on the socialist and other party congresses as well as long stories with large banner headlines on the Democratic and Republican parties congresses in the United States that were held at the same time. Even UFO reports warranted more column inches than did communist activities.

That seemingly misplacement of priorities subsequently fed conspiracy theories that the CIA or other intelligence agencies planted stories of aliens in order to distract the population from more significant and pressing political matters.

For its part, the United States Embassy made some minor passing references to the congress in its weekly updates from Ecuador. Drawing on information published in *El Pueblo*, in March the embassy mentioned the upcoming meeting.[12] At the beginning of the congress, the embassy noted that the socialist newspaper *La Tierra* printed a letter from Saad inviting its editor to attend the inaugural session. For Ambassador Paul Daniels, "this open display is further indication of sympathy between so called Socialist paper and Commies."[13] The ambassador's repeated use of the derogatory term "Commies" is significant. The CIA operative David Atlee Phillips notes that while conservatives employed it, "the typical officer selected his political sobriquets more carefully, making it clear whether he was speaking of a Communist, Marxist, or Socialist (because the distinction could be important, if not vital, in writing intelligence reports as well as planning and conducting most operations)."[14] Those distinctions obviously escaped the ambassador. Either he ignored the fact that political parties routinely invited the media and other public and political figures to their inaugural sessions, or he could not resist the dig at the left. In either case, this comment reveals a failure to understand divisions on the left. At the end of the congress, Daniels dismissively characterized the congress as "vociferously pro peace, anti-US, anti-Plaza, anti-Velasco Ibarra and pro-Soviet."[15] That reactionary portrayal reveals more about the ideological assumptions of the embassy and says nothing about the congress, and could have been written before the meeting or without any surveillance of the event.

In contrast to the mainstream media's disregard for the communist party congress and the embassy's limited appreciation for its dynamics, CIA officers in Ecuador ignored the socialists and other political activities, and instead drafted an unusually lengthy and detailed memo that chronicled discord within the PCE. The congress came after Albert Haney's departure in 1949, and with the available evidence it is difficult to parse out who might have conducted the surveillance and how the information was gathered. One possibility is that this memo is the work of Howard Shetterly who by all indications was a CIA officer. He was from Des Moines, Iowa, was a navy pilot during the Second World War, and graduated from the Ohio State University. Shetterly joined the Guayaquil Consulate as vice consul in March 1950 with the rank of FSS-11.[16] In April 1952 he transitioned to vice consul at the Quito Embassy with a promotion to FSS-9, which is where he would have been stationed during the PCE congress. The following year he moved to public affairs assistant in the embassy with another promotion to FSS-8. In November 1954 Shetterly left Ecuador for a similar post in Mexico City and eventually proceeded on to Porto Alegre and Brasilia, Brazil and finally Barcelona, Spain.[17] Shetterly retired in 1976, and two decades later moved to Albuquerque, New Mexico not only "to be near three of his children" but also "to be surrounded by the Hispanic and Native American culture he so much appreciated."[18] Latin America typically leaves a profound imprint on people, and CIA officers would be no exception.

The CIA report played up long-standing divisions and conflicts that were on full and open display at the congress. Dwight Eisenhower had not yet been elected, and the agency had not yet taken its turn from an intelligence agency to what the dissident CIA operative Ralph McGehee denounced as "the covert action arm of the Presidency" that overthrew democratically elected governments and backed right-wing dictators.[19] The CIA obviously had officers in place in Ecuador, but it is not apparent that they intervened in the assembly's proceedings. Furthermore, without more and better sources of information, it is difficult to ascertain whether the intelligence agency's assessment was an accurate representation of the congress, or whether CIA informers and case officers skewed their portrayal of events to match preconceived notions of how communists would act. As was common practice, sources of information for the memo were either not included in the original or are redacted in the declassified version that the CIA has released to the public. Variances in information, however, would seem to indicate that it drew on multiple sources and that none of these was an eyewitness account by the report's primary author. That alone should hardly be a surprise, as a typically young, clean-cut, European-descent, linguistically challenged, Ivy League–trained US official would hardly pass unnoticed at a leftist meeting whether or not it was a public affair. Despite these limitations, the CIA information report is one of the few extant contemporary accounts of the PCE congress and as such provides a rich source of documentation with valuable insights into internal party debates.[20]

The congress began with a preparatory session in the auditorium of the Liceo Juan Montalvo on the afternoon of Thursday, July 24, 1952, with the attendance of about 150 to 160 communists, including 105 delegates apparently divided between either eighty-two or eighty-eight cell delegates, two foreign fraternal delegates, and either fifteen or twenty-one alternative delegates. The party's interim secretary general Saad presided over the preparatory session. In what surely must have been an ironic gesture, Saad warmly thanked Ambato's conservative mayor for allowing the party to use the auditorium. Others were less generous. Some at the meeting complained about anticommunist graffiti that ARNE members had plastered on the walls throughout the city. Saad urged delegates to take the high road and ignore the provocations. His gracious gestures are in part what gained him support for his leadership role in the party, particularly during these difficult years as political spaces for the left slowly closed.

Delegates at the preparatory session elected the presidium for the congress, with Saad as president. Joining him on the daises were Enrique Gil Gilbert, the secretary general of the party in Guayas; Hernán Acebedo, a party leader from Loja; Jaime Galarza Zavala, the secretary general of the party in Azuay; Aquiles Valencia, PCE member from Manabí; Oswaldo Albornoz Peralta, the secretary general of the party in Pichincha and future leading communist historian; and José María Dávalos, the secretary general of the party in Tungurahua. Even though the presidium already demonstrated a broad geographic reach, a delegate proposed the inclusion of representatives from Cañar, Imbabura, and Esmeraldas because of party gains in those provinces. Delegates did not approve the motion, although the report does not indicate the reasoning behind their exclusion. The preparatory session also established a presidium of honor that included the Soviet leader Joseph Stalin, the Chinese leader Mao Zedong, the Chilean poet Pablo Neruda, the Brazilian Luís Carlos Prestes, as well as other communist leaders from China, France, and Italy.

In addition to the organizational and ceremonial activities, the preparatory session engaged in several substantive discussions. Among the resolutions approved were a protest against United States intervention in the internal affairs of other countries, support for the CTE, opposition to the United States firm Morrison-Knudsen holding a contract to build the Quevedo-Manta Road, and a salute to other communist parties. The discussion that most naturally attracted the CIA's attention was one that Alfredo Vera led on the threat of a global war. According to the CIA, "Vera bitterly blamed the United States for causing the as yet undeclared World War III. He further blasted the American banana companies for ruthlessly exploiting Ecuadoran labor, especially in the Province of Esmeraldas." Attacks on the economic interests of United States corporations always attracted the agency's attention.

With the conclusion of the preparatory session, congress participants moved to the Teatro Inca for the inaugural session that began at 9:00 p.m. that same evening. The theater was packed with one thousand attendees—hardly an indication of a small and insignificant meeting. A large portrait of Stalin hung in the back at the center of the stage, flanked by the Ecuadorian and Soviet flags. Members of the presidium for the congress as well as the fraternal delegates Rubén

Calderón from Cuba and Jaime Barrios from Colombia joined party leaders on the stage. The CIA indicated that Calderón had previously been in Ecuador as an advisor to the PCE. The case officer identified him as a relative of the Cuban party leader Blas Roca, and that he used the pseudonym "Calderio" when traveling.

Gil Gilbert opened the inaugural session, which featured a mixture of pageantry, incendiary speeches, and party resolutions. Ambato's municipal band was the first musical act, reflecting the civic embrace that the communists received from local political leaders. In the middle of the introductory remarks, a Juventud Comunista del Ecuador (JCE, Young Communists of Ecuador) relay team arrived from Quito with a burning "torch of peace." The group carried a large communist flag, and two members, one dressed as a worker and the other as a farmer, crossed a hammer and a sickle on the stage to sustained audience applause. A JCE chorus sang the Ecuadorian national anthem, the "Internationale," and other revolutionary songs. Individuals also recited revolutionary poems and sang revolutionary songs. Organizers opened up significant cultural spaces for youth at the congress.

Significantly, the first speaker at the inaugural session was Olga Muñoz in representation of the Juventud Comunista Femenina (JCF, Young Communist Women). Muñoz praised the work of young women in the party. Both contemporary surveillance operatives as well as subsequent historians largely ignored the role of women, as well as gender relations more generally, in the party. What we do know, however, is that while all of the other parties—including the socialists—were the exclusive domain of literate, urban, European-descent men, the PCE somewhat more closely reflected Ecuador's demographic diversity. The involvement of women, as well as rural peasants, Indigenous peoples, and Afro-Ecuadorians, never approached their proportion in society, but it would also be a mistake to dismiss their presence as mere tokenism as critics have commonly done. Instead, the participation of Muñoz in the inaugural session indicates an attempt to foster and encourage new forms of leadership.

PCE founder and outgoing secretary general Ricardo Paredes followed Muñoz. According to the CIA, Paredes "bitterly attacked the United States and singled out the Military Pact that the United States and Ecuador had recently signed as his principal target. He mouthed standard Communist phrases about world peace and Yankee Imperialism." What the case officer did not mention in the report was that in January of the previous year, United States immigration officials had incarcerated Paredes at Ellis Island as he returned to Ecuador through New York from a peace conference in Warsaw, Poland even though he had the proper travel documents. A rapid mobilization of solidarity networks gained his freedom, but understandably the unjustified detention would have left him with an unpleasant attitude toward that country.[21] The Cuban delegate Calderón also spoke briefly against United States imperialism, and urged his counterparts in Ecuador to oppose military pacts because of how they would compromise national sovereignty. The CIA reported that Calderón was an effective speaker and the audience responded warmly to his comments.

Rafael Echeverría then addressed the assembly in the name of the JCE. He criticized the party for its lack of decision, discipline, and valor. The CIA had tracked Echeverría for several years, and reported that he was not a good speaker. Two years earlier, Echeverría had been elected to the executive committee of the IUS at the Second World Student Congress in Prague, Czechoslovakia, information that made its way through an Army Counter Intelligence Corps (CIC) report to the CIA.[22] Similar to Muñoz, Echeverría's participation in the inaugural session was a reflection of the party's goals to include what would otherwise be disregarded or overlooked voices.

Finally, Saad spoke for almost two hours on a variety of subjects, including the threat of a global war, United States support for reactionary coups and governments in Latin America, the need to nationalize foreign businesses in Ecuador including the petroleum industry, the importance of an agrarian reform program that would turn land over to those who worked it, and the subjugation of Ecuador's domestic economy to United States interests. Saad criticized right-wing socialists who had allied with the Plaza government and highlighted the need to oppose conservative populists including Velasco Ibarra and Juan Perón in Argentina. His targeting of Perón is particularly interesting considering that in the immediate postwar period United States opposition to communism was only rivaled by the fear that Perón's popular appeal fostered anti-imperialist sentiments throughout the region. If United States policy analysts had bothered to step back and examine these political issues in their broader political context, they would have understood that there was no love lost between communists and populists as they competed for the allegiance of the same working-class base of support.

As indication of the reality that internal battles often surpassed international political considerations, ARNE and CFP thugs attacked the theater in the middle of Saad's speech and cut electric power to the building. Outside, a group of fifty opponents shouted anticommunist slogans and damaged a car that belonged to Franklin Pérez Castro. Meanwhile, Saad continued his speech by flashlight. Eventually the police quelled the disturbance, and restored power to the theater. While local authorities welcomed the communist congress, others were determined to make their hostility loudly known. The session ended at midnight with more music and other cultural acts.

The first plenary session opened the following morning, July 25, at the Liceo Juan Montalvo where the party had held its preparatory session the previous afternoon. For the next four days, delegates gathered in three plenary sessions each day. While the inaugural session was an open and public event, the plenary sessions were restricted to the 105 credentialed delegates with others escorted outside of the auditorium. Nevertheless, the CIA report continued with information on specific rules including the time allotted for discussion of each point on the agenda. The level of detail indicates either an infiltrator in the meeting or access to published proceedings, and in the absence of party archives to verify internal organizational minutiae it is difficult to say which might be the case. The CIA reported that the principal characteristic of the congress was "bitter personal strife among the leaders and the delegates present." And, in fact, the balance of the CIA's report extensively cataloged internal conflict in the party, information that would not have been included in published proceedings. Naturally it would be in the United States interest to highlight such disputes within a communist party, and it is difficult to ascertain whether the report accurately communicates the tone of the meeting. The report gives no indication as to whether the CIA fostered these disputes, as Agee famously related a decade later in his book *Inside the Company*. Whether or not the CIA report is faithful to the level of internal conflict, it does provide useful insights into divisions and ideological disputes that had long run through the party.

Paredes and Saad

Front and center at the congress was the long-running conflict between Paredes and Saad. Paredes continued to live in Manta on the coast where he had his medical practice, even though party statutes stipulated that the secretary general should reside the capital. Already in July 1950, party leadership had given him a year to return to Quito, and that time was up. Paredes faced the choice of resigning his position in the party or moving back to the capital. A CIA case officer reported that his wife, Zoila Flor, "who is not a Communist, wishes him to give up the position because it demands so much of his time and effort that it is impossible for him to support his family properly." Furthermore, Saad was "the actual leader of the Party," which created internal tensions. According to an earlier CIA report, the suspected Communist Information Bureau (Cominform) agent Roberto Morena had elevated Saad to nominal head of the party although he would need the formal approval of a party congress to make that designation official.[23]

Regionalism is an overwhelmingly powerful force in Ecuador, but significantly divisions did not fall out along such straightforward geographic nor other easily discernible lines. Coastal labor leader and secretary general of the FPTG Segundo Ramos nominated Paredes for the political commission at the congress. Ramos claimed that Paredes was rightfully the party's secretary general, and that Saad had usurped the position. Saad retorted that the PCE's executive committee elected him to the post after Paredes had asked for an indefinite leave to move to Manta. Whereas personal, ideological, and regional factors may have underlain the discord at the congress, delegates did not address them directly. Instead, divisions in the party were expressed in other ways.

Following the debate over who should lead the party, Paredes faced a flurry of charges. Foremost among them and apparently the most serious was that of entering into direct contact with foreign communist leaders without advising the party's executive committee. Echeverría accused Paredes of writing to Mao Zedong to solicit scholarships for two comrades in Manta of Chinese descent. Paredes had handed Mao's response in Moscow to Echeverría for him to carry to the central committee in Ecuador, but instead Echeverría gave the letter to Saad. According to the CIA report, the letter read:

> Comrade Ricardo Paredes, Secretary General of the PCE, I answer your kind letter in which you ask me to facilitate the further study of the Chung Jurado brothers in Peking. I send you my best wishes and inform you that they may come when they consider it convenient, Mao Tse Tung [Zedong].

The letter was vague and noncommittal, and included no indication of specific dates or financial assistance. Nevertheless, the simple fact that Paredes had written the letter apparently caused extreme concern among the delegates. Many Latin American communists held up the recent Chinese Revolution as an inspiration, and one that they might emulate in their own countries. No indication exists that the dispute was political or ideological in nature, but rather one of a violation of organizational norms and protocol. On the other hand, Saad's partisans simply may have exploited the issue to attack a competitor in the party. Relations between Chinese and Latin American revolutionaries is a significantly understudied topic due in part to language barriers and a lingering Euro-centrism, but this exchange indicates underlying tensions well before the Sino-Soviet split in the 1960s that led to the emergence of avowedly Maoist parties.[24]

In addition to his contact with the Chinese, the Colombian delegate Jaime Barrios accused Paredes of providing a Colombian communist named Suárez with a signed and notarized letter stating that Suárez was an anticommunist conservative. The Colombian press printed the letter, and Barrios brought a copy with him to the congress. Suárez had attended the Warsaw Peace Congress, and allegedly Paredes's support allowed him to reenter the country. Paredes denied the entire affair, and the CIA failed to provide a logical explanation for why a communist leader would provide such a safe conduct pass and how it would carry any weight in the neighboring country, which calls into question the agency's ability to convey those internal discussions accurately. If anything, the letter may have been a plant, an anticommunist ploy to denigrate the leader of the party. The CIA report does not include information on the resolution of these charges, but it might be that Barrios had brought the letter either to clear up the issue or to make the party aware of the types of disinformation campaigns it faced.

In addition to these international concerns, delegates also accused Paredes of violating democratic centralism by attempting to publish a party newspaper in Manta and of collecting money from the FEI to pay for his trip to the Soviet Union. The FEI's secretary general Modesto Rivera led the charges that Paredes solicited funds from the Indigenous federation, and particularly from the Kayambis with whom he had a longstanding relationship, and then raised 8,000 sucres more from the federation upon his return. As with the other charges, the CIA does not include information on a resolution. That did not seem to be the agency's interest or concern. But the reference to the FEI is notable in that it was one of few mentions of Indigenous peoples in the CIA's report on the party's congress. The CIA observed "that no delegates of Indian cells were present at the Congress, nor was any mention made of the existence of such cells." If that were the case, it would represent a change in the party. Famously, the communists had long made space in their ranks for Indigenous militants. Most notably, the long-time Kayambi activists Jesús Gualavisí, Dolores Cacuango, and Tránsito Amaguaña played key roles in the party, with Gualavisí participating in its founding congress in 1926, Cacuango more recently serving on the party's central committee, and Amaguaña subsequently being an active member including traveling internationally on behalf of the party.

The general absence of Indigenous voices in the CIA report either reveals a blindness to those who did not match demographic assumptions about who would be a communist leader, or is an indication of a disinterest in or ignorance of rural struggles. Subsequent observers and scholars have often assumed that one could not be both an Indigenous person and a communist militant or leader, and the silences in the CIA record may reflect those presumptions. In fact, even the information that the CIA officers included contradicts their conclusions about the lack of Indigenous participation in the party. According to Rivera, the FEI "will soon be run entirely by Indians, members of the PCE." He claimed that the FEI has made "considerable progress" in establishing Indigenous unions, including eight in Otavalo, three in Riobamba, and one in Sangolquí in addition to those in Cotacachi and Cayambe that already had a long and well-established history. As a male of European-descent, Rivera's comments may have registered with the CIA officers or their informers in a way that the presence of subaltern voices at the congress might not have.

In addition to attacking Paredes for exploiting Indigenous federations for his own personal gain, Rivera also condemned María Luisa Gómez de la Torre for having "abandoned her work with the Indians." According to Rivera, after working so hard and long with Indigenous schools in Cayambe, Gómez de la Torre had "retired to a position of bourgeois luxury at her comfortable home in Quito." In Ecuadorian leftist circles, Gómez de la Torre is legendary for having set up these schools.[25] And in fact, Paredes shared a similar reputation for his long-term interest in, and petitioning for, Indigenous rights. Rather than condemning Paredes and Gómez de la Torre, Rivera may have been attempting to hold them accountable to their responsibilities as longtime communist militants and party leaders. An outside observer may have mistaken—or intentionally misconstrued—a communist tradition of self-criticism for open and irreconcilable splits in the party.

On the other hand, the infighting may have simply reflected political immaturity. At least this is how it appeared to the Colombian communist leader Barrios. He described for the congress the torture and repression that his party's members confronted. Given the intense wave of violence that was washing over Colombia, Barrios criticized the Ecuadorian delegates for gathering only to hurl insults at one another rather than to work together around a common agenda. He found it colossally stupid to fight when they faced "propitious circumstances for the triumph of Communism." Particularly considering the relative advantages that the Ecuadorians enjoyed, the Colombians appeared to be more politically advanced than their counterparts in the neighboring country. From his perspective, the Ecuadorians should pull together rather than engage in such incendiary fights. If Barrios were correct, these internal disputes would explain in part why the Ecuadorian left lost so much ground in the 1950s.

On the surface, a final complaint against Paredes appears to be much more personal than political in nature. This charge concerned making false accusations against his fellow comrade Nela Martínez. Paredes and Martínez famously had an affair in the late 1930s that resulted in the birth of a child named Leonardo. Martínez subsequently married the French communist Raymond Mériguet and had several more children with him. Apparently Martínez had cut off contact with Paredes, which had led to the spat. Once again, such an open airing of personal laundry may have embodied the weaponization of seemingly trivial matters, or it might indicate the mature reconciliation of personal issues so that comrades could effectively continue their work around a shared political agenda. If that were the case, it would reflect the party's strength and ability to overcome difficulties and rally around a common cause.

The CIA reported that Paredes railed for three hours against his accusers, and in particular against Saad, Echeverría, and Rivera. "His speech reportedly had no coherence," the CIA stated in their account, "and he was several times warned by the Presidium to get back to the point," indicating that the author was not present at the meeting but drew on secondhand evidence. Paredes responded to the charges with a description of his revolutionary activities and years of service to the party. The CIA's account continued, "It has been reported that the general consensus was that he made a complete fool of himself and did not effectively refute any of the charges made against him." Given Paredes's long history of activism, the accusations had repercussions throughout the party. Allegedly, many delegates concluded "that Paredes has degenerated completely as a revolutionary, but that he should be 'put out to pasture' by a Party which must recognize his valuable service in the past." It would, of course, also serve United States imperial interests to eliminate a long-standing communist militant from the political scene.

Paredes was not the only party member to face charges at the congress. Delegates criticized Vera for his "rightist deviations" stemming from his stint as minister of education in Velasco Ibarra's government after the May 1944 revolution. At that time, US ambassador Robert Scotten identified Vera as "known to be closely identified with the extreme Left" and reportedly "affiliated with the Communist Party."[26] According to the FBI, Vera had formally resigned from the communist party after accusations surfaced that his brother-in-law was a Nazi, even though he personally remained sympathetic to communist principles. Velasco Ibarra forced both Vera as well as the socialist minister of social welfare Alfonso Calderón Moreno out of office on January 30, 1945, claiming that the ministers were incompetent, although his actual reason was to lessen leftist influence in his government. A day after the dismissals, the PCE accused the administration of moving to the right and announced that it would no longer collaborate with the government.[27]

Vera also faced charges that he had failed to act with proper revolutionary vigor in his interactions with the CFP leader Carlos Guevara Moreno and his allies with whom he served on Guayaquil's municipal council, and that he had acted in an opportunistic manner. Vera later grumbled of the party's failure to support his leadership on the council. A CIA officer commented that after the party congress Vera had "continued his carping criticism of the PCE leadership without let-up." In particular, Vera protested that the PCE was losing the initiative in opposing Guevara Moreno's actions on Guayaquil's municipal council.[28] These divisions tore at the party and threatened to lead to defections among those who were not committed to a long-term struggle.

Leading the attack on Vera was Primitivo Barreto, whom the executive committee had sent from Quito to Guayaquil to address problems in the coastal regional committee, and a young communist named Bolívar Sandoval from the coastal province of Los Ríos. A group of longtime militants including Ana Moreno, Segundo Ramos, Cesario Valverde, Ricardo Paredes, and Nela Martínez all came to Vera's defense. According to the CIA, this group claimed that Vera's opponents were simply attempting "to make him the scapegoat for all of the errors of the PCE." Paredes considered Vera to be "the most intelligent and loyal of all the members of the PCE." Notably, those who came to Vera's defense represented the left wing of the party even though he had been accused of rightist deviations, but this was also a group who opposed Saad's leadership of the party. Multiple factors intertwined to define conflictual and contradictory alliances.

Similar to Vera, Manuel Medina Castro also faced criticism for his rightist deviations. Medina Castro had led the fight against the Grace Line's dispute with the Port of Guayaquil, but party members complained that he had done so without advising party leaders of his plans. Grace had held a contract since 1943 to transfer cargo from ships docked at Puna Island near the mouth of the Guayas River to the city of Guayaquil. The Ecuadorian government now requested that the United States send an engineer to examine proposals to dredge the Guayas River to circumvent the additional transportation costs of off-loading the shipments. The Truman administration included improvements to the Ecuadorian port in its "Point Four" technical assistance and economic development program.[29] In March 1951, the Ecuadorian congress passed a resolution to cancel the Grace Line contract to handle cargo at Puna Island. Grace and Chilean Lines threatened to stop service if they were not permitted to unload at the island, arguing that it was unsafe to bring their ships directly into the Guayaquil harbor. Opponents retorted that the transshipment simply provided an opportunity to inflate costs.[30]

The Grace contract became a common topic of discussion for the PCE, and provided a convenient battering ram with which to attack United States imperialism. Medina Castro frequently spoke on the topic, and in particular emphasized the advantages of dredging the Guayas River and constructing a new port at Guayaquil. A year and a half earlier, a CIA officer had complained that as a "prominent member of the PCE and member of the Guayas Provincial Council," Medina Castro had denounced the government's contract with the Grace Company in a speech at the Casa de la Cultura in Guayaquil.[31] Another speech at the University of Guayaquil resulted in the publication of a book that placed pressure on the government to cancel the contract and upgrade Guayaquil's port facilities.[32] Medina Castro's vocal opposition led Dario Astudillo, a professor of civil law at the university and the father of several workers at the Grace Line, to complain to US Consul Perry Ellis about undue communist influence at the university.[33] In December 1951, the FPTG, the communist-dominated coastal affiliate of the CTE, invited Medina Castro to address their congress on the topic. Medina Castro complained that the United States government and financial interests wished to conduct work that would not be needed for navigation of the Guayas River, and that laborers and farm workers would be stuck with the bill. He claimed that Grace refused to allow its ships to enter the Guayaquil harbor only because it could make more money by unloading the cargo at Puna and charging extra for transporting the freight up the river on barges.[34] In response, the finance minister Alfredo Peñaherrera announced the government's decision not to renew its contract with the Grace Line because it was harmful to Ecuadorian interests, which influenced the company to threaten to terminate its service to Ecuador because the river lacked sufficient depth for safe navigation.[35] The *New York Times* reported "from a reliable source that the Grace Line had not been interested in renewing the contract," but that "leftist political and labor circles" had latched onto the issue as a topic of agitation.[36] In this case, communist appeals to nationalist sentiments contributed to an alliance with the Ecuadorian government against the economic penetration of a foreign company.

CIA surveillance of the party congress calls into question how united the party was in its opposition to the Grace contract, and whether Medina Castro was simply using the party to advance a pet cause. While Moreno, Ramos, and Valverde had come to Vera's defense, now they accused Medina Castro of acting on his own rather than adhering to party discipline. Medina Castro, for his part, reportedly said that he was fed up with party discipline, and encouraged members to abandon the party if it would not personally benefit them to remain.

The CIA reported that the accusations against Medina Castro were particularly bitter, and almost led to a fistfight between Vera and Medina Castro.

The CIA's report does not indicate to what extent the conflicts with Vera and Medina Castro were personal or political, and what underlying issues might have contributed to the disagreements. Those on the party's left may have had their disagreements with Vera's relatively more moderate political positions, but they appeared to recognize and admire his commitment to socialist struggles. Medina Castro similarly had a trajectory on the left, including working with the FEUE while a student, winning a seat in the 1945 constituent assembly as an elected delegate from the province of Los Ríos, and subsequently serving on the Guayas provincial council. As with many militants, he was imprisoned multiple times for his activism, including later being exiled to Cuba after the 1963 military coup. Even so, apparently Medina Castro's perception of his role in the party did not match that of his comrades. Rather than clear ideological divisions, the issues appeared to concern matters of commitment and opportunism.

Nela Martínez stressed the need for criticism and self-criticism, and whether ironic or not she subsequently became the victim of what the CIA officer characterized as "violent tirades of criticism." She had prepared a political report for the congress, and other delegates condemned it as plagued with "serious political and 'personalist' errors." The CIA summarized Martínez's report as contending that the executive committee of the PCE, and not Vera, had pledged support to the liberal J. Federico Intriago for mayor of Guayaquil in the recent municipal elections, a statement that led to strong criticism from Vera's detractors.[37] Martínez also criticized Paredes for signing a letter that had appeared in the Colombian press. Her insistence that Paredes be investigated and punished if found guilty prompted a strong response from Paredes's defenders.

Delegates also complained that Martínez encouraged young women to join the PCE directly without first going through the JCF, thereby leading to the decline of that feeder organization into the main party. Martínez was a noted feminist and founder of several women's organizations, so it would seem unlikely that she would oppose young women forming their own group particularly given the patriarchal nature of society that bled over into the party. This criticism was especially ironic given that Martínez encouraged more party support for the JCE, the young communist group, including pressing for the appointment of a youth member to the PCE's executive committee. She also advocated for the party to create and support a JCE newspaper. Others echoed Martínez's comments on the JCE and urged that the party dedicate more resources to the promotion of the organization. Efraín Alvarez Fiallo from the JCE in Guayas promoted the establishment of youth groups in each province. Saad responded to the criticism by stating that in the future more attention would be paid to developing the JCE. Martínez's overt support for the JCE naturally led to criticism for her failures as head of the JCF. The documentation is frustratingly silent on why she would not be more supportive of the JCF.

Martínez, in turn, criticized her fellow communists for not raising their children in accord with the party's line. In particular, she called out Alfonso Quijano Cobos for sending his daughters to a convent. Religious education had long been an issue for anticlerical liberals given the assumption that students would emerge from Catholic schools thoroughly indoctrinated into conservative ideologies. For a communist like Martínez, it was completely unthinkable that leftists could willingly send their children to a parochial school even if it meant taking advantage of a higher quality education.

Martínez raised many more issues at the congress, many of them quite personal. For example, she advocated providing funding to Ernesto Rossi Delgado so that he could travel outside of Ecuador to seek medical treatment. One criticism flowed into another, with the tension building up to a crescendo. As was perhaps to be expected, divisions also ran through the JCE. Patricio Cueva Jaramillo, the son of the socialist Carlos Cueva Tamariz who had recently held the portfolio of minister of education in Plaza's government, asked the congress to expel Jorge Maldonado Renella because he spent all his time selling the Cominform newspaper *For a Lasting Peace, For a People's Democracy* rather than dedicating himself to more important JCE activities. The British Embassy noted that Cueva Jaramillo had recently returned from what it described as "a year's Communist education at Prague University."[38] Both Cueva Jaramillo and Maldonado Renella, who had also studied in Prague as well as Warsaw, had attended the World Federation of Democratic Youth (WFDY)–sponsored Berlin Youth Festival the previous year, which probably had drawn them further into communist circles.[39] According to the CIA, Cueva Jaramillo was also one of Martínez's principal accusers, even though he was young and had been in the party for only eight months. The CIA report does not indicate on what authority he made his complaints, or whether in such an open and democratic environment he even needed any special standing other than being a formal delegate to the congress to do so. Nor does the agency indicate how other delegates responded to his demands. Perhaps he had taken Martínez's call for the need for self-criticism too seriously.

A year later, Cueva Jaramillo was named president of the JCE, and one of his principle concerns in that position was the upcoming elections for control of the FEUE. JCE leaders indicated that they were "getting along well" with the socialist student leaders, and were hoping for expanded cooperation.[40] Several years later he traveled to Moscow for the Sixth World Festival of Youth and Students.[41] At the same time, he was slowly drifting away from the PCE and did not subsequently play a significant role in the party. Instead, he went on to work with the political periodical *La Calle* that secular intellectuals founded in 1957 to press a liberal, anticommunist agenda.[42] He later became known as a journalist, including working with *Granma* in Cuba, and as a painter.

In an earlier session Ramos had supported Paredes for the post of secretary general over Saad, and now he continued his attack against Saad for his shortcomings in leading the communist labor movement on the coast. Underlying the criticisms was the fact that Ramos was to have held the post of senator for coastal labor in the federal congress, but instead the position went to Saad. Ramos accused Saad and his allies of cheating him out of the position. Rightfully, Ramos claimed, the post belonged to him because he was a true worker, whereas Saad had "never worked a single day in his lifetime." This charge led to significant debate. According to the CIA, "the few delegates belonging to the laboring class" supported Ramos, while "the 'intellectual' majority" defended Saad. His backers denounced Ramos as "a degenerate drunkard," and claimed "that only Saad has the necessary Party background and political acumen to hold such an important post in the National Assembly." This debate had long been present in the party, with considerable anti-intellectual and proworker sentiments prevalent in the coastal committee. Saad's supporters maintained that having a person of his stature and skills in a leadership position was in the party's best interests. An undercurrent of opposition to intellectuals such as Saad (and the socialist Manuel Agustín Aguirre, who earlier had served as senator for highland workers) was broadly present among the labor rank and file. The argument was that as intellectuals rather than manual workers they did not meet the constitutional qualifications to represent labor in congress, even though they continued to enjoy the support of CTE leaders.[43]

Ramos allegedly also insulted the visiting emissaries Barrios from Colombia and Calderón from Cuba, which triggered a negative reaction from other delegates and elicited an apology from Saad. The party leader then asked for a vote of confidence for Barrios and Calderón, which prompted prolonged applause that forced Ramos to retract his statements. Barrios asked for a committee to investigate Ramos's charges so as to reassure the assembled delegates of the visitor's legitimacy. The CIA reported that it was later revealed that Calderón had participated in the executive committee meeting in which party leaders had decided to support Saad rather than Ramos as labor senator, and in fact Calderón had voted for Saad as the more valuable of the two postulants. Political debates easily bled into personal disputes.

Vera then launched an attack against Pérez Castro, the wealthy son of the founder of *El Universo*. Pérez Castro had a complicated relationship with both his family and the Ecuadorian left. In its earlier investigations, the FBI claimed that Pérez Castro had become involved in the communist party due to his rebellious nature rather than a commitment to "any particular political ideology." The bureau quoted an unnamed "prominent Socialist leader" who characterized Pérez Castro as "young, rich, crazy, imprudent and uncontrollable, and who is used by the Communist Party since he has money and since his family runs the newspaper *El Universo*."[44] At the party congress, Vera accused Pérez Castro of "leftist deviations" that had contributed "to the virtual destruction of the PCE in Guayaquil." Allegedly Pérez Castro had made no effort to adhere to the party line and thereby harmed communist support for building an international peace movement. His actions had led to political confusion in the party at both the cell level and in the Guayas provincial committee. Pérez Castro also faced charges of physically assaulting Gil Gilbert, and of abandoning his party duties to move to Salinas "where he lives like any other bourgeois." As with other party members, Pérez Castro also had his defenders. Juan Pío Narváez claimed that Pérez Castro was "the most faithful, hardworking PCE member in the coastal area," and "had poured all his personal funds into Party work." Narváez returned Vera's accusations, charging that Vera had sabotaged the party's peace movement in order to discredit Pérez Castro. Other delegates also defended Pérez Castro and welcomed his work in organizing the party in Tungurahua. He may have been impetuous, but they valued the work he did.

Next, José María Roura Cevallos accused Paredes, Gómez de la Torre, Martínez, and Mériguet for their "rightist deviations" that had compromised the party's effectiveness. Roura had joined the communist party while studying at the Central University in Quito a decade earlier, and represented university students in the 1945 constituent assembly. A decade later the PCE expelled Roura, together with Jaime Galarza and Nela Martínez, from the party for their leftist "divisive activities."[45] In between those events, in November 1955 Velasco Ibarra sought to transfer Roura from his teaching position at Colegio Mejía in Quito to a new girls' school at Guaranda in an attempt either to exile an opponent or to force him to resign. The students at Colegio Mejía responded to the news with protests and demonstrations that quickly spread to other schools. Those at the Normal Juan Montalvo barricaded themselves in their school and refused to leave. The police and military attacked the school with tear gas and rifle fire and in the process killed a student, severely wounded numerous others (including a thirteen-year-old girl), and arrested others. The murdered student, Isidro Guerrero, subsequently became a cause célèbre for the left.[46] Predictably, rather than granting legitimacy to the protests, Joseph Costanzo, the United States consul in Guayaquil, complained that it was "clear as daylight that the PCE is responsible for keeping the strike going" for none other than the nefarious purpose to cause trouble for the government.[47]

Given this militant history and an apparent ability to inspire others to action, in 1952 Roura launched his complaints against his fellow comrades. According to Roura, these leaders in Pichincha had "converted the Party into a scheming group of gossips and rumor-mongers," and he asked the congress to censure their actions. Roura noted that these "old-timers" enjoyed considerable prestige in the party, and that either they needed to change their behavior or they should be expelled before they corrupted a younger generation. If the CIA's recording of the internal conflicts is accurate, Roura grouped these historical leaders together as a common problem for the party even though they had earlier attacked one another on other issues. Or, perhaps, it was the bickering among themselves that so bothered him. Roura also advocated for an intensification of propaganda among the working class. He promoted the nationalization of foreign businesses as "the only practical way to rid Ecuador of foreign imperialists." Those members he had just denounced represented the party's left wing, and probably would not have disagreed with him on these points.

Both of the visiting communist leaders from Colombia and Cuba had an opportunity to address the congress. Barrios spoke for three hours during which time he detailed the history of the Partido Comunista de Colombia (PCC, Communist Party of Colombia). The CIA highlighted in particular his criticism of Yankee imperialism. Barrios claimed that "the repressive measures of Colombian conservatives, backed by Yankee Imperialism, have served only to strengthen the PCC, causing more persons to join the cause." Barrios discussed the upcoming Peiping [Beijing] Peace Conference, and the opportunities that it would provide for the Ecuadorian party. The PCE could send twelve delegates, and Barrios encouraged the party to assemble a delegation comprised of capable intellectuals. Taking advantage of this opportunity would help them advance their struggle.

The anonymous CIA author was less charitable in an assessment of the contributions of the Cuban representative Calderón. The intelligence officer disregarded his speeches as "more repetitions of the usual Party line." Calderón advised the PCE to purge "its ranks to weed out the weak and vacillating, as well as the infiltrated agents of the 'imperialist powers,'" though apparently, he did not indicate who those agents might be and if an informer for the CIA was one of those. He encouraged the establishment of schools to train new leaders. Given what he had seen at the congress, that was perhaps not bad advice.

The party devoted its closing session to reports from various commissions. According to the CIA, the organization commission's report "marked the temporary end of the bitter personal accusations which had heretofore been the principal activity of the convention delegates." Barreto read the report that laid out the party's new political line, which the assembled delegates approved. Among the recommendations was a new system of party identification cards to be distributed to all members, the establishment of schools to train new leaders, the formation of new working-class and peasant cells, the recruitment of new members, an intensification of a campaign for peace and against military pacts, opposition to decadent imperialist literature, fundraising, creation of a peasant federation, and development of a women's movement and federation. Party leadership planned to draft a new document on party organization for distribution after the congress.

The discipline commission explained charges against several party members, and expelled four: Pedro Barba, Héctor Pazmiño, Ecuador (aka Manuel) Jaya, and Manuel Arenas Coello. Barba had previously been a political prisoner, and was released in June 1946 under an amnesty program.[48] Arenas Coello had been elected to the Guayaquil municipal council on the Popular Alliance ticket. Little information is available on the other two and the CIA report does not detail complaints against them, which indicates that the party targeted marginal members rather than major leaders for sanction. The discipline commission also accused Vera and Medina Castro of "rightist deviation," and instructed them never to promise electoral support for political candidates without first gaining approval from the party's executive committee. Vera would subsequently receive additional charges of being a "renegade" for his work with the municipal council, and eventually he too was expelled from the party.[49]

The final issue facing the congress was election of party leadership, which according to the CIA led to a new wave of angry debates because many nominees "have proven in the past that they lack the necessary attributes of revolutionary vigor." Pérez Castro urged that Saad be elected unanimously as secretary general. Narváez seconded the motion, but revealing divisions in the party Ana Moreno nominated the JCE leader Echeverría instead. Moreno stated that even though Echeverría was young, he was the most outstanding, loyal, and capable member of the party. Others also indicated that Echeverría was a "rising star" in the party, and that members had a great deal of faith in his ability to push the party forward.[50] It was apparent that more would be heard from this youth leader.

For his part, Paredes endorsed Saad in the interests of "harmony within the Communist family," but also declared that his counterpart had committed serious errors. Ramos nominated Barreto, but subsequently voted for Saad with considerable reluctance. In the end, only Moreno withheld her vote for Saad. The CIA document does not indicate whether Calderón or Barrios played a role in this process, but if they had determined a preference for Saad over Ramos as labor representative in the federal congress, it would be reasonable to assume that they had come to the meeting to assure that Saad be installed as the party's new leader. If that were the case, his elevation can be understood as an external imposition rather than the result of an internal democratic process. Understandably, that outside pressure would only have rankled militant members of the party.

The position of secretary general now had formally passed from Paredes to Saad, and the latter remained the head of the party for the next thirty years. With his election, not only did the center of control over the party shift from the highlands to Guayaquil, but also the historic leaders including Paredes, Nela Martínez, María Luisa Gómez de la Torre, César Endara, Dolores Cacuango, Enrique Gil Gilbert, and Gustavo Becerra became marginalized.[51] Furthermore, divisions in the party continued to deepen. A decade later Saad expelled Echeverría who Moreno wanted to elevate to secretary general over the issue of whether communists should seek power peacefully through parliamentary means, as Saad advocated, or take a much more radical turn and prepare for a violent revolution as Echeverría was preparing to do. Echeverría in turn formed a new Maoist party, the PCMLE, although it never gained the strength or presence of the original pro-Soviet PCE. The roots of this division between "bureaucratic" members who opposed engaging in guerrilla activity and generally lacked daring and initiative, and their counterparts who the old-line party leaders criticized as being too headstrong, undisciplined, and foolhardy was already apparent at the 1952 congress.[52]

The delegates' attention then turned to the selection of a central committee. In the name of party solidarity, Vera asked that his name be withdrawn from nomination. He asked to say a few words, and then proceeded to unleash a series of accusations against party leaders in Guayaquil, in particular against Pérez Castro and Medina Castro. Vera denounced Pérez Castro as an irresponsible drunkard and repeated the long-held accusation that the party tolerated his presence only because his familial connections to *El Universo* allowed him to contribute significant sums to the party's finances. According to the CIA, this attack came in the context of attempting to rebuild party unity that prompted a reaction against Vera and support for Pérez Castro. Vera's outburst impelled the Cuban representative Calderón to denounce him as a "populist," something that would be understood in this context to be quite an insult.

Echeverría, Barreto, and Gil Gilbert were elected unanimously to the central committee. In an apparent egotistical move, Martínez "asked that her election be unanimous as well, since the Central Committee desperately needed her services," although she did not indicate exactly what those services might be. The CIA report does not indicate whether delegates granted her the request, but in any case she did retain her post. Other party members elected to the central committee were Oswaldo Albornoz (Quito), Modesto Rivera (Quito), Marco Tulio Oramas (Guayaquil), Aquiles Valencia (Manabí), José María Roura (Quito), Hernán Acebedo (Loja), José María Dávalos (Ambato), Jesús Gualavisí (Ambato), Segundo Ramos (Guayaquil), Neptalí Pacheco León (Milagro), Pascual Palomino, and Franklin Pérez Castro (Guayaquil). Alternatives were Guillermo Cañarte, Eduardo González, José Villacreses, Nelson Segura, and Tirso Gómez.

Two years later, the State Department presented a somewhat different list of party leaders. According to their files in Washington, Saad, Echevarría, and Barreto had been elected to the party's national secretariat. The State Department also listed a seven-person executive committee, with Saad as secretary general, Echevarría as secretary of organization, Roura as secretary of finances, Albornoz as secretary of press and propaganda, Martínez as secretary for political education and the pro-peace movement, Barreto as secretary for labor, and Rivera as secretary for peasants and Indians.[53] The correspondence does not indicate the source of this information, whether it is from embassy reports that have been lost or otherwise have not emerged, or whether it came from another agency such as the CIA.

Equally if not more notable than who was elected to the new central committee is who was excluded. Particularly conspicuous by their absence were the longtime militant and Indigenous rights activist Cacuango and the educator Gómez de la Torre, both of whom had previously played prominent roles in the party. Earlier when they had wanted to drop out of the party Paredes urged them to remain, contending that a true communist never gives up and stays in the struggle come what may.[54] Martínez was the only woman left on the central committee, and her time with the party would soon come to an end as well. If the CIA's list is accurate, not even Paredes retained a seat on the central committee.

One curiosity on the CIA's list of central committee members is the name of Jesús Gualavisí from Ambato. It is unclear from the documentation whether this is the same person who was a longtime Kayambi militant who had participated in the party's founding in 1926.[55] If so, it is curious that he was now listed as from Ambato and that the agency stated that no Indigenous peoples attended the congress, although both statements could be in error. Alternatively, given the fluid nature of ethnic boundaries, the identity of individual delegates may not have been immediately apparent to a foreign observer. Gualavisí was literate, fluent in Spanish, and a leader in his community, all of which may have marked him as mestizo rather than native. If Gualavisí had been at the congress, it would have been unusual that he did not register in the CIA's accounting of the proceedings since in previous gatherings he had played such a prominent role. By the 1950s, the aging Gualavisí was no longer as active in political struggles as he had once been, and he may not have attended the congress. Furthermore, he would not have had to be present to be elected to the central committee, and he may have been nominated because of his legendary contributions to the party and social movements in general. Otherwise, except for Pacheco León, the peasant leader from Milagro, most of the rest of the committee were men of European descent who lived in urban areas. Under Saad, party leadership became less rather than more diverse.

The CIA reported that otherwise qualified and "highly valuable" communists were barred from the central committee due to a party rule that its members must have at least four years of "uninterrupted militancy." Jaime Galarza (Azuay) and Juan Arias (Imbabura) were denied positions for this reason, even though they were both "promising young Communists." Galarza, for example, had joined the party in 1948, had quickly risen to the position of secretary general of the local party in Azuay, and had served on the presidium for the congress. At the time of the congress he was only twenty-one years old (and, in fact, turned twenty-two on July 28, the final full day of the congress). He would subsequently go on to engage in a lengthy career as a communist militant, although he became vocally critical of Saad for his adherence to a dogmatic pro-Soviet line. He helped found the militant Unión Revolucionaria de la Juventud Ecuatoriana (URJE, Revolutionary Union of the Ecuadorian Youth) in the early 1960s, which contributed to his expulsion from the PCE. He became best known for books he published on agrarian issues and the 1970s petroleum boom, as well as an interview he conducted in London in 1975 with Agee.[56] As with many militants, Galarza suffered imprisonment and exile for his activism.

In the months leading up to the congress, Galarza had authored several broadsheets denouncing political violence against leftists. These publications provide a reflection of his ideas at the time and the contributions he made to the communist movement. In advance of the June presidential elections, Galarza blamed political violence in Cuenca and the spreading of anticommunist propaganda for the unpopularity of the government's candidate Salazar Gómez and the provocations of Velasco Ibarra's supporters who attempted to present themselves as victims. Galarza accused all sides of being political reactionaries who represented wealthy capitalist, landholding, and banking interests. He criticized the honest but misled conservative socialists for collaborating with Plaza's government that had led to a three-fold increase in poverty, a rise in unemployment, and more corruption. Galarza called on people regardless of political affiliation or religious conviction to join the communists in a unified struggle against misery and oppression. Rather than putting their hopes in candidates or electoral promises, the masses should rely on the immense force that their numbers would represent once they were united in a struggle for bread, peace, and liberty.[57]

A second flyer denounced an anticommunist campaign in Cuenca that sought to smear the party's good name. Someone, presumably the ARNE and the CFP, had distributed leaflets signed by the communist party with slogans in favor of Plaza and Russia and against religion. Those agitators had also painted similar slogans of "Viva Plaza, Viva Rusia, Muera la Religión" on the city's walls. In light of these harmful acts, Galarza sought to clarify the party's position on Plaza, the Soviet Union, and religion so that everyone would be aware of the types of malicious activities in which the ARNE and the CFP engaged.

As for Plaza, Galarza pointed out that the PCE was the first to denounce his election, and warn that his ascension to office represented the triumph of the enemies of the people, in particular United States capitalists who oppressed Ecuadorians. Subsequently, and in contrast to the socialists, the PCE had never stopped denouncing Plaza's antipopular and antinationalist actions, including the theft of aid destined for the victims of the 1949 earthquake. They continued this campaign by unmasking the wealthy candidate Salazar Gómez as symbolizing a continuation of Plaza's policies. In short, far from supporting Plaza, communists had denounced his government as representing wealthy landholders and functioning as an agent of United States interests that hurt workers.

Galarza declared that communists respected and admired the Soviet Union as a workers' and peasants' state that one day they hoped to emulate in Ecuador. The USSR was a country in which factories were in the hands of the workers, land was in the hands of the peasants, and culture was open to all people. The USSR represented a future of peace and brotherhood, in which war would only be a bad memory from the past. Galarza then proceeded to declare that a true patriotism involved a struggle for a truly free country. "The communists deeply love the land of heroic Indians, bravely resisting Spanish rule," he wrote in tracing out the country's history as one of struggle for a better future. Communists fought to free Ecuador from new conquistadores, the Yankee colonists who subjugated the country to their neocolonial control. Galarza denounced military pacts for placing the country's youth and its wealth at the hands of imperialist forces engaged in a war against the heroic people of Korea. Communists were strong nationalists, but they were also internationalists who supported working-class struggles around the world against capitalist exploitation.

On the third point, Galarza stated that communists "respect religious beliefs." Simply put, people could embrace whichever religious faith they so choose, or none at all. They favored an absolute separation of church and state. What communists opposed was the pernicious tendency to use religion as a political weapon to subjugate working-class interests and halt their struggles for a better life. Particularly objectionable was the actions of some priests and landowners who used religion as a smokescreen to blind people to a true understanding of their class interests and hindered their ability to identify their true enemies: Yankee imperialists and their local allies, reactionary landowners and capitalist speculators who thrived off of the poverty of the people. Galarza denounced the conservative candidate Ruperto Alarcón Falconí in the 1952 presidential race for his desire to return to the days of Gabriel García Moreno who drafted a constitution that denied citizenship to those who were not Catholics. On the other hand, Galarza celebrated priests such as Juan Morales y Eloy who after visiting communist countries declared that the accusations against communists were completely false. Galarza contended that the PCE opposed the exploitation of people, but still maintained a profound respect for religion. He maintained that this was true for all communist parties in the world. Galarza denounced anticommunists for acting under cover of night to try to convince Catholics in Cuenca that communists were something that they were not. Rather than fighting fairly and cleanly, they resorted to lies and deceit. Galarza pledged that communists would continue their battle against all those who impoverished the country, and those who were complicit in such crimes. Galarza closed the pamphlet with a call for liberation of the people.[58] It is not difficult to understand how and why Galarza's fellow comrades would find him such a compelling and inspiring militant for the communist cause.

The PCE congress formally adjourned at 5:00 a.m. on Tuesday, July 29, 1952, after an all-night session. The CIA closed its lengthy report on the congress with a summary of the "extensive and bitter personal enmity among numerous leaders of the Party." The agency included a chart (see table 8.1) that listed the divisions that the report had recounted in great detail. An alternative reading of the chart is that it summarizes healthy and dynamic debates that revealed an ability to articulate differing perspectives without them becoming entrenched into a toxic split that would otherwise divide people over unrelated issues.[59] For example, according to the CIA, Martínez opposed Paredes on one issue, but allied with him on others. Furthermore, what was also remarkable was how the congress concluded on a note of unity with the longtime leader Paredes reaching out to his opponents. The PCE emerged stronger from the congress thanks in large part to their ability to air these issues in an open forum and come together around a common political platform.

The mainstream newspapers in Quito failed to carry news of the congress, though at its closure the *New York Times* published a short note that Saad had been elected the party's secretary general, and that the party would oppose Velasco Ibarra's government that was to be inaugurated a month later.[60] It is ironic that a foreign paper paid attention to Saad's assumption of leadership when a domestic paper of record did not. Similarly, the CIA was so fixated on internal dissension in the party that its officers and informers had not bothered to record the contents of political resolutions that emerged out of the meeting. Or perhaps actual policy initiatives were irrelevant to their surveillance operations. This mismatch in interests and emphasis between the PCE and the CIA also emerges in Agee's account of his efforts to subvert the political process in Ecuador. He notes that the party attempted to keep internal disputes quiet even as the agency's objective was to broadcast this unrest as broadly and loudly as possible.[61]

Several weeks after the conclusion of the congress, *El Comercio* printed a front-page story in which it noted that both Velasquista committees and the ARNE had met in Guayaquil and agreed to support the recently elected president and vowed to battle communism. While the paper had failed to cover the PCE congress, now it reported that the Velasquistas pledged "unity in struggle against the communists who, in their recent congress in Ambato, had resolved to combat the regime of José María Velasco Ibarra." The ARNE similarly promised

TABLE 8.1: Dissension within the PCE

Pedro Saad Rafael Echeverría Modesto Rivera Nela Martínez	vs.	Ricardo Paredes, supported by Alfredo Vera
Primitivo Barreto Bolívar Sandoval	vs.	Alfredo Vera, supported by Ana Moreno Segundo Ramos Cesario Valverde Ricardo Paredes Nela Martínez
Ana Moreno Segundo Ramos Cesario Valverde	vs.	Manuel Medina Castro
Patricio Cueva Jaramillo	vs.	Nela Martínez
Segundo Ramos	vs.	Pedro Saad
Alfredo Vera	vs.	Manuel Medina Castro, and Franklin Pérez Castro, the latter supported by Juan Pío Narváez
José María Roura Cevallos	vs.	Ricardo Paredes María Luisa Gómez de la Torre Nela Martínez Raymond Mériguet
Modesto Rivera	vs.	María Luisa Gómez de la Torre
Ana Moreno	vs.	Pedro Saad

SOURCE: Central Intelligence Agency (CIA), "Fifth Congress of the Communist Party of Ecuador (PCE) Held at Ambato," October 7, 1952, CIA Electronic Reading Room, https://www.cia.gov/library/readingroom/document/cia-rdp82-00457r014100290007-1.

to join the Velasquistas in their opposition to the PCE and to support Velasco Ibarra unconditionally in order to assure that he would be able to complete his four-year term in office.[62] The ARNE and the CFP soon entered into an intense rivalry for influence in Velasco Ibarra's government, and proceeded to throw barbs at each other.[63] Meanwhile, CFP legislators presented a bill in congress to outlaw the PCE. Saad retorted that doing so would only solidify the communist movement in Ecuador.[64] Pressure to proscribe communist activities continued even though the legislature did not ban the party, while both the ARNE and the CFP periodically threatened coup attempts against the government.

Even without media coverage, the echoes of the communist congress could be felt for months afterward. Discussion of tensions within the PCE continued unabated in CIA information reports. One such document conveyed statements that Wilson Durango López, who the CIA identified as a "prominent Communist leader in the University of Guayaquil," had made in September 1953 on conflicts and deep divisions in the party. Durango highlighted in particular the "diversionist tactics" of Vera who advocated allying with any group opposed to Guevara Moreno. According to Durango, "Vera has forgotten his loyalty to the PCE and has undertaken a campaign of hate and mud-slinging." The PCE planned to expel Vera, as well as his supporters, Ana Moreno, Elías Safadi, Vicente Iturralde Rivera, and others.[65]

Several years later, Vera reflected on his expulsion from the PCE in *La Calle*. Vera asserted that he was more of a Marxist than ever and remained firm in his "scientific conviction" that socialism would ultimately prevail. But, he stated, he could not in all honesty belong to a "party that is the exclusive property of such mediocre and small-minded men as Pedro Saad and Enrique Gil." They had done him a favor by expelling him in 1953 for having committed "the crime of having fought relentlessly against the fascistic CFP domination of Guayaquil's municipal council." According to Vera, only the Chilean, Brazilian, and perhaps the Venezuelan parties were doing well. As for the Ecuadorian party, after reaching a high point in the aftermath of the May 1944 revolution, it was falling apart "thanks to the petulant fatuity, opportunistic incompetence, and clumsy sectarianism of Saad and his cronies." Vera criticized Saad for holding on to the seat of labor senator in the federal congress through his speaking ability but without using it to advance the interests of the working class. Furthermore, Vera complained that Saad never supported him when he held the post of minister of education for six months after the May revolution. What goes around comes around. From his perspective, it was not so much that he had left the communist party but that it had left him.[66]

THE MONUMENTAL DECISIONS at the 1952 congress determined the direction the party would take for the next generation. Not only did Saad assume formal control over the party, but doing so laid the groundwork for a militant wing to splinter from the main organization a decade later. Despite all of the internal conflict, a CIA officer reported, "The PCE has been transformed and 'revitalized' as a result of the publication of the resolutions of the Fifth PCE

Congress."[67] The outcome of the congress was mixed, but by no means a defeat. It is therefore ironic and unfortunate that at the time media outlets did not recognize its importance and dedicate more resources to covering the event. The primary source of information we have on the congress is a CIA surveillance document, and ultimately that artifact tells us more about US imperial interests than it does about working-class demands. Inadvertently, in concentrating on internal dissent within the ranks of the party the CIA also shed light on how activists might negotiate conflict and disagreement. Those struggles grew ever more difficult across the 1950s, but the communists remained committed to their cause and were determined to continue onward. They understood that they would not immediately realize their goals, but through engagement with everyday forms of organization they demonstrated their resolve to fight for steady and important advances in society.

CHAPTER 9

Everyday Forms of Organization

WHILE MANY MIGHT NOW fondly reflect back on the 1950s as a period of peace and prosperity, at the time observers saw this decade as anything but that. For example, in its retrospective review of political events of 1953, *El Comercio* observed that few years in the history of the republic had been as turbulent. According to the newspaper, nothing was permanent on the continually shifting political landscape where intense passions could destroy anything and everything. Even respectable institutions came under scrutiny, and important leaders fell from their high pedestals when their feet were shown to be made of clay. The newspaper editors were not convinced that politicians were taking the country in the right direction.[1]

Labor strikes, coup attempts, and other visible manifestations of unrest and protest gained public attention, including coverage in the newspapers. Mundane and less spectacular practices were less apt to register in the media, but more accurately reflected the ongoing organizational processes. Covert surveillance proved to be particularly useful in charting these everyday efforts to build a strong and viable left. Evidence that emanates from CIA records demonstrates that far from disappearing, in the face of overwhelming opposition militants continued to build their organizations across the 1950s. Even more significant, intelligence gathering reveals the types of conversations and debates that took place within the left. What emerges evident is a form of praxis—political action that was informed by serious intellectual reflections.

For the communist party, its most high-profile activity in 1953 was the interpellation that communist party leader and labor senator Pedro Saad conducted in congress of José María Velasco Ibarra's conservative minister of government Camilo Ponce Enríquez. Although Saad lost the censure vote against the person who had become the left's primary opponent, the concerns laid bare in the midst of those debates highlight the issues that were of primary interest to the communists. Furthermore, as became unmistakably apparent, the surveillance and repression of leftist activities did not only come from outside of the country.

Many times, socialists and communists encountered a more ferocious hostility to their activities from domestic opposition. In order to advance their struggles, the communists would need to overcome those exacting challenges.

Theory and Action

On August 25, 1952, a month after the fifth PCE congress, the local committee in Guayaquil held an extraordinary meeting at communist headquarters to receive reports from party leaders.[2] CIA monitoring of that event indicates that the agency's surveillance of the PCE did not end with the party congress but continued at an intense pace. The agency maintained a particular concern with investigating coastal activities where the party unquestionably now had its base of operations. As with the fifth congress, it is not immediately apparent who conducted the investigations or how the documentation was compiled, but detailed information reflects a dedication of significant resources to the surveillance of the party.

Faulty coordination in advertising the August 25 meeting resulted in the attendance of only fourteen members. Party chief Enrique Gil Gilbert was in Quito, so Marco Tulio Oramas presided. Oramas informed those present of plans to reorganize communist cells. The Guayas provincial committee aimed to send delegates to visit all of the cells to verify that they were operating properly. Each cell was to hold regular meetings in a defined location. All members were expected to attend and to be current with their dues payments. Leaders instructed cells to emphasize a campaign against the military assistance pact that Ecuador had recently signed with the United States, and to denounce the treaty through public events, distribution of handbills, and collection of signatures for their peace campaign. According to Lilo Linke, the pact provoked less resistance in Ecuador than elsewhere in the hemisphere "because the Communist Party is so weak." Further hindering their efforts, the government presented the agreement as a logical continuation of the provision of naval bases on the Pacific Coast and Galápagos Islands during the Second World War.[3] While that may be the case, the CIA surveillance reveals the presence of concerted and ongoing efforts to build a campaign against imperial penetration of the country.

At the local committee meeting, Segundo Ramos, the secretary general of the FPTG, discussed labor unrest at the Witting Shipyard. Ramos blamed the problems on the United States supervisor Francis Vincent Coleman. The workers had gone on strike and needed communist support in order to achieve their goals of better pay and working conditions. The strikers' legal representative

Jorge Maldonado Renella, who Patricio Cueva Jaramillo had wanted to expel from the party at the previous month's congress because of his shirking of party responsibilities, cautioned "that the new Velasco administration would attempt to wipe out all labor unions and federations." Perhaps he had taken the criticisms to heart, because now he advocated that the PCE needed to work energetically to mobilize the unions in defense of their interests. A CIA case officer added a comment that the party leadership described the FPTG as "their federation," as if it were an adjunct of the PCE. The economic challenges that labor unions presented to United States hegemonic control over the hemisphere remained at the forefront of the minds of those in the intelligence agency.

Even as the party organized political actions, cadres also engaged in study and theoretical reflection in order to gain a better understanding of their current environment. Jorge Arellano Gallegos held a series of classes in his house in Quito for members of his cell. In addition to Arellano, seventeen cell members attended the meeting, of whom the CIA was able to identify twelve. The first session lasted for about an hour. Arellano traced the history of the Bolshevik Revolution and explained different theories of how a revolution would emerge, including a discussion of Vladimir Lenin and Joseph Stalin's arguments that a revolution could only be victorious through the combined force of the peasants and an urban proletariat. Arellano compared Russia before the revolution to Ecuador's current neocolonial status under Yankee control, and proclaimed "that Ecuador should follow the example set by Lenin and Stalin in throwing off the bonds of capitalism." He pointed to the USSR as the center of a global proletarian revolution. The gatherings were part of a concerted effort to fashion a more dedicated and effective core of party members to advance their revolutionary agenda. The CIA, for its part, dismissed the study sessions as nothing other than political indoctrination.[4]

In addition to charting the contents of the discussions that militants had inside the party, CIA surveillance also serves to record ongoing organizational efforts at local, regional, national, and international levels. CIA officers had a natural tendency to exaggerate internal conflicts—the same discord that party leaders wanted to keep under wraps—but more useful are the insights that information reports provide into how the party structured itself. For example, the CIA reported that the party's Pichincha province central committee sought to strengthen its organizational structure "by insuring that each local cell is directed by energetic well-qualified individuals." To realize this goal, the committee transferred Simón Pérez, a member of the Pichincha executive committee, from the Pedro Saad cell to the new Goya cell (apparently named after the Spanish painter Francisco Goya who through his artwork denounced Napoleon's invasion of the Iberian Peninsula in 1807), with the hope that doing so would strengthen the Goya cell. The provincial committee also instructed each cell to select a complete slate of officers, including a secretary of propaganda.[5] A fortified cell structure was key to advancing the party's ideological agenda.

On the coast where the party was stronger, on August 8, 1953, the Guayas committee of the PCE held a provincial conference in Guayaquil at the home of Franklin Pérez Castro.[6] Gil Gilbert presided over a preparatory session with sixteen members who established an agenda for the conference that would begin that same evening. Twenty delegates attended the inaugural session that commenced with a history of the PCE before proceeding to an examination and critique of the activities of the thirty cells that existed in the city. Of those thirty, only six or eight were truly active, and even among those attendance was sporadic. The session devolved into a long and heated debate late into the night with exchanges of accusations as to wh Narváez o was to blame for the shortcomings. Many of the allegations and underlying conflicts followed along lines similar to those at the previous year's party congress.

The discussions continued the following morning. Cesario Valverde of the Jesús Menéndez cell who had attacked Manuel Medina Castro at the fifth party congress now faced particularly harsh criticism for accusing Pérez Castro of bribing supporters to vote for him in order to retain his position on the provincial committee. In particularly, Valverde had accused Juan Pío Narváez and Marco Tulio Oramas of being blind followers of Pérez Castro, and who had gained their loyal support by providing them with free meals in his home. From interpersonal conflicts, debates swung toward international issues with much broader political implications. Some party members moved from criticizing Valverde for his statements against other party members to denouncing him for claiming that the USSR had ordered Trotsky's assassination and declaring that the expulsion of deputy premier Lavrentiy Pavlovich Beria was unjust. Valverde acknowledged having made these statements, and defended his position with the claim that he was not the only one who held those views. He contended that Oramas had raised the same issue at a FPTG meeting. As for naming Narváez and Oramas as lackeys of Pérez Castro, Valverde said that if they felt guilty perhaps it was because there was some truth to the rumors. As with other conflicts, it is difficult to determine how much of the attacks could be traced to interpersonal tension and how much might be due to political or ideological differences. Rather than the doctrinaire imposition of a party line from outside or above, these debates reflected an environment in which members did not hesitate to articulate their differences of opinion.

The CIA report notes that the meeting then turned on Bernardino Poveda and Abelardo Santos from the Puerto cell. They faced charges of receiving 300 sucres from J. Federico Intriago to support him in his election to the Guayaquil municipal council in exchange for his support for the formation of an agricultural colony. Poveda and Santos allegedly pocketed the money and did nothing to support Intriago, nor did Intriago help the Puerto cell secure the land they needed to form the cooperative. Julio Olmedo Muñoz faced additional accusations of campaigning for Intriago behind the back of the PCE, the same issue that had divided Nela Martínez and Alfredo Vera at the previous year's party congress. Olmedo allegedly told his clients that they did not need to pay their bills if they would vote for Intriago. Opportunism appeared to be a problem on all sides. Although Intriago emerged out of the liberal party, the conservative Ponce later named him as minister of economy after his election as president in 1956. Intriago faced additional charges of involvement in other scandals in that post.[7] It was not without good reason that communist party militants questioned involvement with such a shady character.

Even with all of the complications that involvement in electoral campaigns introduced into party organization, delegates at the conference selected Alfonso Quijano Cobos and Enrique Gil Gilbert to head the ballot for the Guayas provincial council in the upcoming November 1953 elections. Oramas and Olmedo, despite the complaints against their actions, would be the candidates for the Guayaquil municipal council. The meeting concluded with elections for the provincial party committee. A delegate asked the assembly to analyze the activities of each nominee so that only those with clean records would be selected for leadership positions. This led to further acrimonious sparring that eliminated many nominees. Finally, the meeting elected a committee with the labor leader Guillermo Cañarte as the secretary general.

CIA surveillance allows scholars to peer deeply into the organizational structures of a local party. What the agency's information gathering efforts reveal are sincere militants engaged in critical and open debates over how to advance their struggles. As with making sausage, the process was not always pretty but what emerges apparent is a small but devoted group of communists who remained committed to realizing their vision for a more just and equal world.

Interpellation

When Paredes was secretary general the PCE actively engaged with rural struggles in Indigenous communities. Under Saad's leadership, the party turned instead toward strengthening its alliances with labor unions and participating in parliamentary maneuvers. Saad excelled at using his position as labor representative in the federal congress to advance a working-class agenda. He effectively used that space to engage in sustained attacks on the left's archenemy and current minister of government Camilo Ponce Enríquez. One of the most noted examples of Saad's use of parliamentary maneuvers came with his interpellation of Ponce in September 1953.[8]

Opposition to Ponce extended well beyond the left, and in fact the inspiration for the interpellation came from different quarters. The previous December, Velasco Ibarra had exiled his previous ally and CFP leader Carlos Guevara Moreno to Peru under charges of plotting to overthrow his government. On September 12, 1953, Guevara Moreno announced that he would return from Lima to Guayaquil, but Velasco Ibarra bared him from entering the country. Hundreds of Guevara Moreno's supporters gathered at the airport in Guayaquil to welcome him, but when they learned that the government would deny him entry they began to throw rocks at the police. In the melee, one person was killed and sixteen police officers and an undetermined number of civilians were injured. Officials arrested more than thirty people, including four minors. Undersecretary of interior José Bucheli said that "professional agitators" had planned the protest. He attributed the disturbances to the CFP, communists, and elements representing other ideologies.[9]

The decision to bar Guevara Moreno from returning to Ecuador along with shuttering two opposition newspapers led to political pressure to censure Velasco Ibarra's government. Finally, on September 19 after a marathon thirteen-hour session the Ecuadorian congress voted seventy-three to fifteen against a motion of censure of Ponce.[10] Conservative domination of congress, which *El Comercio* described as "a docile instrument of the executive" that blindly followed the president's orders, made the outcome a foregone conclusion.[11] Nevertheless, while the motion failed it provided the left with a visible venue in which to highlight their complaints about the government's rightward drift. It also offered the public an opportunity to observe a direct confrontation between politicians with extremely divergent views.

Rumors had circulated for months that Saad wanted to present a series of charges against the government minister. At the end of August, Saad had told an assembly of workers that the indictments were in the pipeline, although he was vague on details.[12] Over the next several days, the media reported on his plan to bring charges.[13] On Friday, September 11, Saad together with the congressional deputies Joel Cevallos Cedeño, a socialist from Manabí, and Guillermo Grijalva from Carchi presented eight questions to which they wanted Ponce to respond. The government's decision the following day to bar Guevara Moreno's return provided the legislators with the political impetus to bring the accusations in front of the entire body.

The list of complaints against the administration was eclectic, and reflected the range of enemies that Velasco Ibarra had made during his first year in the presidency. The first question asked under what legal authority Ponce had closed the opposition Guayaquil newspapers *La Nación* and *La Hora*. The wealthy banana exporter Simón Cañarte owned both papers and had financed Velasco Ibarra's electoral campaign. His support had assured his victory by building a bridge between the caudillo and Guevara Moreno's populist CFP. When political differences led to a falling out between Velasco Ibarra and Guevara Moreno, Cañarte's newspapers supported the CFP. In revenge for this betrayal, Velasco Ibarra ordered both papers shuttered. Their closure and the arrest of their reporters had led to international condemnation, including from the Inter-American Press Association's Freedom of the Press Committee.[14] The British ambassador quipped that the closing of *La Nación* and *La Hora* was not without merit, but still that "Ecuador is one of the few democratic countries left in South America and the suppression of a newspaper gives a shock to the body politic."[15] Both papers remained closed for four months until Velasco Ibarra finally allowed them to reopen.

The second item questioned Velasco Ibarra's violation of the autonomy of the Central University in Quito. The third raised the issue of illegal detentions. The fourth concerned Ponce's intervention in other ministries to act against worker interests. The fifth touched on the issue of an August 6 massacre of agricultural workers on the Merced hacienda in the parish of Pintag just outside of Quito. The sixth inquired into a loan for the colonization of the Amazon. The seventh concerned the confiscation of material sent from Europe to the bookstore Librería Ecuador. And, finally, the eighth asked why Ponce had ordered the ministry of public works to intercept mail sent to Librería Ecuador.[16] In relation to the third item, one of the petitioners attached a lengthy list of illegal detentions starting with an attack on Evangelicals in Cotocollao on March 8, 1953, and concluding with the arrests in Guayaquil on September 8, 1953, of the student Eduardo Flores, president of the Unión Democrática Universitaria (UDU, University Democratic Union) and Franklin Pérez Castro. The list detailed eleven more alleged violations between those two events, including the illegal detention of labor leaders, political activists, student radicals, journalists, and many more. Miguel Macías Hurtado, a deputy from Guayas and one of Guevara Moreno's closest and most trusted supporters in the CFP, added a ninth question asking what right Ponce had to evict Guevara Moreno from the country and to prevent him from returning.[17] Opposition to Ponce's policies had momentarily united a diverse range of politicians who otherwise would not have collaborated and even might have been mortal enemies. The United States Embassy reported that Ponce was nervous because he knew "that some of his acts were without good legal justification."[18] He had a valid reason to be anxious.

Telegrams flowed into the senate from around the country, some backing Ponce and others Saad.[19] A committee in defense of democracy in the working-class neighborhood of San Roque in Quito distributed a handbill in which they announced their support for the interpellation. "Ponce Enríquez has imprisoned and tortured students, workers, and simple citizens, and has allowed the murder of Indians," the statement read. He "has closed newspapers, seized books, and imprisoned trade union leaders. His government has led to an increase in the misery of the people." In contrast, "the democratic legislators have defended the interests of the people, fighting against new taxes, for an increase in wages and salaries, for price controls on food, for democratic liberties, and for national independence." The interpellation was not against religion, as some opponents had claimed. Rather, "it is the struggle of men and women who live in misery, who have no bread or shelter, against the exploitative landholders headed by Ponce Enríquez." The committee called on all people regardless of political or religious beliefs to support the interpellation and the permanent struggle for democratic freedoms and better life conditions that it represented.[20] Saad hoped to advance his political struggle through such popular expressions of support.

In what strains the limits of credulity, the United States Embassy reported a rumor that communists were considering murdering Saad and blaming the minister for his death. According to this theory, the party leader and deputy's death would trigger a "Bogotazo" similar to the protests that occurred on April 11, 1948, with the assassination of the Colombian populist Jorge Eliécer Gaitán. The PCE responded with a handbill charging Ponce with planning to kill Saad to avoid the interpellation.[21] These competing narratives indicate the heightened level of tension that coursed through the current political environment.

Finally, on Friday, September 18, 1953, the day arrived on which Ponce would have to face the charges leveled against him. *El Comercio* published an editorial in support of the questioning:

> Today the interpellation will be made of the minister of government, which is a legal and democratic act that in no case can be allowed to become cause

for scandals or much less to provoke acts of force or agitation without a civic sense of any kind.

The editorial proceeded to note that it was well known that the government held a majority in congress and undoubtedly the body would vote in favor of the minister. Nevertheless, the paper defended the right of the legal process to proceed forward for the betterment of the country. The editorial called for the interpellation to be conducted in a respectful and measured fashion.[22] Meanwhile, telegrams in support of Saad continued to flow in from labor and other groups.[23]

The joint session of congress convened at 5:15 in the afternoon. *El Comercio* reported that the visitors' gallery was full of spectators who chanted against communism, socialism, liberalism, and the CFP, and cheered in support of the minister of government. The conservatives had packed the hall, and Saad would be facing an antagonistic audience. Alfredo Chiriboga Chiriboga, the country's vice president who presided over the session, asked for quiet in the chamber, and stated that the gallery would be cleared if the visitors did not remain silent. The secretary then read out the constitutional provisions that allowed for the interpellation and the charges that the minister faced. Article 55 of the 1946 Constitution granted a joint session of congress (*congreso pleno*) the right to "examine the official behavior of the ministers of state, and censure them if there is a reason."[24] Legally, Saad could not be denied his day in court.

Saad proceeded to lay out his reasons for initiating the charges against Ponce. He proclaimed that the government's policies and violations of the constitution had brought political unrest and an economic crisis to the entire country. The government had engaged in undemocratic measures. Imprisonments and violations of peoples' rights continued without end. The country faced the choice of remaining under the current autocratic system, or returning to the rule of law. Saad declared that those who brought the charges were simply complying with their responsibilities as representatives of the people. He asserted that this interpellation grew out of respect for the constitution. The communist leader denied that any political interest underlay the interpellation, or that they were seeking political advantage through this process. They were not engaging in the interrogation as members of a political party. In fact, he noted, those who brought the questions came from different parties. Rather, the interpellation reflected the will of the Ecuadorian people, a defense of the constitution that the government had violated countless times, and an act in support of democratic rule.

After a lengthy debate over procedural issues, Ponce began a defense of his actions. He presented an overview of the history of Ecuador's political development, highlighting that for much of its existence the country had followed a path of anarchy and demagoguery. Saad stopped the minister to thank him for the history lesson, but asked him to limit his comments to the questions currently under consideration. Despite the interruption, Ponce continued his exposition, synthesizing the dates of the various constitutions that had been promulgated in Ecuador. The minister contended that Ecuadorians lived under an abstract idea of freedom, something granted by a deity that could be lost if care was not taken to defend those rights.

The minister then proceeded to respond to the charges one by one, starting with the closure of the newspapers *La Nación* and *La Hora*. Ever since he had assumed his cabinet post on February 18, the papers had launched virulent and personal attacks against him, and over the following months this had risen to the point of inciting rebellions that presented a serious threat to the stability of the government. Whereas Saad had charged the minister with having violated the constitution, Ponce countered that the government had taken the step of closing the papers to preserve public order. The minister contended that the constitution not only defended the rights of free speech, but also placed responsibilities on those who made public statements. The problem existed only with certain papers that acted in an irresponsible manner, and therefore was not a systemic issue. When the media operated responsibly, the minister declared, the government respected them, but when they acted in a criminal fashion the government would sanction their activities.

Ponce then read his correspondence with the Central University's rector in response to the second question concerning the alleged violation of the university's autonomy. He asked why a government minister could not correspond with a university rector without risking violation of the law. Furthermore, the accusations concerned the FEUE, which Ponce maintained was an organization that was neither related to the university nor comprised of university students but instead was a political group with its own agenda that attacked the ministry of government on a daily basis. That the FEUE acted in such a fashion was unacceptable, he declared. Ponce also criticized the UDU at the University of Guayaquil that was associated with the IUS based in Prague. Its only concern was to spread Marxist propaganda with the goal of undermining Ecuador's constitutionally established government. As evidence of the UDU's communist orientation, the minister pointed to a telegram he had received from the IUS demanding the release of the student leader Luis Arcentales. Ponce said that as an Ecuadorian and a member of the government, he would fight to prevent Ecuador from falling under Moscow's domination and being trapped behind the "iron curtain." He contended that the government had to act to counter the subversive threats emanating out of the university, and was justified in doing so because Ecuadorians were a Christian and Catholic people.

The third issue concerned allegations of illegal detentions, and Ponce said that he would provide the congress with documentation to respond to each accusation. The minister began with the first charge concerning the arrest of Evangelical preachers in Cotocollao. In March, local Catholics attacked Protestant Evangelicals who were proselytizing in the northern suburb of Quito. Police had to intervene to reestablish order.[25] Ponce justified their arrest as a response to an attack on the Catholic religion that violated Article 168 of the constitution that sanctioned actions that contributed to public unrest. Conflicts with Evangelicals had been going on for some time, and communist support for their rights can be interpreted as either a principled defense of freedom of religion or an opportunistic exploitation of an issue to attack an extremely Catholic and conservative minister.

The second case concerned Nelson Chávez, the secretary general of the railroad union, who for years had been fighting for the rights of those workers. Chávez gained heightened animosity from conservatives when he traveled to Beijing in October 1952 to attend the World Peace Congress. Upon his return Ponce charged him with subversive activities, which led the head of the government-owned railroad company to fire Chávez under accusations "of fomenting disorder for political reasons." Chávez had organized a strike in opposition to the government's rigorous antilabor measures that included a plan to reorganize the railroad and eliminate jobs with the intent of purging leftist workers. Ponce charged that the strike was part of a communist plot and ordered the labor leaders arrested and other workers fired in an attempt to undermine their union.[26]

At this point, the congressional leadership ruled that the documentation regarding the multiple charges that Saad had raised was well known, and that there was no need for Ponce to respond to each one, and therefore they would pass on to the fourth point. Cevallos Cedeño, one of the four deputies who had brought the charges, objected and insisted that the congress should hear a full response to each item. Although several deputies supported Cevallos Cedeño, the procedural vote went against him. Saad protested that the congressional leadership was impeding the interpellation process. Despite these protestations, Ponce proceeded on to the next question.

Ponce denied that he had intervened in other ministries to act against worker interests, including the firing of railroad workers and teachers. Since all of the ministries were part of the same executive branch, Ponce argued, the complaint of intervention in other branches of government logically made no sense and therefore did not violate any constitutional provisions. In terms of the specific issue of separating the leaders of the railroad union from their employment, the minister contended that the government had simply recognized the decision that the company had made in order to maintain internal peace and order in the face of a threatened general strike. In a second case of a fired journalist, the action was justified for security concerns because he had engaged in open opposition to the government.

The fifth question addressed the massacre at La Merced. A long history of exploitation on the estate had led to rising tensions with the Indigenous workers finally forming a union to press their demands for better treatment. On August 6, the workers attacked a particularly abusive overseer when he broke from the tradition of providing women with a portion of the potatoes that they were harvesting for their own domestic use. When the owners called in the police to put down the protest, the officers responded with lethal force leaving three workers dead, fourteen injured, and twenty-five imprisoned.[27] The minister justified the use of violence with the contention that the owners of the hacienda had requested that the police intervene to reestablish order. It was only for that reason that the government had sent a squad of seven police officers. Furthermore, the protesters had injured the police as well as a local priest who accompanied them in the hopes of appeasing the workers. Ponce contended that the violence the officials faced justified the armed response, and that the issue was one of following judicial procedures rather than an administrative matter. In fact, Ponce expressed surprise that only two days earlier a judge had ordered the release of the protesters who had been detained. This action had been taken even though those charged had set fire to a granary on the hacienda and damaged more than 1,200 quintales of wheat.

In terms of the loan for the colonization of the Amazon, the sixth question on the list, the minister justified his actions based on security concerns, that the Amazon was a symbol of Ecuadorian nationality and that the region represented the country's future. The people who lived in the area needed access to transportation, and since the ministry of public works lacked funds the president of the country had requested the loan. As an Ecuadorian and a patriot, Ponce claimed he could not refuse to help his compatriots when they needed his assistance. Furthermore, he did not act alone but with the unanimous support of other administrators. In fact, he maintained, the loan had already been repaid and therefore that no damage had been done.

The minister responded simultaneously to the seventh and eighth questions concerning the confiscation of printed matter from the mail. He denied that he had ordered the ministry of public works to intervene with postal deliveries. In any case, Ponce justified government action in seizing communist propaganda that could damage the country's international relations, claiming that doing so was legal and legitimate. Ecuador was a Western democratic republic, Ponce contended, and needed to defend itself from foreign communist aggression. Upon investigating the existence of the Librería Ecuador, the authorities discovered that the bookstore only existed as a collection of communist propaganda in the house of María Luisa Gómez de la Torre. Although the mail service could have destroyed the books, instead they had returned them to Moscow from whence they had come. The minister argued that he was fully within his constitutional rights to take the action that he did. British ambassador Norman Mayers similarly challenged Gómez de la Torre's claim that the "books were purely literary works and not propaganda material." He maintained that the items "provide the channel for subsidising the Communist party funds, the proceeds of sale not being remitted back," even though the press had not reported their purpose as such.[28] Arguably, one person's propaganda is another person's art, and in either case disruption of mail delivery was a blow to the communist party's political agenda.

After responding to Saad's eight questions, Ponce warned that communist penetration had reached an unprecedented level in Ecuador. He asked how people could remain calm in the face of this threat. It was for this reason that the government would not tolerate the corrupting influence of communist propaganda. Ponce pledged that as minister of government he would apply the country's laws with all of its rigor and might in order to save the country from foreign influences. Anticommunist sentiments ran deeply through his presentation. Leftist sentiments presented the greatest challenge to his conservative politics and Catholic faith.

It was then Saad's turn to interrogate the minister. He began with the closure of *La Nación* and *La Hora*. As CFP publications, they were not sympathetic to a communist agenda. Saad's defense of them can be interpreted as either an opportunistic gesture to seek allies in a campaign against a common enemy, or a principled stance in support of freedom of the press. Saad took this second tack. He asked Ponce whether the government had evidence that the newspapers were engaged in seditious activities. Again, the minister defended his actions with references to the current 1946 Constitution, which led to debates regarding what current legislation regulated press activities and who had the right to interpret constitutional provisions. Saad accused Ponce of leading the government toward a dictatorial regime that would freely engage in arbitrary acts of repression. Referencing specific constitutional articles and other legislation, Saad asserted that Ponce had violated the freedom of the press. The minister, naturally, was not willing to concede this point.

Saad stated that he would leave the second and third questions of violations of the Central University autonomy and of illegal detentions to his colleagues Cevallos Cedeño and Grijalva. Instead, as the senator representing labor, he turned to the fourth question concerning Ponce's intervention in other ministries to act against worker interests. Saad began with the firing of Chávez and fifteen other labor leaders and workers from the railroad under accusations of organizing a strike. The government had denied the workers their constitutional right to strike, Saad asserted. He stated that he had repeatedly asked the ministry of government for copies of documents related to this case but the ministry had never sent them. Fortunately, he received documents from the railroad company that demonstrated collusion between the government and the company to remove the workers. Saad also raised the case of Humberto Vacas Gómez who had been fired from his teaching position at the Colegio Nacional 24 de Mayo for his opposition to the government. Saad produced documents that supported his charges, and asked the minister how it was possible to deny his accusations of collusion between the ministry and those autonomous entities. Saad charged that Ecuadorians had been left subject to the government's political whims. The outcome, he asserted, was a violation of constitutional free speech rights.

In his questioning of Ponce, Saad apparently skipped over the fifth question regarding the massacre of workers at La Merced, or at least neither the official record of congressional debates in the legislative archive nor the newspaper reports in *El Comercio* make mention of any comments he might have made on that topic. In part that absence was predictable, and reflects a long-held division in the PCE between those in the highlands banded around Paredes with an interest in rural peasant and Indigenous communities, and those on the coast grouped around Saad with their base in urban labor movements. Even in both of these camps, the communist reach was limited, which left the PCE open to charges of exploiting other peoples' struggles when the party called attention to their oppression and exploitation. Even if that were the case, it is surprising that Saad would not raise the issue in his interpellation, if for no other reason than to weaken his political opponent.

On the other hand, perhaps that documentary record is in error. In his history of Indigenous struggles, the communist historian Oswaldo Albornoz

Peralta highlights Saad's interpellation of Ponce as putting responsibility for the massacre directly at the feet of the minister of government.[29] Furthermore, Ponce made a similar acknowledgment in his annual report on the ministry's activity. "The upheaval at La Merced immediately preceded the interpellation that senator Saad and others brought against the minister of government," Ponce stated in a summary of his activities, "and coincided with an intense campaign of insults and incitements made in Quito against the minister of government." According to Ponce, the interpellation "was not about isolated events, but on the contrary, planned and directed towards the achievement of an end." According to Ponce, all of this emerged manifestly apparent in newspaper reports at the time.[30] It could be that the ethnocentric attitudes that deemed rural Indigenous struggles not worthy of attention were not those of Saad but rather of the congressional recorder and media outlets. Alternatively, in the absence of an advocate such as Paredes who had long pressed for the rights of Indigenous communities, all sides may have been just as happy to let the issue slide.

Saad then turned to the seventh and eighth questions concerning the confiscation of material from the postal service, and again raised allegations of violations of constitutional rights and other laws. Saad reviewed the legislation regulating the handling of the mail, and declared that no provision existed to confiscate material transmitted through the post office. Furthermore, Saad denied that the publications in question challenged the country's peace and tranquility. Rather, they addressed topics such as philosophy, science, biography, and literature. Saad repeated previous statements that the minister could not demonstrate that the books violated the country's harmony.

Saad attempted to use Ponce's own actions again him. On July 19, 1944, when serving as foreign minister in Velasco Ibarra's second government he had signed Decree 302 that denounced those implicated in the disastrous 1941 war with Peru. That action underscored the inalienable rights of people. At this point, the liberal senator from Esmeraldas César Plaza Monzón angrily protested Saad's statement, declaring that these were personal rather than political issues. Saad responded by saying that he would publish the charges in the press, and ended his statement by once again underscoring his argument that the minister had violated constitutional guarantees.

Cevallos Cedeño and Grijalva then took their turns at bringing charges against the minister, including underscoring points that Saad had already made and touching on other issues that Saad had not addressed. In his responses, Ponce returned to the theme of a fear of communist infiltration, particularly in educational institutions. He declared that the government enjoyed popular support, and would continue to do so regardless of the charges brought against him. He also stated that because of his belief in his god and country the government would not fall. It was those nationalistic and theocratic attitudes that demonstrated a wide gap between Ponce and his communist opponents.

It was almost midnight when the CFP deputy Macías Hurtado finally had an opportunity to raise his question of the expulsion of his party leader Guevara Moreno, which again sparked debates concerning constitutional rights and threats to the country. Furthermore, Ponce charged that in exile Guevara Moreno had maintained contact with Peruvian exiles, which demonstrated the danger he presented to the country. Once again, the minister resorted to nationalistic and xenophobic sentiments to defend his actions.

Numerous representatives came to Saad's defense. Benjamín Carrión, a socialist and senator representing media interests, began his comments by defending the Casa de la Cultura, which he had founded, from the minister's charges that it was a center for communist indoctrination. He emphasized that Ponce had completely evaded the questions placed to him, and failed to provide a constitutional basis for the closure of *La Nación* and *La Hora*. Alfredo Pérez Guerrero, also a socialist and senator for higher education, similarly defended the universities and the CTE from the minister's attacks. Both senators represented a unified left opposition to the conservative minister's political stances.

At 1:45 a.m., Ponce left the chamber and the congress entered into debate over the charges. Saad argued that what they had just witnessed was the reality that the country was currently experiencing. He observed that the minister effectively dodged the questions that they had brought. Saad criticized Ponce for steering the discussion in a doctrinaire direction when in reality the charges had little to do with those issues. The communist deputy denied that he had interviewed Guevara Moreno in Lima as Ponce had charged. Saad pointed out that the PCE had always been opposed to the CFP, and that the minister was only trying to denigrate the legitimacy of his party. Ponce had effectively played at cleavages between his opponents.

In an attempt to refocus the conversation on a united attack against the minister, Saad charged that Ponce had not been able to respond with arguments, but only used sophistry to hide from the charges. If the congress accepted Ponce's contention that a minister could determine whether or not a law was constitutional, Saad contended, Ecuador would be living in a frank and open dictatorship. He accused the minister of attempting to control Ecuador through a repressive political police. Saad closed his statement with a declaration that he was confident that the congress would vote to censor the minister of government.

Despite demands from some deputies to continue the debate, at 4:20 a.m. the chamber moved to a vote on the motion. Despite Saad's best efforts, with a conservative majority in the congress the outcome was a foregone conclusion. The motion failed with seventy-two votes against and fifteen in favor. Elections matter. At 6:20 a.m., the marathon session finally came to a close.

Mail Intercept Operations

The confiscation of communist propaganda from the mail that Saad denounced in the interpellation relates to larger issues of CIA surveillance and the obstacles that the PCE had to overcome to advance their political agenda. From the beginning of CIA operations, information reports point to the presence of undercover agents in the Ecuadorian government. One example is the interception of an airmailed circular with the return address of a commercial firm in Paris that Saad received via a Syrian business in Guayaquil. The CIA case officer was aware of the contents of the circular, which denounced the Marshall Plan and outlined the special conditions that Latin America faced in countering a United States imperial agenda.[31] Subsequent CIA reports reference instructions that Saad received "from Europe through clandestine channels" that indicate the ongoing presence of a successful spy operation despite communist attempts to evade surveillance.[32] PCE treasurer Gómez de la Torre also received a letter from Moscow concerning the provision of paper supplies. The correspondence was the result of a conversation that Paredes had during a recent trip to Warsaw. The particulars in the CIA report, including the date of letter (December 11, 1950) and a description of the letterhead (Mezhduna Rodnaja Kniga, Moscow), in addition to the contents of the letter points to the presence of an intercept in the Ecuadorian post office.[33] All indications are that these operations had been in place for years and probably predated the CIA—most likely as a continuation of FBI and other previous investigations that included collaboration with Ecuadorian state security forces.

In his exposé of CIA operations in the early 1960s, Philip Agee describes the intercept operation in which an agent in the central post office in Quito provided the agency with the incoming airmail pouch. A CIA officer opened, read, and photographed letters of interest, and returned the letters to the post office on the same day for delivery. The officer reported the contents of the most relevant correspondence to CIA Headquarters in Washington and perhaps other stations.[34] Although intelligence officers did not always understand the information they acquired and were willing to exaggerate its importance to satisfy their superiors, these operations provide historians with access to a level of detail on communist activities that otherwise would not be available.

Naturally, communists sought ways to counter this surveillance. A CIA report from 1948 on international communist movements acknowledged that parties only sent routine communications through the mail, preferring instead to communicate important orders verbally. When that was not possible, couriers might carry written instructions, but with the additional protection of codes and secret ink. When the mail was used, correspondence was typically sent to cover addresses, or hand carried across borders and posted domestically to prevent surveillance of international mail. In Ecuador, a communist cell had infiltrated the post office and extracted mail addressed to their comrades for personal delivery. That the CIA was aware of this level of communist penetration of the mail service highlights the detail of information that the agency was able to acquire. Recognizing an awareness that opponents were reading their correspondence, the agency admitted, "documents purporting to contain 'orders' or 'instructions' from one Party to another have thus far been generally found to be forged."[35] While fake documents could be useful for propaganda purposes, they are less valuable as intelligence or historical sources. If the most crucial information was only communicated orally, that also means that some of the most important records of communist activities have been lost to history.

A CIA informer cautioned that Colombian communists could be using greeting cards to communicate with their counterparts in Ecuador. A confidential information report identified Ana Moreno as a "prominent Guayaquil Communist" who received a New Year's card from PCC leader Gilberto Vieira White. The card appeared innocuous, but on careful examination Moreno informed her comrade Medina Castro that a courier would come from Colombia with instructions for the party. Indeed, secretary general Vieira White did presently arrive in Quito by plane from Cali. This sequence of events led the CIA to conclude that the communists were using the mail to communicate surreptitiously with one another. What the CIA report does not explain is how they were able to acquire intimate details on Moreno's actions, or why they were now conducting surveillance on a militant whom they had previously largely ignored.[36]

Similar CIA operations intercepted information from other communication systems, including telegrams. One example concerned a decision to send Nela Martínez to the World Peace Congress in Paris. That congress in 1949 and the World Peace Council (WPC) founded the following year was part of the socialist bloc's "peace offensive" or peace campaign designed to build global political resistance to US "warmongering" and aggression against socialist countries.

Under the guidance of the French physicist and activist Frédéric Joliot-Curie, the WPC advocated for universal disarmament, sovereignty, independence, and peaceful co-existence. It campaigned against imperialism, weapons of mass destruction, and all forms of discrimination.[37] In an information report on this development, a CIA case officer noted "that Martínez had received a personal invitation from Madame [Irène] Joliot Curie to attend the Congress." The source of that intelligence "had seen the cablegram but had not noted the name of the cable company." When the case officer investigated further, he discovered that the All American Cable Company had not transmitted such a cable. This led to the conclusion "that the cable was forged in order to account for Martínez's sudden decision to attend the Congress."[38] The use of the passive voice makes it unclear as to who would have forged the cable and why. Did Martínez take this step to justify her travel, or did the CIA's agent do so in order to have something to report to the agency? And if the person in question indeed did see a cable, was this person a friend of Martínez's, an informer in the cable company, or was this the result of some other surveillance operation? Unfortunately, the available documentation is silent on these issues.

Even though the CIA monitored a variety of correspondence, the agency was particularly concerned with the importation of printed materials. In one curious case, someone had mailed multiple copies of the Russian-language publication *Prazhskie Novosti* from Prague addressed (in English) to "The Legation of the USSR, Quito," even though the Soviet Union did not currently have a diplomatic mission in that country. Apparently the Ecuadorian government gave the mailing to the embassy, and the CIA officer, military attaché, and public affairs officer all independently forwarded a copy of the periodical to their corresponding headquarters in Washington.[39] In February 1951, a case officer reported that A. D. Bolaños, a local agent in Quito, had received fifty copies in Spanish of the weekly newspaper *New Times* from the USSR. The party had also received periodicals in French and English, including a bi-monthly magazine *La Femme soviétique* for circulation among PCE members and Ecuadorian women in general.[40] Not incidentally, this interference in the delivery of material to Quito corresponded to similar meddling in Guayaquil that the CIA had reported as an example of the government's heightened efficiency in the interception of propaganda material.[41]

The mail intercept operations continued throughout the 1950s and beyond. In 1956, the embassy's PAO Walter Bastian reported that a limited amount of printed material reached Ecuador. Before the dissolution of the Cominform earlier that year, about one hundred copies of its periodical *For a Lasting Peace,*

For a People's Democracy was mailed to twenty people weekly who were then responsible for further distribution. Other regularly mailed material included the monthly *Czechoslovakia Today* and the *World Student News*. Not much of this material reached its intended recipients because "Ecuadoran postal authorities regularly and successfully intercept the bulk of the shipments of communist and satellite periodicals mailed into this country, at the rate of ten or twelve sacks the size of diplomatic pouches." Bastian estimated that the confiscations represented a loss of about $500 USD per month for the communists.[42] In 1957, the United States Embassy reported that the ouster of Czech diplomats closed the possibility of receiving funds, propaganda, and messages through that mission. According to the CIA, the communists then turned to the CTE as a venue for the receipt of international messages, and the party received "14 to 16 large mail sacks of communist propaganda" every month via that route. Even so, the current Ponce administration was realizing success in "intercepting and destroying large amounts of incoming communist propaganda," and that made United States officials happy.[43]

The PCE faced overwhelming opposition, both domestically and internationally, to the realization of its political agenda. Ironically, CIA surveillance chronicles communist awareness of the challenges that they faced and the measures that they took in an attempt to overcome these barriers. Even in the face of these challenges, the committed activists were determined to continue their struggles.

Legislative Defeat, Propaganda Victory

The Pichincha provincial committee of the PCE responded to the attacks on Saad that emerged out of the interpellation with a pair of statements condemning Ponce and the ARNE. The communists denounced reactionary attempts to silence Saad, and called their leader the best opponent against fascism and the strongest supporter of democracy and freedom.[44] The PCE pointed out that during Saad's time in congress he had been the firmest and best defender of popular interests and most steadfast opponent of corruption and the violations of human rights and democratic guarantees. The party denounced government charges that the communists opposed religion, repeating what they had proclaimed on multiple occasions that they favored freedom of religion, consciousness, and thought. Furthermore, the communists fought against hunger and misery that resulted from government policies. The PCE pointed out that the government did not discriminate between Catholics and nonbelievers when it engaged in massacres of Indigenous communities or enacted polices that hurt workers. Everyone, regardless of religious beliefs, suffered the consequences of wealthy landholder and capitalist policies. The party also rejected allegations that they were collaborating with the CFP in their attacks on the government. This was an absurd charge, the statement declared, as it repeated Saad's proclamation that communists had long been the firmest opponents of Guevara Moreno and his fascist forces. All of the terrorist attacks on the communists could not stop the forward march of the people. The PCE called on all democratic organizations and political parties to join them in a struggle against fascism.[45]

Although Ponce concentrated most of his fire on the communists, he was equally opposed to the socialists. In his ministerial report the following year, he attacked the socialist party for its opportunistic defense of the interpellation. He accused their members of twisting the truth when they championed the actions of "a distinguished socialist, comrade Joel Cevallos, who advanced the accusations of beaten and massacred workers and peasants." Ponce charged that such statements were political nonsense that included assertions devoid of logic and failed to adhere to ethical standards of political behavior.[46]

The socialists responded to Ponce's attacks with a statement that proclaimed that their party was engaged in a long-term struggle against the government's reactionary and totalitarian actions, and especially against the minister's vain and scandalous deeds. Their statement denounced among other things "the wealthy landholders' open complicity with the police murder of defenseless Indians." At the same time, the party sought to distance itself from communism. The PSE denied that it was under the control of Moscow, that it was part of any international movement, or that it received "Moscow gold." Rather, it was an autonomous organization that fought for the rights of the Ecuadorian people. Similar to the communists, the socialists declared that they were not opposed to religion. Instead, they called on workers, students, members of other democratic parties, and all progressive forces to stand up and fight decisively and energetically for the right to remain free rather than to become miserable slaves.[47]

For his part, British ambassador Mayers belittled Saad's leadership in the interpellation as nothing more than a communist move toward the construction of a united front. He acknowledged that Ponce was guilty "of various arbitrary acts and measures of the last six months which were considered to be derogatory to the freedom of the press, of speech and of opinion." Ponce's adversaries called him "reactionary and illiberal, probably not without reason." Some of the minister's actions, such as the banishment of Guayaquil mayor Guevara Moreno, "were urgently necessary, though unconstitutional." Others, such as the arrest of *El Comercio*'s editor Jorge Mantilla Ortega, "were unnecessary and inexcusable." Unfortunately, his behavior led to a united opposition among liberals and socialists. Opponents selected Saad to lead the attack because "he was the best orator available," and because the passion that Ponce stirred was such that his enemies "cared little who led the attack." Mayers concluded that "Saad did *not* dominate the debate as was expected of him," but nevertheless "he got somehow to the spearpoint of the attack." In providing leadership, Saad gained "well-wishers in quarters where sympathy with Communism is never thought of." But this was also a double-edged sword, and led to the failure of the interpellation because of "the very fact of the improvised communist leadership." Mayers pointed to this as the primary reason why the opposition did not realize more success in their attack. "The spectacle of a Communist, however eloquent and master of debate, declaiming against dictatorship (the alleged dictatorship of the present government of Velasco Ibarra) and demanding the freedom of the press was a bit too much of a good thing." Even so, the interpellation was a propaganda victory for the communists because it was undeniable that Saad led a democratic attack, and he would be remembered for doing so.[48] The interpellation represented a political gain for Saad and his supporters.

The United States Embassy had a similar evaluation. Although Ponce avoided the vote of censure by almost a five to one margin, chargé d'affaires Thomas Maleady commented that from a legal or constitutional perspective Ponce did not perform well. The minister dodged the larger and more important questions rather than confronting them directly, and his answers tended to be vague and inconclusive. Maleady inferred that "while the embassy naturally is fully in favor of scotching Communism," the nationalist and authoritarian tendencies of Velasco Ibarra, Ponce, and the ARNE was not a preferable alternative. "One extreme could be as bad as the other," the chargé declared. He feared that a temporary period of political peace was evaporating in this perennially unstable country.[49]

On October 3, the communists held a meeting in Cotocollao to celebrate Saad's success. The party sold tickets for twenty sucres a piece, which included food and drink. A CIA officer commented that the meeting was more of a success than Saad's interpellation given that the censure vote lost by a large margin. An informer noted that some PCE leaders considered Saad's poor showing to be a major defeat for the party, and that Echeverría and Barreto were making moves to replace Saad as the party's secretary general.[50] But both sides missed the point of the interpellation. At best censoring Ponce might have removed an unpopular minister, but it would not have fundamentally changed the country's rightward drift. In contrast, Saad's strong showing helped brace against rising anticommunist sentiments.

A subsequent CIA information report highlighted the participation of Carlos Cueva Tamariz and Mario Veintimilla at the fiesta. Cueva Tamariz, the socialist party member, rector of the University of Cuenca, and senator, attended with his two sons, Patricio, the communist who had lashed out at fellow members in a self-criticism session at the previous year's party congress, and Mariano. Both in this document and in others, the CIA indicated their concern with the elder Cueva Tamariz's "pro-Communist activities."[51] The British Embassy articulated a somewhat more measured assessment of Cueva Tamariz. Their report characterized him as "a Socialist with tendencies towards the Left of that Party." He was "one of the most qualified for office," and had demonstrated this through his performance in several governmental posts, including as deputy in congress, minister of government and education, and as socialist candidate for vice president in 1948. The British Embassy concluded that Cueva Tamariz was "a respected Socialist but difficult to place."[52] It was Saad's ability to build alliances with such prominent political figures that so worried government officials.

Veintimilla, the other person the CIA officer mentioned in the report on the fete for Saad, had been an alternate for Ponce's seat as senator for highland agricultural interests. Veintimilla was "an elderly man from Cuenca" who said "he was too old to take an active part in the Communist movement, but that he anticipated the coming of a world-wide Communist revolution, and he hoped that it would come soon." Veintimilla also said that he had two sons who were members of the PCE.[53] While that may have been the case, neither the father nor his sons otherwise appeared in the CIA surveillance or played a significant role in the party. His presence, though, does point to the array of forces allied against Ponce.

COMMUNIST DEPUTY PEDRO SAAD's interpellation of Velasco Ibarra's conservative minister of government Camilo Ponce Enríquez provided the left with an opportunity to place their political agenda on public display for all to see. Even though Saad lost the vote in congress, he gained respect because of his conscientious and serious engagement with important issues. That strategy also underscored his embrace of a peaceful and parliamentary path to power. Even so, a rising anticommunist tide in the midst of growing cold war tensions created significant obstacles for the left to advance its agenda. CIA surveillance provides scholars with an opportunity to peek inside communist party structures to understand how militants organized themselves to advance their political agendas. That surveillance reveals that party members understood that their struggle would be long and hard, and despite the forces allied against them they were committed to staying in it for the long haul.

CHAPTER 10

Communist Threats

THE CONSERVATIVE MINISTER OF government Camilo Ponce Enríquez not only survived near constant attacks from his liberal and leftist opponents, but he also won the 1956 presidential election—though with the smallest plurality of the vote in Ecuador's history. Even so, he pressed forward in an unrelenting fashion with his conservative agenda, which in large part was designed to marginalize those on the left. Despite those challenges, his years in office corresponded with a resurgence in leftist strength. Among indications of rising communist fortunes was the party's ability to hold its sixth congress a year after Ponce's election.

Ponce's election and the PCE congress took place in the aftermath of the death of Joseph Stalin on March 5, 1953, and his replacement with Nikita Khrushchev as general secretary of the Communist Party of the Soviet Union (CPSU). Khrushchev undertook a program of liberalization, and famously denounced Stalin's crimes at the twentieth congress of the CPSU in February 1956. Among Khrushchev's complaints was Stalin's cult of personality, his excessive concentration of power in the hands of one individual, and his use of authoritarian and repressive measures to maintain societal control. Following on the heels of the CPSU congress, an October 1956 uprising in Hungary threatened to topple that country's communist government. A large Soviet military force crushed the protests and returned the communists to power. After five years as United States ambassador to Hungary, Christian Ravndal departed on the eve of the uprising to take up his new post in Ecuador. Ravndal said that during his time in Hungary he had observed a move toward liberalization, with a relaxation of political control and more latitude for people to express their views. The uprising did not surprise him, but he had not expected it to happen so quickly.[1]

This sequence of events—Stalin's death, Khrushchev's denunciations, and the repression of the Hungarian uprising—sent shockwaves around the world and eventually led to splits in communist parties as some clung to a Stalinist line while others advocated for more openness. Furthermore, a deterioration of relations between China and the Soviet Union eventually led to the Sino-Soviet split. As elsewhere, all of these issues played out inside the Ecuadorian communist party with dissidents complaining of Saad's bureaucratic and reformist line and demanding that the party take more aggressive and militant action. All of these factors in addition to the triumph of the Cuban Revolution in 1959 contributed to the rise in the 1960s of what came to be known as a "new left" that rejected dogmatic approaches to Marxist theory.

Throughout this entire time, CIA officers and other United States government officials maintained their surveillance of the PCE. A result is a rich documentary record that offers glimpses into how militants responded to these changing landscapes. In confronting the twin challenges of first José María Velasco Ibarra's populist government and then the open hostility of his conservative minister Ponce followed with his subsequent reign as president, the PCE continued to organize along both electoral and social movement axes. Underneath and countervailing what the election of a conservative president would seem to indicate, United States surveillance points to a rising tide of social mobilizations.

CIA Officers

The election of President Dwight Eisenhower in 1952 and his nomination of Allen Dulles as the Director of Central Intelligence (DCI) represented a shift in the CIA from its original purpose as an intelligence-gathering and coordinating agency to one that engaged in covert operations designed to advance the president's political agenda. Harry Rositzke who worked with the CIA during its first quarter century and finished his career as a senior officer in the agency's clandestine services describes this turn to covert action in the mid-1950s. This activity included "distributing propaganda, supporting non-Communist student congresses, sponsoring or subsidizing anti-Communist publications," and creating youth, student, and labor groups that would extend those objectives.[2] During the first years of the Eisenhower administration, CIA information reports continued to trickle out of Ecuador but at a slower rate and with a different emphasis than earlier. Much of the material that the CIA has released discusses mundane topics characteristic of State Department dispatches, such as details on mining operations, wages, roads, and ports.[3] By the mid-1950s, these reports, which initially provided keen insights into internal communist party dynamics, disappear from the cache of documents that the CIA has made available. Oblique references in the diplomatic correspondence to "an officer of the Embassy's staff representing another agency" indicates the continued presence and activity of CIA case officers.[4] What we do know from Philip Agee is that in the early 1960s he continued to draft reports for consumption in Washington, and that the agency's penetration of the PCE resulted in five or six per week.[5] It is not clear if these records were lost, destroyed, or still remain to be declassified. Perhaps with a turn from an intelligence to a covert action arm of the government, the CIA is reticent to release material that would document its illegal activities. If and when their information reports come to light, they will provide a boom for a study of the Latin American left. Meanwhile, a lack of access to this surveillance limits our ability to gain a fuller understanding of communist actions.

After several years in the early 1950s during which it is difficult to pinpoint the identities of individual CIA officers in Ecuador, beginning in 1954 once again their identities emerge out in the open even though we currently have less access to the memos that they drafted than we do for their predecessors. Even so, recognizing who conducted surveillance allows for a fuller and deeper investigation of agency actions. CIA Chief of Station Ned Holman arrived in Quito in November 1954 and his deputy Comer Wiley Gilstrap followed in March 1955. Holman served under the cover of attaché in the embassy, and subsequently went on to similar posts in Argentina, Uruguay, and Guatemala. After his appointment to Argentina, in March 1960 he appears in the *Foreign Service List* as assigned to the State Department in Washington, apparently his official cover while at CIA Headquarters, but then he disappears from the publication although other CIA officers continue to be listed.[6] Gilstrap, whose cover in Quito was political officer, later served in Brazil, Uruguay, El Salvador, Guyana, and ultimately as COS in San José, Costa Rica. With the available information, it is difficult to say whether Holman and Gilstrap were the only two operatives in Ecuador until the expansion of the post in the aftermath of the Cuban Revolution, and who besides Howard Shetterly was present between Albert Haney's departure in 1949 and their arrival.

Holman collaborated closely and seamlessly with the United States Embassy. As one example, Secretary of State John Foster Dulles requested that each embassy designate a liaison officer to work directly with local government officials to exchange information on communist activities.[7] Ambassador Sheldon Mills immediately named "Political Attaché Holman" to this position.[8] His counterpart in the Ecuadorian government was Jaime Sánchez, an official in the police department and a private secretary to the minister of government.[9] Holman was a logical choice, and his designation allowed him to continue his surveillance operations that were already in place. Shortly after his designation the embassy's counselor William Wieland asked for Holman's assistance in digging out information on "known communists," and requested his cooperation in checking the names of those who were reportedly involved in communist activities.[10] Wieland, in turn, passed this information on to Ambassador Mills.[11] Dulles approved of this collaboration, and instructed diplomats to coordinate their anticommunist activities with "CAS" (that is, the CIA station), the PAO, and military attachés in the embassy.[12] The USIA similarly instructed its PAOs to provide the liaison, which in the case of Ecuador was Holman, with copies of anticommunist propaganda.[13] Different branches of the government collaborated extensively around a shared anticommunist agenda.

As a CIA officer, Holman supplied the embassy with services that others could not or did not want to undertake, even to the point of engaging in unpleasant and even illegal activities. One example was when the embassy's PAO Walter Bastian met with two young communist party defectors, Mario Cárdenas and Luis Vargas. Both had joined the party in high school and were active members. Several years earlier, Holman's predecessor had listed Cárdenas as the finance secretary of the JCE.[14] Now both were on the verge of graduating from university and were concerned that their communist affiliation would hinder them in their job searches. Not only were they "outcasts of good society," but their fellow communists also regarded them with suspicion. Bastian surmised that they could "both be bought, probably fairly reasonable." The United States Information Service (USIS), however, was "most eager to get out from under this type of operation." Either recognizing the danger of conceding that propaganda endeavors bled over into covert operations or wishing to keep the two tasks separate in a division of labor that might have also reflected a certain amount of turf battles, Holman changed the text from "get out" to "stay out of this type of operation."[15] Rather curiously, a year later Holman's successor James Noland included both Cárdenas and Vargas on a list of delegates to the Sixth World Festival of Youth and Students in Moscow. He listed both as communists, but provided no indication of their earlier contact with the embassy.[16] In retrospect, it is unclear whether the two were attempting to infiltrate an anticommunist operative, had changed their minds about defecting, were now working for the CIA as agents reporting on communist activities, or simply did not want to pass up the opportunity to travel to Moscow. Agee subsequently worked under Holman in Uruguay and described him as incompetent.[17] His failures in recruiting the two may be an indication of those shortcomings.

Although it could serve the interests of those on many different sides to exaggerate the level of communist support and strength, it is also notable when various parties refused to do so. One example came in the aftermath of an interview that José Ricardo Chiriboga Villagómez, Ecuador's ambassador to the United States, had with State Department officials in Washington. Chiriboga Villagómez had recently returned from a visit to Ecuador after an absence of three years since his failed presidential run in 1952 to test the waters for another attempt in 1956. He recounted "an amazing increase in communist influence in university and school circles," and described the socialists as "tools of the communists." He lamented that the government was "powerless to check such activity."[18] Wieland responded to the memo with a quite different assessment. While Chiriboga Villagómez "is entitled to his own 'impression,'" Wieland wrote, "that is not the feeling of the Embassy." Wieland said he had double-checked his view with "CAS" (presumably Holman or someone in the CIA station) and the PAOs who worked closely with those issues. While they acknowledged "substantial Communist influence," they denied that any "appreciable increase" in communist activity had taken place, "much less an 'amazing increase.'" Chiriboga Villagómez may have exaggerated a communist threat in an attempt to concur favor with United States officials by leaving them with the impression that he alone could rise to the challenge, but if that was his aim, he failed at it. Wieland declared that Chiriboga Villagómez was "in error" in his assessment that socialists were "tools of the communists." United States officials estimated five thousand communists in Ecuador, but there were at least six times as many socialist party members. Furthermore, two-thirds of those socialists came from the moderate wing of the party and wanted nothing to do with the communists. While the remaining ten thousand socialists represented the left wing of the party, they were "by far the weaker section" and in no sense dominated the party. In fact, Wieland predicted that the socialist party might split in two.[19] The CIA typically exaggerated communist threats, whereas State Department officials dedicated more attention to the much larger PSE. Particularly in private internal correspondence, more rational and less sensationalistic reporting could emerge out of United States surveillance.

Minister of Government

British ambassador Norman Mayers described 1953 as "one of continual change, contention and upset, with no apparent benefit to anyone." In large part, this chaos was due to Velasco Ibarra who was "changeable, violent, but not unlikeable." As president, he called "eloquently for national unity and mutual comprehension," even as he was largely responsible for shortcomings in those areas. Mayers found the "Extreme Right" and the "Extreme Left" to be equally dangerous, and urged the country not to desert "the sound political conceptions of an older time . . . to follow strange creeds," whether falangist or communist.[20] As a representative of a country with a long imperial and colonial tradition, he felt situated and entitled to pontificate on what it would take for an impoverished and unequal country to solve their problems.

Mayers contrasted 1953 in Ecuador, which "was a year of continual change and public dissension," with 1954 that provided "a period of consolidation, in which President Velasco Ibarra made himself master of the country, finally settled into the saddle and assured apparent stability of government." Notable for Mayers was the general absence of significant and frequent cabinet changes that had characterized the previous year.[21] Mayers's successor F. Herbert Gamble observed that his predecessors had described Velasco Ibarra as "masterful, difficult, self-willed, changeable, violent, not unlikeable, mercurial, unpredictable, incorrupt, most patriotic, imperious," and he added "courageous and indefatigable." Gamble remarked that such a person as head of state would inevitably lead to "some excitement, and we have indeed had some exciting moments in 1955." Velasco Ibarra had managed to ride out these difficulties, and "at the end of the year he was fully in control of the situation and head and shoulders over those who surround him."[22] While previously these characteristics had led to Velasco Ibarra's removal from office, this time it assured that he would complete his four-year term—the only one of his five times in office that he was able to do so.

In large part, Velasco Ibarra's minister of government Ponce was responsible for imposing strong-armed control over the country that assured his continuance in office. In a report on his ministerial activities, Ponce launched into an extended attack on leftists and their opposition to Velasco Ibarra's government. He made a distinction between an idealist or utopic socialism and the "scientific" socialism of communists who followed a Bolshevik line. He claimed that this division was reflected in the types of people who were attracted to each ideology. He derogatorily referred to those in the second group as "comunistoides" who tried to infiltrate labor and peasant organizations. As a result, the interests of workers and peasants suffered because of the manipulation of outside agitators who pressed revolutionary ideologies that deprived people of their personal freedoms.

Ponce noted that from before his elevation to minister of government, leftists had declared a frontal attack against Velasco Ibarra's government, often without a clear purpose or political agenda. Rather, they forwarded ideas developed in the context of European industrial economies that were entirely inappropriate for Ecuador. They embraced abstract economic and social theories interpreted through a European literary framework that engendered polemical discourses with little relevance for Ecuador's lived realities.

Ponce pointed to the hypocrisy of socialists who previously collaborated actively with Galo Plaza Lasso's government, including holding cabinet posts in education and economics. He asked whether the socialist party that had allied with Plaza was different from the one that now engaged in open combat with Velasco Ibarra. Ponce challenged a statement in a PSE manifesto that "Velasco Ibarra is the man who has caused the most damage to Ecuador." The socialist statement compared Velasco Ibarra to Adolf Hitler, Benito Mussolini, and Francisco Franco, and declared that he had delivered his government into the hands of the most reactionary elements in Ecuador as represented by Ponce, the conservative party, and the ARNE. This led Ponce to inquire whether Plaza's government was any more democratic or popular than the current one. Had it done anything more to foster economic development, or had it paid more attention to the most marginalized sectors of society? The socialist manifesto concluded with a call for workers, students, intellectuals, popular organizations, and other political forces to "to occupy its position of struggle against the obscure conservative-ARNE forces that have seized the country, which threaten to bloody it and reduce it to greater misery and slavery." Ponce warned what they were advocating was a social revolution that would lead to a "dictatorship of the proletariat" with all of its negative manifestations as was currently the case in Moscow.[23]

Ponce then turned his ire against the communists. Beginning in July 1953, "a malaise could be felt, connected with the continuous mobilizations of certain leaders," and he noted that from August through October of 1953 "communists were especially active." Their exploits had caused disruptions in rural communities, as seen in the "serious disorders and lamentable bloody acts" that culminated with massacres at the Galte hacienda in Chimborazo, and the La Merced and Guachalá haciendas in Pichincha. Earlier in 1953, a new owner of the Galte hacienda had tried to expel thirty-nine Indigenous workers, which triggered an eight-month strike that the police put down with considerable force.[24] A January 1954 protest at the Guachalá hacienda over a lack of pay and other abuses similarly resulted in the police killing four unarmed workers and imprisoning many more.[25] All of these protests ended "with the same consequences and without any benefit." Ponce complained that at both La Merced and Guachalá the press distorted the truth in search of sensationalism and reported the news "so that it does not coincide with legal declarations and procedures." In other words, the mainstream media had spread "fake news" about his actions. The minister claimed that a concerted campaign to discredit the government lay behind the protests, and an unfortunate result was "more victims with no public or private benefit for anyone." He particularly blamed the FEI, what he denounced as "foreign elements of the workers federations," and communist party members for all of these troubles.

Ponce contended that in contrast to the charges from labor leaders, Velasco Ibarra's administration was not hostile to the working class. Rather, as it had demonstrated on repeated occasions, it supported workers' right and just demands and sought to elevate their "moral and economic level." At the same time, Ponce justified repressive actions against communist agitators. He contended that the government took such measures not because of their labor activities, but because of their violations of the law and their attacks on authorities. "A portion of the Ecuadorian working class are victims of political deception," Ponce claimed, "of international communism's dialectical seduction." Even though revolutionary activity had not reached the extreme levels that it had in some other countries, the minister observed, workers still suffered the same negative consequences of revolutionary incitements from unscrupulous leaders. He contended that legal labor union organizing was one thing, but that permanent communist agitation disguised as syndicalist action was something else entirely. Ponce argued that legal sanctions were necessary to preserve order.[26]

While the political prospects for both Velasco Ibarra and Ponce appeared to be improving, those for the communists proffered the impression of heading in the opposite direction. Saad warned a communist youth meeting, "We are getting weaker." He complained that communist militants were "spending too much time in cafes" when "victory is to be found in the streets, at the head of the proletariat and the Indians."[27] According to Albert Gerberich at the OSA in Washington, Saad, "allegedly admitted privately that 1953 was a bad year for the Communists in Ecuador and that the party's financial situation is worse, coupled with apparent dishonesty on the part of some members handling party funds." Furthermore, the local committee in Guayaquil faced internal difficulties, including ones related to personal conflicts. Nevertheless, Saad anticipated "a vigorous campaign in 1954" that would include "attacks on the Velasco Government and the U.S., and by the fermentation of strikes where they will have most effect."[28] In order to achieve its goals, however, the party needed to be better organized.

Ponce's anticommunist policies appeared to be having their intended effect. In November 1955, a CIA analyst in Washington described the PCE as "poorly organized" with only about five thousand members—the same number that

US officials had reported for years. The party held "little influence," but at the same time its secretary general Saad was "a member of the Ecuadoran Senate and has considerable prestige among Latin American Communist parties." Perhaps its small size and marginal influence would explain why "The Ecuadoran government does not view Communism as a clear and present danger either to the country or to the continent." The agency complained of Velasco Ibarra's "third way" orientation that "characterized the cold war as 'a struggle between two materialistic powers.'" As further evidence of the president's insufficiently anticommunist credentials, he had "allowed unrestricted freedom of activity to some 45 Communist exiles from Guatemala" who had left that country after the right-wing military coup against the progressive Jacobo Arbenz administration the previous year. Even with Ponce's opposition, CIA analysts feared that unless the government were willing to take even more aggressive and concerted action a communist threat could grow.[29]

The USIA painted a similarly dismal picture of communist strength. In April 1956, it asked its local posts to provide an assessment "of the nature and extent of the communist propaganda program."[30] The embassy's PAO Bastian replied that "the communist press is quite minor in Ecuador." The party's nominally weekly newspaper *El Pueblo* was deeply in debt, which compromised it ability to publish on a regular and consistent basis and as a result only appeared sporadically. Cultural activities were "almost nil." Despite these problems, "in Ecuador communism finds an economic system which with its great inequalities and its underdevelopment offers an opportunity for exploitation found in few other Latin America countries." As a result, the possibilities for communist subversion surpassed its currently limited financial resources, particularly in terms of its potential ability to mobilize students, workers, and intellectuals.[31]

Local and Midterm Elections

Despite concerted anticommunist campaigns, progressive forces appeared to be strengthening in the lead up to Ponce's election in 1956. In addition to presidential elections held regularly every four years on the first Sunday in June, throughout the 1950s Ecuador convoked other ballots on a consistent basis. In June of every other year, the country held congressional elections, and every November voters elected representatives for municipal and provincial offices. In addition to the sequence of presidential terms, the consistency of these local and legislative elections that were largely held without interruption reinforced an impression of a period of political stability. Underlying these votes, however, lay political unrest and discord that highlights ongoing debates over the direction the country should take. These elections provided multiple opportunities to ponder and debate how to advance political agendas, and they contributed to the construction of alliances and the setting of agendas for approaching presidential races. Furthermore, while public attention tends to be drawn toward presidential races, it was on a local level where the left realized most of its gains. Concentrating only on the presidency exaggerates the impression of a weak left and resurgent right.

As an example, a reconstituted Frente Democrático Nacional (FDN, National Democratic Front) coalition of liberals and socialists scored a substantial victory over the conservatives in the November 6, 1955, municipal and provincial elections. In fact, the conservatives won in only one city, Riobamba, where the FDN had not run a candidate. Furthermore, the FDN only lost in one city, and that was in Portoviejo where a Velasquista candidate had emerged victorious. United States Embassy officials identified the November 1955 election as "one of the least turbulent and most honest of recent years." Voters were "acquiring greater confidence in the constitutional process" with assurances that voting outcomes would be respected. Wieland closed a detailed five-page analysis of the election results with the observation that "Ecuador stands in direct contrast to its neighboring countries, still in the grip of dictatorships, or having just undergone the turmoil of revolution and counter-revolution." In comparison, "Ecuador could well be described as an island of relative democratic and institutional stability virtually surrounded by the angry seas of dictatorship and revolution."[32] Furthermore, the outcome of the Guayaquil municipal elections cheered United States consul Joseph Costanzo because "the Communist party evidently got nowhere." The PCE had only run candidates in Guayaquil, and in that city their list E "had no success to speak of."[33] Wieland bluntly characterized their performance as "a miserable showing.[34] The communist contribution to the rise of a progressive alternative never manifested itself in the electoral realm, but it could be felt elsewhere.

The 1955 local elections appeared to place the liberals in a strong position to win the June 1956 presidential elections half a year later. The Catholic Church hierarchy had worked intensively on behalf of conservative candidates to the point where they faced a backlash with liberals charging that it was engaging in undue interference in the electoral process.[35] The outcome resulted in a weakening of the political influence of the Catholic Church, and the conservatives feared that they would again face defeat unless they were able to identify and unify around a suitable candidate. From Wieland's perspective, if the June 1956 election proceeded as planned, "Ecuador may well become one of the most politically stable countries in Latin America."[36] The future appeared bright for the country.

Camilo Ponce Enríquez (1956)

A three-way division among progressive political parties opened a path for the election of the Social Christian Camilo Ponce Enríquez in 1956 with only 29 percent of the vote, the lowest percentage of any winning presidential candidate in Ecuador's history. Conservative support continued to drop across the 1950s, and in the end, Ponce barely polled three thousand more votes than his nearest competitor. A record-breaking six hundred thousand people participated, though they still represented only about 15 percent of the country's almost four million people even with many (literate) women voting for the first time. Observers noted that almost three-quarters of those cast their ballots for nonconservative candidates, but suicidal divisions among liberal candidates handed victory to the right that was opposed to the social and political gains achieved during the last half century of liberal governance.[37] Furthermore, it was never clear that Ponce had won in a clean and fair contest. It became a common trope on the left that the FDN had triumphed but was the victim of a brazen fraud.[38] Even the traditional conservative leader Mariano Suárez Veintimilla accused Ponce of only managing his minor victory through massive electoral chicanery.[39] The right faced as much fractious infighting as did the left, but with the reins of power it could advance its political agenda.

As in previous elections, liberals, leftists and other progressives had sought to form a broad anticonservative alliance to keep the right out of power, but with no more success than with other attempts. Once again, divisions among liberals provided conservatives with their narrow margin of victory. After failing to gain nomination as the official liberal party candidate, Chiriboga Villagómez competed as an independent. The FDN unified other liberals, socialists, and independents in support of liberal stalwart Raúl Clemente Huerta. In addition, the populist Carlos Guevara Moreno ran as a candidate for the CFP. He had his best showing in that election, which further split the anticonservative vote. Left-wing unity could theoretically prevent a conservative victory, but attempts to build a coalition were fraught with fractures and splits. Furthermore, the liberals, socialists, and communists all suffered from internal divisions within their ranks, and these ruptures became even more pronounced in the 1960s. Conservatives took advantage of these cleavages to win elections, which created the impression of a weak left and an ascendant right, even though they never enjoyed majority backing. Underlying all of this were intense debates over socialist ideologies and strategies that point to the presence of a vibrant and dynamic left.

As with all electoral coalitions, the formation of the FDN required a complicated dance around competing interests, which eventually resulted in the exclusion of the communists. As before, the socialists attempted to gain respectability and support by joining an anticommunist chorus. The PCE reacted quite negatively to their exclusion. The communist party denounced the liberal and socialist leaders Augusto Durango, Juan Isaac Lovato, Fernando Chávez, and Oswaldo Tamayo as "four insignificant people, members of the FDN board" who had "declared open war on the PCE." According to the party, the four "revealed their voracious, greedy policy of seeking power for power's sake, without any concern for the interests and the needs of the people." The party accused the FDN leaders of acting as "instruments of wealthy economic interests, which do not appear because of their blatant ambition of profit and exploitation. They are interested more than anyone in maintaining the conditions of injustice in our country." The communists claimed to have had lofty expectations for the FDN, but they denounced Huerta as an "instrument of high finance and exploitative merchants in Guayaquil." His election would represent a victory for coastal bankers and *gamonales*, the wealthy landowners who fed off the poverty and misery of the people.

According to the PCE, the FDN's vice presidential candidate José María Plaza Lasso was a tool of imperialism who had a long history of acting against the interests of the people. They accused him of urging his older brother, the former president and modernizing landowner Galo Plaza Lasso, to hand the entire country over to the United States. Furthermore, and most disturbing, "the vilest conditions of slavery and exploitation of the Indigenous masses continue to persist on his haciendas." The statement claimed that the younger Plaza had even proclaimed arrogantly to his journalist friends that poor people should not have the right to vote. Rather than leading to the liberation of the people, such bourgeois politicians only contributed to their exploitation and misery.

The PCE attacked both the presidential and vice-presidential candidates for their insufficiently radical positions, but they saved their strongest ire for the leaders of the FDN. The PCE denounced them as "the same old reactionary exponents" who had declared that "between communism and democracy there is an abyss." The PCE retorted that the "democracy" of the FDN was "the democracy of injustice, of slavery, of lies and exploitation. TRUTHFULLY THERE IS AN ABYSS BETWEEN COMMUNISM AND THIS PERVERSION

OF DEMOCRACY," their statement shouted.[40] The communists sought to turn the rhetoric of a defense of democracy back on the liberals with the contention that their version was exclusionary and failed to advance the interests of the working class and other marginalized communities. At the same time, turning their ire against other progressives contributed to disunity on the left that permitted victories on the right.

In response to its exclusion from the FDN, the PCE published a sixteen-page pamphlet with its own electoral platform.[41] The cover featured a graphic of a communist worker breaking the chains of African descent and Indigenous peoples with a hammer and anvil (see figure 10.1). The statement began with a declaration that "a profound mobilization of the entire Ecuadorian people" had created a "hope that these elections will serve to transform the harsh realities we now endure." Reflecting the dominant political line that Saad currently championed, rather than calling for an armed struggle the party appealed to the people's "democratic and patriotic spirit" to solve the country's problems. While advocating for peaceful coexistence, the PCE also denounced imperial penetration of the country's economy. It directed its call to workers, peasants, artisans, teachers, students, industrial workers, and all men and women who suffered under the oppression of large United States monopolies that extracted the wealth of the country—petroleum, bananas, fish—and left the country's internal economy underdeveloped. The party charged that the entire country had become subjugated to foreign economic interests. Even the military had fallen under imperial control through the military pact that the government had signed with the United States. "In a word," the statement declared, "an accelerated process of colonization of Ecuador is underway." In contrast to the FDN, the communists sought to break free from foreign domination of the country.

According to the PCE, the current administration of Velasco Ibarra had an equally dismal domestic record compared to what the FDN would implement were it to gain power. Wealthy feudal landowners occupied most of the country's fertile land and oppressed their Indigenous and *montuvio* [coastal peasant] workers with an exploitative regiment descended directly from the Spanish colonial system. Their actions caused the country to remain underdeveloped, both agriculturally and in terms of industrial advancement. Those reactionary groups were constantly violating the liberties that the people had struggled so hard to advance. The party condemned Velasco Ibarra as being responsible for the systematic destruction of democratic rights, the persecution of labor and peasant leaders, and the murders of students and Indigenous peoples. His government had imposed restrictions on the freedom of the press and pursued disastrous

FIGURE 10.1. Graphic of a communist worker breaking the chains of African descent and Indigenous peoples with a hammer and anvil. Source: Comité Central del Partido Comunista del Ecuador, *Por un gobierno democrático al servicio del pueblo; contra la reacción, los golpes de estado y el continuismo; programa electoral del Partido Comunista del Ecuador* (Quito: Ediciones "El Pueblo," February 21, 1956), Private Collection of Leonardo J. Muñoz.

economic policies that impoverished the country and undermined its national sovereignty. The statement condemned conservative candidates in the current election who promised to continue those criminal policies. The June election would be a battle that could either mark a fundamental shift in the country's direction, or a deepening of all of these problems if the reactionaries won. It was not merely a matter of changing leaders, the communists declared, but of the need for a fundamental change in policies to benefit workers, peasants, the popular sectors, and progressive capitalists.

As with most mainline communist parties of the era, rather than pressing for class struggle and a violent revolution the PCE advocated pursuit of a peaceful and gradual path to socialism in coalition with other progressive forces. To that end, the PCE proposed a seven-point platform. The leading issue was democracy, and the party emphasized the importance of preserving existing liberal constitutional guarantees, particularly freedom of the press and assembly, and separation of church and state. The second item proposed economic changes that were necessary to improve the lives of workers and other poor people. This included lowering taxes, raising wages, establishing price controls on basic goods, strengthening social security laws, providing adequate housing, and improving access to healthcare. The third point called for an agrarian reform that would grant land to those who worked it, as well as raising the salaries of agricultural and other Indigenous workers. Fourth was a call for a new economic policy that would restrict foreign companies and implement measures to benefit the country's internal economic development. The program also called for the expulsion of United States technical missions that "direct our economy, our education, our agriculture, health, and the military in a manner contrary to legitimate national interests." In terms of education and culture, the fifth point, the communists called for free and universal education with the goal of eliminating illiteracy. Realizing this objective would require wealthy estate owners to provide schooling for the children of their workers. Furthermore, students should be guaranteed employment upon completion of their studies. The sixth point concerned the implementation of fiscal policies that would benefit poor people, including an increase in funding for education and healthcare and a cut in military and police spending. The implementation of such an economic policy would require the restriction of foreign investments and the encouragement of domestic development. The seventh and final point called for a peaceful foreign policy, including the establishment of diplomatic and commercial relations with the Soviet Union and other socialist countries. This would entail a change in United Nations policies that were too often subjugated to the concerns of United States imperial interests. The communists appealed for a defense of national sovereignty, including revision of the 1942 Rio de Janeiro Protocol that ceded half of Ecuador's territory to Peru, a cancelation of plans to hold the Eleventh Inter-American Conference in Quito, and a refusal to host any foreign military bases in Ecuador. The PCE acknowledged that its program would not definitively resolve all of the country's problems, but it would represent a decisive step toward the discovery of solutions. The party called on the Ecuadorian people to fight together for this program through the election of a government that would implement these measures.

Notable is how relatively moderate the demands were in this communist party platform. It does not include any calls for expropriation of industry or changes in the capitalist mode of production, or even for empowering the working class. In fact, it makes an appeal to progressive capitalists to join a program of national development. While it does attack conservatives, it does so for their reactionary and feudalistic policies that hindered the capitalist economic progress of the country. In keeping with an orthodox Marxist understanding of Ecuador's current stage of economic development, it advocated for bourgeois national development rather than a class struggle. Instead of appealing to acts of violence or armed struggle, as the United States government feared, it called for peaceful participation in electoral contests and achieving reforms through a parliamentary process. At the end of the document, the party returned twice more to appeals to stand firm against military coups, regardless from where they came, because such a step would "circumvent our right to choose our leaders freely and to apply this program of urgent measures for national salvation." The communists did not believe that extraconstitutional changes in power would be in either their interest as a party, nor in that of the country as a whole. This was largely a social democratic platform that party leaders had designed to appeal to as broad of an audience as possible. There was little in it that other leftists and even many liberals would oppose. Furthermore, other than denunciations of foreign economic enterprises and military pacts, it is difficult to understand what precisely United States government officials would find objectionable about this statement, except that it came from the communists. An ever-present anticommunist knee-jerk rejection was at play, as was of course hostility toward any critique of United States economic penetration of Latin America.

Despite the FDN's exclusion of the PCE from their alliance, the conservative ARNE newspaper *El Combate* still engaged in extensive redbaiting. It attacked the coalition as operating under communist control. Despite communist statements to the contrary, the newspaper declared that the PCE leaders had imposed

Huerta as the presidential candidate, "surely fulfilling international communist slogans." *El Combate* proclaimed that the alliance's efforts to distance themselves from communist control were not fooling anyone. "They verbally repudiate communism with false and misleading statements," the paper declared. "But these only happen to be statements to attract the unwary." It presented what it contended was irrefutable proof that communists had worked to undermine the nominations of Galo Plaza Lasso and Eduardo Salazar Gómez whom they accused of being agents of United States imperialism and of working instead to promote Huerta's candidacy.[42]

United States officials made similar types of claims, beginning even before Huerta declared his candidacy.[43] Allegedly the FDN "openly included known communists and communist sympathizers in the entourage which has been accompanying Huerta in his campaign tours of the country." Drawing on information from *El Combate*, embassy officials reported that top FDN leaders in Manabí were active communists, and that "six well-known Quito communists" met with FDN leaders at their headquarters. The CIA similarly asserted that communists supported Huerta's candidacy, including hanging posters on his behalf. Saad allegedly declared that Huerta's nomination "represented a resounding victory for the PCE, which has actively campaigned for him." According to this source, "Huerta would doubtless permit the PCE freedom of action, since his political beliefs coincide with the Party in many respects." Young communists were "working long and hard in behalf of Huerta," including traveling around the country to rally support for his candidacy. These militants "dismissed Huerta's public rejection of Communist Party support as mere campaign strategy, stating that in reality Huerta is sympathetic to the policies of Communism."[44] Whether or not the PCE actively campaigned for or covertly supported Huerta, what does emerge apparent in these discussions is the complicated terrain that the communists tread as they attempted to advance their political agenda.

Even after the election, the CIA continued with its assertions that the communists were behind the Huerta campaign. In May, party members allegedly traveled "throughout Guayas Province to distribute campaign literature and propaganda material in favor of Front Presidential candidate Huerta to the farm workers and residents of small towns." Local communist cells formed committees in support of Huerta and continued to do so up until the June 3 election even in violation of electoral regulations. The CIA quoted communist leader José María Roura Cevallos as stating that it was less important that the party was supporting a bourgeois candidate like Huerta because "the important point was to defeat reactionary candidates in order to insure a favorable atmosphere for the Party in the next four years." His hope was that a Huerta presidency would facilitate realization of "various aspects of the socialist revolution." According to the agency, party members continued campaigning throughout election day for the FDN and gathered at their headquarters to await electoral returns. Afterwards, the communists were more eager to protest Huerta's defeat than were the FDN leaders themselves.[45]

After Ponce emerged at the top of the June 1956 presidential contest, some opponents were determined not to let him take office. These shenanigans included a June 29 coup attempt in Riobamba, an abortive military uprising on August 8 in Manabí, and a boycott of congress on August 10 to prevent the body from certifying his election. A week later, the conservative majority in congress defeated an opposition motion to recount the votes and instead declared Ponce president elect.[46] José María Plaza Lasso, the losing vice-presidential candidate, was later arrested and charged with involvement in the Manabí revolt.[47] CIA analysts in Washington concluded that Ponce feared that anticonservative groups would organize a general strike on August 31 to prevent him from assuming the presidency the following day. Even so, according to the CIA, "The small Ecuadoran Communist Party apparently has not made any significant contribution to recent political unrest."[48] The agency inadvertently acknowledged what the communists had long maintained—that they were committed to orderly societal transformations rather than resorting to palace coups that only resulted in temporary and meaningless disruptions of the political order.

The PCE made its political position clear in a series of statements it produced during the three-month period between the June 3 election and Ponce's inauguration on September 1. The party repeatedly denounced his fraudulent election and condemned a progression of steps that the supreme electoral council and congress had taken to certify his designation as president. The party reminded the public of Ponce's previous actions as minister of government in Velasco Ibarra's administration where he revealed his "retrograde spirit," his systemic opposition to the constitution and the rule of law, "his virulent hatred of public liberties," and his complete disregard for the democratic advances that Ecuador had made in the sixty years since the liberal leader Eloy "Alfaro raised the people against tyranny and the infamy of [Gabriel García Moreno's] conservative regime." The statement pointed to the Manabí uprising and the boycott of congress as evidence of public repudiation of Ponce's criminal attacks on democracy. In this context, the PCE as the "party of the working class and people" called on all Ecuadorians who yearned for progress regardless of whom they supported in the election to join together in an anticonservative coalition and to take to the streets in opposition to Ponce. Through such a mobilization, the people could open a "path to progress and democracy, to national independence, and to the benefit of the masses who today suffer the devastating economic consequences to which the Velasco regime has led them." It no longer mattered whether one had voted for Huerta, Guevara Moreno, or Chiriboga Villagómez, because together they represented the majority and together they would make the difference between reaction and democracy.[49] Despite the heightened rhetoric, notably absent in these party documents was an embrace of extraconstitutional measures to prevent Ponce from taking office.

Upon Ponce's inauguration, the PCE declared that his "conservative-fascist government" was "nothing other than the fruit of a monstrous unholy alliance between the former government of Velasco Ibarra, certain sectors of the national and foreign clergy, imperialism, feudal castes, and fascist advance guards such as ARNE." Together, these groups had conspired against democracy and perpetuated a scandalous electoral fraud on the country. Once again, the party recounted the "crimes and outrages" that Ponce had committed "against democratic freedoms and the rights of citizens and against worker, peasant, popular, and student organizations." These included the massacres of Indigenous peoples on the La Merced and Guachalá haciendas. Ponce had trampled on the constitution and rule of law. The party warned that if he had done all that as minister of government, logically his actions would be much worse as president. He would attempt "to destroy every principle of liberty, democracy and human dignity, guarantees for which our people have struggled and which they have partially gained since that unforgettable year of 1895," the momentous date of Alfaro's liberal revolution. Ponce's program was comprised of nothing other than "the starving of the popular masses and the most brutal repression of men of free thought." His government threatened to undo all of the political and social gains that people had achieved over the past sixty years and would lead to the surrender of Ecuador's natural resources to foreign companies.

The PCE acknowledged that Ponce had threatened to outlaw their party but stated that this was only logical because he was well aware that communists would never compromise with him. Instead, the party would continue to struggle even under the worst of conditions "for the maintenance of democratic freedoms and in defense of the rights and aspirations of the people." The party would continue its battle "until the slavery and exploitation under which the people suffer comes to an end, and until the chains of imperialist oppression are forever broken." In sum, the communists would fight "until an authentically popular and democratic government is installed in our country and our homeland becomes completely independent and sovereign." The party declared that it was not afraid of fascist threats and would continue to fight with more firm resolve than ever before. "We have profound faith that history never marches backward and we know how to comply, with revolutionary honor, the task of socially and nationally liberating our country." The party called on all Ecuadorian democrats, both men and women, to join in their fight against Ponce's "conservative-fascist regime" and in support of common objectives. It was time for struggle and action, the statement declared. Together, united and organized, the party optimistically declared, the people would destroy reactionary forces.[50] The embassy considered this statement to be of sufficient importance to translate it in its entirety, even as it denigrated the party for attacking "Ponce and 'imperialism' in the usual Communist terms." Other than highlighting the statement that the PCE expected that the new administration would drive the party underground, the embassy made no comment on the party's proposed strategies to address Ecuador's longstanding problems.[51]

At the end of August 1956 on the eve of Ponce's inauguration, Reginald Bragonier at the OSA in the State Department prepared a report on communism in Ecuador. In the late 1940s Bragonier was the first secretary and PAO of the Quito Embassy and had only recently started at his current position in Washington after serving at posts in Peru and Germany. He drew on United States intelligence sources in Ecuador including those from the embassy, CIA, and military attachés for his analysis. Bragonier noted that while previous estimates had given the size of the PCE at five thousand members, an army attaché report from April had dropped that figure to 1,500, a number that had "remained static in spite of the setbacks received by the party during the past year." Communists were "numerically insignificant" and "internal bickering and an apparent shortage of funds" prevented the party from wielding more power than it otherwise might have. The army attaché had no evidence of communist penetration of the Ecuadorian military, but its influence continued strong among workers, students, teachers, and intellectuals. It was in those realms, particularly in labor strikes and student protests, where communists made their presence known. "The greatest vulnerability," Bragonier warned, was "the absence of a widespread popular conviction that the activities of the Communists in Ecuador present a danger to the country."[52] This was a concern that other United States officials expressed, and it endlessly bothered them that Ecuadorians did not take the communist threat more seriously.

United States consul Costanzo once expressed his frustration that "people tend to believe that home-grown Communism is a harmless sort of political play which will never get very far."[53] Bragonier was therefore optimistic that Ponce's new conservative government, and the Catholic Church's opposition to the left in general, would provide a barrier to the growth of communism. Whereas previously some United States officials had criticized conservatives for trapping Latin America in a feudal backwardness that blocked any efforts at modernization, now under the Eisenhower administration diplomats openly cavorted with conservatives in their anticommunist campaigns.[54] Bragonier looked forward to strengthening relations with Ponce's government. Depending on how those collaborative efforts developed, they could extend to providing him with "ammunition" that included details on infiltration of the Casa de la Cultura and other USIS operations that have been "active, imaginative and effective."[55] Despite Bragonier's optimism and the new president's promises, Ponce actually took few concrete steps in the direction of curbing communist activity or circumscribing the party, a reality that continued to frustrate embassy officials.[56]

A year after Ponce's election, liberals were still engaged in an earnest postmortem in an attempt to come to terms with their loss. In a lengthy article in *El Comercio*, Huerta denied charges that international communism directed the FDN as Ponce had contended. As evidence, he pointed to the coalition's rejection of the communists' application to join. Instead, Huerta attacked Salazar Gómez and his other opponents in the liberal party. He declared that Chiriboga Villagómez was guilty of treason for dividing the democratic opposition and handing victory to Ponce.[57] In a confidential comment on Huerta's statement, a US Embassy official noted that Huerta did reject an alliance with communism, but that the communists supported the front anyway.[58] Both United States officials and Ecuadorian politicians were eager to see a hidden communist hand at play and were determined to do anything they could to stop it.

As the opposition to Ponce coalesced into an anticonservative front, the embassy's first secretary Walter Dustmann warned that the communists may be providing the spark that would lead to its consolidation.[59] A PCE manifesto presented contradictory statements on the party's relationship to the previous year's electoral campaign and its aftermath. On one hand, according to the embassy's summary of a June 14, 1957, proclamation, Ponce had "charged that international communism was behind the front in order to weaken and divide it." On the other hand, the PCE claimed credit for the "organization and success" of the FDN even though they had been denied entry. "We initiated action for anti-Conservative unity from the very moment Ponce took power," the communists declared.[60] The party never hesitated to exaggerate its ability to influence and lead such a coalition, and United States officials actively encouraged that narrative even as their own surveillance documented communist weakness.

AFTER A PERIOD of fairly insightful reporting during the late 1940s and early 1950s, the frequency and quality of CIA reporting on domestic events in Ecuador dropped off significantly during the second half of the 1950s, and that limits the conclusions we can draw about communist activities. A preponderance of the initial items in the CREST database from Ecuador are intelligence or information reports that case officers sent from the field to agency headquarters in Washington. By 1952, that coverage became much spottier. One of the few reports for that year is the usually lengthy evaluation of the communist party's fifth congress at Ambato. In fact, that twelve-page report is an outlier in the entire run of available documentation in terms of its detail and depth of examination, and it proves to be particularly useful in the absence of other sources on that meeting. After 1954, these regular reports from case officers that provide a fascinating fount of information on domestic leftist organizing efforts disappear entirely from the agency's declassified records. Even finished intelligence in the form of daily and weekly reports produced in Washington that mention Ecuador are largely missing from the archive, although their absence could be a result of the priorities and vicissitudes of the Eisenhower White House. This is the case even as diplomatic officials in the United States Embassy continued to generate a constant flow of reports on domestic political developments. The lack of CIA surveillance underscores just how useful the information the agency did create is to documenting leftist organizing efforts.

Even without full access to CIA records, a series of contradictions becomes readily apparent in the material that the agency has declassified. On one hand, officials contended that the PCE was determined to engage in sabotage even as it adhered to peaceful and parliamentary paths to power, and on the other those same officials denigrated the party's small electoral footprint even though a highly exclusionary political system excluded the vast majority of its potential supporters from voting. Fears outstripped realities, even as communist militants struggled to make their presence known in the political realm.

Even with all of this tension and attacks and counterattacks from multiple sides, political scientist Robert Alexander commented, "The effect of Ponce's election was to tighten the unity among the Liberal, Socialist, and Communist parties." While it had been difficult to rally diverse forces in support of a single candidate or electoral platform, it proved easier to mobilize progressives against a government that all opposed. A result of this harmony, according to Alexander, was that the PCE "remained one of the most successful Communist groups anywhere in the continent as a manipulator of 'fellow travelers,' though it had failed to gain much of a mass base for itself."[61] Out of its apparent weaknesses emerged a continual strength that laid a basis for advances that the communists would make over the next several years, as was to become apparent in its sixth party congress.

CHAPTER 11

Resurgent Left

After repeated delays, in May 1957 the PCE gathered in Quito for its sixth congress, its first since meeting in Ambato in 1952 in the final days of the Galo Plaza Lasso administration. The congress came a year after the election of the conservative Camilo Ponce Enríquez, and highlighted the challenges that the left faced. Divisions among liberal and leftist forces had opened the path to his victory. Despite a recognition of the importance of progressive unity to prevent a conservative triumph, differences had proven to be too great to overcome. Furthermore, communist leaders faced a growing left-wing insurgency within their own party. Reactions against the left's ineffectualness as an electoral force contributed to a rise in these protest actions.

The 1957 party congress received more press attention than did the previous one that faced an almost complete media blackout. As with the 1949 party congress, in 1957 the communists met as the CIA station in Quito was going through a change of personnel. This transition affected the agency's coverage of communist activities, but that does not mean that the surveillance stopped—only that its hand became more hidden. Traces of the agency's reporting emerge in other sources, particularly in dispatches that diplomatic officials sent to the State Department in Washington. These and other sources allow for a reconstruction of the nature and content of discussions that swirled around the assembly and the party in general.

One of the most significant aspects of the sixth party congress were the discussions regarding revisions of the statutes that governed the PCE. Despite common assumptions that political lines were dictated from above or from outside of the local party, surveillance and other documents indicate that rewriting the statutes and the congress itself provided space for vigorous internal debate over the direction that the party should take. In particular, those deliberations highlight the continued presence of a countervailing current that maintained that the party should root itself in rural Indigenous and peasant communities and dedicate itself to advancing working-class struggles rather than pursing an accommodationist position that deferred a transition to socialism to some indeterminate point in the future. These and other issues that delegates thrashed out in the 1957 communist party congress laid the stage for subsequent ruptures that characterized the fractured political landscape of the 1960s.

James Noland

In 1957, both COS Ned Holman and his deputy Comer Wiley Gilstrap left Ecuador for other posts—Holman to Argentina and Gilstrap to Brazil and eventually as COS in Chile in the 1970s.[1] James Noland arrived in Quito in July 1957 to replace Holman. In contrast to Holman, who Agee characterized as not "one of the more outstanding Chiefs of Station," Noland was "one of the best-liked COS's" in the agency.[2] All of the other officers that Agee names arrived after the triumph of the Cuban Revolution, and it is not immediately apparent who if anyone initially accompanied Noland in the Quito station.

Much like Holman, Noland worked closely with embassy officials. In one case, the embassy's counselor Perry Culley asked Noland for a list of communist-sponsored travel for assistant secretary of state for Inter-American Affairs Roy Rubottom. Noland generated a three-page list that documented the actions of many of the party's top functionaries. Secretary general Pedro Saad along with at least seven others traveled to Moscow for the fortieth anniversary celebrations of the 1917 Bolshevik Revolution. Some stayed on for other meetings, trainings, or presentations. The document also contains the names of twenty-four members of the Ecuadorian delegation to the Sixth World Festival of Youth and Students in Moscow July 1957 together with their political affiliations, as well as four labor leaders who traveled to a WFTU congress in Leipzig in October 1957.[3] If nothing else, CIA officers cataloged the extent of travel and the nature of the party's international connections. That is not to say that these interagency relations were without conflict. The embassy's political officer George Jones said that he had his "first run in with CIA" in Quito, apparently with Noland who was convinced that Plaza would win the 1960 presidential election when José María Velasco Ibarra instead emerged on top in a landslide. This was the first of "lots of conflicts and lots of run-ins with the CIA over the years."[4] The close working relationship was not without its tension.

Noland pressed hard on the Ecuadorian government to implement anticommunist measures, and his actions bore fruit. Several months after his arrival, Noland reported that "the recent ouster of the Czech mission in Quito was a 'blow' to the Ecuadoran Communist Party." According to central committee member

Oswaldo Albornoz Peralta, "the departure of the Czech diplomats will hurt the Party because it has received 'considerable aid, both financial and otherwise,' through the Czech Legation." Reporting on a private conversation that Albornoz apparently had with a CIA informer, Noland indicated that "the degree of cooperation between the Party and the Czech mission was not as pictured by the Ecuadoran Government and was insufficient reason to expel the Czechs." Rather, "the ousters were due to 'Yankee pressure.'"[5] That reality, nevertheless, did not halt attempts to circumscribe communist actions.

In a memo to Ambassador Christian Ravndal, Noland outlined the agency's success in denying visas to Soviet journalists as well as other communist groups and representatives including labor and student activists and a Puerto Rican nationalist. Noland also highlighted President Ponce's action in ousting the Czech legation and the repercussions that doing so had across the region, including resulting in the closing of its missions in Peru and Bolivia. No other Latin American country, Noland proclaimed, had cooperated more fully than Ecuador with such anticommunist campaigns. Ravndal proudly passed the memo on to the State Department with all identifying markers removed except to note that it was "prepared by CAS at my request." Ravndal declared that he "strongly endorse[d] the CAS statement," and called for the State Department to extend the Ecuadorian government "some kind of special recognition."[6] And, indeed, Acting Secretary of State Christian Herter responded with a note expressing the department's gratification "over the recent actions taken by Ecuador against international Communism."[7] CIA officers collaborated closely with diplomatic officials to advance United States policy objectives, which suggests the need for caution in exaggerating the distinctions between the competing agencies in providing intelligence on communist party activities. More often than not, the CIA and State Department—as well as the military and other branches of the government—shared the same policy objectives.

Sixth PCE Congress (Quito, May 24–30, 1957)

The communists had been planning their sixth congress for some time, and rumors of the pending assembly swirled throughout the intelligence community in the years leading up to the meeting. Already in April 1954, a CIA officer reported information obtained from Albornoz that the PCE was making arrangements for another assembly. According to the party's bylaws, the party was due for its biannual meeting since it had held its last congress almost two years earlier in Ambato in July 1952. In keeping with a goal to extend the party's geographic reach, some party members mentioned Cuenca in the southern highlands as a possible site for the next congress. According to the case officer, "Albornoz gave the impression that a considerable purge of Party ranks was being contemplated," although the officer did not indicate how, where, or from whom he obtained this information.[8] The year 1954 came and went without the party holding a congress. A list of upcoming communist meetings from July 1955 in the CIA archives indicated that the PCE intended to convene the congress in Guayaquil on April 30, 1956.[9] In February 1957, recently arrived Ambassador Ravndal reported, "the Embassy has learned reliably that Ecuador's Communist Party plans to hold its 6th annual Congress on March 8, 1957, in Quito. The proposed Congress has been postponed time and again during the past year, reportedly due to lack of funds."[10] That situation had not changed, because once again the party delayed the opening of the meeting.

Probably drawing on the same source of information as the embassy, CIA analysts in Washington also reported that the PCE planned to convene its congress on March 8. Notable for the CIA, the Ecuadorian meeting would be the first communist congress in a Latin American country since the Soviets crushed the revolt against the Hungarian People's Republic government the previous November. The agency was eager to examine the political fallout of European conflicts in the American hemisphere.[11] Rather than dedicating their attention to domestic issues and how they might inform local political actions, United States officials were primarily preoccupied with the ramifications of East-West tensions.

In addition to the Hungarian uprising, "certain echoes" of the previous year's CPSU's twentieth congress ran throughout the PCE assembly.[12] When Nikita Khrushchev's accusations became public in June of that year, the PCE published a statement in its party newspaper *El Pueblo* that acknowledged the criticisms of the cult of personality and embraced the importance of collective leadership, but remained silent on the issue of political repression.[13] In April 1957, an unsigned article in the center-left political periodical *La Calle* complained that Joseph Stalin's portrait still hung next to that of Vladimir Lenin in the PCE headquarters, which indicated that destalinization had not yet arrived to Ecuador. In a recent speech Saad discussed the position of intellectuals in the current political situation, which the anonymous author took to indicate a change in the cultural line in the party, particularly in terms of a dogmatic and sectarian attitude toward socialist realist art.[14] Decades later, the communist author and militant Elías Muñoz Vicuña continued to put a positive spin on these events. According to Muñoz, the Soviet's twentieth congress showed "the possibility of new ways of achieving socialism, including a peaceful path."[15] Support for a Stalinist position never completely dissipated.

According to CIA analysts, the party would hold its congress "in an atmosphere of political isolation, unusual governmental hostility, and considerable party dissension." The agency estimated that the party had about two thousand members, which was down from the figure of five thousand that it had earlier given, plus twice as many sympathizers, but its presence was multiplied with "its strong influence in leading labor, student, and intellectual organizations in Ecuador." Reflective of its apparent strength was Saad's involvement in the federal congress as the labor representative. On the other hand, Ponce's election as president the previous year and his continued threats to outlaw the party presented the PCE with its most serious danger. The party lived in constant fear of the possible loss of its legal status, so that was not necessarily a new concern, although attacks from Ponce's conservative administration had heightened that possibility. Worsening the situation, liberal party leader Eduardo Salazar Gómez had organized the Juridical Committees for the Defense of Western Democracy, a hemispheric anticommunist group that contributed to the isolation of the party.[16] The publishers of *La Calle* similarly expected little of significance to come out of the congress.[17] Even so, both US officials and Ecuadorian politicians did everything in their power to suppress the party's activities.

An additional blow to the communists was the concerted effort of conservative students to gain control of the FEUE and withdraw its affiliation with the IUS. A lingering conflict over a decision at its 1953 congress to associate with the IUS came to a head at a student congress at the end of 1956 when dissident students decided to break away from the leftist FEUE.[18] US Embassy officials concluded that while communist control of the FEUE had "been building up stronger and tighter for the past several years" that was no longer the case. The split was a great setback for leftist elements in the student federation. Now the anticommunist faction appeared to be gaining strength at a cost to the communists. "The Embassy is giving full attention to the movement of the dissident groups," the embassy's cultural affairs officer Michael Karnis stated, "and will lend them our program support through the various channels during the coming months." Karnis admitted that "making the best use of this university student split stands as one of our primary short term objectives." The embassy promised to keep the State Department informed as they proceeded with their intent to intervene in the internal affairs of the student federation.[19] It was thus with a bit of duplicity that a CIA analyst in Washington stated that "the party is confronted with a split in one of its major front organizations" as if that development was completely independent of United States intervention.[20]

A greater threat than either Salazar Gómez's anticommunist organization or the FEUE dissidents was Ponce's intent to outlaw the party once his political position was strong enough to do so. The president allegedly intended to exile or imprison Saad and sought a pretext to break relations with Czechoslovakia, the only communist country with diplomatic representation in Ecuador.[21] Such an action, a CIA analyst concluded, "could both damage the PCE's prestige and sever its most available direct link with international Communism." For this and other reasons, the CIA presumed that the congress would concentrate its attacks on Ponce, including opposing "his unpopular economic austerity program." According to the agency, a goal would be to persuade other parties to join the PCE in an "attempt to overthrow the government by violence," even though the party repeatedly had made clear that it would not move in that direction. The agency predicted that delegates would "receive indoctrination on the present Soviet line from Saad, who reportedly attended conferences in Prague and Peiping [Beijing] in late 1956." The secretary general's statements might "foreshadow some of the new international policies which may be considered by the Argentine and Brazilian Communist congresses reportedly to be held in the near future."[22] While Ecuador may have been of marginal interest to policymakers, local developments were worth monitoring because of their broader regional ramifications. The agency's analysis of the threats facing the PCE was not entirely off, even though they framed their discussion in terms of international factors and exaggerated fears of the party turning to armed struggle.

In December 1956, the party's central committee announced the impending congress, without setting a specific date. The agenda for the assembly included receiving a report on the party's activities from the central committee, drafting a program of action, updating the party's statutes, and electing a new central committee. In preparation for the congress, the current central committee called on all members to study documents that the party had prepared, and to engage in an open debate on the party's affairs including a broad examination of "all of the problems related to the activity of the party and its future performance."[23] Rather than imposing a line from above, the implication was that the party needed an honest discussion to fortify its base as a necessary precondition to advance its agenda.

One of the most important topics was a revision of the party's statutes, and in preparation for those discussions the PCE leaders published their proposed changes in the party newspaper *El Pueblo*.[24] The statutes began with a proud statement that the PCE "is the political party of the working class, its conscious and organized vanguard, its highest form of class organization that resolutely defends the interests of the Ecuadorian nation and its broadest masses to which it must be closely linked." The party comprised "the voluntary and militant union of the Ecuadorian communists." Following a pattern that José Carlos Mariátegui had established in neighboring Peru decades earlier, the party was "guided in all its activity by the doctrine of Marxism-Leninism as applied to the national reality." The PCE followed in a long tradition of struggle, and sought to "educate its members in the spirit of proletarian internationalism." The party's current task entailed unifying broad anti-imperialist and antifeudal forces in their "Great Democratic Front of National Liberation" that would be based on a worker-peasant alliance. The goal was to overthrow the wealthy feudal landowners, imperialist forces, and their local agents. In their place the party would "implement a progressive democratic regime of national independence as a preliminary step towards the construction of socialism, the first stage in the building of a communist society in our country." The party remained dedicated to an orthodox Marxist orientation of requiring the establishment of the proper objective economic conditions of a fully developed capitalist economy before attempting to move toward a socialist mode of production.

According to the statutes, the organization of the party was structured around the model of democratic centralism. Cells comprised of at least three members formed the base of the party, and the party congress was the top decision-making body, which was to meet every other year—although in practice it never met that often. Between congresses, the central committee held responsibility for the party's actions, and that body would select an executive committee and secretary general to administer daily affairs. Members elected the leaders, but those members were also expected to adhere to party decisions. Discipline was important and would be applied "not with a sense of punishment, but with the spirit of educating the sanctioned militant, as well as correcting the defects in the work of the party's organizations and militants." The statutes sought to protect the party from antagonistic individuals who might damage it. Not only were members to be ideologically and politically committed to adopting the principals of Marxism-Leninism to their national reality, they were also to be honest and sincere in all aspects of their personal lives. Members were to engage actively in internal debates in the party, including criticizing errors and presenting proposals and suggestions to strengthen the party's work. In the period leading up to a party congress, party members enjoyed "the broadest rights to reopen the discussion on any point of party policy." It was in that spirit that party leaders presented issues for members to debate in anticipation of the pending congress.

Before the congress even started, the PCE faced intense conservative opposition to meeting in a public space. Quito's liberal mayor Carlos Andrade Marín had granted the communists use of the municipal Espejo Theater for their inaugural assembly on May 24, 1957. On the eve of the gathering, José Antonio Baquero de la Calle, a hardcore conservative member of Quito's municipal council, called for an emergency session to challenge the mayor's decision. Baquero was no stranger to these types of battles, and he was well known to United States officials. Almost a decade earlier, while serving as sub-secretary of foreign affairs, Baquero had exploited the political chaos following the assassination of liberal leader and presidential candidate Jorge Eliécer Gaitán during the ninth Pan-American Conference in neighboring Colombia to press an anticommunist agenda with the United States Embassy in Quito.[25] Then as now, Baquero expressed a greater fear of communism than did embassy officials.

In his exposé of CIA operations in the early 1960s, Philip Agee describes Baquero as a "long-time agent," which makes it within the realm of possibility that in 1957 he was already collaborating with the agency to prevent communist access to public venues.[26] We do know that as leader of the conservative party he had ongoing and intimate conversations with embassy officials concerning local political developments.[27] And, in fact, this was broadly the impression that his opponents had of him. At the time of the communist congress, the socialist newspaper *La Tierra* identified Baquero as "a paid agent of imperialism" who followed instructions from the United States in his anticommunist campaigns.[28] Reading between the lines of embassy dispatches would seem to confirm that indeed he was a CIA informer.[29] In the early 1960s, Baquero was a leader of the right wing of Velasco Ibarra's political movement and had presidential aspirations. Velasco Ibarra named him minister of labor and social welfare, and the Quito station paid him a salary and expenses to provide political intelligence on the government. The CIA hoped that Baquero could strengthen noncommunist labor organizations, but his closeness to the conservative Catholic Church hierarchy limited those possibilities. Nevertheless, Agee referred to Baquero as "our" minister, as if he responded to imperial rather than domestic concerns. When in October 1961 Velasco Ibarra forced him out of his government, Agee quipped that he had "been an ineffective minister and not a particularly effective agent either." The Quito station then faced the task of removing him from the agency's payroll.[30] Baquero's inability to convince his colleagues on the Quito city council to join him in opposition to communist use of the municipal theater was just one of his many failures to advance his conservative, anticommunist agenda.

At the municipal council meeting on the evening of Wednesday, May 23, 1957, Mayor Andrade Marín explained that he had made his decision to permit use of the municipal theater based on the precedent that the council had established the previous year in allowing any political organization to use the facilities for their meetings.[31] Baquero retorted that the "so-called" Ecuadorian communist party was neither a political party nor Ecuadorian. He contended that only three political parties existed in Ecuador (the conservatives, liberals, and socialists), but unlike the others the communists did not defend the country's interests but rather received orders from Moscow with the objective of destroying the country and its democratic institutions. Rather than a local party, he denounced the PCE as in reality the "Partido Comunista Soviético, Sucursal del Ecuador," the Ecuadorian branch of the Soviet communist party.

Baquero declared that Ecuadorians could never agree with communist tactics, particularly given recent events in Hungary where the communist party asked for arms and tanks to repress its own people. "We should not and cannot allow this in Ecuador," Baquero declared. He protested that in communist countries no freedoms existed for workers, students, or others who were not communists, and likewise Ecuador should restrict the actions of communists. Granting the party use of the theater would provide it with a level of respectability and legitimacy that it did not deserve and with which he was not willing to be complicit.

The socialist Pablo Duque Arias retorted that given Baquero's political sentiments, it was no surprise that he would oppose communist party use of the theater. Duque Arias pointed out that the ARNE was not a political party and received its marching orders from Madrid, but yet it and other political groupings such as the CFP had met in the theater. Duque Arias saw no problem in extending the same right to the PCE. Although United States officials made no mention of Duque Arias's comments, they must have been particularly troubling for the embassy as he was a labor leader who was willing to meet with diplomatic officials and had worked to break the CTE free from communist control.[32] At the same time, later in the year Duque Arias traveled to Leipzig for a WFTU congress, so apparently he saw no problem in collaborating with communists and perhaps had drifted in that direction.[33] Similarly, the liberal counselor Jaime Mantilla Mata underscored that the council should extend use of its facilities in a spirit of liberty, justice, tolerance, and peace. Mantilla Mata asked when the PCE had been declared illegal. He argued that all political organizations should have the right to use the theater. The communists made effective use of a liberal embrace of freedom of expression to advance their political agenda.

Baquero declared that he did not wish to turn this issue into a political debate. He claimed that he did not disagree with the communist party's right to meet; he only opposed their use of the municipal theater that he considered to be their own house. While he acknowledged that the PCE had not (yet) been declared illegal, neither did it have formal standing and recognition as a registered political party. He added that communists had "cavernous ideas" that were a negation of all democratic principles. If liberals defended them today, Baquero charged, tomorrow they would be the first ones hanging from the lampposts on Plaza Grande. Mantilla Mata retorted that he supported the liberal party's position. While he rejected any form of totalitarianism, he still supported the communist party's right to meet. Since the municipal theater belonged to the people, all parties whether conservative, social Christian, or communist had a right to gather there.

The socialist Juan Isaac Lovato observed that all council members agreed that the mayor had the right to grant the theater to groups for political meetings, and that this should not be a topic of debate. Lovato's defense of the communist use of the municipal facilities was perhaps ironic because only a year earlier in the hard-fought June 1956 presidential election the PCE had attacked him quite personally for excluding the party from the FDN electoral alliance that backed the liberal candidate Raúl Clemente Huerta. At the time, the communists denounced Lovato and other FDN leaders as "insignificant," "voracious," and "greedy" who functioned as "instruments of wealthy economic interests" and sought "power for power's sake, without any concern for the interests and the needs of the people."[34] The communists launched this attack even though in the past party leaders had collaborated quite closely with Lovato. Or maybe they had responded in that fashion because they felt that his refusal to cooperate in the electoral campaign was a betrayal of their previous attempts to advance a common political agenda. If that were the case, his defense now of the communists may have simply been a return to the practice of a long-standing tactical alliance. Or perhaps Lovato's support in the municipal council should just be taken at face value, and that granting the PCE use of the theater was a simple bureaucratic matter of allowing all organizations access to the venue and that politics should be left out of such decisions.

In any case, Lovato acknowledged Baquero's honorable and brilliant defense of his position, even if he disagreed with it. With this comment, the discussion came to an end and the council voted on Baquero's resolution to rescind the communist party's permission to use the theater. Despite Baquero's complaints, after "an elevated and serene debate" in front of a large audience, the council reaffirmed the mayor's decision. Comandante Miguel Espinosa Páez, who had not previously participated in the debate, justified his vote against Baquero's resolution with the argument that ideas should be confronted with ideas, and that the communists should be allowed to use the theater so that they could be exposed for who they were and what they thought. The council's vice president Wilson Córdova Moscosa could not attend the meeting, but he sent a note in which he declared that as a liberal he was eminently anticommunist and antifalangist, but he also deeply disagreed with denying the communists the right to use the facilities. In a telegram to the State Department the following morning, Ambassador Ravndal succinctly summarized the outcome as Baquero being "outvoted by liberal socialist majority."[35] Outside of United States officials, he had gained little support for his position.

Having recently arrived from Hungary, Ravndal highlighted Baquero's contention that the "world has looked with horror on Communist slaughter [of] Hungarian children and on how [the] Hungarian Communist Party called in Soviet tanks, arms 'to smash [their] own country.'" The ambassador reiterated the conservative council member's assertion that the permit placed the communists in the category of being a "respectable party."[36] Ravndal complained, "One of the [PCE's] main accomplishments was obtaining the municipal Espejo High School theater for the opening session, thereby giving the Party and the Congress official city recognition and approval." Although Baquero "vigorously sought to have the permit revoked, arguing that the Party was a branch of international communism," he could not swing the rest of the council to his position. Instead, the ambassador related, "The city council approved a resolution giving the theater on the grounds the Party was legal and therefore entitled to it as other parties have been."[37] From the ambassador's perspective, Baquero's defeat was a blow for the diplomatic mission's anticommunist agenda. Even more distressing to the ambassador was a CIA report that the mayor had told the party "you have the good wishes of a majority of the council and also my own." This response surprised Ravndal because "in the past the Mayor has not been overly sympathetic to communism but has gone out of his way to be friendly to the American Embassy and Americans generally in Quito."[38] He feared that the United States was losing its hegemonic control over ideological battles in the region.

The archival record does not mention whether the CIA or embassy staff had encouraged Baquero or otherwise taken steps to disrupt the party congress. Nor is the documentation complete enough to know whether the communists always faced such opposition to their use of public facilities, and whether the United States government previously had a hidden hand in such subversions. But in this case, there is no mistaking the embassy's active anticommunist agenda. Just as the congress was starting Maurice Bernbaum, who had previously served as deputy chief of mission in the Quito Embassy and was currently director of Inter-American Affairs at the State Department in Washington (and a future ambassador to Ecuador from 1960 to 1965), returned to the country after an absence of seven years.[39] In an interview with *El Comercio*, Bernbaum stated:

> As for the Ecuadorian communist party, it is an internal matter of your country. In general, I can tell you that world communism is not an ideology but it represents a subversive apparatus everywhere. It divides people and sows hatred.[40]

Publicly, Bernbaum articulated the double discourse that typified most diplomatic statements: The United States government formally embraced policies of nonintervention in the internal affairs of other countries, but was also unrelentingly opposed to the presence of any communist activities. It was a fundamental logical contradiction that liberals in Ecuador understood but that apologists for United States imperialism never acknowledged or could justify.

Regardless of the United States government's position toward communism, domestically winds were blowing against the communist party. Ponce's conservative minister of government Enrique Arroyo Delgado announced his desire to outlaw the communist party, particularly in light of what he contended was an increase in the flow of international communist leaders and propaganda into the country.[41] At the same time, Arroyo made what the US Embassy interpreted as a contradictory statement regarding communist participation in local elections. The minister said that "all parties with a national character are recognized," but the administration would "not recognize those parties that receive instructions from abroad to the detriment of Ecuadorian sovereignty." The embassy was only "mildly impressed" with the government's "apparent sincerity and earnestness" in pursuing anticommunist measures. According to the embassy, "Arroyo's apparent pussyfooting on the local communist issue may indicate the Government has not yet come to a firm decision on whether to crack down on them, despite repeated indications to this effect from various high officials," perhaps a reference to Baquero.[42] Typically, "creole" anticommunist statements were stronger and more aggressive than those from United States officials. Obviously, despite what diplomatic officials had stated for public consumption, they wanted

Ecuadorian government officials to take even more strident measures against communism than what they were already contemplating.

A month after the congress, the communist success at gaining access to the municipal theater still ate at embassy officials and they were determined to get to the bottom of the issue. A lengthy dispatch summarized information that they had already reported and outlined new information diplomats had uncovered. Apparently, the communists had been attempting for quite some time to gain access to a municipal building for the congress. Saad persuaded city council member and socialist party secretary general Lovato to ask permission for use of the Espejo Theater at a special council meeting when he knew Baquero would be out of town on business. The embassy characterized Lovato's maneuver as "ramming" the resolution through the council, which was met with Baquero's "angry" denunciation of the action at a subsequent "stormy" session. Baquero denounced Andrade Marín as "a political weakling who is afraid of offending anyone," whereas others described him as "'a meathead' and 'a muddled liberal' who has never been successful at anything." Salazar Gómez "thought the action was taken primarily to 'attract attention' and in effect to show that the Council majority was not subservient to United States interests and independent enough to make its own decision in the matter." These comments led embassy officials to conclude that the mayor was "not too mature politically and probably was led into a trap by Lovato and Saad, veteran political Machiavellis, when politically-wise Conservative Baquero was not present to dissuade him." Andrade Marín's willingness to "put into writing a note of good wishes to the communists" further underscored "the Mayor's political naiveté." The comments of both the conservative Baquero and liberal Salazar Gómez led the embassy to recommend that in response the State Department not consider Andrade Marín for a leadership grant to visit the United States, and that it has been a mistake to invite Central University rector and council member Alfredo Pérez Guerrero because of his refusal to kowtow to Salazar Gómez's anticommunist line.[43] Salazar Gómez presumed, and perhaps hoped, that Andrade Marín's actions would result in his defeat in November's mayoral election. To his surprise and disappointment, the mayor won reelection. The United States Embassy, however, pointed to this outcome as a result of "the successful communist infiltration of the Quito city Government," and supposed that his victory would mean that the mayor would be further beholden to the socialists and communists.[44] United States officials did not willingly accept their defeats in Latin American elections.

With the municipal council's reaffirmation of its use of the space and despite conservative opposition, the communist party congress began as planned on the evening of Friday, May 24, traditionally celebrated as Ecuador's Independence Day. In fact, right next to the front-page article in *El Comercio* that reported the municipal council's decision to allow the party to use the theater appeared an official proclamation from President Ponce commemorating the 135th anniversary of the 1822 battle of Pichincha that secured Ecuador's separation from Spain.[45] Inadvertently, Baquero had drawn more attention to the communist congress than it otherwise might have enjoyed.

In a lengthy article, *El Comercio* reported that the communists had filled the Espejo Theater when it gathered for its inaugural session.[46] In a detailed summary of the congress, Ambassador Ravndal noted that around one hundred delegates and four hundred sympathizers from across the country were in attendance, in truth a respectable turnout despite his tendency to understate its significance.[47] Former leader Ricardo Paredes presided over the assembly, presumably in an effort to smooth over divisions in the party after he had been ousted as secretary general in the previous congress.[48] Ravndal incorrectly reported that Paredes had been expelled in 1952 (Saad had simply replaced him as secretary general), and included a rumor that "he recently gave some $15,000 to the Party he had been withholding from [the] sale of a Guayaquil house willed to the Party."[49] Current party leaders Pedro Saad and Enrique Gil Gilbert together with provincial delegates joined Paredes on the stage. The plenum read notes of congratulations that it had received from communist parties in Argentina, Chile, Colombia, and Germany, as well as a message from the CPUSA that criticized the Eisenhower administration for its policies toward Latin America. The audience responded to the CPUSA greeting with shouts of "long live the people of the United States and down with the imperialists."[50] The assembly voted to send a note of acknowledgment to Mayor Andrade Marín as well as the other Quito council members for allowing their use of the theater.

As was common in such assemblies, representatives from other sympathetic political forces joined the communists in their opening pageantries. Gonzalo Oleas addressed the congress in the name of the PSE. Echoing what had long been a communist goal, he advocated joining all anticonservative forces into a front to restore democratic freedoms. Referring to Baquero's charge in the municipal council the previous evening that communists had "cavernous ideas," the socialist leader countered that "the cavernous are those who are part of the falangist fold where they learn to be servile to dictators," a not-so-subtle jab at President Ponce. Oleas declared that free people had the right to meet on any national holiday, whether it was August 10 (Quito's first declaration of independence in 1809), May 24 (the 1822 battle of Pichincha that gained Ecuador its independence), or October 9 (Guayaquil's independence in 1820), to celebrate their freedoms. CTE leader Víctor Zúñiga proclaimed a need to unify all workers in the country to struggle for the restoration of democracy. Finally, the Indigenous leader Tránsito Amaguaña spoke in the name of highland peasants. She denounced the indignities to which they had been subjected.

Ravndal summarized these opening comments in a telegram to the State Department that largely matched the narrative arch of the standard media coverage. Since inaugural assemblies are staged pageantry designed for maximum public relations benefit, that parallel should not be surprising, particularly since *El Comercio* probably was the source of his information. Ravndal added that Oleas had told the congress that despite the fact that the socialists and communists had "profound differences" in their conceptualization of how to transform the country socially and politically, they should unite in an anticonservative front because the parties shared the "common task" of saving Ecuador from pain and misery. Oleas predicted that Ponce's "fraudulent" government would "not last another year against [the] will [of] 4 million Ecuadorans."[51] In a subsequent weekly summary of political developments, Ravndal mischaracterized Oleas as a "leftist" who "harangued the gathering" even though he came from the conservative wing of the socialist party. Ravndal feared that his presence underscored "the continued split between moderate and leftist Socialists" that would strengthen the communists' hand. The ambassador seemingly confused political rhetoric with policy positions. While he noted Zúñiga's call to unify workers "to safeguard democracy," he completely ignored Amaguaña's presence. Such neglect contributed to writing Indigenous peoples (as well as women and people of African descent) out of history.[52]

After these preliminary greetings, party leaders read a resolution that recognized the origins of the party in the May 23, 1926, socialist assembly in Quito. That date was also linked to the anniversary of the May 24 battle of Pichincha that represented social liberation for the Ecuadorian people. Secretary General Saad then read his report that examined the country's political situation and laid out the party's future goals. He presented an analysis of the Democratic Front's errors in the electoral campaign the previous June that led to Ponce's victory. His report denounced Ponce's conservative government as representing feudal reaction and declared that the president presented an enormous danger to democracy and the country's sovereignty by bringing it under the subjugation of Yankee imperialism. Every day discontent rose along with the cost of living, the communist leader contended. He called for the formation of a "broad, anti-Conservative coalition against the Government of oligarchs, reactionaries, and plutocratic trusts, supported by imperialism" that won by election fraud.[53] Ravndal characterized Saad's comments as "a typical communist-line speech with little or nothing new in it," and his charges of Ponce only winning through electoral fraud as a "threadbare argument." The ambassador was not convinced with the assertion that the "ferocious Social-Christian-Conservative rulership" was destroying the country.[54] Despite the ambassador's reaction, underlying Saad's radical rhetoric was a continued adherence to an evolutionary and parliamentary path to socialism that over the next several years would lead a radical left wing to break away from the party in search of more militant solutions to Ecuador's problems.

El Comercio reported that mounted police along with others in motorized vehicles surrounded the theater while the communists met inside. A group of leftist students charged that authorities had arrested them upon leaving the theater, although the officers claimed that those who had been detained were released immediately after providing their declarations.[55] Despite the city council's decision to allow the party to occupy the space, the state's repressive forces still engaged in attempts to disrupt the meeting. That fact was an indication of the political realities that the communists confronted as they sought to advance their political agenda. For his part, Ravndal noted that the police had briefly detained the students "for information" but otherwise he had no disorders to report.[56] After the first two days of the congress the police withdrew their forces. The embassy characterized the public reaction to the congress as "complete apathy," with a religious population more interested in simultaneous first communion pageantry than leftist agitation.[57] Ravndal reported with some apparent relief that "some prominent Communists" including youth leader Jorge Arellano Gallegos had boycotted the congress due to "internal bickerings." The ambassador described attendance as "small, unenthusiastic," and advised that even though the congress was scheduled to last through May 28 it might close the following day, May 27. Plans that anticommunist students at the Central University had to protest the congress failed to materialize. Even so, according to Ravndal, the party's ability to hold the "congress after [a] year of attempts, particularly in [the] municipal building, is [a] moral, legal victory for [the] Communists despite reputed continued split." He anticipated, however, that these gains would be offset if the meeting fizzled as he expected. A lack of media attention also cheered the embassy.[58]

In a subsequent summary of the week's events, the ambassador reiterated his impression that the congress was more of a moral victory than a political advance for the communists. Rather than reporting a full auditorium as the press had done, Ravndal pointed to the presence of "around one hundred delegates." This was instead of referencing the entire attendance, although later in the same dispatch he acknowledged a total number of "some 500 delegates and sympathizers." He repeated his previous observations that in terms of press coverage, "The Congress suffered from [a] severe lack of publicity which appeared to be almost a boycott by the liberal dailies of Quito and Guayaquil. Only [the] leftist Socialist *La Tierra* gave the Congress page 1 play."[59] It was with a sense of relief that he reported that after the original brouhaha over access to the municipal theater that the remainder of the congress passed with little attention.

At 5 p.m. on May 26, Ravndal notified the State Department that the congress had reportedly met only for half an hour that day "in [a] poorly attended public session [at] party headquarters which accomplished little, then hierarchy moved [to a] private home for strategy talks." The newspaper carried little to nothing on the meeting, "possibly because [it] made little news." Ravndal reported that Quito appeared normal with no signs of anticommunist demonstrations, which he credited to the extra police presence and a lack of publicity around the congress, not to mention general public apathy. "Religious Quito appears more interested [in] dozen first communion ceremonies with girls parading [in the] streets [with] beautiful communion gowns," the ambassador concluded.[60]

In part, Ravndal's report on press coverage was correct, though he somewhat understated its significance. Indeed, *El Comercio*, the newspaper of record, published only two stories on the congress. The first was a lengthy front-page story regarding debates in the municipal council over whether to allow the party use of its municipal theater. The second the following day reported on the opening session of the congress. The ambassador characterized that article as "buried in [the] back pages." True, the story was on page eleven out of an eighteen-page edition, but it was lengthy and detailed. Furthermore, *El Comercio* described the theater as packed and gave the impression of an energetic and uplifting meeting. The ambassador also ignored, or did not understand, that it was not uncommon for the press and broader public to attend opening sessions with all of the pageantry before party militants retreated into smaller gatherings for intense and private deliberations that were not intended for public consumption. The embassy cast the assembly in as negative of terms as possible.

Several days later, Ravndal reported that much to his surprise the PCE was still meeting in secret sessions, despite his earlier report that the congress would conclude early due to a lack of interest. Obviously, he had underestimated or misunderstood the level of the militants' dedication to their discussions so he had to backtrack on his previous assessment. Now, according to his intelligence, the assembly would wrap up on May 31 with the reelection of Saad as secretary general. The ambassador noted that there was a complete media blackout on the congress, including the socialist newspaper *La Tierra* that US officials had repeatedly accused of being a communist mouthpiece.[61] That newspaper had only given the congress any real publicity on the first day of its meetings. The sole published editorial on the meeting was also in *La Tierra*, and that was "somewhat weak" although it labeled the inauguration as "remarkably successful" and noted that the "relentless anti-communist campaign" and "tremendous police deployment" had not intimidated Saad.[62] Without media reports, the embassy had no access to reliable information to report to Washington, which indicates both the source and limitations of their surveillance operations.

It is therefore curious that only a day later the ambassador submitted a report on the party's "secret strategy sessions." A subsequent dispatch that summarizes the highlights and accomplishments of the congress inadvertently indicates that new information from "CAS sources," or, in other words, CIA informers provided the intelligence that altered the ambassador's reporting patterns.[63] While earlier Ravndal had denigrated what he considered to be the inaugural session's small size, now the party found its headquarters to be too cramped for the forty-seven delegates who participated in the discussions. Despite ongoing interparty tensions, the socialist party granted the communists access to their headquarters to continue the meetings, except for private discussions that took place in individual homes. The ambassador conveyed his concern that communist use of the socialist headquarters "may indicate that the moderate wing may be veering to the left." Rather than indicating a merging of the parties, the gesture could be better understood as one of collegiality and camaraderie.

The party drew up plans to publish a daily newspaper and a monthly magazine, hopefully with socialist collaboration, in addition to the current weekly *El Pueblo*, which appeared irregularly due to a chronic shortage of funds. Embassy personnel had previously expressed apprehension of the potential for a collaboration between the PCE and the CFP, and Ravndal stoked those fears in his report with the mention of a delegation representing Carlos Guevara Moreno's party. Ravndal highlighted Saad's comment that the CFP was "a great group that has managed to get along despite the demagoguery of its directors." Guevara Moreno continually denied charges that he was a communist, "and this action therefore appears to be playing directly into Ponce's hands."[64] These discussions foreshadowed a momentous change in political attitudes and policies, both for the PCE and the CFP, and one that culminated in the two previously antagonistic forces collaborating in an anticonservative alliance in the 1960 elections.

Ravndal flagged what he considered to be an interesting aspect of the meeting: "It was reported that throughout the sessions, Communist China repeatedly was pointed to as the great example of world communism, particularly on land reform, rather than the Soviet Union."[65] CIA analysts in Washington expressed similar concerns that Latin American communist leaders were turning to China as a model for revolution. This was reflected in the size of the delegations to the Chinese communist party's eighth congress in September 1956. The CIA pointed to Saad's attendance at that congress as possibly having "inspired the laudatory discussions on China." Delegates at the Quito congress "reportedly praised Communist China rather than the USSR as an example for world Communism, making specific reference to land reform—a socio-economic problem in Ecuador which the PCE attempts to exploit in its domestic political program."[66] Party leaders faced growing discontent with an adherence to a relatively moderate political line, and mounting pressure to move in more radical directions.

Among the actions taken in the PCE meeting, "the Congress tightened party discipline, suppressed internal critics who have long badgered the party ranks and punished two of its severest critics: Nela Martínez, suspended for six months; and Primitivo Barreto, expelled." Martínez was once again removed from the party at its next congress in 1963, although the historian Tatiana Salazar Cortez states she had never rejoined after her first expulsion.[67] In her autobiography, Martínez simply states, "Although I officially suspended my communist militancy, in the fifties and sixties I was still immersed in strong feminist activism."[68] Martínez always represented the left wing of the party, and repeatedly tangled with the current leadership's more moderate and conciliatory attitudes. She subsequently became sympathetic to, and closely associated with, the Cuban Revolution.

Ravndal concluded his report on the congress with a confidential comment that the party's "success in finally holding the Congress, particularly in a municipal building, is considered a moral and legal victory for the party." He observed that Saad and other party leaders were "elated over 'the great success,'" and acknowledged that they had "a point, in so far as the Party apparently overcame its internal troubles, tightened party discipline, moved closer to the Socialists with an opening wedge for further infiltration through the projected newspaper and magazine and increased party morale with these ambitious plans." Overall,

Ravndal concluded, "the Congress was successful and will undoubtedly help reinvigorate the Party."[69] That outcome, of course, was not in the best interests of the United States.

Four months after the congress and toward the end of 1957, the embassy conducted a thorough survey of the party and came to a somewhat different conclusion than what Ravndal had earlier stated. Now, the embassy described the PCE as "weaker at the present time than at any period in recent years, although its potential always is present to a greater or lesser degree in poverty-ridden, still largely feudal Ecuador, with its predominant but downtrodden Indian population." In large part, that assessment was due to viewing the party through an electoral lens rather than as a social movement force. The CIA estimated party strength at one thousand (down from the five thousand that it had regularly reported earlier in the decade) along with three thousand sympathizers. The party could count on eight thousand votes, but out of a total voting population of six hundred thousand this was insignificant. CIA and embassy sources attributed the decline to internal splinters in the party, dissatisfaction with Saad's intellectual leadership that ignored the party's working-class base, a chronic lack of funds, confusion over what party to support in elections, the failure of a general strike, the ouster of Czech diplomats who provided the party with international connections, and a loss of support from Indigenous communities. Furthermore, communist influence in the Casa de la Cultura declined, and divisions in the labor federation CTE and student federation FEUE undermined the party's strength. Intriguingly, the survey pointed primarily to domestic rather than international factors such as the revelations that emerged out of the twentieth congress of the CPSU that were echoing throughout the communist world to explain the party's current situation. The embassy concluded, "The Party as such is too small and ineffective to pose any threat to the stability of Ecuador but it must always be regarded as a potential threat to stability through its capability to infiltrate and exploit other political parties or to exploit strikes and disorders."[70] Despite public attempts to exaggerate communist threats, internal and more careful assessments painted a quite different picture. It would appear that anticommunist paranoia and fears were largely misplaced.

Socialist Congress

Both United States officials and the mainstream press gave more and better coverage to a regional socialist congress held in Riobamba May 25–26 that met at the same time as the PCE congress. Delegates attended the congress from the central highland provinces of Bolívar, Cotopaxi, Chimborazo, and Tungurahua. The party's secretary general Juan Isaac Lovato as well as other members of the national executive board from Quito along with representatives from youth groups, students, workers, and women's groups also participated. The purpose of the congress was to discuss the current political situation and to study laws that the conservative Ponce government was seeking to implement, particularly those related to labor. A goal was to build a united anticonservative front, a continuously contentious and difficult goal for the left.[71] As had always been the case, socialist party goals were not that different from those of the communists.

The socialist assembly's inaugural session on May 25 received greetings from various individuals and groups, including, as the United States Embassy was keen to point out, from the communist congress that was meeting at the same time.[72] Raúl Clemente Huerta, the losing Democratic Front presidential candidate in the previous June election, also sent his regards. He said he could not attend but wished the assembly success. The congress approved a series of resolutions, including applauding the country's democratic and progressive media that contributed to the betterment of the working class. The assembly appealed for the creation of an anticonservative front for participation in the November 1957 municipal and provincial elections, and recommended holding future regional party conferences to advance its struggle. In this spirit, the assembly passed a resolution to continue the party's "relentless and belligerent opposition to the Government of Camilo Ponce." Finally, the evening concluded with a celebration to recognize and celebrate Lovato for his work on behalf of the party, as well as the labors of Gonzalo Oleas and José Jaramillo.[73]

The two meetings did not operate in isolation from each other. The socialist assembly received a fraternal message from the communist congress, which led Walter Dustmann at the US Embassy to express concern that the communists might be planning "to continue their prior efforts to infiltrate and dominate the Socialist Party, already divided into moderate and leftist factions." Dustmann worried that this infiltration may be succeeding, as evidenced by Lovato's collaboration with Saad to gain access to the Espejo Theater for the opening assembly of the communist party congress.[74] On the other hand, while both parties called for a united front against the government, both wanted to provide leadership and neither wanted to play second fiddle, which inevitably and ultimately hurt their efforts at collaboration.[75] These internal divisions were as much of a barrier to their success as were anticommunist policies, whether they originated inside or outside the country.

Communist Party Platform

What was missing in both the mainstream media reporting on the Ecuadorian party congress as well as the United States intelligence investigations was a discussion of the substance of the communist party's platform. When the central committee announced plans for the sixth congress half a year earlier, it published a draft program in *El Pueblo*.[76] The party followed this publication with a thirty-two-page pamphlet containing the same lengthy, detailed program with a note highlighting two small but significant corrections to the text that it had published in its party newspaper. First, the party blamed what it claimed to be a "printing error" that the version in *El Pueblo* "appears as approved by the party congress when it is nothing but a PROPOSAL." The central committee emphasized that this was a draft, and they sought feedback on it before presenting a revised version for final approval. Second, toward the end of the document they had omitted a key phrase "under the leadership of the working class in close alliance with the peasantry" when referencing the formation of their proposed Great Democratic Front of National Liberation that would group "all Ecuadorian patriots, all of us who suffer today under the rule of foreign monopolies and large feudal landowners."[77] The party leadership wished to underscore that workers and peasants remained at the heart of their political project, rather than it being guided by an urban intellectual vanguard. We may never know whether these were honest mistakes, or "corrections" that resulted from internal pushback against Saad's command of the party.

A common assumption that United States government officials held and that most cold war historians subsequently shared was that these party documents were imposed from above and outside to serve Soviet aims that were divorced from local realities. Strict Stalinist control would leave no room for debate or dissension, and those who dared question the party line faced a threat of expulsion (or worse). A new generation of scholars have challenged these interpretations. While the party sought to present a unified public face, internally more room for discussion existed than critics have wished to acknowledge. Intense debates at party congresses demonstrates that, and the drafting of this program provides another case in point. Several weeks before the party congress, Indigenous leaders met at party headquarters and proposed various changes to the proposed program. Some of their suggestions were rather cosmetic, such as adding references to Indigenous peoples in a discussion of the feudal exploitation of the peasantry. What is noteworthy, however, is their proposal to add a new section on social classes with a special mention of "Ecuadorian Indians who occupy a special place within the peasant masses." Their statement asserts that "this Indian mass unquestionably has a series of national elements, a language, Kichwa and other autochthonous tongues, a tradition, their own cultural manifestations." They were denied education in their own language, and the right to vote through the imposition of literacy restrictions. These small changes added up to altering a document from one that minimized the importance of Indigenous struggles to one that made an Indigenous consciousness central to the communist struggle. If previously communists had influenced Indigenous discourse, now the reverse was true with Indigenous activists shaping a leftist agenda.[78]

The party congress approved the revised text appropriately titled "Democracy, Independence and Peace for the People of Ecuador."[79] Unlike the electoral platform that the party had drafted a year earlier in the run-up to the June 1956 elections that was quite moderate in tone, this document is radical and militant, both in terms of its rhetoric and political analysis as well as its specific policy proposals. The contrast may have been due to a difference in audience, with an electoral platform facing outward in an attempt to convince others to join them in a popular front campaign while this document was designed to solidify internal cohesion among already committed militants. It may also be an early sign of the strengthening of radical tendencies in the party.

The party platform begins with a description of Ecuadorians' difficult lives that were full of suffering, insecurity, and uncertainties. The party asked why people confronted so many problems if Ecuador was a rich country with many possibilities for developing its wealth in a way that would dramatically benefit the entire population. As a "party that examines the national reality in light of the doctrine of Marxism-Leninism," the statement read, "we believe that if we proceed with a realistic analysis of Ecuador's characteristics, the forces that drive its development and those that halt it, we can reach conclusions that will serve to modify the face and life of the country and allow future transformations that lead to the complete liberation of the people." Rather than describing short-term goals that included intermediary steps of embracing a nationalist bourgeois revolution, it mapped out larger and longer-term objectives of a communist revolution with a sense of how to achieve them.

The document then followed with a series of key points to address the difficult issues that the country currently faced. First was the problem that only a small privileged minority of the population benefited from the country's economic growth. In fact, from 1950 to 1954, the working class's share of national income had dropped from 49 to 47 percent even as the size of the working class had grown. Workers earned insufficient and shrinking salaries. Peasants and

Indigenous peoples suffered under subhuman living conditions. Unemployment was high, housing was inadequate, and infant mortality rates were among the highest in the world, while at the same time oligarchs, feudal landowners, and foreign businesses took the lion's share of the country's wealth. In a common refrain, the statement declared, "We are facing a situation that is making the rich richer while the poor get poorer and poorer." Under the current conservative political regime, the country was sliding backward rather than moving forward.

That first point set the tone for the entire document. From there it moved on to a critique of how feudal landowners had underdeveloped the entire country, with the peasant and Indigenous masses subjected to barbarous exploitation. In addition to this semifeudal situation, the United States colonized Ecuador through its large capitalist monopolies such as the United Fruit Company and Standard Oil. International Monetary Fund (IMF) policies benefited United States companies to the detriment of those based in Latin America. That imperial intervention extended to education and training programs, as well as attempts to intervene in labor and student organizations such as the CTE and the FEUE, with the intent to destroy their unity and strength. All of these factors limited democracy, with half of the population excluded from voting because they were not literate. Women and young people did not enjoy equal rights. Despite these problems, the Latin American masses, the statement proclaimed, were rising up against imperial domination in a struggle for national sovereignty and independence. On one side were the wealthy landowners and bourgeois oligarchy allied with imperial forces that sought to defend their privileges as they handed the country over to the Yankees, and on the other side were the workers, peasants, and poor people who had not sold their souls to imperialism. It was clear on which side the communist party stood.

The party recounted the country's recent history that led to Ponce's current conservative government. Plaza represented landowners and bourgeois sectors, and even though he appeared to respect formal democracy, he ruled in favor of Yankee imperialism. Popular discontent with his government led to the election of the demagogue Velasco Ibarra who allied with feudal sectors of the conservative party. While the 1956 election should have opened a path to a progressive democracy, the most reactionary sectors of the country took control with Ponce. Instead, the PCE advocated for the establishment of a democratic coalition government comprised of workers, peasants, and members of the middle class who had not sold out to imperialism. The working class in alliance with peasants would take a leading role in the formation of this new administration that would guide the country forward.

The party declared that it did not hide its position in a global communist movement. The scientific doctrine of Marxism-Leninism guided its actions, and its final goal was the establishment of a communist society. In such a world, workers would control the means of production and distribution, which would eliminate "the exploitation of man by man." Wars would disappear, and complete equality would emerge without special privileges for anyone. The party fought for socialism, the first stage on the path to communism comparable to that which had already been achieved in the Soviet Union where class exploitation and slavery had disappeared. The party acknowledged that these triumphs would not be immediate but required a lengthy historical process. Here the statement turned back to an orthodox interpretation of how that goal might be achieved. The first step was the establishment of a democratic coalition government that would fight for national independence. To lay out concretely what such an administration would look like, the party offered a summary of the rather moderate electoral platform that it had presented a year earlier. Broadly, this program called for democracy, agrarian reform, economic policies that would develop the country, improvements in living conditions, advances in education and culture, and an independent foreign policy. The party expressed confidence that this program would benefit the great majority of the country's population and lead to a free, sovereign, and prosperous country.

Throughout the country's entire history, the Ecuadorian people had been fighting tirelessly for democracy and independence, and the party argued that this program was achievable. The PCE placed itself at the head of this struggle. It acknowledged that the battle would be difficult, because the wealthy would never give up their privileges willingly. As the famed abolitionist Frederick Douglass had observed in the United States, "Power concedes nothing without a demand. It never has and it never will."[80] But struggling together men and women could achieve these gains, and their future depended on doing so.

A quarter century later, the communist militant Elías Muñoz Vicuña reflected fondly on this statement as representing a key step in the progression of the Ecuadorian communist party. Muñoz asserted that as part of a democratic struggle, the PCE played an "outstanding role in the organization of workers, peasants, teachers, artisans, and professionals." A key point of the document was its identification of "imperialism as the primary enemy and the national liberation front as the instrument of victory." According to Muñoz, it was "a first-class historical document for the development of Ecuadorian democracy."[81] For the historian Hernán Ibarra, the proclamation reflected Saad's influence on the party. Similar to Muñoz, Ibarra highlights its emphasis on the imperialist penetration of Ecuador, but also ties its analysis to the lingering negative effects of domestic feudalism that drug the economy down. Local oligarchs were complicit with this foreign imperial penetration. The solution required the unification of a working-class struggle with that of the peasantry, the middle classes, and a progressive bourgeoisie. Together, they would carry out a democratic transformation that would lead to social and national liberation. As an indication of the importance that Ibarra places on this statement, it is the only document from a sixteen-year period between 1944 and 1960 that he included in his massive compilation of Ecuadorian communist thought.[82]

THE 1957 PCE platform contributed to an accelerated growth in communist, and more broadly leftist, activity in Ecuador. Beginning in 1958, social movements gained more visibility and their strength only grew in 1959. No longer were conflicts confined to local areas, and as they increased in size they influenced public opinion. The importance and resilience of rural mobilizations from 1959 to 1963 eventually forced promulgation of agrarian reform legislation.[83] It was in this context that defense minister Alfonso Calderón Moreno asked the United States Embassy for assistance in training his officers in counterintelligence activities. He claimed to be no alarmist, but stated that he was completely convinced that Ecuador had become a prime communist target in Latin America.[84] Such comments only fed CIA fears as well as those of other United States government officials that they were losing an ideological battle as the entire region tilted leftward.

Surveillance documents indicate the direction that the left was taking, not only in Ecuador but also across Latin America and throughout the world. Rather than moderating their demands, a militant wing pushed the PCE to take ever more radical action. These actions laid the groundwork for the emergence of a more combative and aggressive left in the 1960s. External events provide a broader context necessary to understand those advances and contribute to a proper appreciation of internal developments. At the same time, that "new" left did not emerge out of a vacuum or only as a result of the Cuban Revolution, but built on a longer trajectory of sustained domestic grassroots organizing that political surveillance thoroughly documented.

Conclusion

1959

On January 1, 1959, Cuba's authoritarian leader Fulgencio Batista fled into exile with a personal fortune of more than $300 million USD that he had amassed through years of corrupt dealings. The Argentine guerrilla leader Ernesto "Che" Guevara had just defeated Batista's military forces at the battle of Santa Clara, signaling the end of the regime. Guevara was part of Fidel Castro's 26th of July Movement that had landed insurgent forces in the eastern Sierra Maestra Mountains two years earlier. A week after the battle of Santa Clara, the rebel army rolled victoriously into the capital city of Havana to the cheers and open embrace of the general public. The guerrillas occupied key military posts and called for a general strike to put down any remaining support for the dictatorship. Their new government quickly implemented policies to transform society, including an agrarian reform law, a literacy campaign, and the nationalization of foreign-owned businesses with the goal of creating a more equal and just distribution of resources.

Symbolically, 1959 and the Cuban Revolution represent a turning point in Latin America. The triumph of revolutionary forces in Cuba is arguably one of the most significant political events of the twentieth century. If insurgent forces could remove an entrenched pro-United States military dictatorship just off the shores of Miami, then leftists surely would be able to do likewise anywhere in the world. To aid in this endeavor, Guevara penned a how-to manual called *Guerrilla Warfare* that described how you too could overthrow your government. All it would take is a dedicated cadre of revolutionaries to trigger a mass insurrection that would lead to a fundamental transformation of society.[1] The entire world appeared to be on the cusp of revolutionary change.

The Cuban example inspired leftists across the hemisphere to engage in similar guerrilla campaigns against established administrations in their countries.[2] Disillusioned with a gradual, peaceful road to socialism that orthodox communist parties had long backed, a new and younger generation of activists advocated for more immediate and direct action to achieve what the Cubans had just realized. This wave of revolutionary activity has drawn significant public and academic attention to what has come to be known as the "global sixties." Not only in Latin America but also around the world workers, students, and others took to the streets and the mountains with the ambition of realizing a new and different world. Both those mobilizations and the predictable conservative, cold war, anticommunist reactions against them have led to a sizable literature.

Despite heightened hopes and aspirations, none of the attempts to emulate the Cuban Revolution through a violent uprising proved to be immediately successful. Exiles returned to their home countries only to be crushed by superior military forces. In perhaps the most high-profile debacle, a guerrilla force that Guevara led into Bolivia with the vision of turning the Andean Mountains into the Sierra Maestra of South America failed to gain traction with the local population. Instead, in October 1967 US-trained counterinsurgency troops captured and executed Guevara. Other guerrilla leaders had met failure and death before him, but Guevara's defeat called into question the entire Cuban model of shooting one's way into power.

Three years later, Salvador Allende won election in Chile, the first Marxist to gain the presidency through peaceful, democratic means—precisely the model that revolutionaries had rejected in following the Cuban example. That achievement together with the failure of a sequence of guerrilla insurgencies led activists and scholars to ponder whether they had fundamentally misunderstood what had brought about the triumph of the Cuban Revolution. Castro had led his troops in a seemingly rapid and unexpected ascension to power. But what that presupposition ignores are the decades of organizing that had laid the groundwork for the triumph, much as a long history of labor movements precipitated Allende's election a decade later.[3] Armed insurrections naturally incite emotions and draw attention, but ultimately the specific path to success—whether armed, electoral, or a general strike—was less significant than that victory itself. And such victories were only the result of long and difficult struggles.

All of these larger issues of how best to gain that elusive triumph for the left that were playing out across Latin America—and, indeed, around the world—were at work in Ecuador. The triumph of the Cuban Revolution succinctly placed the contrast between orthodox Marxist assumptions that Latin America did not yet possess the objective economic conditions for a transition to socialism and much more militant aspirations for immediate revolutionary action into dramatic relief. As elsewhere, these tensions that had long underlay internal debates within communist parties now spilled out on the open stage for all to see.

The social protest and violent governmental repression of radical desires that swept across Ecuador in 1959 represented the end of an unusual period of institutional stability that had reigned since Galo Plaza Lasso's inauguration as president in 1948. A full exploration of the transformative importance of that one year could probably and usefully fill an entire book. Highlighting only a couple of key points illustrates and summarizes how the 1950s laid the groundwork for the transformative decade that was to follow. As long-term surveillance of the PCE makes readily apparent, those heightened levels of protest did not emerge out of a vacuum.

Eleventh Inter-American Conference

1959 was as active and dynamic in Ecuador as anywhere in the hemisphere, and as elsewhere the shockwaves emanating out from Cuba could most definitely be felt. The year began with a bang on January 7 with a police massacre of five Otavalos and the injuring of others and the damaging and looting of several homes at Lago San Pablo in the northern Imbabura Province. Rural community members at Pucará Bajo de Velásquez had been protesting plans to build a tourist hotel and casino on their land in preparation for the eleventh Inter-American Conference of American states planned for Quito the following year. Víctor Alejandro Jaramillo, a conservative senator to the federal congress and the president of the city of Otavalo's municipal council that intended to build the hotel, justified the bloody repression. He and other members of the white ruling class wanted to pursue the project as a mechanism to encourage tourism and create jobs. Others, including activists with the FTP and lawyers for the CTE, came to the community's defense, and demanded the dismissal of officials who were responsible for the massacre.[4]

The tenth Inter-American Conference in Caracas, Venezuela in 1954 had named Quito as the site for the eleventh conference. Preparations began slowly, and by 1959 they were in full swing. For the Ecuadorian government, it was to be an opportunity to let the country shine. The government received a $2.5 million loan from the Export-Import Bank to build new airport terminals in Quito and Guayaquil, a new hotel (the Quito Hotel) to house the delegates, a new building (subsequently used as the legislative palace) to host the sessions, and for the installation of radio and other equipment. Even the government palace and ministry of foreign affairs buildings underwent extensive renovation. All of these projects were intended to present the image of a modern and developed country. The extensive construction faced repeated delays, and ultimately the conference was never held. The planned conclave encountered many other problems that contributed to its breakdown, including ongoing border tensions with neighboring Peru that led to that country's withdrawal from the meeting.[5]

The failure of the Quito conference was due in part to the success of leftist organizing against its imperialist trajectory. The ninth conference in Bogotá, Colombia in 1948 had seen the birth of the OAS as well as a pledge by member states to fight communism in the Western Hemisphere. The tenth conference at Caracas six years later affirmed and extended that declaration, particularly as it targeted the progressive Jacobo Arbenz government in Guatemala. Communists denounced the conference as only serving "U.S. imperialist aims in the struggle against the democratic movement." The communist party in neighboring Colombia launched a campaign to highlight the exploitative nature of the eleventh conference, and at the same time called on the meeting to "speak out in favor of world peace, disarmament and against the nuclear weapon tests." The Colombian party welcomed opposition to the conference as marking "another step in the growing resistance of the Latin American peoples to North American imperialism."[6] Opponents mobilized grassroots resistance against a meeting that would only benefit the ruling class and their imperial masters to the harm of the workers.

Both government officials and media outlets responded to opposition to the conference with fear and trepidation. The *New York Times* published a report that the PCE was "preparing a campaign to discredit and if possible disrupt the conference." The paper claimed that it had access to "a secret resolution of the party's Central Committee" that detailed plans to attack the meeting. The campaign against the conference was "one of the top current Communist objectives in the hemisphere." That goal was "accompanied by increased Communist activities in Ecuador in recent months," including "a clandestine but substantial flow of Communist propaganda into the country." Weapons and "four Cuban Communist leaders" had also arrived. In light of these developments, President Camilo Ponce Enríquez charged that Ecuador had become "one of communism's prime targets in South America."[7] His administration pleaded with United States government officials for aid to confront this menace.

This *New York Times* article should be immediately seen for the exaggerations, paranoia, and scaremongering that it represented. To be sure, "Cuban Communist leaders" had indeed visited Ecuador. In fact, their arrival in Quito on February 25 received extensive media coverage, including on the front page of *El Comercio*. The *New York Times* even reported on their visit. The "bearded revolutionaries" were in the midst of a tour of the Americas, not to overthrow other regimes but to communicate the truths about the programs their new government planned to implement.[8] The United States government responded to this diplomatic initiative with a psychological disinformation campaign that included the distribution of materials to the Ecuadorian government designed to undermine the communist stance with explicit encouragement to confront opposition to the Inter-American Conference.[9] Theoretically, United States diplomats claimed adherence to the tenets of nonintervention, though how these ideas played out in practice could be quite at odds with those declarations.

Despite its overt propagandistic intent, or perhaps because of it, *El Comercio* in Quito and *El Telégrafo* in Guayaquil translated and republished the *New York Times* article on the alleged communist plot to sabotage the Inter-American Conference.[10] The publication led to a fiery retort from the PCE, asserting that the media did not need to resort to hidden conspiracies because their position on the conference was not a secret. Their "firm and tenacious political line of opposition to imperialist aggression of which the inter-American conferences were a part" was public and well known. Instead, the party favored policies that would lead to world peace, disarmament, and the suspension of nuclear tests. It also denounced military pacts, defended the sovereignty of Ecuador and other Latin American countries, opposed the anticommunist declarations from the last Inter-American Conference that propped up right-wing military dictatorships, and condemned the United States for plundering the wealth from Latin America. More than anything, the party called on the eleventh conference to revise the 1942 Rio Protocol and return the land that had been taken away from Ecuador. Expanding out from this overtly nationalistic position, the PCE proceeded to denounce the imperialist penetration of Latin America and those members of the domestic ruling class who collaborated with these endeavors. The party denied that it had received any weapons, and declared that the only arms that flowed to Latin America were the ones that the United States sent to local governments. The statement joked that the communists did not need to discredit the Inter-American Conferences because the organizers discredited themselves with policies that led in Bogotá in 1948 to the assassination of the progressive populist leader Jorge Eliécer Gaitán and the resulting violence of the conservative administration in Colombia, and in Caracas in 1954 to the overthrow of Arbenz's democratic government in Guatemala. From this pattern, the PCE extrapolated that the intent of the Quito conference was to bring down the Cuban Revolution, and communist activists promised to stand firm against such ventures. Rather than a conference in which dictators such as Luis Somoza from Nicaragua, Rafael Trujillo from the Dominican Republic, and Alfredo

Stroessner from Paraguay attended, they called for an open and democratic encounter of workers, students, and intellectuals that represented freedom and independence.[11]

Communist assertions of innocence did not receive much public attention, particularly in the context of rising anticommunist sentiments and cold war fears that made the media susceptible to propaganda. In fact, the *New York Times* repeatedly returned to its conspiratorial reporting. The following year, the paper once again detailed the assertions of diplomatic and intelligence sources that Cuba and Ecuador were developing closer ties intended to undo hemisphere solidarity. United States government officials fanned these anticommunist sentiments. Once again, they claimed to have intercepted communist party documents indicating plans for "major violence at the conference in order to discredit the inter-American system."[12] Ecuador's ambassador to the United States José Ricardo Chiriboga Villagómez pressed similar issues with the State Department. In one meeting he asserted that Ponce was "extremely concerned over the Communist situation and the possibility that the Communists might take action to interfere with the Inter-American Conference." Chiriboga Villagómez claimed that the Ecuadorian government was not equipped to confront the communist challenge, and exploited this perceived weakness as an excuse to request assistance from the United States—a common ruse that diplomats employed.[13] Similar charges of communist plans to disrupt the meeting of foreign ministers had been raised fourteen years earlier in Bogotá. Then as now, the accusations of communists organizing riots fed fear and an anticommunist narrative rather than reflecting political realities. Leftists indeed opposed the meeting and planned to use their opposition to it to advance their agenda, but as had been the case for the previous decade they had no intentions of resorting to violence to achieve their political goals.

Political strife in Ecuador continued at a similar pace for the rest of the year. In February, one thousand dockworkers went on strike in Guayaquil to protest the firing of eight union leaders. That industrial action brought commerce to a standstill in the port, which led Ponce's government to declare the strike illegal and to send in military troops. Workers in other industries responded with sympathy strikes, and the demonstrations spread as far as the law school at the Central University in Quito under the leadership of future president Rodrigo Borja. In what by now had become a common trope, Ponce charged that communists had instigated the strike to sabotage the upcoming conference of American states.[14] United States officials in Guayaquil responded positively to the president's "prompt and drastic measures against communist leaders." According to consul general William Moreland, this action represented "an entirely new chapter in the current administration." Until this point, communists had "become increasingly brazen and proud of being communists," and the administration's action "undoubtedly have lost to the Ecuadoran communists a tremendous amount of prestige." The consul anticipated that the repression would make it more difficult for the communists to mobilize their forces.[15]

At the same time that dockworkers faced repression on the coast, Indigenous workers on the Chaupi hacienda in Pesillo in the northern highlands successfully convinced the labor inspector to address their concerns of low salaries, mistreatment, and abuses.[16] Ponce accused the communists of "under the pretext of raising the Indians' condition, abusing their ignorance and turning them into cannon fodder." Ecuador, he claimed, had become "one of communism's prime targets in South America."[17] Since he did not believe Indigenous peoples could struggle for themselves, their demonstrations must be the result of "actions instigated by 'expert communist agitators.'"[18] Both CIA officials as well as their counterparts in Latin America were unable or unwilling to recognize that people were capable of organizing themselves to improve their own lives without the intervention of "outside" agents. What Ponce and the CIA faced and feared were these heightened levels of mobilization that echoed across the country.

June Protests

At the end of May, military conscripts at Portoviejo mutinied against their abusive commanding officer, Captain Galo Quevedo. One of the conscripts, José García Macías, committed suicide after attempting to assassinate Quevedo. In reaction to his death, the other draftees proceeded to lynch Quevedo and together with local civilians attacked the army garrison. Five people, including two students, were killed and fifty wounded in the exchange of gunfire.[19] Paratroopers from Quito arrived to put down the mutiny, but rather than quelling the unrest the revolt spread. On June 2, police broke up a student demonstration held in solidarity with the Portoviejo conscripts at the Vicente Rocafuerte High School in Guayaquil, killing six people in the process. Ponce imposed martial law, a twenty-four-hour curfew, press censorship, and sent in the army to restore order. The following day, the inhabitants of Guayaquil's poor neighborhoods joined the protests by burning and looting stores, resulting in the deaths of twenty-five more.[20] The government responded to the vandalism and robberies with indiscriminate violence, including issuing orders to shoot to kill at the masses. By the end, at least thirty-seven people were dead, 150 wounded, and five hundred more held for questioning, although the numbers may have been much higher.[21]

The protests at Portoviejo and Guayaquil came in the context of growing student unrest. In May, demonstrations shut down three high schools in Loja, Machala, and Guayaquil. The US Embassy monitored those developments and reported that the Loja situation was "potentially dangerous" because communists were active in the school system and strove to take advantage of legitimate grievances to advance their own political agenda. "Although strikes are rarely instigated by Communists," the embassy commented, "they usually leap into [the] conflict for [their] own purposes."[22] These troubles were unlikely to end any time soon. The level of repression the government used to put down the protests only caused them to spread. In Quito, university students marched on the presidential palace to demand Ponce's resignation although the absence of their leaders in Loja for a FEUE convention limited the success of their demonstration. The CTE also announced plans for a general strike in sympathy with labor leader Segundo Ramos who had been imprisoned in Guayaquil.[23]

Despite a lack of any factual evidence, Ponce immediately blamed communists for the unrest and proceeded to implement draconian anticommunist and antilabor policies. The president claimed that he needed to act to defend the republic from "foreign Communist aggression." In order to justify his action, he released two documents, one from a plenary meeting of the PCE in Guayaquil in December 1958 and a second from the Pichincha provincial committee of the PCE from April 1959. The documents called for a concerted campaign against the forthcoming Inter-American Conference, which was already the party's public stance and therefore no great news.[24] Even so, it is difficult to know whether these were fabricated or planted documents. The senior clandestine services officer Harry Rositzke describes the CIA's operations in Ecuador as "typical" for the agency, including infiltrating the communist party, working with diplomatic officials, supporting the propaganda efforts of the USIA, and assisting the USAID with its training and equipping of police and military forces—all with the goal of countering the growth of the left.[25] Philip Agee describes disinformation campaigns that deployed such tactics in his book *Inside the Company*, but he did not arrive in Ecuador until December of the following year and so does not discuss these specific events. But United States Embassy personnel present at the time recount providing the press secretary in the president's office—the same source for these items—with communist party material, and that might have been their provenance.[26] In any case, the party made no secret of its political platform and as such these documents were not necessarily out of line with what it publicly advocated. The way the presidency released the documents, however, indicates a blatant attempt to instigate anticommunist sentiments.

Ponce's government charged that communist agitators as well as CFP leaders had encouraged the demonstrations in Portoviejo and Guayaquil, an accusation that State Department analysts willingly echoed, even as military officials acknowledged that the unrest was not political in nature. Nevertheless, once again Ponce contended that communists had smuggled weapons into the country and were following a prepared plan to force cancellation of the Inter-American Conference and to overthrow the government, even though that had never been their modus operandi. The president declared that his actions were necessary "to save the republic from anarchy and aggression." The PCE responded with a statement denouncing the government's "criminal repression" and calling for "a great front of popular and democratic unity to prevent dictatorship."[27] As had been the case across the 1950s, their rhetoric was radical but returning yet again to the formation of a broad electoral front was a moderate solution that did little to assuage the demands of a militant membership that desired more transformative policies.

In the midst of this political discord, Ecuador's ambassador Chiriboga Villagómez once again met with State Department officials in Washington. Chiriboga Villagómez immediately blamed the communists for the disturbances and claimed that they were part of their "known plans for disrupting the Quito Conference." The ambassador exploited the protests and their alleged communist inspiration to appeal once more for United States aid, and in particular for military assistance to put down the subversive threats.[28] Interestingly, in private internal communications the United States consul Moreland had not blamed the communists but instead "hoodlums and vandals" who infiltrated and tarnished what otherwise had "started out to be strictly a student show." Rather than premeditated, the uprising was "spontaneous, and not even the Communists were organized to capitalize on a situation made to order for Communist agitators." In fact, the consul reported that the PCE was significantly behind the curve with its mobilizations. At a funeral procession that quickly became a demonstration with some twenty thousand people, "a youth came dashing through the crowd with handbills which he shoved under the armpits of the persons present." The communist manifesto called on the people to launch a general strike to demand the president's resignation. Most people ignored the handbills which, according to Moreland, "indicated that the Communists were behind schedule."[29] Similar to rank-and-file militants in the party, the consul disregarded communist statements as long on incendiary language and short on implementing concrete measures to achieve their stated objectives.

Apparently the PCE manifesto Moreland references is the same one mentioned in news reports, although the statement itself is not included in depositories where other party documents can be found.[30] One item that has survived is from the party's provincial committee in Pichincha in the highlands far removed from the unrest on the coast and is dated June 7—several days after the events. As with other statements, this one does not so much directly engage the bloody events in Portoviejo and Guayaquil as use those as an opportunity to attack the communists' archenemy, the conservative president Ponce, for his reactionary policies that contributed to hunger, misery, and oppression. The party charged that the president was stirring up fears of alleged foreign communist aggression in order to provide a pretext to advance the interests of feudalistic landowners and to implement a bloody and repressive dictatorship. As with the manifesto in Guayaquil, the Pichincha provincial committee issued its standard call for a "great front of popular and democratic unity" that would stand firm against a criminal dictatorship that massacred the people. The party instead favored policies that would open a path toward liberal freedoms, democratic guarantees, independence for the country, and well-being for the people.[31] While this was hardly a course of action that would appeal to those inspired by the recent triumph of the Cuban Revolution, it does reveal the presence of a persistently active and engaged party that was consistent in its proposed strategy and tactics.

Subsequent consular reports from Guayaquil continued a similar narrative that "the usual Communist actions and declarations were noticeably absent during the height of the troubles," and that "Communists appear to be laying low."[32] The situation had caught the communists by surprise, and as a result they "were too poorly organized to be immediately effective." Before they could act, the government declared martial law and jailed their leaders.[33] Nevertheless, in case any questions might remain as to where alliances ultimately lay, Moreland reported that he was surreptitiously supporting anticommunist students in their efforts to wrestle control of the FEUE away from the communists.[34]

In Quito and farther away from the center of activities in Guayaquil, the United States Embassy was less charitable in their assessment of the communist role than was their consulate on the coast. In a weekly report on developments in the country, chargé d'affaires Frederick Leatherman complained that local newspapers "still did not take [the] threat of Communist intervention as more than [a] minor annoyance."[35] He was more eager to fan the flames of anticommunist sentiments than his counterparts at the center of activity. The closer one was to the action and the more information one had the less scary the communists appeared, and the more accurate of a picture of their actions and intents emerged.

The *New York Times* Latin American correspondent Tad Szulc inadvertently acknowledged the presence of different explanations for communist actions. He observed that Ponce's contention in Quito that the protests "were part of a Communist-directed effort to overthrow the Government . . . differed substantially from the views of military commanders and civilian political observers on the scene" in Guayaquil. Instead, he reported, "there had been no evidence of major Communist involvement" in the unrest. While "the Communists may have had some plan to disrupt public order . . . surprisingly, they failed to take advantage of the riots." Szulc blamed their failures on poor leadership and the military's rapid response in quelling the altercations. Even so, the government arrested fifteen communist leaders. Further weakening the communists' hand, right-wing elements in the FEUE voted in Loja to disaffiliate with the leftist IUS.[36]

Szulc followed with a series of articles in which he warned of the rise of communist threats across the hemisphere. He cautioned that communist parties were more active "than they have been in a long time and apparently better-coordinated than ever before" as they sought "to exploit situations that were ready made for them." As evidence of his claim, he pointed to a Moscow radio broadcast that "gloatingly commented that 'democratic forces' in the Americas were being channeled toward the final objective of freeing the area of Yankee imperialism" and "that the Ecuadorian Communists were with 'the people.'"[37] While numerically small and legal in less than half of the countries, "the Latin American Communist parties are exercising influence that is completely out of proportion to the size of their memberships or even the 'fellow traveling' grass roots support they occasionally command." Their leaders were "extremely skilled" in appealing to nationalist sentiments, fostering resentment over deep social and economic problems, and infiltrating government structures. Still, the limits of Szulc's understanding of communist operations are apparent in his reporting. While he acknowledged that the current orthodox communist line continued to be one of cooperation with progressive bourgeois parties and a desire to gain respectability, Szulc contended that "the Communist hand is almost invariably seen in most strikes and incidents of violence that are cropping up with growing frequency," as well as in "riots in protest against economic austerity measures." The tendency of media sources and the government to label protests as "riots" implies an irrationality of action that deprecates serious attempts to advance legitimate concerns. Szulc repeatedly references the claims of "intelligence experts" that communists planned to disrupt the Inter-American Conference by violent means, and that travel between Latin America and socialist countries meant that Moscow directed their strategies.[38] This narrative of foreign agitators as being responsible for the discord in Latin America served the political and economic interests of local government officials who did not want to give up their ruling-class privileges. It ignores a long trajectory of sustained organizing efforts.

Szulc traced the disturbances in Ecuador—as well as recent attempts to oust governments in Panama, Nicaragua, and Paraguay—back to "the victory of Fidel Castro and the Cuban revolutionaries at the beginning of the year."[39] The Cubans, of course, denied that they intended to export their revolution. The militant leftist Jaime Galarza Zavala later stated that the Cuban Revolution only distantly influenced the events in Ecuador. Rather, he saw the unrest as a natural reaction to the current socioeconomic situation and the government's repressive responses.[40] The *New York Times* acknowledged Castro's statement, "We have been asked if revolution should be exported and we have said no, that revolution cannot be exported, that revolution must be carried out by the people themselves." Nevertheless, the paper responded that the Cuban Revolution "has fanned the flames of revolution throughout the Latin world." The newspaper contended that Latin America was "in the midst of two distinct revolutions." One was to oust the dictatorships of Somoza in Nicaragua, Stroessner in Paraguay, and Trujillo in the Dominican Republic. A second, and perhaps more significant, was "the deep desire of the people for economic improvement and social betterment." According to the paper, "Latin America's small but well-organized Communist parties" aggravated the situation with their efforts to exploit it.[41] The *New York Times* editorial board made this claim even as Szulc acknowledged that the Ecuadorian government had no proof to support its charges that the unrest was communist inspired. Even so, Szulc concluded that regardless of the origins of these events, "the explosions demonstrated how near the surface violence lay in Ecuador."[42] By all appearances, a revolution was breaking out in Ecuador, and the PCE was not positioned to lead it even though its years of engaged activism laid the organizational basis for these developments.

Social conflict continued without let up throughout the rest of the year. On October 1, another protest broke out in Guayaquil when an Ecuadorian navy shore patrol attempted to stop hoodlums from molesting drum majorettes who were practicing their routines. Two people were killed and four injured in the resulting melee. The police proved unable to restore order so once again the government called in the army to patrol the streets. Observers noted that the disturbances unfolded in a similar fashion to what had happened in June. Teeming social and economic problems set the stage for an explosive situation in which jobless and hungry workers welcomed opportunities to loot stores.[43] The United States consulate in Guayaquil complained that communists, socialists, and other left-wing groups systematically exploited the volatile situation to attack Ponce's government. Moreland feared that the strife could rapidly escalate to a point where the army would not be able to maintain control. Unlike his rational explanation of the June disturbances, this time the consul eagerly blamed local communist leaders for the unrest.[44] The consulate even repeated rumors that the political opposition to Ponce paid hoodlums to disrupt public gatherings.[45]

What failed to register on the radar of the diplomats was much more serious and significant political organizing efforts. Several days before the October protest, 850 Indigenous farmers from thirty-five rural syndicates and community organizations converged on Quito to demand higher pay for their labor and the promulgation of an agrarian reform program that would give them access to land. Their urban allies in the FTP and CTE came to their defense when the police refused to let them march from their meeting place at the Casa del Obrero to the federal congress to present their demands directly to the legislators.[46] "For the Indians, history has stopped," the writer Pedro Jorge Vera editorialized. "Servitude is the same in the 20th century as it was in the 16th. Independence only meant that creole landholders could continue to exploit Indians without the intervention of the crown." Even with this long and bloody history, the current government was unequalled in its contempt for Indigenous peoples. Its goal was to outlaw Indians together with the communists.[47]

In a repeat of 1953, Pedro Saad, the communist representative for coastal labor, along with the socialist representative for highland labor Miguel Angel Guzmán cited Ponce's minister of government Carlos Bustamante Pérez for an interpellation to respond to these violations of people's rights. The list of complaints that the two presented quickly expanded to touch on all of the problems that Ecuador had suffered during this pivotal year, including the massacre of Indigenous community members at San Pablo del Lago in January, the protests at Portoviejo and Guayaquil in May and June, attacks on the students in the FEUE, and other issues.[48]

After almost a week of long and exhausting all-night interpellation sessions, the minister and the entire administration remained firmly in place. Saad had made a good showing, but as in 1953 did not possess sufficient political strength to shift policy. Even so, as with the earlier interpellation, the United States

Embassy gave a shout out to Saad for his sincere and principled opposition, notably unlike that of the "demagogic" CFP. As evidence of a certain amount of grudging respect for their ideological foe, the embassy reported that "Saad, using reasonable language but following the Communist line, attacked the proposal for an inter-American police force as a pretext for U.S. intervention in internal affairs of the American Republics."[49] Saad's long history of political agitation provided him with the skills and strength necessary to advance a communist agenda even though his adherence to parliamentary strategies failed to appease those to his left in the party.

Divisions

On September 1, 1960, José María Velasco Ibarra returned to the presidency for his fourth of five times in office. In a four-way race, Velasco Ibarra won with almost 50 percent of the vote, somewhat of an improvement over the 43 percent he had won in 1952. Only three-quarters of a million people out of a total population of 4.3 million participated in the election, making the whole affair still a highly exclusionary event. As in previous outings, the left's champion, the diplomat and current rector of the University of Guayaquil Antonio Parra Velasco, hardly registered in the polls, finished last with about 6 percent of the vote. With literacy restrictions excluding most workers and peasants from the franchise, an electoral path to power hardly seemed viable. Some conservative socialists supported previous president Plaza because he appeared to be a more viable candidate and in comparison to those who had come after him, his government in retrospect appeared to be downright progressive. Even with that backing, Plaza barely outpolled the conservative candidate Gonzalo Cordero Crespo for runner-up status.[50]

In a remarkable policy reversal, the CFP unexpectedly joined the PCE and left-wing socialists in an anticonservative alliance known as the Unión Democrática Nacional Anti-Conservadora (UDNA, National Democratic Anti-Conservative Union) in support of Parra Velasco. While previously progressives had categorically rejected any suggestion of collaborating with the populist CFP, a debate had run through the left as to whether Ponce and the right or Guevara Moreno and the CFP represented a greater threat. After its sixth congress in 1957, the PCE called on liberals to join them and the PSE and the CFP in an anticonservative coalition to advance a common platform of democracy, development, and sovereignty.[51] While some liberals advocated casting a broad tent to include everyone in this alliance, others preferred the conservatives over the CFP. From their perspective, the first was more *culta y controlado* (cultured and controlled) than the CFP, and the idea of a left wing in the CFP with which other progressives could collaborate was nothing more than an illusion.[52] Politics can make for strange bedfellows.

The 1956 presidential election represented a highpoint of electoral strength for the CFP, and by the time of the 1957 PCE congress it was already coasting into a slow and long decline. The CFP subsequently collapsed due to its disastrous administration of Guayaquil's municipal government, which led to the ouster of Guevara Moreno from the party.[53] Even without Guevara Moreno's leadership, populist parties continued to play a significant role in Ecuadorian public life. Politics was shifting in a myriad of different directions.

Beginning with Velasco Ibarra's inauguration, it was immediately apparent that Ecuador had returned to its status quo ante of political volatility and instability. Velasco Ibarra had attacked his predecessor and former ally and protégé Ponce relentlessly during the campaign, which left the incumbent president so angry that he resigned on his last day in office rather than preside over the inauguration of his successor. The resignation technically represented a break in an otherwise unprecedented sequence of constitutional transfers of power, but more significantly it foreshadowed a complete unraveling of institutional structures. As with all except the immediately preceding mandate, Velasco Ibarra's administration quickly degenerated into a military regime, bringing an end to a succession of elected civilian governments. After fourteen months in office and amid a general strike and violent unrest precipitated by worsening economic conditions, the military deposed Velasco Ibarra and installed his vice president Carlos Julio Arosemena Monroy in his place. The military, in turn, expressed discontent with Arosemena Monroy's pro-Cuban rhetoric and, fearing the emergence of a domestic left-wing insurgency, ousted the president in 1963. The military junta that took power outlawed the communist party. In the process, soldiers captured and probably destroyed the party's archives, leaving historians to search for other sources (including the CIA) to document their activities.

Rather than radicalizing the communist party, the Cuban Revolution divided an already fragmented left into pro-Soviet, pro-China, and pro-Cuba wings.[54] Competing leftist factions criticized the PCE for having lost its revolutionary fervor with its adherence to a pro-Soviet line that advocated for peaceful coexistence with imperialism. Young people in particular wanted to engage in more aggressive political action. Rather than embracing Castro and Guevara as heroes, orthodox communist leaders in Cuba had initially denounced them as a radicalized petty bourgeoisie who were provocateurs and adventurers engaged in inappropriate ultra-leftist activities. Party leaders in Ecuador now hurled the same criticism against the young revolutionaries in their own ranks. Two entirely different visions emerged as to how a socialist revolution might be realized—one peaceful and evolutionary and other violent and rapid. These tensions had long run through the left and had been building inside the party for some time, but the Cuban Revolution brought them fully out into the open for all to see.

Shortly after the 1957 PCE congress, the United States Embassy reported "a newly-developed potentially serious schism in the Communist Party." Several "higher-echelon leaders" had "expressed their complete disillusionment over Soviet leadership" as well as Saad's domination of the party. These quarrels played out even as the party proceeded with their plans to build a leftist coalition, publish a daily newspaper, and increase their presence in labor unions. The diplomats anticipated that these divisions "may curtail somewhat the Party's upsurge" after the congress.[55] Cracks in the party did not emerge out of nowhere but could be traced to different visions that had long been present on the left.

The most serious, visible, and long-lasting of these rifts was the Sino-Soviet split. Global conflicts reached into the heart of what otherwise might be seen as marginalized sectors of an international communist movement. In Ecuador, the Cuban Revolution influenced Jaime Galarza and Édison Carrera to found the Unión Revolucionaria de la Juventud Ecuatoriana (URJE, Revolutionary Union of the Ecuadorian Youth). In April 1962 under the leadership of the PCE's Pichincha provincial committee members Jorge Rivadeneyra and Rafael Echeverría, the URJE launched a failed guerrilla uprising at the Toachi River in Santo Domingo. Saad, who remained committed to a Soviet line that advocated for a peaceful path to power through the formation of electoral alliances with progressive and nationalistic sectors of the bourgeoisie, evicted these radical "ultra-leftists" from the party. Rivadeneyra and Echeverría in turn formed the pro-Chinese PCMLE in 1964.[56] Meanwhile, the socialists also suffered a series of divisions, with longtime leader and intellectual Manuel Agustín Aguirre leaving in March 1963 to form the PSRE, which assumed a pro-Cuban position. Other independent radical groups emerged during the 1960s, including the Movimiento de Izquierda Revolucionaria (MIR, Movement of the Revolutionary Left), Vencer o Morir (VM, Win or Die), and Unión Revolucionaria de Mujeres del Ecuador (URME, Revolutionary Union of Ecuadorian Women).[57] Contributing to these divisions were the actions of left-wing women such as Nela Martínez and María Luisa Gómez de la Torre who were critical of the communist party's patriarchal and hierarchical structure that favored the prevalence of men in leadership roles. Similar to those who engaged in armed struggle, these women activists faced attempts from the mainline communist party to proscribe their political agency. Despite these challenges and eventual exclusion, these militants had honed their organizing skills within the ranks of the communist party.[58]

Documentation

After a gap of several years in the late 1950s, the level of CIA attention to Latin America rebounded significantly in the aftermath of the Cuban Revolution. In the final months of 1959, CIA intelligence bulletins drafted at CIA Headquarters in Washington once again centered attention on internal developments in Ecuador. After not saying anything about the June protests, now these analysts discussed the October demonstrations and contextualized them with the earlier events. The bulletins identified Guayaquil as "a center of explosive labor and economic unrest which the Communists are attempting to exploit with aggressive new tactics." Ultimate goals included unseating Ponce and disrupting the Inter-American Conference.[59] Subsequent reports continued the narrative that communists sought to capitalize on social discord with the intent of halting the conference.[60]

A lengthy 1963 CIA report on the ramifications of the Sino-Soviet split for Latin America includes a probing section on Ecuador that details the tensions between Saad's pro-Soviet wing centered in Guayaquil that favored adherence to a peaceful transition to power and Echeverría's much more militant pro-Chinese faction in Quito.[61] Those divisions became a frequent topic of careful analysis for the agency.[62] The depth of investigation during the militant 1960s is perhaps uncharacteristic in relation to what the agency generated during the second half of the 1950s, but not necessarily so if compared to what it produced in the immediate postwar period. Nevertheless, what is missing from the declassified records are the information reports similar to those that CIA case officers generated during the early years of the agency's operation. The raw data that those officers collected from their informers and other sources provide rich detail on domestic developments that contributes to a deeper understanding of the left.

As with all things related to secret surveillance, it is difficult to say what might account for changes in the nature, quality, and quantity of information. Was it a staffing issue? One exceptionally highly qualified and motivated individual could generate useful intelligence that logically would dissipate when the agency transferred that person to a new post. Alternatively, the change could be a result of higher-level policy decisions and priorities, both in terms of where to position staff and what tasks to assign to them. In this case, the disappearance of the CIA's information reports in the 1950s may reflect the Eisenhower administration's shift toward using the agency for covert actions to achieve foreign policy objectives. In that environment, officials probably communicated the most important information and decisions orally so as not to leave written traces. As the historian Charles Ameringer observes, "Successful covert operations are rarely documented; only the failures receive publicity."[63] Furthermore, it is possible that records were lost or destroyed. Or more mundane explanations for missing reports may relate to the vulgarities of what documentation the agency has been willing to release and even the constraints of the search features of the CREST database.

Even with these limitations, what emerges evident from the declassified documentation available to researchers is that during the 1950s the CIA hardly ignored the Western Hemisphere, even marginal countries like Ecuador with small and weak communist parties. Together with other sources of information, these reports assist historians in filling in details on the history of the left. The archival record that the CIA inadvertently left behind serves to challenge stereotypes of the 1950s as a period that experienced a turn toward the right. Rather than a decade dominated by conservatives, the 1950s witnessed the emergence of mass popular movements in the context of a fragmenting and complicated political environment. Marginalized and disenfranchised sectors of the population, including Indigenous peoples, women, workers, and students, provided significant leadership to those mobilizations. Their roles disappear from dominant narratives, but recovering their contributions is key to gaining a fuller and more complete understanding of the left. While the Communist Party of Ecuador never had a large membership, it nonetheless exercised significant influence in these movements. CIA and other surveillance documentation offer opportunities for a renewed study of these different tendencies on the left.

Multiple factors contribute to a heightened state of political mobilization and ultimate victory and it goes without saying that each individual situation is unique, and it is not the intent of this work to unwrap and analyze all of those various considerations. Rather, a goal has been to illustrate how despite appearances to the contrary political conflicts and actions do not emerge out of a vacuum. Furthermore, not considering a broader and longer context that lays the groundwork for subsequent political action can lead to a misunderstanding of the causes and intent of militant movements. It is for that reason that a study of the left in the 1950s is key to understanding how 1959 became such a pivotal year that led to advancements in the 1960s. Today's struggles contribute to tomorrow's victories.

NOTES

Abbreviations in the Notes

APL	Archivo Palacio Legislativo, Quito
BEAEP	Hojas Volantes (Handbills) collection of the Biblioteca Ecuatoriana Aurelio Espinosa Pólit, Cotocollao
CAS	Controlled American Source
CIA	Central Intelligence Agency
CIG	Central Intelligence Group (immediate forerunner of the CIA)
FBI	Federal Bureau of Investigation
FTP	Federación de Trabajadores de Pichincha
FRUS	Foreign Relations of the United States
NARA	National Archives Records Administration, College Park, MD, which includes:
	RG59 Central Decimal Files (CDF) of Record Group 59
	RG84 Record Group 84
OIR	Office of Intelligence Research at the Department of State
PCE	Partido Comunista del Ecuador
PSE	Partido Socialista Ecuatoriano
TNA	The National Archives, London

Introduction

1. For contemporary newspaper reports of the broadcast of "The War of the Worlds," see "Pueblo enardecido incendia El Comercio," *La Tierra*, February 13, 1949, 1; "Diligencias hachas sobre sucesos del 12," *El Comercio-El Día*, February 15, 1949, 1; "Redención por la cultura," *El Comercio-El Día*, February 16, 1949, 1; "El Comercio aparecerá mañana," *El Comercio-El Día*, February 18, 1949, 1; "'Mars Raiders' Cause Quito Panic," *New York Times*, February 14, 1949, 1; "20 Dead in the Quito Riot," *New York Times*, February 15, 1949, 5; "Wrecked Quito Paper to Resume," *New York Times*, February 21, 1949, 4. Also see Gosling, *Waging The War of the Worlds*, 103–13.

2. CIA, "Investigation of Terrorist Radio Program in Quito," March 16, 1949, https://www.cia.gov/library/readingroom/document/cia-rdp82-00457r002500190008-0; Memo, American Embassy, February 17, 1949, RG84, Entry #2396, Box 51, NARA.

3. Aguirre, *Economía de laisser faire*, 71.

4. Department of State, "Policy Statement Ecuador," October 2, 1950, RG59, 611.22/10-250, NARA.

5. A large literature exists on United States interventions in Latin America. For an accessible introduction, see McPherson, *A Short History of U.S. Interventions in Latin America and the Caribbean*, as well as his other works including *The Invaded*. Also see Grandin, *Empire's Workshop*.

6. Becker, *The FBI in Latin America*.

7. This tendency to skip the 1950s is apparent in works such as Paredes Ruiz, *Ricardo Paredes y la antorcha revolucionaria* and Martínez Espinosa, *Yo siempre he sido Nela Martínez Espinosa*.

8. Ibarra, "Conflictos rurales," 411.

9. Personal communication. "Indigenous" and its variations ("Indian," "native," "aboriginal," "autochthonous," etc.) are part of an inherently complicated and contested colonial nomenclature that gloss over significant ethnographic diversity. The terms traditionally have communicated negative connotations of referencing savage, primitive people who lack intelligence or reason, and often imply an essentialized and racialized notion of a primordial, unchanging existence. Some countries have resorted to synonyms to avoid these inherent problems, including "original peoples" in Bolivia and "first nations" in Canada. One of the most disastrous attempts was that of General Juan Velasco Alvarado who in a 1969 agrarian reform law in Peru announced that he was elevating Indians to the status of *campesinos* (roughly "peasants," or literally people from the countryside). His attempt to abolish the negative term *indio* led to charges of ethnocide, that he sought to eradicate and homogenize unique ethnic identities. In response, militant activists in neighboring Bolivia reclaimed the term "Indian," and in a queering of the language proclaimed that since they were colonized as indios they would liberate themselves as indios. This study recognizes all of those complications, and employs the term "Indigenous" carefully, deliberately, and intentionally even as it attempts to reflect and respect self-referential terms in common usage at the time. The *Chicago Manual of Style*, 17th ed., 8.38, calls for the names of ethnic and national groups to be capitalized, including adjectives associated with those names. Pursuant to that provision, "Indigenous" is capitalized in this book because descendants of the first inhabitants of the Americas have embraced it as an ethnic and national identifier, and doing so accords it with the dignity and recognition that it deserves. This convention is also based on, and followed in respect for, the explicitly stated preference of the board of directors of the South and Meso American Indian Rights Center (SAIIC) as an affirmation of their ethnic and national identities.

10. Ramón, *Actores de una década ganada*.

11. We see evidence of these trajectories in recent treatments of the Cuban Revolution that argue that it emerged triumphant only thanks to a much longer history of labor organizing. See, for example, Cushion, *A Hidden History of the Cuban Revolution*.

12. See "Lineamientos programáticos del Partido Comunista del Ecuador" (1957), in Ibarra, *El pensamiento de la izquierda comunista*, 275–302.

13. Duncan, "The 1970s," 29; see Duncan, *Finally Got the News*.

14. Other scholars have made similar observations about the utility of police archives for writing the history of social movements. For example, the historian Teishan Latner calls the FBI an inadvertent "clandestine biographer" and "unauthorized archivist" as the bureau engaged in surveillance of the Venceremos Brigade with the goal of criminalizing its sponsorship of solidarity travel to Cuba. In the process, it assembled the largest cache of material on the group. See "'Agrarians or Anarchists?'" 132; and Latner, *Cuban Revolution in America*.

15. For a solid analysis of the relationship between anthropology and the cold war and how to employ intelligence sources to interrogate that relationship, see Price's trilogy *Threatening Anthropology*; *Anthropological Intelligence*; and *Cold War Anthropology*.

16. Marchetti and Marks, *The CIA and the Cult of Intelligence*, 44.

17. For critical studies on the CIA, see Prados's many books, most recently *The Ghosts of Langley*; Weiner, *Legacy of Ashes*; and Jeffreys-Jones, *The CIA and American Democracy*. Most critical studies as well as memoirs of dissident case officers who left the agency generally do not question United States policy objectives but argue instead for a more effective intelligence agency that would enhance an imperial project. An exception is William Blum who provides a popular condemnation of the CIA in *Killing Hope*.

18. The diplomatic historian Piero Gleijeses relied heavily on the CIA's finished intelligence to fill in gaps where no other sources existed in his study of Cuba's involvement in Africa. He notes the trustworthy and insightful nature of these reports, and states that he was "highly impressed" with their "superior quality and objectivity." See *Conflicting Missions*, 11. Dissident officers, on the other hand, paint a more skeptical picture of the quality of the information the agency generated. See, for example, McGarvey, *CIA*; Marchetti and Marks, *The CIA and the Cult of Intelligence*; Agee, *Inside the Company*; Stockwell, *In Search of Enemies*; and McGehee, *Deadly Deceits*. For a broader discussion on the utility of using the CIA to study the history of Latin America, see Becker, "The CIA on Latin America."

19. Since the release of the CREST database at https://www.cia.gov/library/readingroom, a team of research assistants (starting with Kelsey Smugala who introduced me to the database, and continuing with Dusty Davis, Jared Favero, Colin Garrett, Baylee Hatter, Kaitlin Lewis, Austin Miller, Amatista Pearson, Tom Sebacher, Chloe Shoulders, Taylor Tucker, Meghan Walker, and Artemis Winkeler) have entered these and other supporting newspaper articles and archival documents into a bibliographic database to facilitate their organization and retrieval. I could not have completed this project without their collaboration, and I am deeply appreciative of their efforts. Cheryl Musch and Tim Block generously assisted with the collection of corroborating documentation from the National Archives. The American Philosophical Society awarded a Franklin Research Grant that provided funding for investigation in the National Archives. As always, Su Flickinger and Doris Bartel graciously extend hospitality during those research trips.

20. Much has been written about the cold war and the surveillance state, and little need exists to rehash that literature here. Suffice it to note that much of the leading work approaches the topic from a traditional, conservative, patriarchal, Euro-centric perspective. For example, see Gaddis, *The Cold War* and Leffler, *For the Soul of Mankind.* Even works that purport to present a global perspective, such as that of leading historian Westad in *The Global Cold War* and *The Cold War,* minimize Latin America. Brands, *Latin America's Cold War* suffers from some of these same deficiencies, while newer works seek to address them. See, for example, Garrard-Burnett, Lawrence, and Moreno, *Beyond the Eagle's Shadow* and Keller, *Mexico's Cold War.* Also see Joseph and Spenser, *In from the Cold* and Grandin and Joseph, *A Century of Revolution.*

21. McPherson, "Afterword," 307.

22. Grandin, "Living in Revolutionary Time," 7.

23. Carr, "Escribiendo la historia de los comunismos en las américas," 19.

24. Carr, "Escribiendo la historia de los comunismos en las américas," 16–17.

25. Kuhns, "The Office of Reports and Estimates," 40.

26. McGehee, *Deadly Deceits,* xi.

27. Garrard-Burnett, Lawrence, and Moreno, "Introduction," 11.

Chapter 1

1. Bethell and Roxborough, *Latin America between the Second World War and the Cold War.*

2. Poppino, *International Communism in Latin America,* 34.

3. Alexander, *Communism in Latin America,* 27.

4. Poppino, *International Communism in Latin America,* 35–36.

5. Mayers, "Reply to Questionnaire Sent Out on PR 101/33/G," May 22, 1953, 2195/4/53, FO 1110/592, TNA. Thanks to Aaron Coy Moulton for graciously sharing copies of documents from this archive.

6. Henderson, *Gabriel García Moreno and Conservative State Formation in the Andes.*

7. Ayala Mora, *Historia de la Revolución Liberal Ecuatoriana.* Spanish names typically carry two surnames, both a patronymic (from the father's first surname) and matronymic (from the mother's first surname, which in turn was her father's first surname). Formal usage dictates a person's full name, which typically includes a first and second forename and both surnames. In practice, how these names are rendered varies widely, with sometimes one or both forenames and surnames included (and less commonly only the first initial of one of the forenames or the second, matronymic, surname). Eloy Alfaro, for example, is most commonly known only by his patronymic ("Alfaro") whereas Gabriel García Moreno is almost always referenced with both his patronymic ("García") and matronymic ("Moreno") surnames. A variety of factors influence these conventions, including the social prestige of a surname and attempts to avoid confusion between people with similar names. This work follows the most common usage of how individuals were known, which sometimes means including both surnames when a complete

name is first mentioned, but then only the patronymic on subsequent usage (for example, Galo Plaza Lasso, and subsequently "Plaza," and Camilo Ponce Enríquez followed by "Ponce").

8. Paz y Miño Cepeda, *Ecuador.*

9. Coronel, "The Ecuadorian Left during Global Crisis"; Páez Cordero, *Los orígenes de la izquierda ecuatoriana*; Rodas Chávez, *Partido Socialista.*

10. Scholars have long carried out a debate over the precise nature of populism in Ecuador. In particular see Quintero, *El mito del populismo en el Ecuador*; Cueva, *The Process of Political Domination in Ecuador*; and Maiguashca and North, "Orígenes y significado del velasquismo."

11. Blanksten, *Ecuador*, which strongly influenced subsequent works. See in particular Maier, *The Ecuadorian Presidential Election of June 2, 1968*; and Martz, *Ecuador.*

12. A particularly large literature exists on Velasco Ibarra. A useful introduction to his political career is Sosa, "Populism in Ecuador" and Sosa, *Hombres y mujeres velasquistas 1934-1972.* A detailed biography based on extensive interviews and personal correspondence is Norris, *El gran ausente.*

13. Luna Yepes, *Explicación del ideario de ARNE.*

14. Clark to Eden, "Ecuador: Annual Review for 1952." February 3, 1953, AE 1011/1, in *British Documents on Foreign Affairs*, series D, pt. 5, vol. 3, doc. 53.

15. Mayers to Eden, "Ecuador: Annual Review for 1953." January 7, 1954, AE 1011/1, in *British Documents on Foreign Affairs*, series D, pt. 5, vol. 4, doc. 53.

16. Linke, *Ecuador*, 42.

17. Mayers to Eden, "Ecuador: Annual Review for 1953." January 7, 1954, AE 1011/1, in *British Documents on Foreign Affairs*, series D, pt. 5, vol. 4, doc. 53.

18. Sam Pope Brewer, "Ecuador Fearful of Military Coup," *New York Times*, May 29, 1952, 11. Brewer worked for the Office of Strategic Services (OSS) during the Second World War and collaborated with the CIA on his reporting from Latin America. See Salisbury, *Without Fear or Favor*, 504.

19. Ricardo Paredes, "El cuartelazo de la UPERRA Fascista ha fracasado," July 1950, BEAEP. For an authoritative account on Guevara Moreno and the CFP, see Martz, "The Regionalist Expression of Populism.

20. Milk, *Movimiento obrero ecuatoriano*; Ycaza, *Historia del movimiento obrero ecuatoriano.*

21. Boggs, "Organization and Operation of the National Communist Party of Ecuador," May 19, 1947, RG84, Entry #2396, Box 43, NARA.

22. OIR, "Key Communist Centers and Communist Sympathizers in Certain Latin American Countries," March 10, 1952, in *OSS/State Department Intelligence and Research Reports.*

23. Dearborn to Hall, April 22, 1947, RG59, 822.00B/4-2247, NARA.

24. Sowell to Bernbaum, July 12, 1949, RG84, Entry #2396, Box 52, NARA.

25. Studer, *The Transnational World of the Cominternians*, 147.

26. Mayers, "Reply to Questionnaire Sent Out on PR 101/33/G," May 22, 1953, 2195/4/53, FO 1110/592, TNA.

27. Linke, *Ecuador*, 40.

28. Alexander, *Communism in Latin America*, 235.

29. Barnard, "Chilean Communists, Radical Presidents and Chilean Relations with the United States," 363–74; Pavilack, *Mining for the Nation*; Salgado Muñoz, "'El tribunal está abierto para críticas y para autocríticas,'" 170; Huneeus, *La guerra fría chilena*.

30. Alexander, *Communism in Latin America*, 238–39.

31. Ayala Mora, "Ecuador since 1930," 704.

32. CIA, "Weekly Contributions," July 18, 1950, https://www.cia.gov/library/readingroom/document/cia-rdp79-01090a000200050029-4.

33. Marx, *Karl Marx*, 288. Also see Lenin, *State and Revolution*, 126.

34. CIA, "Communist Candidates for the Municipal Elections in Ecuador," November 26, 1948, https://www.cia.gov/library/readingroom/document/cia-rdp82-00457r002100160004-1.

35. Cueva, *The Process of Political Domination in Ecuador*, 41–45. For a good general overview of Ecuadorian history, see Pineo, *Ecuador and the United States*, and in particular chapter 5 on Ecuador during the 1950s.

36. Cabrera Hanna, *La Gloriosa*.

37. On Plaza, see Coronel Valencia and Salgado Gómez, *Galo Plaza Lasso*; and de la Torre and Salgado, *Galo Plaza y su época*.

38. For an excellent examination of these economic changes, see Kofas, "The IMF, the World Bank." Also see Striffler, *In the Shadows of State and Capital*.

39. The other elected conservative presidents were León Febrés Cordero in 1984 and Sixto Durán Ballén in 1992. In September 1947, the conservative leader Mariano Suárez Veintimilla briefly served as president after a coup removed Velasco Ibarra from office, but he was not elected. Many observers would characterize Velasco Ibarra's policies as de facto conservative, though he always claimed to be fundamentally a liberal secularist.

40. Ibarra, "Los idearios de la izquierda comunista ecuatoriana," 57.

41. Political scientist Martz provides a summary of this sequence of governments in *Ecuador*, 127–45.

42. Cueva, *The Process of Political Domination in Ecuador*, 43.

43. Ayala Mora, "Ecuador since 1930," 703.

44. Grandin, *The Last Colonial Massacre*, 16.

Chapter 2

1. Much has been written about the CIA. Arthur Darling, the CIA's first historian, wrote an internal history of the agency in 1953 that was later published as *The Central Intelligence Agency*. Thomas Troy provides a second official internal history in *Donovan and the CIA*. Published collections provide extensive documentation on the formation of the agency. See, for example, Warner, *The CIA under Harry Truman*; United States Department of State, *Emergence of the Intelligence Establishment*; Merrill, *Documentary*

History of the Truman Presidency; and United States Department of State, *The Intelligence Community*.

2. Marchetti and Marks, *The CIA and the Cult of Intelligence*, 119.

3. See for example, Dulles, *The Craft of Intelligence*; Colby, *Honorable Men*; and Kinzer's biography, *The Brothers*. The CIA did not begin to move into its new headquarters building in Langley, Virginia, until 1961, and for the entire period under study in this book the agency was located in Washington, DC.

4. Cline, *The CIA under Reagan, Bush & Casey*, 13.

5. Donald Daughters, interview by Anton Daughters, 1998, transcription of an interview in Anton Daughters's personal possession.

6. The most common exemption from declassification that the CIA employs is 25X1, which concerns the identity of intelligence sources or methods. One example of the vagaries of claiming this exemption is a Central Intelligence Bulletin from April 3, 1951 with redactions not clearly protecting any sources or methods, and with the restricted information sourced from other previously released documentation. See CIA, "Central Intelligence Bulletin," April 3, 1951, https://www.cia.gov/library/readingroom/document/cia-rdp79t00975a000100470001-8 compared with another copy with fewer redactions at https://www.cia.gov/library/readingroom/document/02003044. Furthermore, the restricted information was included in "Hamlin to State," April 1, 1951, RG59, 722.00/4-151, NARA and was also reported in CIA, "Daily Digest," April 2, 1951, https://www.cia.gov/library/readingroom/document/cia-rdp79t01146a000100280001-1.

7. Johnson, *The Sorrows of Empire*, 10.

8. Winks, *Cloak & Gown*, 475. Also see Price, "Uninvited Guests," 36. William August Fisher, alias Rudolf Ivanovich Abel, who some consider to be the most important Soviet spy captured in the United States (and whose story is related in Steven Spielberg's 2015 historical drama film *Bridge of Spies*), reportedly acquired the information he transmitted to the Soviet Union from reading the *New York Times* and *Scientific American*.

9. The Department of State Central Decimal Files (Record Group 59) at the National Archives and Records Administration (NARA) in College Park, Maryland represents the largest and most important repository of United States diplomatic correspondence. This collection contains communications with United States diplomatic and consular posts as well as internal memorandums, reports, and correspondence with other government agencies. The CIA has withdrawn its correspondence with other government agencies from RG59, and as of this writing still has not responded to Freedom of Information Act (FOIA) requests to have documents related to Ecuador released even though it has made much of the same information available in its CREST database. In contrast to RG59, Record Group 84, the Records of Foreign Service Posts of the Department of State, contains items originally filed at United States diplomatic and consular offices. Researchers spend less time with RG84 because much of the material duplicates that found in RG59, but it also includes internal correspondence and memos that were only summarized or otherwise never made it into reports to State Department headquarters in Washington and hence are not included in RG59. Curiously, copies of some

documents that the CIA withdrew from RG59 remain available in RG84, including correspondence that references the seemingly innocuous sounding "controlled American source" (a.k.a. the CIA station) or quote material from CIA sources that apparently led to the withdrawals from RG59. In some cases, a corresponding memo in RG84 provides documentation of the information's provenance. In cases where such a memo is missing, a simple extrapolation points to the source of information.

10. Batvinis, *Hoover's Secret War against Axis Spies*, 269.

11. Phillips, *The Night Watch*, 3. CIA operative and future director of the agency's Western Hemisphere division David Atlee Phillips does not identify Haney by name—he calls him "Brad"—but the description of his trajectory including his future work in Korea and Guatemala makes it apparent that the person he is discussing is Haney. In this account, Phillips has Haney declaring that he "was the first CIA officer in one of the Central American republics," rather than Ecuador. That vague reference might be either an error or a deliberate attempt to obfuscate Haney's identity.

12. Bissell, *Reflections of a Cold Warrior*, 83.

13. *Foreign Service List*, October 1, 1945, 12. The available documentation does not indicate exactly when or why Haney left his position in Colombia.

14. *Foreign Service List*, July 1, 1947, 155.

15. *Foreign Service List*, October 1, 1949, 10.

16. Schlesinger and Kinzer, *Bitter Fruit*, 109; Eveland, *Ropes of Sand*, 29–31. For an outstanding analysis of the United States campaign against Germans in Latin America during World War II, see Friedman, *Nazis and Good Neighbors*.

17. Bissell, *Reflections of a Cold Warrior*, 83.

18. Gleijeses, *Shattered Hope*, 288.

19. Weiner, *Legacy of Ashes*, 63. The civil liberties attorney Frank Donner criticizes the substitution of operational terms such as "informer" with the more professional sounding "informant," "confidential source," or "asset" as a "semantic facelifting" designed to justify questionable activities. For that reason, this work returns to the more accurate "informer." See Donner, *The Age of Surveillance*, 464.

20. Schlesinger and Kinzer, *Bitter Fruit*, 109.

21. Weiner, *Legacy of Ashes*, 106, 108. Curiously, in the analysis of the coup in Guatemala that the historian Nick Cullather wrote for the CIA, Haney is repeatedly referenced in the published book's index although all mentions of him are redacted from the text. See Cullather, *Secret History*, xxxvii. Haney seems to disappear after the Guatemalan operation. Phillips relates a story of all of those involved receiving promotions and going "on to other chores" except for one field officer who likely was Haney who requested a double promotion from Dulles. That power play "did not fare well," and the officer in question retired twenty years later without receiving a promotion or another COS assignment. See Phillips, *The Night Watch*, 51.

22. FBI, *History of the Special Intelligence Service Division*, 143–63, 171, 408, 416–17.

23. McGarvey, *CIA*, 57.

24. Stockwell, *In Search of Enemies*, 52.

25. Marchetti and Marks, *The CIA and the Cult of Intelligence*, 255.

26. McGarvey, *CIA*, 57. Eisenhower was the president who originated the practice of designating the ambassador as head of a country's Foreign Service team. See Marchetti and Marks, *The CIA and the Cult of Intelligence*, 320.

27. Stockwell, *In Search of Enemies*, 178.

28. Agee, *Inside the Company*, 138.

29. Agee, *Inside the Company*, 109.

30. Agee, *On the Run*, 250.

31. Stockwell, *In Search of Enemies*, 136.

32. Phillips, *The Night Watch*, 4, 8.

33. McGarvey, *CIA*, 55–57.

34. See, for example, Hull to Quito, January 6, 1944, RG84, Entry #2396, Box 14, NARA.

35. John Prados (personal communication) comments that the origins of the term "controlled American source" lies in obscurity and "probably originated as an indicator that information came from a U.S. asset, but it came to be a stand-in for CIA station." The term formed part of the fiction that the agency attempted to preserve for many decades that there was "no such thing as a CIA station." Former State Department intelligence officer John Marks provides guidelines for identifying CIA officers in his essay "How to Spot a Spook," but even those methods are not foolproof.

36. *Foreign Service List*, January 1, 1947, 16–17.

37. *Foreign Service List*, January 1961, 18–19.

38. Agee, *Inside the Company*, 109. The State Department lists Weatherwax as a public safety adviser with the ICA. See *Foreign Service List*, January 1961, 19.

39. The Association for Diplomatic Studies and Training Foreign Affairs Oral History Project, "George F. Jones," August 6, 1996, http://www.adst.org/OH%20TOCs/Jones,%20George%20F.pdf. Marks observes "we don't really need this kind of information from Third World countries unless we intend to muck about in their internal affairs." See Marks, "How to Spot a Spook," 11.

40. McGarvey, *CIA*, 57.

41. Agee, *Inside the Company*, 110, 179.

42. CIG, "Italian Economic Commission in Ecuador," May 19, 1947, https://www.cia.gov/library/readingroom/document/cia-rdp82-00457r000600050005-9.

43. CIG, "Communist Party Activities," May 21, 1947, https://www.cia.gov/library/readingroom/document/cia-rdp82-00457r000600140010-3.

44. Haney to Chargé, May 26, 1947, RG84, Entry #2396, Box 43, NARA.

45. Shaw to Ambassador, "Visa Application by Pedro Saad," December 31, 1947, RG84, Entry #2398, NARA.

46. Haney to Chargé, July 2, 1947, RG84, Entry #2396, Box 43, NARA.

47. Haney, "Communist Matters. Francisco Arechandieta Ortega," July 14, 1947, RG84, Entry #2396, Box 43, NARA.

48. Shaw to State, July 7, 1947, RG59, 822.00B/7-747, NARA. Neither the CIA nor State Department officials identified their sources by name but instead reported on their reliability. The origin of the information was not necessarily a person, and could be from

a variety of sources including mail intercepts and wiretaps. Marchetti and Marks, *The CIA and the Cult of Intelligence*, 201. According to Prados (personal communication), the grade B-3 refers to a system that the Joint Chiefs of Staff developed during the Second World War to rate intelligence sources and the accuracy of reporting. It followed the following system:

Source:	Content:
A: Completely reliable	1: Confirmed by other sources
B: Usually reliable	2: Probably true
C: Fairly reliable	3: Possibly true
D: Not usually reliable	4: Doubtfully true
E: Unreliable	5: Improbable
F: Cannot be judged	6: Cannot be judged

If that is the case, it would appear that embassy officials considered Haney to be "usually reliable" and the information he provided "possibly true."

49. Shaw to State, July 15, 1947, RG59, 822.00B/7-1547, NARA.

50. Haney to Ambassador, July 16, 1947, RG84, Entry #2396, Box 43, NARA.

51. One of the rare exceptions is Haney's investigation into the February 12, 1949 "War of the Worlds" broadcast, in which case the "date of info" is given as February 12–17, 1949, and the date of distribution is a month later, March 16, 1949. On February 17, Ambassador Simmons drafted a memo for distribution to the Division of North and West Coast Affairs at the Department of State that quoted information from a "controlled American Source" in only a lightly edited form as compared to what appeared in the CIA information report. See CIA, "Investigation of Terrorist Radio Program in Quito," March 16, 1949, https://www.cia.gov/library/readingroom/document/cia-rdp82-00457r002500190008-0; and Memo, American Embassy, February 17, 1949, RG84, Entry #2396, Box 51, NARA.

Chapter 3

1. PCE, *Por la paz, por la democracia y el progreso*, 29, 31, 35–36, 39.

2. Becker, "General Alberto Enríquez Gallo."

3. CIA, "Communist Activity in Guayaquil," August 18, 1948, https://www.cia.gov/library/readingroom/document/cia-rdp82-00457r001800240006-4.

4. CIA, "Communist Anti-Government Propaganda Efforts," September 21, 1948, https://www.cia.gov/library/readingroom/document/cia-rdp82-00457r001900050003-7.

5. Huggins, *Political Policing*.

6. CIA, "Weekly Summary," April 14, 1950, https://www.cia.gov/library/readingroom/document/cia-rdp78-01617a002300160001-8.

7. CIA, "Political Unrest in Ecuador," October 6, 1948, https://www.cia.gov/library/readingroom/document/cia-rdp82-00457r001900490009-3.

8. Military Attaché, "Weeka," November 19, 1948, RG59, 822.00(W)/11-1948, NARA.

9. Military Attaché, "Weeka," November 29, 1948, RG59, 822.00(W)/11-2948, NARA.

10. Military Attaché, "Joint Weeka 1," December 4, 1948, RG59, 822.00(W)/12-448, NARA.

11. CIA, "Weekly Contributions," April 19, 1949, https://www.cia.gov/library/readingroom/document/cia-rdp79-01090a000200020003-5.

12. CIA, "Political Tension in Ecuador," December 15, 1948, https://www.cia.gov/library/readingroom/document/cia-rdp82-00457r002100780001-6.

13. Quito to State, "Leftist, Subversive Troop Movements in Ecuador," April 12, 1949, RG84, Entry #2396, Box 51, NARA.

14. CIA, "Opposition Groups to Plaza Administration," December 13, 1948, https://www.cia.gov/library/readingroom/document/cia-rdp82-00457r002100590008-0.

15. CIA, "Strengthening of the Guevara-Trujillo Opposition Faction," January 13, 1949, https://www.cia.gov/library/readingroom/document/cia-rdp82-00457r002200380011-8.

16. CIA, "Disaffection in the Armed Forces of Ecuador," December 24, 1948, https://www.cia.gov/library/readingroom/document/cia-rdp82-00457r002200050001-5.

17. CIA, "Threatened Revolt in Ecuador," January 12, 1949, https://www.cia.gov/library/readingroom/document/cia-rdp82-00457r002200680007-0.

18. CIA, "Weekly Contributions," January 15, 1948, https://www.cia.gov/library/readingroom/document/cia-rdp79-01090a000200010003-6.

19. Quito to State, "Subversive Activities of the Ecuadoran Socialist Party: General Alberto Enríquez Gallo," April 18, 1949, RG84, Entry #2396, Box 51, NARA.

20. "Estudiantes de izquierda están por la reforma de la constitución vigente," *El Comercio*, March 31, 1949, 1.

21. Quito to State, "Discourse by Pedro Saad," April 11, 1949, RG84, Entry #2396, Box 51, NARA; CIA, "Pedro Saad's Remark on the Progress of Democracy in Ecuador," May 23, 1949, https://www.cia.gov/library/readingroom/document/cia-rdp82-00457r002700670004-9.

22. CIA, "Political Tension in Ecuador," December 31, 1948, https://www.cia.gov/library/readingroom/document/cia-rdp82-00457r002200350001-2.

23. CIA, "Communist Interest in Vencedores Revolt," February 23, 1949, https://www.cia.gov/library/readingroom/document/cia-rdp82-00457r002400130003-2; Simmons to State, "Communist Aspects of Threatened Troop Revolution of 16 January 1949," January 27, 1949, RG59, 822.00/1-2748, NARA.

24. CIA, "Popularity of Carlos Mancheno," April 7, 1949, https://www.cia.gov/library/readingroom/document/cia-rdp82-00457r002600140005-7.

25. CIA, "Weekly Contributions," April 19, 1949, https://www.cia.gov/library/readingroom/document/cia-rdp79-01090a000200020003-5.

26. "Revolt in Ecuador Quelled Speedily," *New York Times*, July 27, 1949, 13; also see "Revolt That Wasn't," *Newsweek*, August 8, 1949, 32; Bernbaum to State, "Political Situation Following the Unsuccessful Coup of July 26," August 4, 1949, RG59, 822.00/8-449, NARA.

27. CIA, "Weekly Contributions," August 16, 1949, https://www.cia.gov/library/readingroom/document/cia-rdp79-01090a000200030007-0.

28. Quito to State, "Particular Development of Carlos Mancheno Movement Noted within the Ecuadoran Army," June 30, 1949, RG84, Entry #2396, Box 51, NARA.

29. Bernbaum to State, "Possible Change in Tactics of Communist Party of Ecuador," July 22, 1949, RG59, 822.00B/7-2249, NARA.

30. Quito to State, "Decision of PCE to Join Leftist Coalition Group against Plaza Government," July 28, 1949, RG84, Entry #2396, Box 51, NARA.

31. Quito to State, "Decision of PCE to Join Leftist Coalition Group against Plaza Government," July 28, 1949, RG84, Entry #2396, Box 51, NARA.

32. Quito to State, "Attempted Military Coup d'état by Col. Carlos Mancheno Cajas," July 29, 1949, RG84, Entry #2396, Box 51, NARA.

33. Quito to State, "Official PCE Reaction to Mancheno Attempted Coup," August 4, 1949, RG84, Entry #2396, Box 51, NARA.

34. Bernbaum to State, "Political Developments in Connection with Recent Arrests of Alleged Revolutionary Plotters," July 7, 1949, RG59, 822.00/7-749, NARA.

35. Quito to State, "Decision of PCE to Join Leftist Coalition Group against Plaza Government," July 28, 1949, RG84, Entry #2396, Box 51, NARA.

36. Bernbaum to State, "Joint Weeka 32," July 29, 1949, RG59, 822.00(W)/7-2949, NARA.

37. CIA, "Weekly Contributions," August 16, 1949, https://www.cia.gov/library/readingroom/document/cia-rdp79-01090a000200030007-0.

38. Simmons to State, "Foreign Minister's Views on Revolution Threats in Ecuador," December 12, 1949, RG59, 822.00/12-1249, NARA.

39. Bernbaum to State, July 7, 1949, RG59, 822.00/7-749, NARA.

40. "Ecuador," *Hispanic World Report*, August 1949, 18. In 1950, this publication became the *Hispanic American Report*.

41. "Ecuador," *Hispanic World Report*, December 1949, 21.

42. The CIA's fake radio shows were taped in Miami and broadcast from Nicaragua but "set" in Guatemala. See Cullather, *Secret History*, 76.

43. CIA, "Weekly Contributions," February 15, 1949, https://www.cia.gov/library/readingroom/document/cia-rdp79-01090a000200010006-3.

44. "Declaraciones de Eduardo Alcaraz sobre los resultados d' dramatización de obra de Wells," *El Comercio-El Día*, February 16, 1949, 3; "Quito Holds 3 for 'Mars' Script," *New York Times*, February 16, 1949, 15. Páez defends his actions in *Los que siembran el viento*.

45. "Sin tener mayores datos no se puede explicar los platillos voladores," *El Comercio*, February 12, 1949, 7.

46. Quito to State, "Radio Quito Incident of 12 February 1949," March 4, 1949, RG84, Entry #2396, Box 51, NARA.

47. Quito to State, "Radio Quito Incident of 12 February 1949," March 4, 1949, RG84, Entry #2396, Box 51, NARA.

48. Ellis to State, "Summary of Political Items Appearing in Guayaquil Newspapers during February 1949," March 3, 1949, RG59, 822.00/3-349, NARA.

49. Styles to State, "Transmitting Memorandum Prepared by Walter P. Houk," July 25, 1949, RG59, 822.00/7-2549, NARA.

50. Quito to State, "Manuel Popoca Estrada, President Confederación de Jóvenes Mexicanos," March 10, 1949, RG84, Entry #2396, Box 51, NARA.

51. Quito to State, "Radio Quito Incident of 12 February 1949," March 4, 1949, RG84, Entry #2396, Box 51, NARA.

52. Quito to State, "Leading Ecuadorian Communist's Views of Situation in Ecuador," March 4, 1949, RG84, Entry #2396, Box 51, NARA.

53. Quito to State, "Radio Quito Incident of 12 February 1949," March 4, 1949, RG84, Entry #2396, Box 51, NARA.

54. Kofas, "Politics of Conflict and Containment," 85.

55. CIA, "Ecuador Handbook," October 1, 1970, https://www.cia.gov/library/reading room/document/cia-rdp79-00891a000700010001-5.

56. CIA, "Ecuador," July 1973, https://www.cia.gov/library/readingroom/document /cia-rdp79t00975a021300020001-2.

Chapter 4

1. Alexander, *Communism in Latin America*, 239.

2. Blasier, *The Giant's Rival*, 81.

3. CIA, "Communist Activities in Guayaquil," May 3, 1951, https://www.cia.gov /library/readingroom/document/cia-rdp82-00457r007400210011-9.

4. CIA, "Reorganizational Program for Guayaquil Cells," January 27, 1949, https:// www.cia.gov/library/readingroom/document/cia-rdp82-00457r002200750006-3.

5. Boggs, "Organization and Operation of the National Communist Party of Ecuador," May 19, 1947, RG84, Entry #2396, Box 43, NARA.

6. "Proyecto de reformas a los estatutos del Partido Comunista del Ecuador aprobado por el Comité Central," *El Pueblo*, December 22, 1956, 6–8.

7. CIA, "Financial Report of Guayaquil Local Committee of Communist Party of Ecuador," March 1, 1949, https://www.cia.gov/library/readingroom/document/cia-rdp82 -00457r002400350006-5.

8. CIA, "PCE Finances," May 16, 1949, https://www.cia.gov/library/readingroom /document/cia-rdp82-00457r002700520008-1; Quito to State, "Finances of the Ecuadoran Communist Party," April 18, 1949, RG84, Entry #2396, Box 51, NARA.

9. CIA, "Meeting of the Pedro Saad PCE Cell," April 10, 1953, https://www.cia.gov /library/readingroom/document/cia-rdp80-00810a000900170009-5. The available documentation does not provide any indication of why militants in Quito would name their cell after a current communist leader from Guayaquil, although it may have been to gain his good graces.

10. CIA, "Fifth Congress of the Communist Party of Ecuador (PCE) Held at Ambato," October 7, 1952, https://www.cia.gov/library/readingroom/document/cia-rdp82-00457r014100290007-1.

11. CIA, "Guayaquil Local Conference of the Partido Comunista del Ecuador (PCE)," September 10, 1953, https://www.cia.gov/library/readingroom/document/cia-rdp80-00810a002200280013-3.

12. Dustmann to State, "Analysis of Ecuador's Communist Party," November 25, 1957, RG59, 722.001/11-2557, NARA.

13. CIG, "Collection of Funds by PCE for Printing Press," October 29, 1947, https://www.cia.gov/library/readingroom/document/cia-rdp82-00457r001000460008-6.

14. Quito to State, "Developments of Plans for Forthcoming Fourth National Congress of the Partido Comunista del Ecuador," June 21, 1949, RG84, Entry #2396, Box 51, NARA.

15. CIA, "Communist Activity in Guayaquil," August 18, 1948, https://www.cia.gov/library/readingroom/document/cia-rdp82-00457r001800240006-4.

16. CIA, "PCE Finances," May 16, 1949, https://www.cia.gov/library/readingroom/document/cia-rdp82-00457r002700520008-1; Quito to State, "Finances of the Ecuadoran Communist Party," April 18, 1949, RG84, Entry #2396, Box 51, NARA.

17. CIA, "Weekly Contributions," April 11, 1950, https://www.cia.gov/library/readingroom/document/cia-rdp79-01090a000200050015-9.

18. Quito to State, "Alleged Seizure of Communist Documents by Ecuadoran Government," April 8, 1949, RG84, Entry #2396, Box 51, NARA.

19. Bragonier to State, "Questionnaire on Soviet Propaganda," December 23, 1949, RG84, Entry #2396, Box 51, NARA; Evans, "Report on Soviet Propaganda," July 28, 1949, RG84, Entry #2396, Box 51, NARA.

20. CIA, "PCE Finances," May 16, 1949, https://www.cia.gov/library/readingroom/document/cia-rdp82-00457r002700520008-1; Quito to State, "Finances of the Ecuadoran Communist Party," April 18, 1949, RG84, Entry #2396, Box 51, NARA.

21. CIA, "Communist Activities in Guayaquil," May 3, 1951, https://www.cia.gov/library/readingroom/document/cia-rdp82-00457r007400210011-9.

22. CIA, "PCE Finances," May 16, 1949, https://www.cia.gov/library/readingroom/document/cia-rdp82-00457r002700520008-1. The agency invoked exemption 25X1, which, according to the Department of Justice, allows the withholding of information from declassified documents that might "reveal the identity of a confidential human source, a human intelligence source, a relationship with an intelligence or security service of a foreign government or international organization, or a non-human intelligence source; or impair the effectiveness of an intelligence method currently in use, available for use, or under development." See https://www.justice.gov/open/declassification/declassification-faq. The CIA officer (presumably Haney) provided the same information to the ambassador, but without naming the treasurer in question. See Quito to State, "Finances of the Ecuadoran Communist Party," April 18, 1949, RG84, Entry #2396, Box 51, NARA. Alternatively, of course, the redaction could be an error, and merely a reflection of the inefficiencies in the release of previously classified information.

23. OIR, "Communism in the Other American Republics," October 24, 1951, in OS-S/State Department Intelligence and Research Reports.

24. CIA, "Daily Digest," July 13, 1951, https://www.cia.gov/library/readingroom/document/cia-rdp79t01146a000300150001-3.

25. OIR, "Communism in Latin America," April 18, 1956, in *FRUS*, 1955–1957, 6:88.

26. CIA, "Ecuador," July 1973, https://www.cia.gov/library/readingroom/document/cia-rdp79t00975a021300020001-2.

27. "Periódicos que quedan sin venderse," *El Pueblo*, May 22, 1954, 2.

28. CIA, "Fifth Congress of the Communist Party of Ecuador (PCE) Held at Ambato," October 7, 1952, https://www.cia.gov/library/readingroom/document/cia-rdp82-00457r014100290007-1.

29. Ibarra, "Conflictos rurales," 417.

30. "La lucha del pueblo y el papel de nuestro periódico," *El Pueblo*, September 1, 1956, 2.

31. CIA, "Meetings of PCE Propaganda Committee," April 17, 1953, https://www.cia.gov/library/readingroom/document/cia-rdp80-00810a000800120004-6.

32. CIA, "PCE Propaganda Activities in Guayas Province," December 23, 1953, https://www.cia.gov/library/readingroom/document/cia-rdp80-00810a003200140001-0.

33. CIA, "Communist Candidates for the June Elections," May 4, 1954, https://www.cia.gov/library/readingroom/document/cia-rdp80-00810a004100040007-5.

34. Adams to USIA, "Estimated Communist Expenditures on Propaganda Directed at Free World," March 18, 1957, RG84, Entry #2396, Box 73, NARA.

35. CIA, "PCE Propaganda Activities in Guayas Province," December 23, 1953, https://www.cia.gov/library/readingroom/document/cia-rdp80-00810a003200140001-0.

36. CIA, "PCE Fundraising Activities in Guayaquil," May 21, 1953, https://www.cia.gov/library/readingroom/document/cia-rdp80-00810a001300020003-2.

37. McLean, "Ismael Pérez Castro," July 2, 1956, RG84, Entry #2396, Box 73, NARA

38. CIA, "Statements of Wilson Durango Lopez," October 27, 1953, https://www.cia.gov/library/readingroom/document/cia-rdp80-00810a002700010003-8.

39. "Casa del partido comunista de Guayaquil fue asaltada por 6 sujetos desconocidos," *El Comercio*, June 28, 1951, 14. I have not located the referenced party statement.

40. CIA, "PCE Newsstand in Guayaquil and Sale of Communist Publications," August 21, 1953, https://www.cia.gov/library/readingroom/document/cia-rdp80-00810a002000460007-2.

41. Mills, "Communist Propaganda Burned by Ecuador," August 25, 1954, RG84, Entry #2396, Box 65, NARA

42. CIA, "Propaganda Efforts of Communist Party of Ecuador (PCE)," April 8, 1954, https://www.cia.gov/library/readingroom/document/cia-rdp80-00810a003900460007-2.

43. "Feo incidente se produjo cuando se proyectaba 'La Cortina de Hierro,'" *El Comercio*, December 19, 1948, 14.

44. Simmons to State, December 29, 1948, RG84, Entry #2396, Box 49, NARA.

45. CIA, "Communist Disturbances at Showing of the 'Iron Curtain,'" January 31, 1949, https://www.cia.gov/library/readingroom/document/cia-rdp82-00457r002200690004-2.

46. "¿Comunismo en el Ecuador?" *El Comercio*, December 20, 1948, 4.

47. Simmons to State, December 29, 1948, RG84, Entry #2396, Box 49, NARA.

48. Quito to State, "Communist Plans for Motion Picture Propaganda," April 7, 1949, RG84, Entry #2396, Box 51, NARA; CIA, "Activities of the Communist Party of Ecuador," April 28, 1949, https://www.cia.gov/library/readingroom/document/cia-rdp82-00457r002600660006-9.

49. CIA, "Circulation of Soviet Propaganda," February 5, 1951, https://www.cia.gov/library/readingroom/document/cia-rdp82-00457r006800200010-1.

50. CIA, "PCE Propaganda Activities in Guayas Province," December 23, 1953, https://www.cia.gov/library/readingroom/document/cia-rdp80-00810a003200140001-0.

51. Kirkpatrick, *Target*, 28.

52. Bureau of Intelligence and Research, "International Communism Annual Review – 1958," December 1958, https://www.cia.gov/library/readingroom/document/cia-rdp81-01043r003200210001-8.

Chapter 5

1. Boggs, "General Summary of Communist Activities for the month of May," June 12, 1947, RG84, Entry #2396, Box 43, NARA.

2. For a biography of Paredes, see Paredes Ruiz, *Ricardo Paredes*. Paredes's best-known book is *El imperialismo en el Ecuador*. As secretary general of the PCE, he wrote many party manifestos and descriptions of current struggles that were often published unsigned in leftist periodicals and as handbills. No central repository of his writings exists, although a preliminary collection is at http://www.yachana.org/earchivo/comunismo/.

3. Ellis to Simmons, June 30, 1948, RG84, #2396, Box 49, NARA.

4. Styles to State, "Notice of Communist Meeting," December 21, 1949, RG59, 822.00B/12-2149, NARA.

5. Moreland to State, "Communist Activities in Manabí Province," January 9, 1959, RG59, 722.001/1-959, NARA.

6. No standard biography of Saad exists, but see Roberts, *The Lebanese Immigrants in Ecuador*, 83–89. Saad was a prolific author of political tracts and many of these are easily available. In 1971, the PCE decided to publish his collected works. They planned six volumes, but only the fourth and fifth volumes covering the years 1960 to 1966 were completed. See Saad, *Obras escogidas*.

7. Ibarra, "Acción colectiva rural," 151–52.

8. Hoover to Lyon, January 27, 1945, RG59, 822.00B/1-2745, NARA.

9. CIA, "Activities of the Communist Party of Ecuador," April 28, 1949, https://www.cia.gov/library/readingroom/document/cia-rdp82-00457r002600660006-9; Quito to State, "Communist Denial of Responsibility for Present Economic Situation in Ecuador," March 11, 1949, RG84, Entry #2396, Box 51, NARA; Quito to State, "Ecuadoran

Communist Party's Views of International Situation," April 1, 1949, RG84, Entry #2396, Box 51, NARA.

10. CIA, "Reaction to Election of Pedro Saad as Secretary General of Ecuadoran Communist Party," January 3, 1949, https://www.cia.gov/library/readingroom/document/cia-rdp82-00457r002200160009-5; CIA, "Communist Efforts to Regain Control of CTE," December 27, 1948, https://www.cia.gov/library/readingroom/document/cia-rdp82-00457r002200070008-6.

11. Gil Gilbert, *Nuestro pan*; Gil Gilbert, *Our Daily Bread*.

12. See, for example, CIA, "Roberto Morena's Visit to Colombia and Ecuador," November 4, 1948, https://www.cia.gov/library/readingroom/document/cia-rdp82-00457r002000340010-5; Donnelly to State, December 6, 1948, RG59, 822.00B/12-648, NARA.

13. Marshall to Caracas, November 26, 1948, RG59, 822.00B/11-2648, NARA.

14. Beaulac to State, December 2, 1948, RG84, Entry #2396, Box 49, NARA.

15. CIA, "Activities of Enrique Gil Gilbert in Colombia," December 18, 1948, https://www.cia.gov/library/readingroom/document/cia-rdp82-00457r002200120003-5.

16. Donnelly to State, November 29, 1948, RG59, 822.00B/11-2948, NARA; Donnelly to State, December 6, 1948, RG59, 822.00B/12-648, NARA.

17. CIA, "Visit of Enrique Gil Gilbert to Peru," August 3, 1949, https://www.cia.gov/library/readingroom/document/cia-rdp82-00457r003000040006-2.

18. CIA, "Decision of Pedro Saad to Reside in Guayaquil," March 3, 1949, https://www.cia.gov/library/readingroom/document/cia-rdp82-00457r002400370007-2.

19. CIA, "Reorganization of Ecuadoran Communist Party," January 19, 1949, https://www.cia.gov/library/readingroom/document/cia-rdp82-00457r002200750004-5.

20. CIA, "New PCE Leader for Guayaquil Local Committee," February 28, 1949, https://www.cia.gov/library/readingroom/document/cia-rdp82-00457r002400280004-5.

21. Quito to State, "Alleged Instructions from French Communist Party, Regarding Policy of Passive Resistance," March 10, 1949, RG84, Entry #2396, Box 51, NARA; CIA, "PCE Policy of Passive Resistance," April 4, 1949, https://www.cia.gov/library/readingroom/document/cia-rdp83-00415r002600040002-6.

22. Ellis to State, "Recent Activities of the Communist Party in Guayaquil," March 3, 1949, RG59, 822.00B/3-349, NARA.

23. CIA, "Operational Plan for the Guayaquil Cells," March 4, 1949, https://www.cia.gov/library/readingroom/document/cia-rdp82-00457r002400350007-4.

24. CIA, "Operational Plan for the Guayaquil Committee of the PCE," May 10, 1949, https://www.cia.gov/library/readingroom/document/cia-rdp83-00415r002900080009-2; CIA, "Operational Plan for Guayaquil Cells," May 16, 1949, https://www.cia.gov/library/readingroom/document/cia-rdp82-00457r002700520006-3; Quito to State, "Local Committee Directive for Communist Activities in Guayaquil for Period 20 March– 20 June 1949," April 12, 1949, RG84, Entry #2396, Box 51, NARA.

25. CIA, "Pending Reorganization of Communist Cells in the Sierras," February 23, 1949, https://www.cia.gov/library/readingroom/document/cia-rdp82-00457r002400130002-3.

26. CIA, "Handbill of Partido Comunista del Ecuador," April 8, 1949, https://www.cia.gov/library/readingroom/document/cia-rdp83-00415r002600040002-6.

27. PCE, "Por la defensa de la vida del pueblo: Manifiesto del Comité Central del Partido Comunista," March 1, 1949, in CIA, "Handbill of Partido Comunista del Ecuador."

28. CIA, "Weekly Contributions," October 25, 1949, https://www.cia.gov/library/readingroom/document/cia-rdp79-01090a000200040004-2.

29. For a discussion of the 1946 congress, see Becker, *The FBI in Latin America*, 215–20.

30. CIG, "Proposals for a PCE Congress in Guayaquil," October 29, 1947, https://www.cia.gov/library/readingroom/document/cia-rdp82-00457r001000430001-6. None of these documents in the CREST database are signed, but presumably Haney was the author.

31. CIA, "Plans for Proposed Meeting of Latin American Communist Leaders," June 15, 1948, https://www.cia.gov/library/readingroom/document/cia-rdp82-00457r001600140007-6. At other points, the CIA reported on instructions that the party allegedly received from Mexico. See, for example, CIA, "Instructions Received by the Ecuadoran Communist Party," January 13, 1949, https://www.cia.gov/library/readingroom/document/cia-rdp82-00457r002200390001-8; CIA, "Mexican Communists Urge Ecuadoran Party to Control Military Enslavement," January 18, 1949, https://www.cia.gov/library/readingroom/document/cia-rdp82-00457r002200670013-4.

32. CIA, "Activities of the Communist Party of Ecuador," April 28, 1949, https://www.cia.gov/library/readingroom/document/cia-rdp82-00457r002600660006-9; Quito to State, "Forthcoming Fourth National Congress of the Ecuadoran Communist Party," April 7, 1949, RG84, Entry #2396, Box 51, NARA.

33. Quito to State, "Developments of Plans for Forthcoming Fourth National Congress of the Partido Comunista del Ecuador," June 21, 1949, RG84, Entry #2396, Box 51, NARA.

34. Quito to State, "Developments of Plans for Forthcoming Fourth National Congress of the Partido Comunista del Ecuador," July 14, 1949, RG84, Entry #2396, Box 51, NARA.

35. "El primero de agosto se inaugurá en el Puerto congreso comunista del Ecuador," *El Día*, July 19, 1949, 2.

36. Quito to State, "Developments of Plans for Forthcoming Fourth National Congress of the Partido Comunista del Ecuador," July 28, 1949, RG84, Entry #2396, Box 51, NARA.

37. "Comunismo," *La Tierra*, August 3, 1949, 3.

38. Paredes Ruiz, *Ricardo Paredes*, 239.

39. Ibarra, "¿Qué fue la revolución de 1944?," 202; Ibarra, "Los idearios de la izquierda comunista ecuatoriana," 49–51.

40. Styles to State, "Transmitting Memorandum Prepared by Walter P. Houk," July 25, 1949, RG59, 822.00/7-2549, NARA.

41. CIA, "International Communist Movements," September 1, 1949, https://www.cia.gov/library/readingroom/document/cia-rdp78-00915r000100260002-0.

42. CIA, "Weekly Contributions," October 25, 1949, https://www.cia.gov/library/readingroom/document/cia-rdp79-01090a000200040004-2.

43. Bernbaum to State, "Extraordinary Congress of the Socialist Party of Ecuador," June 28, 1949, RG59, 822.00/6-2849, NARA.

44. CIA, "Communist Infiltration of New Socialist Party Directorate," August 9, 1949, https://www.cia.gov/library/readingroom/document/cia-rdp82-00457r003000440004-0; Military Attaché, "Weeka," November 29, 1948, RG59, 822.00(W)/11-2948, NARA.

45. Quito to State, "New Directory of the Partido Socialista del Ecuador," July 20, 1949, RG84, Entry #2396, Box 51, NARA; CIA, "Communist Infiltration of New Socialist Party Directorate," August 9, 1949, https://www.cia.gov/library/readingroom/document/cia-rdp82-00457r003000440004-0. Also see Conklin to State, "Comment on Labor Chapter in Weekly Review," January 19, 1951, RG59, 822.062/1-1951, NARA.

46. *Foreign Service List*, July 1, 1949, 21, 10.

47. *Foreign Service List*, April 1, 1949, 19.

48. CIA, "PCE Propaganda against Government Taxation," December 22, 1949, https://www.cia.gov/library/readingroom/document/cia-rdp83-00415r004000060006-4.

49. Bragonier to State, "Submission of Communist Circular Matter," December 23, 1949, RG84, Entry #2396, Box 51, NARA. Since all of this material was forwarded to Washington, none of it survived in the embassy's files together with this copy of the dispatch, nor have these publications surfaced in the Washington files.

50. PCE, *Por la paz, por la democracia y el progreso.*

51. PCE, *Por la paz, por la democracia y el progreso*, 29, 31, 35–36, 39.

52. "Terrible destrucción de Ambato por terremoto," *La Tierra*, August 6, 1949, 1; "Muerte, desolación y daños calculados entre 80 y 100 millones de sucres produjo el terremoto en una zona de cien kilómetros de largo," *El Comercio*, August 7, 1949, 1; "200 Reported Killed by Quake in Ecuador," *New York Times*, August 6, 1949, 7; "Ecuador," *Hispanic World Report*, September 1949, 15–16; "Death in the Andes," *Time*, August 15, 1949, 27; "Disaster in the Andes," *Newsweek*, August 15, 1949, 40.

53. "Partidos de izquierda del Guayas hacen llamamiento para ayudar a víctimas," *El Comercio*, August 8, 1949, 5.

54. "Congreso Mundial de la Paz y P. Socialista Popular de Cuba con Ecuador," *La Tierra*, August 16, 1949, 1.

55. CIA, "Weekly Contributions," October 25, 1949, https://www.cia.gov/library/readingroom/document/cia-rdp79-01090a000200040004-2.

56. Carvell to Bevin, "Annual Review of Events for 1949," February 10, 1950, AE 1011/1, in *British Documents on Foreign Affairs*, series D, pt. 4, vol. 8, doc. 16.

57. PCE, "Luchemos defensa de la vida de las masas populares," September 19, 1949, included in CIA, "PCE Propaganda against Government Taxation," December 22, 1949, https://www.cia.gov/library/readingroom/document/cia-rdp83-00415r004000060006-4.

58. Quito to State, "Joint Weeka no. 40," October 6, 1950, RG59, 822.00(W)/10-650, NARA.

Chapter 6

1. Muñoz Vicuña, *Temas obreros*, 240.

2. CIA, "Influence in Ecuador of Communist Victories in China," February 24, 1949, https://www.cia.gov/library/readingroom/document/cia-rdp82-00457r002400130 001-4.

3. CIA, "Personal Views of Pedro Saad on Influence on Ecuadorans of Communist Victories in China," March 3, 1949, https://www.cia.gov/library/readingroom /document/cia-rdp82-00457r002400370006-3.

4. CIA, "Influence in Ecuador of Communist Victories in China," February 24, 1949, https://www.cia.gov/library/readingroom/document/cia-rdp82-00457r002400130 001-4.

5. CIA, "Establishment of Communist 'Revolutionary Committee,'" December 22, 1948, https://www.cia.gov/library/readingroom/document/cia-rdp82-00457r002100730002-0.

6. CIA, "Personal Views of Pedro Saad on Influence on Ecuadorans of Communist Victories in China," March 3, 1949, https://www.cia.gov/library/readingroom /document/cia-rdp82-00457r002400370006-3.

7. CAS to Ambassador, "Communist Propaganda in China," February 10, 1949, RG84, Entry #2396, Box 52, NARA.

8. PCE, "Gran Asamblea Popular Pro China Democrática," 1949, BEAEP.

9. Simmons to State, "Communist Meeting in Celebration of Communist Victories in China," February 17, 1949, RG59, 822.00B/2-1749, NARA.

10. CIA, "Influence in Ecuador of Communist Victories in China," February 24, 1949, https://www.cia.gov/library/readingroom/document/cia-rdp82-00457r002400130001-4; Simmons to State, "Local Influence of Communist Victories in China," January 27, 1949, RG84, Entry #2396, Box 51, NARA.

11. CIA, "Weekly Summary," June 13, 1957, https://www.cia.gov/library/readingroom /document/cia-rdp79-00927a001300030001-6.

12. CIA, "Weekly Summary," July 3, 1957, https://www.cia.gov/library/readingroom /document/cia-rdp79-00927a001300060001-2.

13. "Declaran legal y licita la huelga en La Industrial," *El Comercio*, April 1, 1950, 1.

14. "Huelga nacional de textiles del país ha decretado la FNT," *El Comercio*, April 18, 1950, 5; "FTP realizará huelgas de solidaridad con los sindicatos afiliados," *El Comercio*, April 21, 1950, 2; "Huelga de brazos caídos inician hoy esposas e hijos de obreros de La Industrial," *El Comercio*, April 21, 1950, 2; "Obreros de fábrica La Internacional y realizan huelga de solidaridad," *El Comercio*, April 22, 1950, 5.

15. "La policía disolvió anteanoche una manifestación obrera," *El Comercio*, April 22, 1950, 5.

16. "Obreros de La Industrial iniciaron anoche huelga de hambre indefinida," *El Comercio*, April 20, 1950, 18; "Cuatro obreros que declararon huelga de hambre se hallan enfermos de gravedad," *El Comercio*, April 22, 1950, 5.

17. "Hija de una obrera ha muerto de desnutrición," *El Comercio*, April 22, 1950, 14.

18. "Se efectuó el sepelio de la niña muerta cuando su madre, obrera textil, se hallaba en huelga," *El Comercio*, April 23, 1950, 2.

19. "Mensaje de ternura a la niña muerta," *Surcos*, May 1950, 10.

20. "Gerente de La Industrial pide a Policía haga salir de la fábrica a los obreros," *El Comercio*, April 25, 1950, 1; "Gobierno no ordenará el desalojamiento de los obreros de La Industrial," *El Comercio*, April 26, 1950, 1.

21. "Trabajadores de La Industrial abandonaron la fabrica ayer," *El Comercio*, April 28, 1950, 5.

22. "Cadáver de hija de obrera huelguista ha servido para una fea explotación," *El Comercio*, April 25, 1950, 14.

23. "La FTP protesta por acusación falsa lanzada contra la señorita Nela Martínez," *El Comercio*, April 26, 1950, 9. "La Alianza Femenina reitera su confianza a la Señora Nela Martínez," *El Comercio*, April 29, 1950, 2.

24. "La Señora Nela Martínez fue apresada ayer por la policia," *El Comercio*, May 4, 1950, 7.

25. "Orden la libertad de Nela Martínez," *El Comercio*, May 5, 1950, 16.

26. Martínez Espinosa, *Yo siempre he sido Nela Martínez Espinosa*.

27. CIA, "Efforts by Quito Police to Discredit Activities of Women Communists," June 14, 1950, https://www.cia.gov/library/readingroom/document/cia-rdp82-00457r005000400005-1.

28. CIA, "Efforts by Quito Police to Discredit Activities of Women Communists," June 14, 1950, https://www.cia.gov/library/readingroom/document/cia-rdp82-00457r005000400005-1.

29. CIA, "Weekly Contributions," July 18, 1950, https://www.cia.gov/library/readingroom/document/cia-rdp79-01090a000200050029-4.

30. CIA, "Weekly Contributions," March 7, 1950, https://www.cia.gov/library/readingroom/document/cia-rdp79-01090a000200050010-4.

31. CIA, "Weekly Contributions," April 11, 1950, https://www.cia.gov/library/readingroom/document/cia-rdp79-01090a000200050015-9.

32. Carvell to Bevin, "Annual Review for 1950," February 16, 1951, AE 1011/1, in *British Documents on Foreign Affairs*, series D, pt. 5, vol. 1, doc. 17.

33. Milton Bracker, "South American Ills Reflected in Revolt," *New York Times*, May 28, 1950, 100.

34. Herbert Matthews, "Democratic Life Waxes in Ecuador," *New York Times*, April 14, 1951, 5.

35. Mayers to Eden, "Leading Personalities in Ecuador," November 12, 1953, AE 1012/2, in *British Documents on Foreign Affairs*, series D, pt. 5, vol. 3, doc. 55.

36. "New Cabinet in Ecuador," *New York Times*, May 12, 1951, 3; "Ecuador," *Hispanic American Report*, June 1951, 25. For an outstanding examination of the socialist party's decision to ally with the Plaza administration, see Ibarra, "Entre la oposición y la colaboración."

37. Hamlin to State, May 6, 1951, RG59, 722.00/5-651, NARA.

38. "Como juzgan los partidos políticos la crisis del gabinete," *El Comercio*, May 8, 1951, 1.

39. Hamlin to State, May 8, 1951, RG59, 722.00/5-851, NARA.

40. Hamlin to State, "Joint Weeka 19," May 11, 1950, RG59, 722.00(W)/5-1150, NARA.

41. CIA, "Daily Digest," June 13, 1951, https://www.cia.gov/library/readingroom/document/cia-rdp79t01146a000200390001-8.

42. OIR, "Communism in the Other American Republics," July 19, 1951, in *OSS/State Department Intelligence and Research Reports*.

43. CIA, "Daily Digest," June 13, 1951, https://www.cia.gov/library/readingroom/document/cia-rdp79t01146a000200390001-8.

44. "A defender y luchar por la educación Laica," September 5, 1951, BEAEP.

45. Williams, *Through the Russian Revolution*, 174.

46. Paredes Ruiz, *Ricardo Paredes*, 249.

47. CIA, "Roberto Morena's Activities in Guayaquil," January 4, 1950, https://www.cia.gov/library/readingroom/document/cia-rdp82-00457r004000360003-9. The CIA's reference to Trotskyists is unclear, because Ecuador never had strong Trotskyist organizations. In 1956, the CIA reported that Ecuador was one of forty-six countries in which "there was evidence or claims of activity" of a revolutionary party affiliated with the Fourth International, and perhaps that is the reference here. See CIA, "The Fourth International," November 15, 1956, https://www.cia.gov/library/readingroom/document/cia-rdp83-01042r000600100008-8.

Chapter 7

1. Paredes, "Los graves problemas de la patria ecuatoriana en la hora actual," February 25, 1951, BEAEP. Paredes had previously emphasized social movement strategies over electoral politics, and this statement may reflect the consensus of the central committee rather than his own personal views.

2. See "Intervenciones del delegado ecuatoriano ante la ONU, Dr. Antonio Quevedo, en los grandes problemas mundiales," *El Comercio*, January 28, 1951, 1.

3. Paredes, "Los graves problemas de la patria ecuatoriana en la hora actual," February 25, 1951, BEAEP.

4. Maiguashca and North, "Orígenes y significado del velasquismo," 173; Linke, "The Political Scene in Ecuador," 132.

5. "Ecuador," *Hispanic American Report*, July 1952, 25. "*Descamisados*," or "the shirtless ones," is a reference to the impoverished followers of Juan Perón in Argentina.

6. "Ecuador," *Hispanic American Report*, December 1951, 25.

7. Mayers to Eden, "Ecuador: Annual Review for 1951," January 23, 1952, AE 1011/1, in *British Documents on Foreign Affairs*, series D, pt. 5, vol. 2, doc. 34.

8. "Ecuador," *Hispanic American Report*, January 1952, 27.

9. "Ecuador," *Hispanic American Report*, February 1952, 26.

10. Mayers to Eden, "Ecuador: Annual Review for 1951," January 23, 1952, AE 1011/1, in *British Documents on Foreign Affairs*, series D, pt. 5, vol. 2, doc. 34.

11. PCE, "Por la liberación nacional," February 21, 1952, BAEAP.

12. CIA, "Current Intelligence Digest," April 15, 1952, https://www.cia.gov/library/readingroom/document/cia-rdp79t01146a000900110001-1.

13. Hamlin to State, "Appraisal of Presidential Candidates from Point of View of United States Interest and Forecast of Winning Candidate," March 14, 1952, RG59, 722.00/3-1452, NARA.

14. "Ecuador," *Hispanic American Report*, March 1952, 24.

15. "Ecuadoreans Testify on Plot," *New York Times*, March 6, 1952, 10; "Ecuador," *Hispanic American Report*, April 1952, 26.

16. "Ecuador Quells Revolt," *New York Times*, March 4, 1952, 4.

17. "Candidate in Ecuador Stoned," *New York Times*, March 11, 1952, 2.

18. "One Dead in Ecuador Riot," *New York Times*, March 24, 1952, 2; "Ecuador," *Hispanic American Report*, April 1952, 26-27.

19. "Ecuadorean Rioters Kill One," *New York Times*, April 14, 1952, 3; CIA, "Current Intelligence Digest," April 15, 1952, https://www.cia.gov/library/readingroom/document/cia-rdp79t01146a000900110001-1. The number injured varied in different accounts, with one giving the number as thirty-seven.

20. Mayers to Eden, "Leading Personalities in Ecuador," November 12, 1953, AE 1012/2, in *British Documents on Foreign Affairs*, series D, pt. 5, vol. 3, doc. 55.

21. "Partido comunista dirige carta abierta al congreso socialista," *El Día*, March 31, 1952.

22. "El comunismo no tiene derecho a impugnar candidatos de ADN," *El Sol*, April 3, 1952, 1. Also see Hamlin to State, "Fifth Special Congress of the Ecuadoran Socialist Party," April 9, 1952, RG59, 722.00/4-952, NARA.

23. "Aclarase que el congreso socialista no insinuó la renuncia de Salazar Gómez," *El Comercio*, April 11, 1952, 1. Also see Hamlin to State, "Fifth Special Congress of the Ecuadoran Socialist Party," April 15, 1952, RG59, 722.00/4-1552, NARA.

24. PCE, "Unidad de las fuerzas democráticas: El Partido Comunista y la renuncia de Salazar Gómez," April 21, 1952, BEAEP.

25. "Ecuador Electioneering Heated," *New York Times*, April 19, 1952, 4.

26. CIA, "Central Intelligence Digest," April 21, 1952, https://www.cia.gov/library/readingroom/document/cia-rdp79t01146a000900150001-7.

27. CIA, "Current Intelligence Digest," April 25, 1952, https://www.cia.gov/library/readingroom/document/cia-rdp79t01146a000900190001-3.

28. CIA, "Central Intelligence Bulletin," April 26, 1952, https://www.cia.gov/library/readingroom/document/cia-rdp79t00975a000600540001-5.

29. "Ecuadorean Move Fails," *New York Times*, April 26, 1952, 3.

30. Hamlin to State, April 30, 1952, RG59, 722.13/4-3052, NARA.

31. "Ecuador Cabinet Named," *New York Times*, May 1, 1952, 4.

32. "2 Die in Clash in Quito," *New York Times*, April 27, 1952, 2.

33. "Rioting Quelled in Ecuador," *New York Times*, April 28, 1952, 5.

34. Hamlin to State, April 26, 1952, RG59, 722.13/4-2652, NARA.

35. Hamlin to State, April 27, 1952, RG59, 722.13/4-2752, NARA.

36. Herbert Matthews, "Latin America Unrest Due to Basic Causes," *New York Times*, April 27, 1952, 161.

37. CIA, "Increased Instability in Latin America," April 28, 1952, https://www.cia.gov/library/readingroom/document/cia-rdp91t01172r000300300009-4.

38. CIA, "Central Intelligence Bulletin," May 24, 1952, https://www.cia.gov/library/readingroom/document/cia-rdp79t00975a000700110001-1.

39. CIA, "Current Intelligence Digest," May 28, 1952, https://www.cia.gov/library/readingroom/document/cia-rdp79t01146a001000120001-8.

40. Sam Pope Brewer, "Guayaquil Tense as Mayor Flees," *New York Times*, May 28, 1952, 8.

41. Milton Carr, "Plaza declara que el Ejército respaldará a Gobierno que sea elegido en próximos comicios," *El Comercio*, May 30, 1952, 1; Sam Pope Brewer, "Ecuadorean Chief Sees Vote, No Coup," *New York Times*, May 30, 1952, 6.

42. "Suspendese orden de detención contra Guevara Moreno y otros," *El Comercio*, May 30, 1952, 1; Sam Pope Brewer, "Ecuador Warned by an Army Group," *New York Times*, May 31, 1952, 10.

43. Sam Pope Brewer, "Ecuador Fearful of Military Coup," *New York Times*, May 29, 1952, 11.

44. Mayers to Eden, "Leading Personalities in Ecuador," November 12, 1953, AE 1012/2, *British Documents on Foreign Affairs*, series D, pt. 5, vol. 3, doc. 55.

45. Mayers to Eden, "Presidential Elections," June 17, 1952, AE 1015/5, in *British Documents on Foreign Affairs*, series D, pt. 5, vol. 2, doc. 35.

46. "Ecuador Protests to Nuncio," *New York Times*, May 15, 1952, 14; "Nuncio Warns Ecuador's Clergy," *New York Times*, May 16, 1952, 4.

47. Sam Pope Brewer, "Ecuador Fearful of Military Coup," *New York Times*, May 29, 1952, 11.

48. Sam Pope Brewer, "Ecuador Warned by an Army Group," *New York Times*, May 31, 1952, 10.

49. "A la nación," *El Comercio*, May 31, 1952, 1.

50. CIA, "Current Intelligence Digest," June 5, 1952, https://www.cia.gov/library/readingroom/document/cia-rdp79t01146a001000170001-3.

51. "Ecuadorean Move Fails," *New York Times*, April 26, 1952, 3.

52. Hamlin to State, April 27, 1952, RG59, 722.13/4-2752, NARA.

53. Of a total 357,675 votes cast, Velasco Ibarra received 153,934; Alarcón Falconí 118,186; Chiriboga Villagómez 67,307; and Larrea Jijón 18,248. See "El Dr. Velasco Ibarra fue proclamado Presidente Electo," *El Comercio*, July 18, 1952, 7.

54. Sam Pope Brewer, "Ousted Head Seen Victor in Ecuador," *New York Times*, June 3, 1952, 11; Sam Pope Brewer, "Ex-President Wins Ecuador Election," *New York Times*, June 4, 1952, 11.

55. Mayers to Eden, "Presidential Elections," June 17, 1952, AE 1015/5, in *British Documents on Foreign Affairs*, series D, pt. 5, vol. 2, doc. 35.

56. "Ecuador," *Hispanic American Report*, July 1952, 25.

57. Mayers to Eden, "Presidential Elections," June 17, 1952, AE 1015/5, in *British Documents on Foreign Affairs*, series D, pt. 5, vol. 2, doc. 35.

58. PCE, "Partido Comunista frente a las elecciones presidenciales y al futuro nacional," *El Pueblo*, May 24, 1952, 4.

59. Mayers to Eden, "Presidential Elections," June 17, 1952, AE 1015/5, in *British Documents on Foreign Affairs*, series D, pt. 5, vol. 2, doc. 35.

60. McGinnis, "Memorandum to Assistant Secretary Miller," June 3, 1952, RG722.00/6–352, in *FRUS*, 1952-1954, 4:970.

61. OIR, "Communism in the Other American Republics," August 12, 1952, in *OSS/State Department Intelligence and Research Reports*.

62. CIA, "Current Intelligence Digest," June 5, 1952, https://www.cia.gov/library/readingroom/document/cia-rdp79t01146a001000170001-3.

63. CIA, "Current Intelligence Digest," April 22, 1952, https://www.cia.gov/library/readingroom/document/cia-rdp79t01146a000900160001-6; Daniels, *Latin America in the Cold War*, 110.

64. "Democracy in Ecuador," *New York Times*, June 5, 1952, 30.

65. Sam Pope Brewer, "First Free Election Surprises Ecuador," *New York Times*, June 8, 1952, 157.

66. "Ecuador," *Hispanic American Report*, July 1952, 25.

67. Herbert Matthews, "Democratic Life Waxes in Ecuador," *New York Times*, April 14, 1951, 5.

68. Linke, "The Political Scene in Ecuador," 136.

69. Wight to State, "Labor Report," October 15, 1952, RG59, 822.06/10-1552, NARA.

70. OIR, "Communism in the Other American Republics," October 20, 1952, in *OSS/State Department Intelligence and Research Reports*.

71. Linke, "The Political Scene in Ecuador," 137.

72. Clark to Eden, "Ecuador: Annual Review for 1952," February 3, 1953, AE 1011/1, in *British Documents on Foreign Affairs*, series D, pt. 5, vol. 3, doc. 53.

73. Mayers to Eden, "Ecuador: Annual Review for 1953," January 7, 1954, AE 1011/1, in *British Documents on Foreign Affairs*, series D, pt. 5, vol. 4, doc. 53.

74. "Party Cuts Tie to Quito Regime," *New York Times*, June 8, 1953, 22; "Ecuador," *Hispanic American Report*, July 1953, 28-29.

75. "Quito Party Drops 3 Envoys," *New York Times*, March 18, 1953, 3.

76. "Resumen del año político de 1953," *El Comercio*, January 1, 1954, 21.

77. Norris, *El gran ausente*, 149.

78. Gonzalo Villalba, "Contra las maniobras y la provocación fascistas: Unión Combativa del Pueblo," May 16, 1953, BEAEP.

79. See, for example, CIA, "Congress of Federación Provincial de Trabajadores del Guayas (FPTG)," February 12, 1952, https://www.cia.gov/library/readingroom

/document/cia-rdp82-00457r010500210007-9; and CIA, "Activities of the Federación Provincial de Trabajadores del Guayas (FPTG)," October 17, 1952, https://www.cia.gov/library/readingroom/document/cia-rdp82-00457r014300020005-0.

Chapter 8

1. "Hacia el V congreso del Partido Comunista del Ecuador," *El Pueblo*, February 17, 1952, 2. Also see "El V congreso y la reforma de los estatutos del PCE," *El Pueblo*, March 8, 1952, 2.

2. Higdon to FBI, "Communist Movement in Latin America," September 13, 1944, FBI Subject file 064-HQ-200 SUB 212, FOIPA Request 1381938–000.

3. Boggs, "Organization and Operation of the National Communist Party of Ecuador," May 19, 1947, RG84, Entry #2396, Box 43, NARA.

4. Simmons to State, "Political Implications of Government Decision Declaring Three Strikes Illegal," October 15, 1948, RG59, 822.5045/10-1548, NARA.

5. Hamlin to State, "Joint Weeka 15," April 13, 1951, RG59, 722.00(W)/4-1351, NARA.

6. Ibarra, "Acción colectiva rural" 375.

7. "El hombre en quien el pueblo de Ambato confía," *La Calle*, August 29, 1959, 19.

8. Quito to State, "Joint Weeka 38," September 22, 1950, RG59, 822.00(W)/9-2250, NARA.

9. FTP, "Federación de Trabajadores de Pichincha," October 6, 1950, BEAEP.

10. Agee, *Inside the Company*, 193, 242.

11. Quito to State, "Developments of Plans for Forthcoming Fourth National Congress of the Partido Comunista del Ecuador," July 14, 1949, RG84, Entry #2396, Box 51, NARA.

12. Daniels to State, "Joint Weeka 62," March 7, 1952, RG59, 722.00(W)/3-752, NARA.

13. Daniels to State, "Joint Weeka 82," July 27, 1952, RG59, 722.00(W)/7-552, NARA.

14. Phillips, *The Night Watch*, 36.

15. Daniels to State, "Joint Weeka 83," August 1, 1952, RG59, 722.00(W)/8-152, NARA.

16. *Foreign Service List*, July 1, 1950, 15.

17. *Foreign Service List*, July 1, 1952, 16; Foreign Service List, October 1, 1953, 11; *Biographic Register*, 1961, 642.

18. "Shetterly," *Albuquerque Journal*, October 30, 2004, http://obits.abqjournal.com/obits/show/148474.

19. McGehee, *Deadly Deceits*, xi.

20. The following information is largely drawn from CIA, "Fifth Congress of the Communist Party of Ecuador (PCE) Held at Ambato," October 7, 1952, https://www.cia.gov/library/readingroom/document/cia-rdp82-00457r014100290007-1.

21. "El Dr. Ricardo Paredes fue detenido en Ellis Island por autoridades," *El Comerico*, January 27, 1951, 1; "El doctor Ricardo Paredes, comunista ecuatoriano, ha sido apresado en los EE.UU.," *El Día*, January 28, 1951; "Prisión de líder comunista ecuatoriano

en Estados Unidos ha originado una serie de protestas de elementos progresistas," *La Tierra*, January 28, 1951; "Protestas por la detención del Doctor Ricardo Paredes," *El Sol*, January 28, 1951; Hamlin to State, January 28, 1951, RG59, 722.001/1-2851, NARA.

22. CIA, "Executive Committee of the International Union of Students," January 5, 1951, https://www.cia.gov/library/readingroom/document/cia-rdp83-00415r007000110001-0.

23. CIA, "General Communist Activities in Ecuador," July 19, 1950, https://www.cia.gov/library/readingroom/document/cia-rdp82-00457r005200630010-8; CIA, "Roberto Morena's Activities in Guayaquil," January 4, 1950, https://www.cia.gov/library/readingroom/document/cia-rdp82-00457r004000360003-9.

24. Rothwell, *Transpacific Revolutionaries*.

25. Rodas, *Nosotras que del amor hicimos*; Rodas, *Crónica de un sueño*; Rodas, *Maestras que dejaron huellas*; Almeida Cabrera, *Antología*.

26. Scotten to State, July 29, 1944, RG59, 822.00/7-2944, NARA.

27. Hoover to Lyon, March 14, 1945, RG59, 822.00B/3-1445, NARA; Hoover to Lyon, April 20, 1945, RG59, 822.00B/4-2045, NARA.

28. CIA, "Extraordinary Meeting of the PCE in Guayaquil," October 17, 1952, https://www.cia.gov/library/readingroom/document/cia-rdp82-00457r014300070009-1. The CIA notes that this report was based on "unevaluated information."

29. "Ecuador to Improve Port," *New York Times*, January 29, 1951, 37. Plaza's government requested a total of eighteen technical commissions under the Point Four program, with an emphasis on agricultural development and hydroelectric power generation. "Ecuador," *Hispanic American Report*, March 1951, 22.

30. "Grace Line Contract Hit," *New York Times*, March 10, 1951, 27.

31. CIA, "Communist Activities in Guayaquil," May 3, 1951, https://www.cia.gov/library/readingroom/document/cia-rdp82-00457r007400210011-9.

32. Medina Castro, *El Guayas*.

33. Ellis to Simmons, March 23, 1949, RG84, Entry #2396, Box 52, NARA.

34. CIA, "Congress of Federación Provincial de Trabajadores del Guayas (FPTG)," February 12, 1952, https://www.cia.gov/library/readingroom/document/cia-rdp82-00457r010500210007-9.

35. "Ecuador Bars Grace Stop," *New York Times*, January 25, 1952, 41; "Ecuador," *Hispanic American Report*, February 1952, 26.

36. "Ecuador Takes Over Cargo Task at Port," *New York Times*, February 17, 1952, 148.

37. Martínez in fact was correct that it was a party decision to support Intriago's campaign. See "El Partido Comunista del Guayas resolvió apoyar la candidatura del señor Antriago para la alcaldía," *El Sol*, October 8, 1951. Unfortunately, we do not have a copy of the report she presented at the congress.

38. Mayers to Eden, "Leading Personalities in Ecuador," November 12, 1953, AE 1012/2, in *British Documents on Foreign Affairs*, series D, pt. 5, vol. 3, doc. 55.

39. Daniels to State, "Communist and Border Line Activities in Ecuador," March 5, 1952, RG59, 722.001/3-552, NARA.

40. CIA, "Activities of the Juventud Comunista del Ecuador (JCE)," November 4, 1953, https://www.cia.gov/library/readingroom/document/cia-rdp80-00810a002700690010-6.

41. Ravndal to State, July 5, 1957, RG84, Entry #2396, Box 73, NARA; Culley to Noland, 1958, RG84, Entry #2396, Box 73, NARA.

42. Arcos Bastidas, "Revista Política La Calle," 23, 53.

43. Daniels to State, "Joint Weeka 86," August 22, 1952, RG59, 722.00(W)/8-2252, NARA.

44. Hoover to Lyon, November 26, 1945, RG59, 822.00B/11-2645, NARA.

45. According to Agee, Roura traveled to China in 1963 without communist party authorization and was arrested at the airport in Quito when he returned with $25,000 USD in cash, allegedly to launch a guerrilla campaign. Agee subsequently tried and failed to recruit Roura as a CIA agent. Agee, *Inside the Company*, 274–80, 315–19. Also see "Dirigente comunista José María Roura detenida ayer al retornar del exterior," *El Comercio*, May 20, 1963, 1; "Papales y dinero que traía Roura eran calvez para el plan subversivo comunista," *El Comercio*, May 21, 1963, 1; "Estudian documentos comisados al comunista J. M. Roura," *El Comercio*, May 22, 1963, 3; José María Roura, "José María Roura, a la opinion popular," *El Comercio*, May 22, 1963, 1.

46. "Trágicos sucesos en Normal Juan Montalvo," *El Comercio*, November 29, 1955, 1; "A la 1.50 de la madrugada de hoy se dio sepultura al estudiante Isidro Guerrero," *El Comercio*, November 29, 1955, 1; CIA, "Central Intelligence Bulletin," December 3, 1955, https://www.cia.gov/library/readingroom/document/cia-rdp79t00975a002300170001-7; Jorge Vivanco, "Yo vi matar a Isidro Guerrero," *La Calle*, June 8, 1957, 11.

47. Costanzo to Wieland, November 9, 1955, RG84 Entry #2408-B, Box 18, NARA.

48. "Ecuador Grants Amnesty," *New York Times*, June 9, 1946, 34.

49. CIA, "PCE Propaganda Activities in Guayas Province," December 23, 1953, https://www.cia.gov/library/readingroom/document/cia-rdp80-00810a003200140001-0.

50. CIA, "Statements of Wilson Durango Lopez," October 27, 1953, https://www.cia.gov/library/readingroom/document/cia-rdp80-00810a002700010003-8.

51. Paredes Ruiz, *Ricardo Paredes*, 239.

52. On the expulsions from the PCE in 1963, see CIA, "Weekly Summary," June 21, 1963, https://www.cia.gov/library/readingroom/document/cia-rdp79-00927a004100020001-6, and Agee, *Inside the Company*, 296.

53. Murphy, "Members of Communist Party Organs in Non-Orbit Countries," June 1, 1954, RG84, Entry #2396, Box 65, NARA.

54. Rodas, *Dolores Cacuango*, 158; Rodas, *Nosotras que del amor hicimos*, 85.

55. Becker, *Indians and Leftists in the Making of Ecuador's Modern Indigenous Movements*, 17.

56. See Galarza Zavala, *El yugo feudal*; *Los campesinos de Loja y Zamora*; *El festín del petróleo*; and *Piratas en el golfo*; Agee, Galarza Zavala, and Herrera, *The CIA Case Against Latin America*.

57. Jaime Galarza Zavala, "Sangre en Cuenca," April 20, 1952, BEAEP.

58. Jaime Galarza Zavala, "Armas sucias de los anticomunistas," April 1952, BEAEP.

59. Fisher and Ury, *Getting to Yes*.

60. "Ecuador Red Leader Named," *New York Times*, August 13, 1952, 4.

61. Agee, *Inside the Company*, 261–62.

62. "Los velasquistas formarán un frente de lucha contra el Comunismo," *El Comercio*, August 11, 1952, 1.

63. Enderton to State, "Joint Weeka 98," November 17, 1952, RG59, 722.00(W)/11-1752, NARA.

64. Daniels to State, "Joint Weeka 89," September 12, 1952, RG59, 722.00(W)/9-1252, NARA.

65. CIA, "Statements of Wilson Durango Lopez," October 27, 1953, https://www.cia.gov/library/readingroom/document/cia-rdp80-00810a002700010003-8.

66. Alfredo Vera, "El comunismo ecuatoriano," *La Calle*, January 3, 1959, 21.

67. CIA, "Statements of Wilson Durango Lopez," October 27, 1953, https://www.cia.gov/library/readingroom/document/cia-rdp80-00810a002700010003-8.

Chapter 9

1. "Resumen del año político de 1953," *El Comercio*, January 1, 1954, 21.

2. CIA, "Extraordinary Meeting of the PCE in Guayaquil, 25 August 1952," October 17, 1952, https://www.cia.gov/library/readingroom/document/cia-rdp82-00457r014300070009-1.

3. Linke, *Ecuador*, 162. On communist resistance to foreign military bases in Ecuador, see Becker, "Ecuador's Early No-foreign Military Bases Movement."

4. CIA, "Political Indoctrination in Pedro Saad Cell," May 8, 1953, https://www.cia.gov/library/readingroom/document/cia-rdp80-00810a001100630004-6.

5. CIA, "Measures of the Pichincha Provincial Committee to Strengthen PCE Cells," June 1, 1953, https://www.cia.gov/library/readingroom/document/cia-rdp80-00810a001300540001-7.

6. CIA, "Guayaquil Local Conference of the Partido Comunista del Ecuador (PCE)," September 10, 1953, https://www.cia.gov/library/readingroom/document/cia-rdp80-00810a002200280013-3.

7. "Quito Cabinet Is Named," *New York Times*, August 31, 1956, 5; "Ecuador," *Hispanic American Report*, November 1958, 619.

8. An "interpellation" is a parliamentary procedure in which members of the legislative body may submit questions to a government official demanding justification for a policy. It is a mechanism drawn from a French constitutional tradition by which a parliament can censure executive branch actions.

9. "Cefepistas tuvieron choque con política de Guayaquil: un muerto y varios heridos," *El Comercio*, September 13, 1953, 1; "One Dead, Many Hurt in Guayaquil Rioting," *New York Times*, September 13, 1953, 26.

10. "Por 73 votos contra 15 se negó la moción de censura al Ministro Ponce Enríquez," *El Comercio*, September 20, 1953, 1; "Quito Backed On 2 Papers," *New York Times*, September 20, 1953, 13.

11. "Resumen del año político de 1953," *El Comercio*, January 1, 1954, 21.

12. "Afirmase que el Senador Pedro Saad interpelaré al Ministro de Gobierno," *El Comercio*, September 1, 1953, 1.

13. "Nada hay concreto sobre posible interpelación al Ministro Ponce Enríquez," *El Comercio*, September 2, 1953, 1; "El Ministro de Gobierno será interpelado por el Sr. Saad próxima semana," *El Comercio*, September 4, 1953, 1; "Ministro de Gobierno dice que concurrirá complacido a ser interpelado en Congreso," *El Comercio*, September 6, 1953, 1; "El viernes será interpelado el Ministro Ponce Enríquez," *El Comercio*, September 8, 1953, 1.

14. Norris, *El gran ausente*, 125, 142–48; "Ecuador Arrests Protested," *New York Times*, April 25, 1953, 4; Sydney Gruson, "Ecuadorian Chief Backs Press Curb," *New York Times*, May 16, 1953, 6; Gardner, *The Inter American Press Association*, 83; "Resumen del año político de 1953," *El Comercio*, January 1, 1954, 21.

15. Mayers to Eden, "Ecuador: Annual Review for 1953," January 7, 1954, AE 1011/1, in *British Documents on Foreign Affairs*, series D, pt. 5, vol. 4, doc. 53.

16. "Senador Saad presenta ocho preguntas que deberá responder el Ministro de Gobierno," *El Comercio*, September 11, 1953, 1.

17. "Se depositó era pregunta que contestara el Ministro Ponce," *El Comercio*, September 15, 1953, 1. On Macías Hurtado, see Martz, "The Regionalist Expression of Populism," 312n6.

18. Maleady to State, "Interpellation of Minister of Government Ponce," September 21, 1953, RG59, 722.00/9-2153, NARA.

19. "Congreso Nacional de 1953," *El Comercio*, September 12, 1953, 3.

20. Comité de Defensa de la Democracia del Barrio de San Roque, "Por el pan y la libertad," 1953, BEAEP.

21. Maleady to State, "Interpellation of minister of government Ponce," Quito, September 21, 1953, RG59, 722.00/9-2153, NARA.

22. "En torno de la interpelación," *El Comercio*, September 18, 1953, 4.

23. "Federación de Trabajadores del Guayas respalda a los que interpelarán al ministro de gobierno," *El Comercio*, September 18, 1953, 16.

24. The follow discussion draws from the congressional record of the debate included in Congreso Pleno Congreso Ordinario de 1953, "Sesión del 18 de setiembre–vespertina," September 18, 1953, AFL, as well as newspaper reports: "Efectuose la interpelación al Ministro de Gobierno Dr. Ponce," *El Comercio*, September 19, 1953, 1; "Por 73 votos contra 15 se negó la moción de censura al Ministro Ponce Enríquez," *El Comercio*, September 20, 1953, 1.

25. Daniels to State, "Proselytizing Activities of Protestant Evangelists Provoke Reaction," March 12, 1953, RG59, 822.413/3-1253, NARA.

26. "Exposición de los ferroviarios ecuatorianos," *El Comercio*, January 18, 1953, 1; Warner to State, "Controversy between Railroads President and Union Leader," January 27, 1953, RG59, 822.062/1-2753, NARA; Maleady to State, "Minister of Government Says Administration Has Knowledge of Subversive Plot," March 18, 1953, RG59, 722.00/3-1853, NARA; Gray to State, "Annual Labor Report, Ecuador 1953," January

28, 1954, RG59, 822.06/1-2854, NARA; Kofas, "Politics of Conflict and Containment," 73–74.

27. "Hechos de sangre ocurrieron en la hacienda la Merced, Pintag," *El Comercio*, August 7, 1953, 14; "Los disturbios en la hacienda La Merced dejaron saldo de 2 muertos y 14 heridos," *El Comercio*, August 8, 1953, 16; "Cura de Píntag y tres sindicados por los sucesos de La Merced rinden declaración," *El Comercio*, August 9, 1953, 19; "Otra victima de disturbios en la hacienda La Merced falleció," *El Comercio*, August 12, 1953, 16; Ibarra, "Acción colectiva rural," 294–305; Albornoz Peralta, *Luchas indígenas*, 77–79.

28. Mayers, "Comments on the Memorandum on 'Current Developments in Communist Strategy and Tactics in Latin America,'" September 30, 1953, 2195/7/53, FO 1110/592, TNA.

29. Albornoz Peralta, *Luchas indígenas*, 101.

30. Ponce Enríquez, *Informe a la nación, 1954*, 28.

31. CIG, "Latin America Presents Problem to Communists in Plan For "One World,"" October 13, 1947, https://www.cia.gov/library/readingroom/document/cia-rdp82-00457r001000110004-8.

32. CIA, "Latin American Continental Control Headquarters," March 23, 1949, https://www.cia.gov/library/readingroom/document/cia-rdp82-00457r002500190010-7.

33. CIA, "Circulation of Soviet Propaganda," February 5, 1951, https://www.cia.gov/library/readingroom/document/cia-rdp82-00457r006800200010-1.

34. Agee, *Inside the Company*, 115.

35. CIA, "Co-ordination and Control of the International Communist Movement," November 1, 1948, https://www.cia.gov/library/readingroom/document/cia-rdp78-00915r000100200003-5.

36. CIA, "Communication between Ecuadoran and Colombian Communists," February 18, 1949, https://www.cia.gov/library/readingroom/document/cia-rdp82-00457r002300680007-9.

37. Roberts, "Averting Armageddon."

38. CIA, "PCE Delegate to World Peace Congress," May 23, 1949, https://www.cia.gov/library/readingroom/document/cia-rdp82-00457r002700720007-0.

39. CIA, "Transmittal of Russian Language Magazine from Prague," November 21, 1949, https://www.cia.gov/library/readingroom/document/cia-rdp83-00415r003800020007-0; Bragonier to State, "Questionnaire on Soviet Propaganda," December 23, 1949, RG84, Entry #2396, Box 51, NARA; Bragonier to State, "Submission of Communist Circular Matter," December 23, 1949, RG84, Entry #2396, Box 51, NARA.

40. CIA, "Circulation of Soviet Propaganda," February 5, 1951, https://www.cia.gov/library/readingroom/document/cia-rdp82-00457r006800200010-1.

41. CIA, "PCE Newsstand in Guayaquil and Sale of Communist Publications," August 21, 1953, https://www.cia.gov/library/readingroom/document/cia-rdp80-00810a002000460007-2.

42. Bastian to USIA, "Analysis of Communist Propaganda Effort," May 29, 1956, RG84, Entry #2396, Box 73, NARA.

43. Dustmann to State, "Analysis of Ecuador's Communist Party," November 25, 1957, RG59, 722.001/11-2557, NARA.

44. PCE, "Se habla de víctima a Pedro Saad, interpelante al Ministro de Gbno," September 1953, BEAEP.

45. PCE, "A cerrar el paso al fascismo y a impedir la explotación del pueblo," September 1953, BEAEP.

46. Merlo Vasquez, *Informe a la nación, 1958*, 26.

47. PSE, "El Partido Socialista frente a la interpelación del Mtro. de Gobierno," September 17, 1953, BEAEP.

48. Mayers, "Comments on the Memorandum on 'Current Developments in Communist Strategy and Tactics in Latin America,'" September 30, 1953, 2195/7/53, FO 1110/592, TNA.

49. Maleady to State, "Interpellation of Minister of Government Ponce," September 21, 1953, RG59, 722.00/9-2153, NARA.

50. CIA, "Communist Manifestation in Honor of Pedro Saad," October 26, 1953, https://www.cia.gov/library/readingroom/document/cia-rdp80-00810a002700010006-5.

51. CIA, "Communist Manifestation in Honor of Pedro Saad," November 4, 1953, https://www.cia.gov/library/readingroom/document/cia-rdp80-00810a002700860003-5.

52. Mayers to Eden, "Leading Personalities in Ecuador," November 12, 1953, AE 1012/2, in *British Documents on Foreign Affairs*, series D, pt. 5, vol. 3, doc. 55.

53. CIA, "Communist Manifestation in Honor of Pedro Saad," November 4, 1953, https://www.cia.gov/library/readingroom/document/cia-rdp80-00810a002700860003-5.

Chapter 10

1. "Satellite Trend Cited," *New York Times*, October 23, 1956, 19; "U.S. Is Cut Off from Budapest," *New York Times*, October 25, 1956, 8.

2. Rositzke, *The CIA's Secret Operations*, 189.

3. CIA, "Significant Mining Developments," March 1, 1954, https://www.cia.gov/library/readingroom/document/cia-rdp80-00809a000500420002-0; CIA, "Wage Scales/Other Benefits," October 1, 1954, https://www.cia.gov/library/readingroom/document/cia-rdp83-00423r001700590002-7; CIA, "Description of Roads and Railroads," December 8, 1954, https://www.cia.gov/library/readingroom/document/cia-rdp80-00926a007500260002-1; CIA, "Ports of Guayaquil/Puerto Bolivar/Water Depths/Port Requirements and Facilities," September 28, 1954, https://www.cia.gov/library/readingroom/document/cia-rdp80-00809a000500640247-5. This last item relates information from the Office of Naval Intelligence.

4. Mills to State, "Communist Sponsored International Meeting of Rural Youth," Quito, September 29, 1954, RG84, Entry #2396, Box 61, NARA.

5. Agee, *Inside the Company*, 110, 179.

6. *Foreign Service List*, March 1960, 89. Stockwell complained about the agency's tendency to shift personnel between overt and undercover roles both domestically and internationally, which he said "makes a mockery of the CIA's pretenses of clandestinity." See *In Search of Enemies*, 36.

7. Dulles to ARA Diplomatic posts, February 8, 1956, RG84, Entry #2396, Box 73, NARA.

8. Mills to State, February 17, 1956, RG59, 722.001/2-1756, NARA.

9. Wieland to State, May 16, 1956, RG84, Entry #2396, Box 73, NARA.

10. Wieland to Holman, "Front Leaders Reported Communists," March 2, 1956, RG84, Entry #2396, Box 73, NARA.

11. Counselor to Ambassador, March 22, 1956, RG84, Entry #2396, Box 73, NARA.

12. Dulles, "Briefing of Visitors to the Soviet Bloc," April 19, 1956, RG84, Entry #2396, Box 73, NARA.

13. Streibert, "Contacts with Communists and Other Unfriendly Elements Abroad," April 26, 1956, RG84, Entry #2396, Box 73, NARA.

14. CIA, "Activities of the Juventud Comunista del Ecuador (JCE)," November 4, 1953, https://www.cia.gov/library/readingroom/document/cia-rdp80-00810a002700690010-6.

15. Bastian to Wieland and Holman, "Local CP Youth Defectors," May 2, 1956, RG84, Entry #2396, Box 73, NARA.

16. Culley to Noland, 1958, RG84, Entry #2396, Box 73, NARA. Also see Ravndal to State, July 5, 1957, RG84, Entry #2396, Box 73, NARA.

17. Agee, *Inside the Company*, 404.

18. Bragonier and Blankinship, "Communism in Ecuador," December 12, 1955, RG59, 722.001/12-1255, NARA.

19. Wieland to Blankinship, December 30, 1955, RG84, Entry #2408-B, Box 18, NARA.

20. Mayers to Eden, "Ecuador: Annual Review for 1953," January 7, 1954, AE 1011/1, in *British Documents on Foreign Affairs*, series D, pt. 5, vol. 4, doc. 53.

21. Mayers to Eden, "Ecuador: Annual Review for 1954," January 3, 1955, AE 1011/1, in *British Documents on Foreign Affairs*, series D, pt. 5, vol. 5, doc. 35.

22. Gamble to Lloyd, "Ecuador: Annual Review for 1955," January 17, 1956, AE 1011/1, in *British Documents on Foreign Affairs*, series D, pt. 5, vol. 6, doc. 30.

23. Ponce Enríquez, *Informe a la nación, 1954*, 23–25.

24. "Gamonales y autoridades arnistas atropellan a indígenas de Galte," *El Pueblo*, January 10, 1953, 4; "Los campesinos de Galte obtienen gran victoria," *El Pueblo*, August 15, 1953, 5–6; Albornoz Peralta, *Luchas indígenas*, 77.

25. Ibarra, "Conflictos rurales," 436–48.

26. Ponce Enríquez, *Informe a la nación, 1954*, 28–30.

27. Maleady to State, "Joint Weeka 35," August 31, 1953, RG59, 722.00(W)/8-3153, NARA.

28. Gerberich, "Ecuador," January 26, 1954, RG59, 722.00/2-2354, NARA.

29. CIA, "Weekly Summary," November 10, 1955, https://www.cia.gov/library/readingroom/document/cia-rdp79-00927a000600170001-9. The presence of Guatemalan exiles in Ecuador stirring up political problems was a continual concern. See,

for example, letter from Wieland to State, "Analysis of Ecuadoran Political Situation," December 20, 1955, RG59, 722.00/12-2055, NARA.

30. Streibert, "Estimated Cost of World-Wide Communist Propaganda Activities," April 25, 1956, RG84, Entry #2396, Box 73, NARA.

31. Bastian to USIA, "Analysis of Communist Propaganda Effort," May 29, 1956, RG84, Entry #2396, Box 73, NARA.

32. Wieland to State, "Analysis of Ecuador's Municipal and Provincial Council Elections," December 1, 1955, RG59, 722.00/12-155, NARA.

33. Costanzo to Wieland, November 9, 1955, RG84, Entry #2408-B, Box 18, NARA.

34. Wieland to Blankinship, December 30, 1955, RG84, Entry #2408-B, Box 18, NARA.

35. "Frente Democrático obtuvo 13 de las 15 alcaldías del país," *El Comercio*, November 24, 1955, 1.

36. Wieland to State, "Analysis of Ecuador's Municipal and Provincial Council Elections," December 1, 1955, RG59, 722.00/12-155, NARA.

37. Tad Szulc, "Conservative Leads in Ecuador Election," *New York Times*, June 4, 1956, 1; "Ecuador," *Hispanic American Report*, July 1956, 294–97.

38. "Verdadero atraco a la voluntad popular se ha cometido en las votaciones del Azuay," *La Tierra*, July 3, 1956, 1; "Mujeres democráticas del país se agrupan para impedir que se sancione el fraude," *La Tierra*, July 19, 1956, 1; Wieland to State, July 28, 1956, RG59, 722.00/7-2856, NARA; Muñoz Vicuña, *Temas obreros*, 241.

39. Maier, *The Ecuadorian Presidential Election of June 2, 1968*, 59.

40. PCE, "Entre comunismo y democracia hay un abismo," 1956, BEAEP.

41. PCE, "Por un gobierno democrático al servicio del pueblo; contra la reacción, los golpes de estado y el continuismo; programa electoral del Partido Comunista del Ecuador," February 21, 1956, private collection of Leonardo J. Muñoz. I thank Sandra Fernández Muñoz for facilitating access to this collection.

42. "Miente José María Plaza al decir que el Frente rechaza al Comunismo," reprinted from *El Combate*, March 17, 1956, in private collection of Leonardo J. Muñoz.

43. Costanzo to Wieland, November 30, 1955, RG84, Entry #2408-B, Box 18, NARA.

44. Counselor to Ambassador, March 22, 1956, RG84, Entry #2396, Box 73, NARA.

45. Dustmann to State, "Additional Reports on Communist Support of National Democratic Front in Ecuadoran Presidential Election," July 21, 1956, RG84, Entry #2396, Box 73, NARA.

46. CIA, "Weekly Summary," August 16, 1956, https://www.cia.gov/library/readingroom/document/cia-rdp79-00927a000900080001-6; "Ecuador," *Hispanic American Report*, September 1956, 387–89; "Ecuador," *Hispanic American Report*, October 1956, 438.

47. "Ecuador," *Hispanic American Report*, December 1956, 538–39.

48. CIA, "Central Intelligence Bulletin," August 26, 1956, https://www.cia.gov/library/readingroom/document/cia-rdp79t00975a002700160001-4.

49. PCE, "¡Todos contra Ponce!" August 14, 1956, BEAEP. Also see "Forjemos una coalición popular anticonservadora," August 3, 1956, BEAEP.

50. "El partido comunista frente al nuevo gobierno," *El Pueblo*, September 1, 1956, 1.

51. Wieland to State, "Manifesto of the Communist Party of Ecuador," September 10, 1956, RG59, 722.001/9-1056, NARA.

52. Bragonier to King and Sanders, "Communism in Ecuador," August 28, 1956, RG84, Entry #2396, Box 73, NARA. A typed note attached to this document from the CIA's chief of station Holman states: "This looks generally O.K. A summary of activities which we have since submitted, however, may cause some changes." It is not clear which summary he references, or what those modifications might be.

53. Costanzo to Wieland, December 14, 1955, RG84, Entry #2408-B, Box 18, NARA.

54. Rabe, *Eisenhower and Latin America*; Schmitz, *Thank God They're On Our Side*.

55. Bragonier to King and Sanders, "Communism in Ecuador," August 28, 1956, RG84, Entry #2396, Box 73, NARA.

56. Dustmann to State, "Anti-Communist Activity of Ponce Administration," December 20, 1956, RG59, 722.00/12-2056, NARA.

57. Raúl Clemente Huerta, "El comunismo internacional y Frente Democrático Nacional," *El Comercio*, June 11, 1957, 1.

58. Dustmann to State, "Former Presidential Candidate Denies Communist Ties, Counterattacks President Ponce," June 12, 1957, RG59, 722.001/6-1257, NARA.

59. Dustmann to State, "Anti-Conservative Front May Be Developing in Ecuador," June 14, 1957, RG59, 722.00/6-1457, NARA.

60. Culley to State, "Joint Weeka 25," June 21, 1957, 755, RG59, 722.00(W)/6-2157, NARA.

61. Alexander, *Communism in Latin America*, 242.

Chapter 11

1. Kornbluh, *The Pinochet File*, 410.

2. Agee, *Inside the Company*, 404, 12.

3. Culley to Noland, 1958, RG84, Entry #2396, Box 73, NARA.

4. The Association for Diplomatic Studies and Training Foreign Affairs Oral History Project, "George F. Jones," August 6, 1996, http://www.adst.org/OH%20TOCs/Jones,%20George%20F.pdf.

5. Dustmann to State, "Ecuadoran Communist Reaction to Czech Ousters," October 31, 1957, RG84, Entry #2396, Box 73, NARA.

6. Ravndal to State, "Ecuadoran Government Cooperation on Matters Pertaining to International Communism," June 18, 1958, RG84, Entry #2396, Box 73, NARA.

7. Herter to Quito, "Recent Ecuadoran Government Actions against International Communism," July 11, 1958, RG84, Entry #2396, Box 73, NARA.

8. CIA, "Congress of Communist Party of Ecuador (PCE) in Near Future," April 8, 1954, https://www.cia.gov/library/readingroom/document/cia-rdp80-00810a003900460006-3. No evidence exists that Albornoz was an informer, but he may have inadvertently passed information on to an infiltrator who was.

9. CIA, "The Communist Party Penetration Program," December 1, 1955, https://www.cia.gov/library/readingroom/document/cia-rdp78-00915r000300240005-7.

10. Ravndal to State, "Joint Weeka 5," February 1, 1957, RG59, 722.00(W)/2-157, NARA.

11. CIA, "Weekly Summary," March 7, 1957, https://www.cia.gov/library/readingroom/document/cia-rdp79-00927a001100120001-8.

12. Ibarra, "Los idearios de la izquierda comunista ecuatoriana," 55.

13. "La verdad sobre Stalin y las resoluciones del XX Congreso del PCUS," *El Pueblo*, June 9, 1956.

14. "Acierto y desacierto de Pedro Saad," *La Calle*, April 13, 1957, 20–21.

15. Muñoz Vicuña, *Temas obreros*, 241.

16. CIA, "Weekly Summary," March 7, 1957, https://www.cia.gov/library/readingroom/document/cia-rdp79-00927a001100120001-8.

17. "Los comunistas," *La Calle*, June 1, 1957, 18.

18. "Prodúcense discrepancies entre los delegados al congreso de la FEUE," *El Comercio*, November 30, 1956, 11; "El XIII Congreso Nacional de la FEUE terminó sus labores," *El Comercio*, December 1, 1956, 3; Olmedo Castro Alvarado, "Manifiesto del XIII Congreso Nacional de la FEUE a la opinión pública de la patria," *El Comercio*, December 1, 1956, 1.

19. Karnis to State, "Report on the Split in FEUE at its 13th Annual Congress in Quito," December 4, 1956, RG59, 822.422/12-456, NARA.

20. CIA, "Weekly Summary," March 7, 1957, https://www.cia.gov/library/readingroom/document/cia-rdp79-00927a001100120001-8.

21. Ponce did expel the Czechoslovakian diplomatic mission in September 1957 under allegations that it had meddled in Ecuador's internal affairs. "Ecuador Ousts Czech Mission," *New York Times*, September 28, 1957, 2.

22. CIA, "Weekly Summary," March 7, 1957, https://www.cia.gov/library/readingroom/document/cia-rdp79-00927a001100120001-8.

23. "El Comité Central del Partido Comunista del Ecuador convoca al Sexto Congreso del Partido Comunista del Ecuador," *El Pueblo*, December 22, 1956, 1.

24. "Proyecto de reformas a los estatutos del Partido Comunista del Ecuador aprobado por el Comité Central," *El Pueblo*, December 22, 1956, 6-8. For a discussion of the previous communist party statutes, see Becker, *FBI*, 218–20.

25. Becker, "The *Bogotazo* in Ecuador," 169–72.

26. Agee, *Inside the Company*, 122.

27. Hamlin to State, "Conversation between Conservative Party Director General and Counselor of Embassy," April 9, 1952, RG59, 722.00/4-952, NARA.

28. Dustmann to State, "Ecuadoran Communist Party Holds First Congress in Five Years," May 31, 1957, RG59, 722.001/5-3157, NARA.

29. Dustmann to State, "Analysis of Quito 'Mayor's Apparent Aid to Communists," June 27, 1957, RG59, 722.001/6-2757, NARA.

30. Agee, *Inside the Company*, 198.

31. The following account of Quito's city council decision to let the PCE use the municipal theater is from "Concejo ratifica la concesión hecha por el Alcalde de Teatro Espejo para que se realice el Congreso Comunista," *El Comercio*, May 24, 1957, 1. My thanks to Juan Paz y Miño Cepeda for his gracious assistance in identifying people on the council.

32. Bernbaum to State, "Visit of Mr. Arturo Jauregui, Secretary-General of the Inter-American Confederation of Labor," March 20, 1950, RG59, 822.062/3-2050, NARA; Conklin to State, "Visit of Mr. Arturo Jauregui, Organization Secretary of the Inter-American Confederation of Labor," April 11, 1950, RG59, 822.062/4-1150, NARA.

33. Culley to Noland, 1958, RG84, Entry #2396, Box 73, NARA. Also see Duque Arias, "Corrientes del sindicalismo."

34. PCE, "Entre comunismo y democracia hay un abismo," 1956, BEAEP.

35. Ravndal to State, May 24, 1957, RG59, 722.001/5-2457, NARA.

36. Ravndal to State, May 24, 1957, RG59, 722.001/5-2457, NARA.

37. Ravndal to State, "Joint Weeka 20," May 31, 1957, RG59, 722.00(W)/5-3157, NARA.

38. Dustmann to State, "Ecuadoran Communist Party Holds First Congress in Five Years," May 31, 1957, RG59, 722.001/5-3157, NARA. Baquero appears to be the CIA's source of the content of Andrade Marín's note of congratulations to Saad, which the embassy then confirmed with Salazar Gómez, though it is not clear how or why either would have access to such a written communication, and whether their famously and reactionary anticommunist positions would disqualify them as legitimate sources of information. See Dustmann to State, "Analysis of Quito Mayor's Apparent Aid to Communists," June 27, 1957, RG59, 722.001/6-2757, NARA.

39. "El Sr. Maurice Berbaum, el embajador de E.U. y Tte. General Robert Montagne visitaron ayer al president Ponce E.," *El Comercio*, May 23, 1957, 1.

40. "Capitales privados van a lugares en donde se les da la bienvenida," *El Comercio*, May 25, 1957, 3.

41. "No se ha modificado política contra la infiltración comunista," *El Comercio*, May 17, 1957, 1.

42. Dustmann to State, "Minister of Government's Views on Communism," May 17, 1957, RG59, 722.00/5-1757, NARA.

43. Dustmann to State, "Analysis of Quito Mayor's Apparent Aid to Communists," June 27, 1957, RG59, 722.001/6-2757, NARA.

44. Dustmann to State, "Analysis of Ecuador's Communist Party," November 25, 1957, RG59, 722.001/11-2557, NARA.

45. "Presidente Dr. Ponce saluda al pueblo del Ecuador con motivo de la festividad patria de hoy," *El Comercio*, May 24, 1957, 1.

46. "En congreso comunista se enjuició la acción del Gobierno y de los partidos," *El Comercio*, May 25, 1957, 11.

47. Dustmann to State, "Ecuadoran Communist Party Holds First Congress in Five Years," May 31, 1957, RG59, 722.001/5-3157, NARA.

48. "En congreso comunista se enjuició la acción del Gobierno y de los partidos," *El Comercio*, May 25, 1957, 11.

49. Ravndal to State, "Joint Weeka 20," May 31, 1957, RG59, 722.00(W)/5-3157, NARA.

50. Dustmann to State, "Ecuadoran Communist Party Holds First Congress in Five Years," May 31, 1957, RG59, 722.001/5-3157, NARA.

51. Ravndal to State, May 26, 1957, RG59, 722.001/5-2657, NARA.

52. Ravndal to State, "Joint Weeka 20," May 31, 1957, RG59, 722.00(W)/5-3157, NARA.

53. Ravndal to State, "Joint Weeka 20," May 31, 1957, RG59, 722.00(W)/5-3157, NARA.

54. Dustmann to State, "Ecuadoran Communist Party Holds First Congress in Five Years," May 31, 1957, RG59, 722.001/5-3157, NARA.

55. "En congreso comunista se enjuició la acción del Gobierno y de los partidos," *El Comercio*, May 25, 1957, 11.

56. Ravndal to State, May 26, 1957, RG59, 722.001/5-2657, NARA.

57. Dustmann to State, "Ecuadoran Communist Party Holds First Congress in Five Years," May 31, 1957, RG59, 722.001/5-3157, NARA.

58. Ravndal to State, May 26, 1957, RG59, 722.001/5-2657, NARA. Agee reported that almost ten years later the Quito station recruited Arellano as a penetration agent after collecting "vulnerability data" on him "for a long time." Those efforts may have dated to this congress. Agee, *Inside the Company*, 495. Soon after that, Arellano left the party and became rabidly anticommunist. See Arellano Gallegos, *La subversión en Ecuador*.

59. Ravndal to State, "Joint Weeka 20," May 31, 1957, RG59, 722.00(W)/5-3157, NARA.

60. Ravndal to State, May 26, 1957, RG59, 722.001/5-2657, NARA.

61. Ravndal to State, May 30, 1957, RG59, 722.001/5-3057, NARA. Unfortunately, a follow-up telegram from May 27 has been removed from the National Archives because it contains "security-classified information." Considering a certain degree of randomness that accompanies the withholding of documentation, it would be surprising if this communication contained significantly different assessments of the congress than those that the State Department released, if indeed that is the subject of its contents.

62. Dustmann to State, "Ecuadoran Communist Party Holds First Congress in Five Years," May 31, 1957, RG59, 722.001/5-3157, NARA.

63. Dustmann to State, "Ecuadoran Communist Party Holds First Congress in Five Years," May 31, 1957, RG59, 722.001/5-3157, NARA. The CIA removed this dispatch from RG59 because it contains "security-classified information" but a declassified copy is in RG84 (Entry #2396, Box 73). Apparently, the CIA withdrew the copy from RG59 because of the two passing references to "CAS sources," otherwise the information largely parallels that which is included in other declassified documentation.

64. Dustmann to State, "Ecuadoran Communist Party Holds First Congress in Five Years," May 31, 1957, RG59, 722.001/5-3157, NARA.

65. Dustmann to State, "Ecuadoran Communist Party Holds First Congress in Five Years," May 31, 1957, RG59, 722.001/5-3157, NARA.

66. CIA, "Weekly Summary," June 13, 1957, https://www.cia.gov/library/readingroom/document/cia-rdp79-00927a001300030001-6.

67. "Resolución de la sesión plenaria del Partido Comunista del Ecuador respecto a la situación de la Sra. Nela Martínez de Mériguet," *El Pueblo*, May 4, 1963, 3; Salazar Cortez, "La militancia política femenina en la izquierda marxista ecuatoriana de la década de los sesenta," 94.

68. Martínez Espinosa, *Yo siempre he sido Nela Martínez Espinosa*, 113.

69. Ravndal to State, "Joint Weeka 20," May 31, 1957, RG59, 722.00(W)/5-3157, NARA.

70. Dustmann to State, "Analysis of Ecuador's Communist Party," November 25, 1957, RG59, 722.001/11-2557, NARA.

71. "Mañana se instalará en Riobamba la I asamblea regional del socialismo," *El Comercio*, May 24, 1957, 12; "Hoy se instalará en Riobamba el Congreso Regional Socialista," *El Comercio*, May 25, 1957, 3.

72. Ravndal to State, "Joint Weeka 20," May 31, 1957, RG59, 722.00(W)/5-3157, NARA.

73. "La Primera Conferencia Regional del Partido Socialista Ecuatoriano se inauguró el sábado en Riobamba," *El Comercio*, May 27, 1957, 3; "El Consejo Provincial Socialista del Chimborazo aprobó agenda para la conferencia regional," *El Comercio*, May 27, 1957, 5; "La Conferencia Regional trazó plan de actividades socialistas, dice Dr. Lovato," *El Comercio*, May 28, 1957, 3.

74. Dustmann to State, "Socialist Congress Reaffirms Belligerent Opposition," May 28, 1957, RG59, 722.001/5-2857, NARA.

75. Ravndal to State, "Joint Weeka 20," May 31, 1957, RG59, 722.00(W)/5-3157, NARA.

76. "Democracia, independencia y bienestar para el pueblo del Ecuador (Programa inmediato del Partido Comunista del Ecuador)," *El Pueblo*, December 22, 1956, 3–5.

77. PCE, *Proyecto de programa inmediato del Partido Comunista del Ecuador.*

78. "Conferencia campesina de Pichincha, Imbabura y Cotopaxi," *El Pueblo*, May 6, 1957, 6. For the changed text, see PCE, *Democracia, independencia y paz para el pueblo del Ecuador*, 14. Also see Albornoz Peralta, "Sobre algunos aspectos del problema indígena," 64.

79. PCE, *Democracia, independencia y paz para el pueblo del Ecuador.*

80. Douglass, *Frederick Douglass*, 367.

81. Muñoz Vicuña, *Temas obreros*, 241.

82. Ibarra, "Los idearios de la izquierda comunista ecuatoriana," 55–56. The document "Lineamientos programáticos del Partido Comunista del Ecuador" is included on pp. 275–302.

83. Ibarra, "Acción colectiva rural," 9.

84. Ravndal to Rubottom, March 4, 1958, RG84, Entry #2396, Box 73, NARA.

Conclusion

1. Guevara, *Guerrilla Warfare.*

2. Gott, *Guerrilla Movements in Latin America.*

3. Cushion, *A Hidden History of the Cuban Revolution*; Winn, *Weavers of Revolution.*

4. "Ocurrió levantamiento de indígenas a orillas Lago San Pablo: 3 muertos," *El Comercio*, January 8, 1959, 20; "5 muertos y numerosos heridos cerca de Lago San Pablo," *El Comercio*, January 9, 1959, 22; Huerta, "Ha comenzado la matanza de indios como respuesta a sus reclamaciones"; Ibarra, "Conflictos rurales," 452–59. Also see Kincaid, "The Hotel Casino Project that Put Ecuador's Tourism Hopes on Pause."

5. Pineo, *Ecuador and the United States*, 155–56; Martz, "Ecuador and the Eleventh Inter-American Conference."

6. "Against the Forthcoming Interamerican Conference," 59. Also see Friedman, "Fracas in Caracas."

7. Tad Szulc, "Reds in Ecuador Accused of Plot," *New York Times*, May 15, 1959, 4.

8. "Ocho barbudos revolucionaros cubanos llegaron ayer a Quito," *El Comercio*, February 26, 1959, 1; "Mexico Cool to Cubans," *New York Times*, February 17, 1959, 11. Also see Ravndal to State, "Joint Weeka 9," February 27, 1959, RG59, 722.00(W)/2-2759, NARA.

9. Leatherman to State, "Joint Weeka 25," June 19, 1959, RG59, 722.00(W)/6-1959, NARA.

10. "Plan comunista para desbaratar la XI Conferencia Panamericana denunciase en diario de N. York," *El Comercio*, May 16, 1959, 3.

11. PCE, "El Partido Comunista del Ecuador y la XI Conferencia Interamericana," May 17, 1959, BEAEP.

12. Tad Szulc, "Cuba Is Reported Wooing Ecuador," *New York Times*, December 15, 1960, 20.

13. "Communist Activity in Ecuador," May 20, 1959, RG59, 722.001/5-2059, NARA.

14. "Quito Unrest Spreads," *New York Times*, February 24, 1959, 12; "Quito Students Riot," *New York Times*, February 25, 1959, 15; "Ecuador," *Hispanic American Report*, February 1959, 103.

15. Moreland to State, "Customs House Laborers Strike Loses Steam When Declared Illegal," February 25, 1959, RG59, 822.062/2-2559, NARA.

16. "Los trabajadores de Chaupi han presentado un reclamo," *El Pueblo*, February 7, 1959, 7; "Victoria de los trabajadores de Chaupi-Muyurco," *El Pueblo*, February 21, 1959, 7.

17. Merlo Vasquez, *Informe a la nación, 1958*, 17; Tad Szulc, "Reds in Ecuador Accused of Plot," *The New York Times*, May 15, 1959, 4.

18. Guerrero Arias, *El saber del mundo de los condores*, 53.

19. "Ecuador Conscripts Mutiny," *New York Times*, May 30, 1959, 5.

20. "4 muertos, 38 heridos en disturbios anoche en Guayaquil," *El Comercio*, June 3, 1959, 1; "Turbas incendian y saquean en Guayaquil: 8 muertos," *El Comercio*, June 4, 1959, 1; "16 muertos y numerosos heridos por sucesos de antenoche en Guayaquil," *El*

Comercio, June 5, 1959, 1; "Ecuador Disperses Crowd," *New York Times*, June 3, 1959, 25; "19 Dead in Ecuador as Riots Continue," *New York Times*, June 4, 1959, 1; Tad Szulc, "Ecuador Troops Rule Guayaquil," *New York Times*, June 5, 1959, 3.

21. "Ecuador," *Hispanic American Report*, June 1959, 334; Moreland to State, "Comments on Guayaquil Riots of June 3, 1959," June 8, 1959, RG59, 722.00/6-859, NARA.

22. Leatherman to State, "Joint Weeka 22," May 29, 1959, RG59, 722.00(W)/5-2959, NARA.

23. "Estudiantes de FEUE y de secundaria resolvieron ayer un paro indefinido," *El Comercio*, June 4, 1959, 3; "La CTE y la FTP protestan por sucesos últimos y se adhieren a estudiantes," *El Comercio*, June 4, 1959, 3; Leatherman to State, June 3, 1959, RG59, 722.00/6-359, NARA.

24. "Sala de prensa de presidencia de la república da a conocer un plan de acción comunista," *El Comercio*, June 4, 1959, 17.

25. Rositzke, *The CIA's Secret Operations*, 190–92.

26. Leatherman to State, "Joint Weeka 25," June 19, 1959, RG59, 722.00(W)/6-1959, NARA.

27. "Stores Are Looted," *New York Times*, June 4, 1959, 8; "U. S. Lacks Details of Riots," *New York Times*, June 4, 1959, 8.

28. Perry to State, "Current Emergency Situation in Ecuador," June 4, 1959, RG59, 722.00/6-459, NARA.

29. Moreland to State, "Martial Law Restores Order in Guayaquil," June 8, 1959, RG59, 722.00/6-859, NARA.

30. "Stores Are Looted," *New York Times*, June 4, 1959, 8.

31. PCE, "¡Alto a las provocaciones y el terror gubernamental!" June 7, 1959, BEAEP.

32. Moreland to State, "Communist Students Gain Control of Student Strike Committee," June 17, 1959, RG59, 722.00/6-1759, NARA; Moreland to State, June 10, 1959, RG59, 722.00/6-1059, NARA.

33. Leatherman to State, "Joint Weeka 25," June 19, 1959, RG59, 722.00(W)/6-1959, NARA.

34. Moreland to State, "Communist Students Gain Control of Student Strike Committee," June 17, 1959, RG59, 722.00/6-1759, NARA.

35. Leatherman to State, "Joint Weeka 26," June 26, 1959, RG59, 722.00(W)/6-2659, NARA.

36. Tad Szulc, "Source of Riots Disputed in Quito," *New York Times*, June 7, 1959, 32; "7 personas fueron reducidas a prisión en ciudad de Riobamba," *El Comercio*, June 6, 1959, 22; "Con cinco prisiones efectuadas ayer, presos políticos en Quito llegan a 21," *El Comercio*, June 6, 1959, 22; "El congreso de la FEUE acordó desafilares de UIE, organismo comunista financiado por URSS," *El Comercio*, June 5, 1959, 3; "FEUE no se ha desafilado de UIE; sólo suspendió relaciones," *El Comercio*, June 7, 1959, 1.

37. Tad Szulc, "Danger Signals Flare in Latin America," *New York Times*, June 7, 1959, 171. For a report on the broadcast, see "Dijo anoche Radio Moscú: Comunista acompañaron al pueblo de Guayaquil en ultimas disturbios," *El Telégrafo*, June 5, 1959.

38. "Communists Prey on Latin-American Ills," *New York Times*, June 21, 1959, 132.

39. "Storm Over Latin America," *New York Times*, June 5, 1959, 26.

40. Villamizar Herrera, *Ecuador*, 19.

41. "The World," *New York Times*, June 7, 1959, 169.

42. Tad Szulc, "Ecuador Troops Rule Guayaquil," *New York Times*, June 5, 1959, 3.

43. "Una turba cometió desafueros anoche en las calles de Gquil.," *El Comercio*, October 2, 1959, 1; "2 Killed in Riots in Ecuador," *New York Times*, October 3, 1959, 2; "Ecuador," *Hispanic American Report*, October 1959, 559; Moreland to State, October 2, 1959, RG59, 722.00/10-259, NARA.

44. Moreland to State, "Political Oppositionist Groups and Vandals Exploit Guayaquil's Social Unrest," October 2, 1959, RG59, 722.00/10-259, NARA.

45. Somerford to State, "More Public Disorders in Guayaquil," October 5, 1959, RG59, 722.00/10-559, NARA.

46. "Delegados de campesinos e indígenas del país llegarán hoy para presentar memorándum de aspiraciones a congreso," *El Comercio*, September 25, 1959, 18; "En la cámara de diputados se protestó por haberse impedido la manifestación de indígenas," *El Comercio*, September 26, 1959, 1; "Intendente negó autorización para el desfile de campesinos," *El Comercio*, September 26, 1959, 5; "Varios legisladores, dirigentes sindicales y delegaciones campesinas tuvieron asamblea," *El Comercio*, September 26, 1959, 11; "Manifestación de campesinos no fue permitida por intendente de policía," *El Comercio*, September 26, 1959, 15; "Para los indios ¡nada!" *La Calle*, October 3, 1959, 4–5.

47. Pedro Jorge Vera, "Indios y señoríos," *La Calle*, October 3, 1959, 7.

48. "Mtro de Gobierno será interpelado por congreso pleno, próximo martes," *El Comercio*, October 1, 1959, 1; "Preguntas que deberán ser contestadas por el ministro de gobierno, el martes," *El Comercio*, October 1, 1959, 1; "Presenta dos preguntas más para que las conteste el ministro de gobierno," *El Comercio*, October 2, 1959, 1; "Diputado presenta otras preguntas para que las conteste el ministro de gobierno," *El Comercio*, October 2, 1959, 1.

49. Summ to State, "1959 Congressional Session Turned Out Better Than Expected," November 19, 1959, RG59, 722.00/11-1959, NARA.

50. Linke, "Ecuador's Politics."

51. Pedro Saad, "El Partido Comunista propone unidad anticonservadora a la Asamblea Liberal," 1957, BEAEP.

52. Saúl Mora and Ignacio Andra de Arízaga, "Debate sobre la unidad democrática," *La Calle*, June 8, 1957, 13.

53. Martz, "The Regionalist Expression of Populism," 309.

54. Bonilla, *En busca del pueblo perdido*, 34, 72. In the 1930s the left had already been divided into communist, socialist, and vanguardist wings representing different histories and traditions.

55. Dustmann to State, "Analysis of Ponce Administration After First Year," August 26, 1957, RG59, 722.00/8-2657, NARA.

56. Salazar Cortez, "La militancia política femenina en la izquierda marxista ecuatoriana de la década de los sesenta," 98.

57. Bonilla, *En busca del pueblo perdido*; Villamizar Herrera, *Ecuador*.

58. Salazar Cortez, "La militancia política femenina en la izquierda marxista ecuatoriana de la década de los sesenta."

59. CIA, "Central Intelligence Bulletin," October 7, 1959, https://www.cia.gov/library/readingroom/document/cia-rdp79t00975a004700320001-4.

60. CIA, "Central Intelligence Bulletin," December 5, 1959, https://www.cia.gov/library/readingroom/document/cia-rdp79t00975a004800300001-5; CIA, "Communist Plans to Disrupt OAS Conference," December 7, 1959, https://www.cia.gov/library/readingroom/document/cia-rdp78-03061a000100010008-3.

61. CIA, "The Sino-Soviet Struggle in Cuba and the Latin American Communist Movement" November 1, 1963, https://www.cia.gov/library/readingroom/document/5077054e993247d4d82b6a80.

62. CIA, "The Sino-Soviet Dispute within the Communist Movement in Latin America," June 15, 1967, https://www.cia.gov/library/readingroom/document/5077054e993247d4d82b6a9b.

63. Ameringer, *U.S. Foreign Intelligence*, 83.

BIBLIOGRAPHY

Archives

Archivo Palacio Legislativo (APL), Quito
Biblioteca Ecuatoriana Aurelio Espinosa Pólit (BEAEP), Cotocollao
Central Intelligence Agency (CIA) Freedom of Information Act Electronic Reading Room, https://www.cia.gov/library/readingroom
The National Archives (TNA), London
National Archives Records Administration (NARA), College Park, MD
Private collection of Leonardo J. Muñoz, Quito

Periodicals

British Documents on Foreign Affairs: Reports and Papers from the Foreign Office Confidential Print (Bethesda, MD: University Publications of America).

Foreign Relations of the United States (FRUS) (Washington, DC: US Government Printing Office).

OSS/State Department Intelligence and Research Reports, Part XIV, Latin America, 1941–1961 (Washington, DC: University Publications of America, 1979).

United States Department of State, *Biographic Register* (Washington, DC: US Government Printing Office).

United States Department of State, *Foreign Service List* (Washington, DC: US Government Printing Office).

Newspapers

La Calle (Quito)
El Comercio (Quito)
El Día (Quito)
Hispanic American Report (Stanford, CA)
Hispanic World Report (Stanford, CA)

El Pueblo (Quito; Guayaquil)
New York Times
El Sol (Quito)
Surcos (Quito)
El Telégrafo (Guayaquil)
La Tierra (Quito)
El Universo (Guayaquil)

Books and Articles

"Against the Forthcoming Interamerican Conference." *World Marxist Review* 2 (March 1959): 59.

"Death in the Andes." *Time*. August 15, 1949, 27.

"Disaster in the Andes." *Newsweek*. August 15, 1949, 40.

"Revolt that wasn't." *Newsweek*. August 8, 1949, 32.

"Shetterly." *Albuquerque Journal*. October 30, 2004, http://obits.abqjournal.com/obits/show/148474.

Agee, Philip. *Inside the Company: CIA Diary*. New York: Bantam Books, 1975.

———. *On the Run*. Secaucus, NJ: L. Stuart, 1987.

Agee, Philip, Jaime Galarza Zavala, and Francisco Herrera Arauz. *The CIA Case against Latin America*. Quito: Ministry of Foreign Affairs and Human Mobility, 2014.

Aguirre, Manuel Agustín. *Economía de laisser faire, liberal, capitalista vs. economía planificada socialista*. Quito: Imprenta de la Universidad Central, 1949.

Albornoz Peralta, Oswaldo. *Las luchas indígenas en el Ecuador*. Guayaquil: Editorial Claridad S.A., 1971.

———. "Sobre algunos aspectos del problema indígena." *Cuadernos de la Realidad Ecuatoriana*, no. 1 (October 1984): 45–77.

Alexander, Robert. *Communism in Latin America*. New Brunswick, NJ: Rutgers University Press, 1957.

Almeida Cabrera, Laura. *Antología*. Quito: Ediciones La Tierra, 2007.

Ameringer, Charles. *U.S. Foreign Intelligence: The Secret Side of American History*. Lexington, MA: Lexington Books, 1990.

Arcos Bastidas, Diego Rubén. "Revista Política La Calle: prácticas intelectuales y opinión pública en Quito (1957–1960)." Master's thesis. Universidad Andina Simón Bolívar Sede Ecuador, 2018.

Arellano Gallegos, Jorge. *La subversión en Ecuador*. Quito: Editor Luz de América, 2003.

Ayala Mora, Enrique. "Ecuador since 1930." In *The Cambridge History of Latin America, vol. VIII–Latin America since 1930: Spanish South America*, edited by Leslie Bethell, 687–725. Cambridge: Cambridge University Press, 1991.

———. *Historia de la Revolución Liberal Ecuatoriana*. Quito: Corporación Editora Nacional, 1994.

Barnard, Andrew. "Chilean Communists, Radical Presidents and Chilean Relations with the United States, 1940–1947." *Journal of Latin American Studies* 13, no. 2 (November 1981): 347–74.

Batvinis, Raymond J. *Hoover's Secret War against Axis Spies*. Lawrence: University Press of Kansas, 2014.

Becker, Marc. "The *Bogotazo* in Ecuador." *The Latin Americanist* 62, no. 2 (June 2018): 160–85.

———. "The CIA on Latin America," *Journal of Intelligence History* (forthcoming).

———. "Ecuador's Early No–Foreign Military Bases Movement." *Diplomatic History* 41, no. 3 (June 2017): 518–42.

———. *The FBI in Latin America: The Ecuador Files*. Durham, NC: Duke University Press, 2017.

———. "General Alberto Enríquez Gallo: Soldier, Populist, Leftist." *Journal of Latin American Studies* 50, no. 3 (May 2018): 323–53.

———. *Indians and Leftists in the Making of Ecuador's Modern Indigenous Movements*. Durham, NC: Duke University Press, 2008.

Bethell, Leslie, and Ian Roxborough. *Latin America between the Second World War and the Cold War, 1944–1948*. Cambridge: Cambridge University Press, 1992.

Bissell, Richard. *Reflections of a Cold Warrior: From Yalta to the Bay of Pigs*. New Haven: Yale University Press, 1996.

Blanksten, George. *Ecuador: Constitutions and Caudillos*. Berkeley: University of California Press, 1951.

Blasier, Cole. *The Giant's Rival: The USSR and Latin America*. Revised ed. Pittsburgh: University of Pittsburgh Press, 1987.

Blum, William. *Killing Hope: U.S. Military and CIA Interventions since World War II*. 2nd ed. Monroe, ME: Common Courage Press, 2004.

Bonilla, Adrián. *En busca del pueblo perdido: diferenciación y discurso de la izquierda marxista en los sesenta*. Quito: FLACSO-Editorial Abya-Yala, 1991.

Brands, Hal. *Latin America's Cold War*. Cambridge: Harvard University Press, 2010.

Cabrera Hanna, Santiago, ed. *La Gloriosa ¿revolución que no fue?* Quito: Universidad Andina Simón Bolívar, 2016.

Carr, Barry. "Escribiendo la historia de los comunismos en las américas: retos y nuevas oportunidades." In *El comunismo en América Latina. Experiencias militantes, intelectuales y transnacionales (1917–1955)*, edited by Patricio Herrera González, 13–32. Chile: Universidad de Valparaíso, 2017.

Cline, Ray S. *The CIA under Reagan, Bush & Casey: The Evolution of the Agency from Roosevelt to Reagan*. Washington, DC: Acropolis Books, 1981.

Colby, William Egan. *Honorable Men: My Life in the CIA*. New York: Simon and Schuster, 1978.

Coronel, Valeria. "The Ecuadorian Left during Global Crisis: Republican Democracy, Class Struggle and State Formation (1919–1946)." In *Words of Power, the Power of Words. The Twentieth-Century Communist Discourse in International Perspective*, edited by Giulia Bassi, 315–37. Trieste, Italy: EUT Edizioni Università di Trieste, 2019.

Coronel Valencia, Valeria, and Mireya Salgado Gómez. *Galo Plaza Lasso: Un liberal del siglo XX, democracia, desarrollo y cambio cultural en el Ecuador*. Quito: Museo de la Ciudad, 2006.

Cueva, Agustín. *The Process of Political Domination in Ecuador*. New Brunswick, NJ: Transaction Books, 1982.

Cullather, Nick. *Secret History: The C.I.A.'s Classified Account of Its Operations in Guatemala, 1952–1954*. Stanford: Stanford University Press, 1999.

Cushion, Steve. *A Hidden History of the Cuban Revolution: How the Working Class Shaped the Guerrilla Victory*. New York: Monthly Review Press, 2016.

Daniels, Walter, ed. *Latin America in the Cold War*. New York: Wilson, 1952.

Darling, Arthur. *The Central Intelligence Agency: An Instrument of Government, to 1950*. University Park: Pennsylvania State University Press, 1990.

de la Torre, Carlos, and Mireya Salgado, eds. *Galo Plaza y su época*. Quito: FLACSO, 2008.

Donner, Frank. *The Age of Surveillance: The Aims and Methods of America's Political Intelligence System*. New York: Vintage Books, 1981.

Douglass, Frederick. *Frederick Douglass: Selected Speeches and Writings*. Chicago: Lawrence Hill Books, 1999.

Dulles, Allen. *The Craft of Intelligence*. New York: Harper & Row, 1963.

Duncan, Brad. *Finally Got the News: The Printed Legacy of the US Radical Left, 1970–1979*. Brooklyn, NY: Common Notions, 2017.

———. "The 1970s: Finally Got the News!" *Against the Current* 33, no. 1 (March/April 2018): 27–29.

Duque Arias, Pablo. "Corrientes del sindicalismo." *Trabajadores* 2, no. 1 (January 1951): 8.

Eveland, Wilbur. *Ropes of Sand: America's Failure in the Middle East*. New York: W. W. Norton, 1980.

Federal Bureau of Investigation (FBI). *History of the Special Intelligence Service Division*. Washington, DC: Federal Bureau of Investigation, 1947.

Fisher, Roger, and William Ury. *Getting to Yes: Negotiating Agreement without Giving In*. Boston: Houghton Mifflin, 1981.

Friedman, Max Paul. "Fracas in Caracas: Latin American Diplomatic Resistance to United States Intervention in Guatemala in 1954." *Diplomacy & Statecraft* 21, no. 4 (December 2010): 669–89.

———. *Nazis and Good Neighbors: The United States Campaign against the Germans of Latin America in World War II*. Cambridge: Cambridge University Press, 2003.

Gaddis, John Lewis. *The Cold War: A New History*. New York: Penguin Press, 2005.

Galarza Zavala, Jaime. *Los campesinos de Loja y Zamora*. Quito: Universidad Central del Ecuador, 1973.

———. *El festín del petróleo*. Quito: Ediciones Solitierra, 1972.

———. *Piratas en el golfo*. Quito: Ediciones Solitierra, 1973.

———. *El yugo feudal: visión del campo ecuatoriano*. Quito: Editorial Espejo, 1962.

Gardner, Mary. *The Inter American Press Association: Its Fight for Freedom of the Press, 1926–1960*. Austin: University of Texas Press, 1967.

Garrard-Burnett, Virginia, Mark Atwood Lawrence, and Julio Moreno, eds. *Beyond the Eagle's Shadow: New Histories of Latin America's Cold War*. Albuquerque: University of New Mexico Press, 2013.

———. "Introduction." In *Beyond the Eagle's Shadow: New Histories of Latin America's Cold War*, edited by Virginia Garrard-Burnett, Mark Atwood Lawrence, and Julio Moreno, 1–20. Albuquerque: University of New Mexico Press, 2013.

Gil Gilbert, Enrique. *Nuestro pan*. Guayaquil: Librería Vera, 1942.

———. *Our Daily Bread*. New York: Farrar & Rinehart, 1943.

Gleijeses, Piero. *Conflicting Missions: Havana, Washington, and Africa, 1959–1976*. Chapel Hill: University of North Carolina Press, 2002.

———. *Shattered Hope: The Guatemalan Revolution and the United States, 1944–1954*. Princeton: Princeton University Press, 1991.

Gosling, John. *Waging The War of the Worlds: A History of the 1938 Radio Broadcast and Resulting Panic, Including the Original Script*. Jefferson, NC: McFarland & Co., 2009.

Gott, Richard. *Guerrilla Movements in Latin America*. Garden City, NY: Doubleday, 1971.

Grandin, Greg. *Empire's Workshop: Latin America and the Roots of U.S. Imperialism*. New York: Metropolitan Books, 2006.

———. *The Last Colonial Massacre: Latin America in the Cold War*. Chicago: University of Chicago Press, 2004.

———. "Living in Revolutionary Time: Coming to Terms with the Violence of Latin America's Long Cold War." In *A Century of Revolution: Insurgent and Counterinsurgent Violence during Latin America's Long Cold War*, edited by Greg Grandin and Gilbert Joseph, 1–42. Durham, NC: Duke University Press, 2010.

Grandin, Greg, and Gilbert Joseph, eds. *A Century of Revolution: Insurgent and Counterinsurgent Violence during Latin America's Long Cold War*. Durham, NC: Duke University Press, 2010.

Guerrero Arias, Patricio. *El saber del mundo de los condores: Identidad e insurgencia de la cultura andina*. Quito: Ediciones Abya–Yala, 1993.

Guevara, Ernesto. *Guerrilla Warfare*. New York: Monthly Review Press, 1961.

Henderson, Peter. *Gabriel García Moreno and Conservative State Formation in the Andes*. Austin: University of Texas Press, 2008.

Huerta, Francisco. "Ha comenzado la matanza de indios como respuesta a sus reclamaciones." *Vistazo*, January 1959, 62–64.

Huggins, Martha Knisely. *Political Policing: The United States and Latin America*. Durham, NC: Duke University Press, 1998.

Huneeus, Carlos. *La guerra fría chilena: Gabriel González Videla y la Ley maldita*. Santiago: Debate, 2009.

Ibarra, Hernán. "Acción colectiva rural, reforma agraria y política en El Ecuador, ca. 1920–1965." PhD dissertation. Universidad Complutense de Madrid, 2016.

———. "Conflictos rurales, violencia y opinión pública en los años cincuenta." In *Transiciones y rupturas. El Ecuador en la segunda mitad del siglo XX*, edited by Felipe Burbano de Lara, 411–64. Quito: Flacso, 2010.

———. "Entre la oposición y la colaboración: El Partido Socialista Ecuatoriano durante el gobierno de Galo Plaza (1948–1952)." *Ecuador Debate* 67 (April 2006): 37–60.

———. "Los idearios de la izquierda comunista ecuatoriana (1928–1961)." In *El pensamiento de la izquierda comunista (1928–1961)*, edited by Hernán Ibarra, 11–64. Quito: Ministerio de Coordinación de la Política y Gobiernos Autónomos Descentralizados, 2013.

———, ed. *El pensamiento de la izquierda comunista (1928–1961)*. Quito: Ministerio de Coordinación de la Política y Gobiernos Autónomos Descentralizados, 2013.

———. "¿Qué fue la revolución de 1944?" In *La Gloriosa ¿revolución que no fue?*, edited by Santiago Cabrera Hanna, 191–204. Quito: Universidad Andina Simón Bolívar; Corporación Editora Nacional, 2016.

Jeffreys-Jones, Rhodri. *The CIA and American Democracy*. 3rd ed. New Haven: Yale University Press, 2003.

Johnson, Chalmers. *The Sorrows of Empire: Militarism, Secrecy, and the End of the Republic*. New York: Metropolitan Books, 2004.

Joseph, Gilbert, and Daniela Spenser, eds. *In From the Cold: Latin America's New Encounter with the Cold War*. Durham, NC: Duke University Press, 2008.

Keller, Renata. *Mexico's Cold War: Cuba, the United States, and the Legacy of the Mexican Revolution*. New York: Cambridge University Press, 2015.

Kincaid, Kenneth R. "The Hotel Casino Project that Put Ecuador's Tourism Hopes on Pause." In *The Business of Leisure: Tourism History in Latin America and the Caribbean*, edited by Andrew Grant Wood. Lincoln: University of Nebraska Press, forthcoming.

Kinzer, Stephen. *The Brothers: John Foster Dulles, Allen Dulles, and Their Secret World War*. New York: Time Books/Henry Holt, 2013.

Kirkpatrick, Evron Maurice. *Target: The World; Communist Propaganda Activities in 1955*. New York: Macmillan, 1956.

Kofas, Jon. "The IMF, the World Bank, and U.S. Foreign Policy in Ecuador, 1956–1966." *Latin American Perspectives* 28, no. 5 (September 2001): 50–83.

———. "Politics of Conflict and Containment: Ecuador's Labor Movement and U.S. Foreign Policy, 1944–1963." *Journal of Third World Studies* 13, no. 2 (Fall 1996): 61–118.

Kornbluh, Peter. *The Pinochet File: A Declassified Dossier on Atrocity and Accountability*. Updated edition. New York: The New Press, 2013.

Kuhns, Woodrow. "The Office of Reports and Estimates: CIA's First Center for Analysis." *Studies in Intelligence* 51, no. 2 (2007): 27–46.

Latner, Teishan. "'Agrarians or Anarchists?' The Venceremos Brigades to Cuba, State Surveillance, and the FBI as Biographer and Archivist." *Journal of Transnational American Studies* 9, no. 1 (2018): 119–40.

———. *Cuban Revolution in America: Havana and the Making of a United States Left, 1968–1992*. Chapel Hill: University of North Carolina Press, 2017.

Leffler, Melvyn. *For the Soul of Mankind: The United States, the Soviet Union, and the Cold War*. New York: Hill and Wang, 2007.

Lenin, Vladimir Il'ich. *State and Revolution*. Chicago: Haymarket Books, 2014.

Linke, Lilo. *Ecuador: Country of Contrasts*. 2nd ed. London: Oxford University Press, 1955.

———. "Ecuador's Politics: President Velasco's Fourth Exit." *The World Today* 18, no. 2 (February 1962): 57–69.

———. "The Political Scene in Ecuador: President Velasco Ibarra Takes Over." *The World Today* 9, no. 3 (March 1953): 130–38.

Luna Yepes, Jorge. *Explicación del ideario de ARNE*. Quito: Gráficas Sánchez, 1949.

Maier, Georg. *The Ecuadorian Presidential Election of June 2, 1968: An Analysis*. Washington, DC: Institute for the Comparative Study of Political Systems, 1969.

Maiguashca, Juan, and Liisa North. "Orígenes y significado del velasquismo: Lucha de clases y participación política en el Ecuador, 1920–1972." In *La cuestión regional y el poder*, edited by Rafael Quintero, 89–159. Quito: Corporación Editora Nacional, 1991.

Marchetti, Victor, and John Marks. *The CIA and the Cult of Intelligence*. New York: Dell, 1974.

Marks, John D. "How to Spot a Spook." *Washington Monthly* (November 1974): 5–11.

Martínez Espinosa, Nela. *Yo siempre he sido Nela Martínez Espinosa: Una autobiografía hablada*. Quito: CONAMU–UNIFEM, 2006.

Martz, John. *Ecuador: Conflicting Political Culture and the Quest for Progress*. Boston: Allyn and Bacon, 1972.

———. "The Regionalist Expression of Populism: Guayaquil and the CFP, 1948–60." *Journal of Interamerican and World Affairs* 22, no. 3 (August 1980): 289–314.

Martz, Mary Jeanne Reid. "Ecuador and the Eleventh Inter-American Conference." *Journal of Inter-American Studies and World Affairs* 10, no. 2 (April 1968): 306–27.

Marx, Karl. *Karl Marx: A Reader*. Cambridge: Press Syndicate of the University of Cambridge, 1986.

McGarvey, Patrick. *CIA: The Myth and the Madness*. New York: Saturday Review Press, 1972.

McGehee, Ralph. *Deadly Deceits: My 25 Years in the CIA*. New York: Sheridan Square Publications, 1983.

McPherson, Alan. "Afterword: The Paradox of Latin American Cold War Studies." In *Beyond the Eagle's Shadow: New Histories of Latin America's Cold War*, edited by Virginia Garrard-Burnett, Mark Atwood Lawrence, and Julio Moreno, 307–20. Albuquerque: University of New Mexico Press, 2013.

———. *The Invaded: How Latin Americans and Their Allies Fought and Ended U.S. Occupations*. Oxford: Oxford University Press, 2014.

———. *A Short History of U.S. Interventions in Latin America and the Caribbean*. Chichester: Wiley Blackwell, 2016.

Medina Castro, Manuel. *El Guayas, río navegable; esposición*. Guayaquil: Imp. de la Universidad, 1951.

Merlo Vasquez, Jorge. *Informe a la nación, 1958*. Quito: Talleres Gráficos Nacionales, 1958.

Merrill, Dennis, ed. *Documentary History of the Truman Presidency*. Bethesda, MD: University Publications of America, 1995.

Milk, Richard. *Movimiento obrero ecuatoriano el desafío de la integración*. Quito: Ediciones Abya-Yala, 1997.

Muñoz Vicuña, Elías. *Temas obreros*. Guayaquil: Departamento de Publicaciones de la Facultad de Ciencias Económicas de la Universidad de Guayaquil, 1986.

Norris, Robert. *El gran ausente: Biografía de Velasco Ibarra*. Quito: Ediciones Libri Mundi, 2005.

Páez Cordero, Alexei. *Los orígenes de la izquierda ecuatoriana*. Quito: Ediciones Abya–Yala, 2001.

Páez, Leonardo. *Los que siembran el viento*. Caracas: Editorial Arte, 1982.

Paredes, Ricardo. *El imperialismo en el Ecuador: Oro y sangre en Portovelo*. Quito: Editorial Artes gráficas, 1938.

Paredes Ruiz, Lenín Eduardo. *Ricardo Paredes y la antorcha revolucionaria: Ensayo Biográfico sobre el fundador del Partido Comunista del Ecuador*. Quito: Casa de La Cultura del Ecuador, 2014.

Partido Comunista del Ecuador (PCE). *Democracia, independencia y paz para el pueblo del Ecuador: Lineamientos programáticos del Partido Comunista del Ecuador. Aprobados por su VI Congreso*. Quito: Editorial El Pueblo, 1957.

———. *Por la paz, por la democracia y el progreso*. Quito: Partido Comunista del Ecuador, 1949.

———. *Proyecto de programa inmediato del Partido Comunista del Ecuador*. Quito: Ediciones El Pueblo, 1956.

Pavilack, Jody. *Mining for the Nation: The Politics of Chile's Coal Communities from the Popular Front to the Cold War*. University Park: Pennsylvania State University Press, 2011.

Paz y Miño Cepeda, Juan. *Ecuador: los gobiernos julianos 1925–1931: la constitución de la izquierda política*. Quito: Pontificia Universidad Católica del Ecuador, 2018.

Phillips, David Atlee. *The Night Watch*. New York: Atheneum, 1977.

Pineo, Ronn. *Ecuador and the United States: Useful Strangers*. Athens: University of Georgia Press, 2007.

Ponce Enríquez, Camilo. *Informe a la nación, 1954*. Quito: Talleres Gráficos Nacionales, 1954.

Poppino, Rollie. *International Communism in Latin America: A History of the Movement, 1917–1963*. London: The Free Press of Glencoe, 1964.

Prados, John. *The Family Jewels: The CIA, Secrecy, and Presidential Power*. Austin: University of Texas Press, 2014.

———. *The Ghosts of Langley: Into the CIA's Heart of Darkness*. New York: The New Press, 2017.

Price, David H. *Anthropological Intelligence: The Deployment and Neglect of American Anthropology in the Second World War.* Durham, NC: Duke University Press, 2008.

———. *Cold War Anthropology: The CIA, the Pentagon, and the Growth of Dual Use Anthropology.* Durham, NC: Duke University Press, 2016.

———. *Threatening Anthropology: McCarthyism and the FBI's Surveillance of Activist Anthropologists.* Durham, NC: Duke University Press, 2004.

———. "Uninvited Guests: A Short History of the CIA on Campus." In *The CIA on Campus: Essays on Academic Freedom and the National Security State*, edited by Philip Zwerling, 33–60. Jefferson, NC: McFarland & Company, 2011.

Quintero, Rafael. *El mito del populismo en el Ecuador: análisis de los fundamentos del estado Ecuatoriano moderno (1895–1934).* Quito: FLACSO, 1980.

Rabe, Stephen G. *Eisenhower and Latin America: The Foreign Policy of Anticommunism.* Chapel Hill: University of North Carolina Press, 1988.

Ramón, Galo, ed. *Actores de una década ganada: tribus, comunidades y campesinos en la modernidad.* Quito: COMUNIDEC, 1992.

Roberts, Geoff. "Averting Armageddon: The Communist Peace Movement, 1948–1956." In *The Oxford Handbook of the History of Communism*, edited by S. A. Smith, 322–38. Oxford: Oxford University Press, 2014.

Roberts, Lois. *The Lebanese immigrants in Ecuador: A History of Emerging Leadership.* Boulder, CO: Westview Press, 2000.

Rodas Chávez, Germán. *Partido Socialista: Casa adentro, Aproximación a sus dos primeras décadas.* Quito: Ediciones La Tierra, 2006.

Rodas, Raquel. *Crónica de un sueño: las escuelas indígenas de Dolores Cacuango: una experiencia de educación bilingüe en Cayambe.* 2d ed. Quito: Proyecto de Educación Bilingüe Intercultural, MEC–GTZ, 1998.

———. *Dolores Cacuango: Gran líder del pueblo indio.* Quito: Banco Central del Ecuador, 2006.

———, ed. *Maestras que dejaron huellas: Aproximaciones biográficas.* Quito: Grupo de Educadoras María Angélica, 2000.

———. *Nosotras que del amor hicimos . . .* Quito: Raquel Rodas, 1992.

Rositzke, Harry. *The CIA's Secret Operations: Espionage, Counterespionage, and Covert Action.* New York: Reader's Digest Press, 1977.

Rothwell, Matthew. *Transpacific Revolutionaries: The Chinese Revolution in Latin America.* New York: Routledge, 2012.

Saad, Pedro. *Obras escogidas.* Guayaquil: Editorial Claridad, 1977.

Salazar Cortez, Tatiana. "La militancia política femenina en la izquierda marxista ecuatoriana de la década de los sesenta: La URME y el PCE." *Procesos: revista ecuatoriana de historia*, no. 46 (July–December 2017): 91–118.

Salgado Muñoz, Alfonso. "'El tribunal está abierto para críticas y para autocríticas'. Luchas de poder y radicalización del Partido Comunista de Chile, 1945–1946." *Revista Historia* 51, no. 1 (2018): 165–200.

Salisbury, Harrison E. *Without Fear or Favor: The New York Times and Its Times*. New York: Times Books, 1980.

Schlesinger, Stephen, and Stephen Kinzer. *Bitter Fruit: The Untold Story of the American Coup in Guatemala*. Garden City, NY: Doubleday, 1982.

Schmitz, David F. *Thank God They're On Our Side: The United States and Right-Wing Dictatorships, 1921–1965*. Chapel Hill: University of North Carolina Press, 1999.

Sosa, Ximena. *Hombres y mujeres velasquistas 1934–1972*. Quito: FLACSO/Editorial Abya Yala, 2020.

———. "Populism in Ecuador: From José M. Velasco Ibarra to Rafael Correa." In *Populism in Latin America*, edited by Michael L Conniff, 159–83. Tuscaloosa: University Alabama Press, 2012.

Stockwell, John. *In Search of Enemies: A CIA Story*. New York: W. W. Norton, 1978.

Striffler, Steve. *In the Shadows of State and Capital: The United Fruit Company, Popular Struggle, and Agrarian Restructuring in Ecuador, 1900–1995*. Durham, NC: Duke University Press, 2002.

Studer, Brigitte. *The Transnational World of the Cominternians*. Houndmills, Basingstoke, Hampshire: Palgrave Macmillan, 2015.

Troy, Thomas. *Donovan and the CIA: A History of the Establishment of the Central Intelligence Agency*. Frederick, MD: Aletheia Books, 1981.

United States Department of State. *Emergence of the Intelligence Establishment*. Washington, DC: US Government Printing Office, 1996.

———. *The Intelligence Community 1950–1955*. Washington, DC: US Government Printing Office, 2007.

Villamizar Herrera, Darío. *Ecuador: 1960–1990, Insurgencia, democracia y dictadura*. 2nd ed. Quito: Editorial El Conejo, 1994.

Warner, Michael, ed. *The CIA under Harry Truman*. Washington, DC: Center for the Study of Intelligence.

Weiner, Tim. *Legacy of Ashes: The History of the CIA*. New York: Doubleday, 2007.

Westad, Odd Arne. *The Cold War: A World History*. New York: Basic Books, 2017.

———. *The Global Cold War: Third World Interventions and the Making of Our Times*. Cambridge: Cambridge University Press, 2005.

Williams, Albert Rhys. *Through the Russian Revolution*. Westport, CT: Hyperion Press, 1978.

Winks, Robin W. *Cloak & Gown: Scholars in the Secret War*, 1939–1961. 2nd ed. New Haven: Yale University Press, 1996.

Winn, Peter. *Weavers of Revolution: The Yarur Workers and Chile's Road to Socialism*. New York: Oxford University Press, 1986.

Ycaza, Patricio. *Historia del movimiento obrero ecuatoriano: De la influencia de la táctica del frente popular a las luchas del FUT*. Quito: Centro de Documentación e Información Sociales del Ecuador, 1991.

INDEX

Italicized page numbers refer to illustrations.

Acebedo, Hernán, 135, 152
Adams, Clifford, 63
ADN (Alianza Democrática Nacional, National Democratic Alliance), 115, 117–18, 120, 122, 125
AFE (Alianza Femenina Ecuatoriana, Ecuadorian Women's Alliance), 16, 100. *See also* women
AFL (American Federation of Labor), 78
Agee, Philip: CIA campaigns against PCE, 138, 156, 278n45, 288n58; CIA disinformation campaigns, 240; CIA informants, 214, 278n45, 288n58; CIA mail interception, 176; CIA organization in Ecuador, 31–32, 34, 186–87, 208
agrarian reform, 12–13, 23, 88, 232, 245, 252n9
Aguirre, Manuel Agustín, 3, 125, 147, 248
Alarcón Falconí, Ruperto, 23, 115–16, 120–23, 155
Albornoz Peralta, Oswaldo, 135, 152, 173–74, 209–10
Alcarás, Eduardo, 49–50
Alcívar Zevallos, Clodoveo, 115
Alexander, Robert, 11, 19–20, 54–55, 205–6
Alfaro, César, 43, 45
Alfaro, Eloy, 13, 201–2, 254n7
All American Cable Company, 178
Allende, Salvador, 234
Alvarez Fiallo, Efraín, 145–46
Amaguaña, Tránsito, 140, 221
Amazon colonization, 166, 171
Ambato, 130–32, 134
Ambursen Engineering Company, 111
American Philosophical Society, 253n19
Ameringer, Charles, 250
anarchists, 9
Andrade, Bernardino, 76
Andrade Marín, Carlos, 214–16, 219–20
Antorcha (PCE), 85
Arbenz government, 3, 30, 49, 192, 236–37
Arcentales, Luis, 169
Arechandieta Ortega, Francisco, 36–37
Arellano Gallegos, Jorge, 56, 162, 222
Arenas Coello, Manuel, 150
Arias, Juan, 153
Army Counter Intelligence Corps (CIC), 137
ARNE (Acción Revolucionaria Nacionalista Ecuatoriana, Ecuadorian Nationalist Revolutionary Action): and 1952 elections, 121–22; on FDN, 199–200; formation of, 14–15; and Guevara Moreno, 43; and PCE, 64, 137–38, 154; and Spanish and Italian fascist movements, 14, 215; and Velasco Ibarra, 15, 123, 156–57
Arosemena Monroy, Carlos Julio, 23, 126, 247
Arroyo Delgado, Enrique, 218
Arroyo del Río, Carlos Alberto, 21, 47
Asia and Pacific Rim Peace Conference (Beijing, 1952), 149

Astudillo, Dario, 144
Ayala Mora, Enrique, 19–20, 23

Bacon, John, 31
Baquero de la Calle, José Antonio, 131, 214–20, 287n38
Barba, Pedro, 150
Barreto, Primitivo, 72, 78, 132, 143, 150–52, 157, 181, 225
Barrezueta, Enrique, 79
Barrios, Jaime, 136, 140–41, 147, 149, 151
Bartel, Doris, 253n19
Bartonova de Echeverría, Ana, 65
Bastian, Walter, 178–79, 187, 192
Batista, Fulgencio, 119, 233
Batvinis, Raymond, 28–29
Beaulac, Willard, 72–73
Becerra, Gustavo, 40, 76, 151
Beria, Lavrentiy Pavlovich, 163
Bernbaum, Maurice, 30, 44, 47–48, 82, 218
Blasier, Cole, 55
Block, Tim, 253n19
Blum, William, 253n17
Boggs, Adelbert, 17, 70, 130
Bogotazo, 50–51, 167
Bolaños, A. D., 178
Bolivian revolution (1952), 119, 125
Borja, Rodrigo, 238
Bracker, Milton, 104
Bragonier, Reginald, 58, 203–4
Brewer, Sam Pope, 121, 124, 255n18
British Embassy, 105, 115, 117, 120–23, 126, 146, 180–82
Browderism, 81, 86
Bucheli, José, 165
Bustamante Pérez, Carlos, 245–46

Cabeza de Vaca, Alberto, 118
Cacuango, Dolores, 140, 151–52
Calderón, Rubén (Calderio), 136–37, 147, 149–52
Calderón Moreno, Alfonso, 142, 232
Calle, La (Quito), 147; and 6th PCE congress (1957), 211; PCE and destalinization, 210
Cañarte, Guillermo, 152, 164
Cañarte, Simón, 166
Cárdenas, Mario, 187
Carr, Barry, 8–9
Carrasco Miño, José Arcadio, 131
Carrera, Édison, 248
Carrión, Benjamín, 106, 175
Carvajal, Mariana, 98–103
Carvajal Ruiz, Luis, 99–101
Carvell, John, 90, 104
CAS (controlled American source), 32, 37, 84. *See also* CIA (Central Intelligence Agency)
Casa de la Cultura (House of Culture): organization and political importance, 12, 17; and PCE, 59–61, 72–73, 106, 144, 175, 204, 226; USIS infiltration of, 204
Castro, Fidel, 3, 53, 233–34, 244, 247
Catholic Church: Catholic attacks on Evangelicals, 170; and CIA, 214; Concordat (1862), 121; and García Moreno government, 121, 155; and interpellation of Ponce, 170, 172; and Latin American political structures, 12–13; PCE and, 146, 155; support for conservatives, 23, 108, 121, 193–94, 204; and Velasco Ibarra government (1952–1956), 126–27
Central University (Quito), 166, 169, 173, 219, 222, 238
Cevallos, Luis, 52
Cevallos Cedeño, Joel, 165, 170, 173–74, 180
CFP (Concentración de Fuerzas Populares, Concentration of Popular Forces): and 5th PCE congress (1952), 137–38, 154; and 6th PCE congress (1957), 224–25; and 1952 elections, 121–22; and 1956 elections, 194, 247;

and 1960 elections, 246; and coup attempts, 116, 157; formation and early strength, 15–16; PCE on, 112, 115, 119, 121, 123, 158, 180; and Velasco Ibarra government (1952–1956), 123, 157, 166
Chaupi hacienda labor action (Pesillo, 1959), 239
Chávez, Fernando, 195
Chávez, Nelson, 170, 173
Chiang Kai-shek, 94
Chicago Manual of Style (17th edition), and capitalization of names, 252n9
Chiefs of Base (COB), 31
Chilean Line, 143
Chinese Communist Party, 94, 225
Chinese Nationalist Party (Kuomintang), 94
Chinese Revolution (1949), 87, 249; establishment of People's Republic of China, 94; international influence of, 93, 139; and PCE, 94–98, 108, 225; and Soviet Union, 185, 248
Chiriboga, Alfredo, 168
Chiriboga family, 12
Chiriboga Villagómez, José Ricardo: and 1952 elections, 115–17, 120–22; and 1956 elections, 194, 204; on PCE, 188, 238, 241; and Velasco Ibarra government (1952–1956), 126
Chung Jurado brothers, 139
CIA (Central Intelligence Agency): covert action in Ecuador, 2, 16, 65, 102–3, 132, 172, 176–79, 208–9; covert action in Guatemala, 22, 30; formation and organization of, 6, 30–33, 36, 96, 186–87, 207–9; surveillance procedures, 6–8, 28–29, 34–38, 69, 75, 83–86, 176–77, 185–88, 249–50, 264n22; surveillance reliability, 27–28, 34, 37–38, 52–53, 134, 138, 140–41, 205; surveillance value for scholars, 2–7, 25–27, 33, 129, 182–83, 205; as US covert action arm, 26–27, 65, 134, 185–88
CIG (Central Intelligence Group), 28, 35–37, 57. *See also* CIA (Central Intelligence Agency)
civil attaché, 36
Clark, James McAdam, 14–15
Cline, Ray, 27
Coello Serrano, Rafael, 15, 112
cold war: and CIA, 38, 96; and historians and media, 228, 234, 238; and Latin American politics, 3, 11–12, 19, 24, 105, 182–83, 192; study of, 7–9
Colegio Mejía (Quito), 148
Coleman, Francis Vincent, 161
Coloma, Enrique, 118
Combate, El (ARNE), 199–200
Comercio, El (Quito): on events of 1953, 160; on interpellation of Ponce, 167–68; as paper of record, 132, 223; on PCE, 66–67, 80, 132, 156, 220, 222–23, 237; on Velasco Ibarra government (1952–1956), 126; and War of the Worlds broadcast (Radio Quito, 1949), 1–2, 49–50
Cominform (Communist Information Bureau), 138–39, 146, 178
Comintern (Communist International), 8, 13, 18–19, 70
Comité de Defensa de la Democracia del Barrio de San Roque, 167
Communist Party, Section of the Communist International (Ecuador), 15
"Communist Party Activities" (CIG, 1947), *35*
Concordat (1862), 121. *See also* Catholic Church
conservatives. *See* PC (Partido Conservador, Conservative Party)
Constitution (1946), 44
Cordero Crespo, Gonzalo, 246
Córdova Moscosa, Wilson, 217
Corporación de Fomento, 59
Corral, Luz María, 98–103

COS (Chief of Station), 30–31
Costanzo, Joseph, 149, 193, 203
CPUSA (Communist Party USA), 220
CREST (CIA Records Search Tool) database, 7, 34, 205, 250
Crisol (PCE), 86
CTAL (Confederación de Trabajadores de América Latina, Confederation of Latin American Workers), 16, 78
CTE (Confederación de Trabajadores del Ecuador, Confederation of Ecuadorian Workers): American Federation of Labor and, 78; organization, 16; and PCE, 17, 88, 125, 179, 221, 226, 230; and popular protests, 235, 240, 245; and PSE, 125
Cuban Communist Party, 53, 90, 136, 236–37
Cuban Revolution (1959), 20, 185, 225, 232–35, 237, 244, 247–49, 252n11
Cueva Jaramillo, Mariano, 182
Cueva Jaramillo, Patricio, 146–47, 157, 162, 182
Cueva Tamariz, Carlos, 105, 108, 146, 182
Cullather, Nick, 258n21
Culley, Perry, 208
Czechoslovakia, 208–9
Czechoslovakia Today, 179

Daniels, Paul, 133
Darling, Arthur, 256n1
Daughters, Anton, 27
Daughters, Donald, 27
Dávalos, José María, 135, 152
Davis, Dusty, 253n19
Dearborn, Henry, 18
Decree 302 (1944), 174
"Democracy, Independence and Peace for the People of Ecuador" (PCE), 228–32
Democratic Alliance (ADN, Alianza Democrática Nacional), 115, 117–18, 120, 122, 125
democratic spring (Latin America, 1944–1954), 10–12, 21–22
Día, El (Quito), 2, 80
Díaz Granados, Manuel, 50, 66, 116, 118–20
Donnelly, Walter, 73
Donner, Frank, 258n19
Don Pepe (PCE), 65
Dulles, Allen, 30, 185
Dulles, John Foster, 186–87
Duncan, Brad, 5
Duque Arias, Pablo, 83, 215
Durán Ballén, Sixto, 14, 256n39
Durán Carrión, Corsino, 52
Durango, Augusto, 195
Durango López, Wilson, 158
Dustmann, Walter, 204, 227

earthquake (1949), 89–91
Echeverría, Rafael, 137, 142, 150–52, 157, 181, 248–49
Eisenhower administration: and assassinations and military coups, 3; and CIA covert action, 41, 65, 134, 250; and conservatives in Ecuador, 204; election of in 1952, 185
Eleventh Inter-American Conference, 199, 235–39, 244, 249
Ellis, Perry, 70, 74, 144
Endara, César, 76, 151
Enríquez Gallo, Alberto, 39–40, 44, 46, 105
Espejo Theater (Quito), 214–17, 219–20, 225
Espinosa Páez, Miguel, 217
Estrada family, 12
Evangelicals, 166, 170
Export-Import Bank (Eximbank), 111, 235

FAS (Foreign Agricultural Service), 32
fascism: ARNE and, 14; CFP and Guevara Moreno and, 112, 115, 119, 121, 123, 158, 180; PCE and, 18–19,

62, 72, 127, 179–80; Ponce Enríquez and, 203
Favero, Jared, 253n19
FBI (Federal Bureau of Investigation), 6, 28–32, 36, 40, 59, 176
FBI in Latin America, The (Becker), 3–4, 6
FDN (Frente Democrático Nacional, National Democratic Front), 13, 193–96, 199–201, 204–5, 216
Febrés Cordero, León, 256n39
FEI (Federación Ecuatoriana de Indios, Ecuadorian Federation of Indians), 16, 70, 140–41, 191. *See also* Indigenous peoples
Femme soviétique, La (Moscow), 178
feudalism, 22, 131, 199, 232, 242
FEUE (Federación de Estudiantes Universitarios del Ecuador, Federation of Ecuadorian University Students): and IUS, 16, 243; and La Industrial strike (1950), 99, 102; PCE and, 61, 211, 226, 230, 242, 245; and Velasco Ibarra government (1952–1956), 169
Finally Got the News (Duncan), 5
Fisher, William August (Rudolf Ivanovich Abel), 257n8
Flickinger, Su, 253n19
Flor, Zoila, 138
Flores, Eduardo, 166
Flor Torres, Manuel Elicio, 23, 39–40
For a Lasting Peace, For a People's Democracy (Cominform), 146, 178
Foreign Service List (Department of State), 186
"For Peace, Democracy, and Progress" (PCE, 1949), 86
FPTG (Federación Provincial de Trabajadores del Guayas, Provincial Federation of Workers of Guayas), 16, 74, 144, 161–62
Franco, Francisco, 88
Frank, Waldo, 73
Freedom of Information Act (FOIA) Electronic Reading Room, 7
French Communist Party, 74, 79
FTP (Federación de Trabajadores de Pichincha, Pichincha Workers Federation), 16, 99–100, 125, 132, 235, 245

Gaitán, Jorge Eliécer, 50, 167, 214, 237
Galarza Zavala, Jaime, 135, 148, 153–56, 244, 248
Galte hacienda massacre (Chimborazo, 1953), 190–91
Gálvez, Bolívar, 48
Gamble, F. Herbert, 189
Gangotena, Emilio, 82, 125
García Macías, José, 239
García Moreno, Gabriel, 12–13, 155
García Moreno, Juan Esteban, 107
Garrett, Colin, 253n19
gender relations, 66, 136, 190. *See also* women
Gerberich, Albert, 191
Gil Gilbert, Enrique, 40, 72–74, 135–36, 151–52, 161, 163–64, 220
Gilstrap, Comer Wiley, 186, 208
Gleijeses, Piero, 253n18
global sixties, 234
Gómez, Tirso, 152
Gómez de la Torre, María Luisa: and La Industrial strike (1950), 100, 102–3; and mail interception, 172, 176; and PCE finances, 57; and PCE handbill (1949), 76; and political dissension in PCE, 141, 148, 151–52, 157, 248–49
González, César Florencio, 99
González, Eduardo, 152
González Videla, Gabriel, 19, 107
Goya, Francisco, 162
Goya cell, 162
Grace Line, 143–44
"Gran Asamblea Popular Pro China Democrática" (PCE), *97*

Gran Concierto, El (movie), 67
Grandin, Greg, 7, 25
Granma (Cuba), 147
Grijalva, Guillermo, 165, 173–74
Guachalá hacienda massacre (Pichincha, 1953), 190–91, 202
Gualavisí, Jesús, 140, 152–53
Guayaquil city council, 59
Guayaquil dockworkers strike (1959), 238
Guayaquil protests (1959), 244–45
Guerrero, Isidro, 149
guerrilla activity, 52, 151, 233–34, 248, 278n45
Guerrilla Warfare (Guevara), 233
Guevara, Ernesto "Che," 233–34, 247
Guevara Moreno, Carlos: ARNE and, 43; and CFP, 15–16, 194, 247; and coup attempts, 43, 116, 119–20; expulsion from Ecuador, 165–67, 175; and PCE, 16, 43, 112, 115, 119, 121, 123, 143, 158, 180; and Velasco Ibarra, 15, 121–22
Guzmán, Miguel Angel, 245

Hamlin, John, 106, 116
Haney, Albert Richard, 28–30, 36–37, 40–41, 58, 69, 84–85, 96
Haney, Irene Budlong, 29
Hatter, Baylee, 253n19
Hernández Martínez, Maximiliano, 21
Herter, Christian, 209
Higdon, Charles, 130
Hispanic World Report (Stanford University), 48, 114, 124
hispanismo, 14
Historia del Partido Comunista de la URSS, 64
Holman, Ned, 186–87, 208, 285n52
Hoover, J. Edgar, 6, 28–29
Hora, La (Guayaquil), 120, 166, 169, 172–73, 175
Houk, Walter, 51, 81
Huerta, Raúl Clemente, 194–95, 200–202, 204, 216, 227
Hungarian uprising (1956), 184–85
Hurley, Sharon, 31

Ibáñez del Campo, Carlos, 125
Ibarra, Hernán, 4, 22, 62, 71, 231–32
ICA (International Cooperation Administration), 32
IMF (International Monetary Fund), 230
Indigenous peoples: FEI (Federación Ecuatoriana de Indios, Ecuadorian Federation of Indians), 16, 70, 140–41, 191; and PCE, 136, 140–41, 152–53, 164, 221, 228–30; terminology, 252n9
Inside the Company (Agee), 31, 138, 240
Inter-American Press Association, 166
interpellations: of Bustamante Pérez, 245–46; origin and use of term, 279n8; of Ponce Enríquez, 160, 163–76, 179–82
Intriago, J. Federico, 145, 164
Iron Curtain (1948), 65–67
Italy, 34
Iturralde Rivera, Vicente, 158
IUS (International Union of Students), 16, 137, 169, 211

Jaramillo, José, 227
Jaramillo, Víctor Alejandro, 235
Jaya, Ecuador (aka Manuel), 150
JCE (Juventud Comunista del Ecuador, Young Communists of Ecuador), 136–37, 145–47
JCF (Juventud Comunista Femenina, Young Communist Women), 136, 145. *See also* women
Jijón family, 12
Johnson, Chalmers, 28
Joliot-Curie, Frédéric, 178
Jones, George, 33, 208
Juridical Committees for the Defense of Western Democracy, 211

Karnis, Michael, 211
Karolys, Gonzalo, 118

Kent, Sherman, 28
Khrushchev, Nikita, 184–85, 210
Kofas, Jon, 52
Kuhns, Woodrow, 9

Labor Code (1938), 98
La Industrial strike (1950), 98–104
La Merced hacienda massacre (Pichincha, 1953), 166, 171, 173–74, 190–91, 202
Larrea Alba, Luis, 43, 46
Larrea Benalcazar, Hugo, 118
Larrea Jijón, Modesto, 117, 120–22
Lasso, Guillermo, 66
latifundia, 12–13. *See also* agrarian reform
Latner, Teishan, 253n14
Leatherman, Frederick, 242–43
legal attaché, 36
Lenin, Vladimir, 162
Lester, Allen, 84
Lewis, Kaitlin, 253n19
Liberal Revolution (1895), 13, 22, 121, 201–2
liberals. *See* PLR (Partido Liberal Radical, Radical Liberal Party)
Librería Ecuador, 166, 172, 174
Linke, Lilo, 15, 18, 124–26, 161
literacy, 13, 21, 23–24, 114, 246
Lombardo Toledano, Vicente, 36
Lovato, Juan Isaac, 49, 195, 216, 219, 227
Ludeña, Eduardo, 43
Luna Yepes, Jorge, 14

Macías Hurtado, Miguel, 166, 175
Maiguashca, Juan, 114
mail interception, 172, 176–79
Maldonado Estrada, Luis, 118
Maldonado Renella, Jorge, 146, 162
Mancheno, Carlos, 14, 45
Manosalvas, Juan, 44
Mantilla Mata, Jaime, 215
Mantilla Ortega, Carlos, 49–50
Mantilla Ortega, Jorge, 50
Maoist parties, 9, 139, 151
Mao Zedong, 94, 135, 139
Mariátegui, José Carlos, 213
Marks, John, 259n35
Márquez, Pompeyo, 82
Marshall, George, 72
Marshall Plan, 87, 176
Martínez, Nela: and Cuban Revolution, 225; and dissension in PCE, 142–43, 145–46, 148, 151–52, 156–57, 225, 248–49; and La Industrial strike (1950), 99–103; and mail interception, 177–78; and PCE in 1940s, 76, 79; and women's organizing and leadership, 93, 145–46
Marx, Karl, 20
Matthews, Herbert, 104–5, 119, 124
Mayers, Norman, 12, 18, 122, 172, 180–81, 188
May revolution (1944), 21, 88
MCDN (Movimiento Cívico Democrático Nacional, National Democratic Civic Movement), 14, 107, 115
McGarvey, Patrick, 34
McGehee, Ralph, 9, 134
McGinnis, Edgar, 123
McPherson, Alan, 7
Medina Castro, Manuel, 143–45, 150–51, 157, 177
Mendoza Avilés, Rafael, 15
Mera, Mentor, 65
Mériguet, Raymond, 52, 142, 148, 157
Miller, Austin, 253n19
Ministry of Economy, 46, 105, 164
Ministry of Education, 59, 61, 105–8, 126, 142, 146, 158, 182, 190
Miño, Reinaldo, 98
MIR (Movimiento de Izquierda Revolucionaria, Movement of the Revolutionary Left), 248
MNR (Movimiento Nacionalista Revolucionario, Revolutionary Nationalist Movement), 119, 125

Molestina, Raúl, 52
montuvios, 88, 196
Morales y Eloy, Juan, 155
Moreland, William, 70, 239, 241–42, 245
Morena, Roberto, 139, 144
Moreno, Ana, 46–48, 79, 143, 150, 157–58, 177
Moreno, Julio, 48
Morrison-Knudsen, 135
Moscow gold, 2, 54–55, 57, 59, 63, 68, 180
MSC (Movimiento Social Cristiano, Social Christian Movement), 14
Mujer Soviética, La (Moscow), 64
Muñoz, Olga, 136
Muñoz Vicuña, Elías, 73–74, 93, 210–11, 231
Musch, Cheryl, 253n19
Mussolini, Benito, 34

Nación, La (Guayaquil), 166, 169, 172–73, 175
Naranjo, Plutarco, 82
Narváez, Juan Pío, 148, 150, 157, 163
National Security Act of 1947, 6
NATO (North Atlantic Treaty Organization), 87
Navarro, César Humberto, 99
Neruda, Pablo, 135
new left, 185, 232
New Times (USSR), 178
New York Times: on 5th PCE congress (1952), 156; on 1952 elections, 121, 123–24; on Grace Line dispute, 144; on social and political upheaval in Ecuador and Latin America, 104–5, 119, 236–38, 243–44
Nicolalde, Hipatia, 99
Noland, James, 187, 208–9
Normal Juan Montalvo (Guaranda), 148–49
North, Liisa, 114
Nuestro pan (*Our Daily Bread,* Gil Gilbert), 72

OIR (Office of Intelligence Research), 17–18, 107, 123, 125–26
Oleas, Gonzalo, 83, 220–21, 227
Olmedo Muñoz, Julio, 164
Oña (cafe owner), 56
Operation PBSUCCESS, 30
Oramas, Marco Tulio, 152, 161, 163
Ortiz Aldas, Pedro, 62
OSA (Office of South American Affairs), 123, 203–5
Otavalo massacre (Lago San Pablo, 1959), 235

Pacheco León, Neptalí, 152–53
Páez, Leonardo, 49
Palomino, Pascual, 152
Paredes, Ricardo: and 4th PCE congress (1949), 81, 86; and 5th PCE congress (1952), 136, 138–43, 145, 148, 151–53, 156–57; and 6th PCE congress (1957), 220; and conflicts in PCE, 70–72, 81, 86, 111, 138–43, 145, 148, 151–53, 156–57, 220; and Indigenous movement, 70, 140–41, 164; international travel, 136–37, 176; and PCE formation and organization, 13, 62–63, 70–72, 93, 151, 164, 220; personal life, 70–71, 138
Paredes Martínez, Leonardo, 142
Parra Velasco, Antonio, 246
Pazmiño, Héctor, 150
Paz y Miño Cepeda, Juan, 287n31
PC (Partido Conservador, Conservative Party): and 5th PCE congress (1952), 131, 134; and 6th PCE congress (1957), 214–17, 220; and 1948 elections, 23; and 1952 elections, 23, 105–6, 108, 115–17, 120–23; and 1955 midterm elections, 193; and 1956 elections, 23, 184, 194, 201; and 1960 elections, 246; and 1984 and 1992 elections, 256n38; and Catholic Church, 23, 108, 121, 193–94, 204; founding of, 13–14; and interpellation of Ponce,

165, 168, 176; support in 1950s and 1960s, 14, 19, 22–24, 194–95; United States officials on, 204; and Velasco Ibarra government (1944–1947), 14; and Velasco Ibarra government (1952–1956), 126–27
PCC (Partido Comunista de Colombia, Communist Party of Colombia), 136, 140–41, 147, 149, 151, 236
PCE (Partido Comunista del Ecuador, Communist Party of Ecuador), 17; 4th congress (1949), 69, 78–92; 5th congress (1952), 129–59; 6th congress (1957), 207–32; and 1948 elections, 39–49; and 1952 elections, 110–15, 117, 122, 125; and 1955 elections, 193; and 1956 elections, 195; and 1960 elections, 246; and Afro-Ecuadorians, 136; and ARNE, 64, 137–38, 154; and bourgeois national development, 21, 87–89, 199; and Casa de la Cultura, 226; and CFP, 16, 112, 224–25, 246; and Chinese Revolution (1949), 108, 225, 248; coups and illegal activity, 2, 38, 43–48, 58, 86, 201; and Cuban Revolution (1959), 20, 237, 247–49; and earthquake (1949), 90–91, 111–12; and Eleventh Inter-American Conference, 236–39; and fascism, 18–19, 62, 72, 127, 179–80; and FEUE, 61, 211, 226, 230, 242, 245; formation, 13; in Guayaquil, 75, 161–64; and guerrilla actions, 52, 151, 278n45; and Indigenous peoples, 136, 140–41, 152–53, 164, 221, 228–30; internal dissent, 70–78, 81, 93–94, 108–9, 138–59, 173, 225, 232; and *Iron Curtain* movie disruption, 65–67; and June 1959 protests, 241–46; and Khrushchev revelations (1956), 210–11, 226; and La Industrial strike (1950), 98–104; mail interception, 65, 177–79; and military, 94–95; Moscow gold and control, 2, 54–59, 61, 63, 68, 80, 180, 215; organization, 17–18, 34–36, 54–68, 70, 76–78, 95–96, 162–64, 191–92, 207–8, 212–13; outlawing of, 157, 202, 211–12, 218, 247; and peaceful and parliamentary road to power, 17–18, 24, 38–41, 46, 86–89, 127–28, 151, 182, 196–99, 205, 247–49; and peasants, 2–3, 88, 136, 207–8; and Plaza Lasso, 38–49, 66, 90–91, 94, 105–6, 112–13, 230; and Ponce Enríquez, 165, 179–82, 201–3, 212; and popular fronts, 19–21, 86, 110, 113–15, 117, 216, 229; and PSE, 83; publications and distribution, 61–65, 74, 85, 166, 172, 174, 192, 224, 228; religion and religious groups, 146, 155, 170; on Rio de Janeiro Protocol (1942), 237; and Salazar Gómez, 116; and social movements, 20, 71, 109, 153, 185, 226, 232, 272n1; and social security system, 111; and Soviet Union, 154–55, 163, 225, 248; strength and influence, 17–21, 65, 74–75, 161, 188, 191, 203–6, 211, 226, 250; and Velasco Ibarra, 127, 142; and War of the Worlds broadcast (1949), 49–52; and women, 103, 136, 145–46
"PCE Finances" report by CIA, *60*
PCMLE (Partido Comunista Marxista Leninista del Ecuador, Marxist–Leninist Communist Party of Ecuador), 81, 151, 248
peaceful and parliamentary road to power: and Communist parties, 4, 10, 18, 211, 233–34; and PCE, 17–18, 24, 38–41, 46, 86–89, 127–28, 151, 182, 196–99, 205, 247–49
Pearson, Amatista, 253n19
Pedro Saad cell, 56
Peñaherrera, Alfredo, 144
Peñaherrera, Luis Antonio, 64–65, 126
People's Republic of China, 94. *See also* Chinese Revolution (1949)
Pérez, Simón, 162

Pérez Castro, Franklin, 62–63, 75, 79, 137, 148, 150–52, 157, 163, 166
Pérez Castro, Ismael, 63
Pérez Guerrero, Alfredo, 175, 219
Perón, Juan, 123–24, 137
Phillips, David Atlee, 31, 133, 258nn11, 21
Plaza family, 12
Plaza Gutiérrez, Leónidas, 22
Plaza Lasso, Galo: and 1948 elections, 14, 22; and 1952 elections, 105, 114–28; and 1960 elections, 246; and coup threats, 39, 104–6, 116, 120; and earthquake (1949), 90–91; government of and stability, 22, 24; and imperialism, 22, 107–8; and MCDN, 14; PCE and, 38–49, 66, 94, 105–6, 112–13, 230; and PLR, 14; PSE and, 94, 105–8, 246; US officials on, 106–8, 208
Plaza Lasso, José María, 195, 201
Plaza Monzón, César, 174
PLR (Partido Liberal Radical, Radical Liberal Party): and Liberal Revolution (1895), 13; and 1948 elections, 39; and 1952 elections, 115–17, 120–22, 126; and 1955 midterm elections, 193; and 1956 elections, 194, 196, 204; and 1960 elections, 246–47; coalitions with socialists and communists, 13; and Mancheno coup (1949), 45–47; and populist candidates, 14, 24
Point Four program, 143
Ponce Enríquez, Camilo, 14, 65; election and government (1956–1960), 22, 184, 194–206; and feudalism, 22; interpellation of, 160, 163–76, 179–82; and June 1959 protests, 239–41; and PCE, 165, 212, 218, 230, 236, 238–39; and Velasco Ibarra government (1944–1947), 189–91; and Velasco Ibarra government (1952–1956), 126
Popoca Estrada, Manuel, 51
Poppino, Rollie, 11–12
Popular Alliance coalition, 74–75
popular front, 18–21, 86, 107, 110, 114–15, 117, 229
populism, 13–16, 24, 110, 124–25, 127–28, 192, 247, 255n10
Por la defensa de la vida del pueblo: Manifiesto del Comité Central del Partido Comunista (1949), 76–78, *77*
Portoviejo protests (1959), 239, 245
¡Por una paz duradera, Por una democracia popular! (Cominform, Bucharest), 64
Por un gobierno democrático al servicio del pueblo; contra la reacción, los golpes de estado y el continuismo; programa electoral del Partido Comunista del Ecuador (PCE, 1956), *197*
Poveda, Bernardino, 164
Prados, John, 259nn35, 48
Prazhskie Novosti (Prague), 178
Prestes, Luís Carlos, 135
PSE (Partido Socialista Ecuatoriano): and 4th PCE congress (1949), 80–81; and 5th PCE congress (1952), 133; and 6th PCE congress (1957), 220–21, 223–24; and 1952 elections, 115–18, 122, 124–25; and 1960 elections, 246; formation and early history, 13, 70; and interpellation of Ponce, 165, 170, 173–74, 180; and *Iron Curtain* movie disruption, 67; *La Tierra,* 67, 80–81, 107, 133, 214, 223–24; and Plaza government, 82–83, 90–91, 94, 105–8, 118, 246; political dissension in, 82–83, 248; Riobamba regional congress (1957), 226–27; and Velasco Ibarra government (1944–1947), 142; and women, 136
PSRE (Partido Socialista Revolucionario del Ecuador, Socialist Revolutionary Party of Ecuador), 132, 248
Pueblo, El (PCE), 61–65, 74, 192, 224, 228
Puerto cell, 164

Quevedo, Antonio, 113
Quevedo, Galo, 239
Quevedo-Manta Road, 111, 135
Quijano Cobos, Alfonso, 62, 146, 164
Quintana (Colonel), 46
Quintana, Jorge, 99–100
Quito city council, 59

Radio Quito, 1–3, 49
Ramírez Gutiérrez, Gustavo, 52
Ramos, Segundo, 90–91, 139, 143–44, 148, 151–52, 157, 161, 240–41
Ravndal, Christian, 184, 209–10, 217, 220–21, 224–26
Realidad (PCE), 86
Record Group 59 (Department of State Central Decimal Files), 257n9
Record Group 84 (Records of Foreign Service Posts of the Department of State), 257n9
Red Cross, 90
red scare and redbaiting, 105, 199
Revolución Gloriosa (1944), 21, 88
Revolution of July 1925, 21
Revue Partisans de la Paix (World Peace Council), 103
Rio de Janeiro Protocol (1942), 88, 199, 237
Rio Treaty (1948), 87
Rivadeneyra, Jorge, 248
Rivera, Modesto, 140–42, 152, 157
Roca, Blas, 90, 136
Rojas, Angel F., 106
Romo-Leroux, Ketty, 52
Roosevelt, Franklin D., 6
Rositzke, Harry, 185, 240
Rossi Delgado, Ernesto, 146
Roura Cevallos, José María, 148–49, 152, 157, 200–201, 278n45
Rubottom, Roy, 208
Rumiñahui press (Quito), 56
Russian Revolution (1917), 93, 162. *See also* Soviet Union

Saad, Kalil, 36
Saad, Pedro: and 4th PCE congress (1949), 79–81, 86, 89; and 5th PCE congress (1952), 129, 132–35, 137–39, 142–43, 146–48, 150–53, 156–58; and 6th PCE congress (1957), 219–22, 224–28, 231–32; and 1949 coup attempt, 43–44, 46; and 1949 earthquake relief, 90–91, 132; and 1952 elections, 125; becomes PCE secretary general, 81, 93, 129, 150–52, 156, 158; and Bustamante Pérez, 245–46; and conflicts in PCE, 70, 81, 138–39, 142–43, 146–48, 150–51, 157–58, 220; international travel, 36, 55, 208, 225; interpellation of Ponce Enríquez (1953), 160, 165–76, 179–82; political approach of, 70–71, 80–81, 86, 89, 137, 153, 164–65, 222, 248; and War of the Worlds broadcast (Radio Quito, 1949), 51–52
Safadi, Elías, 158
Safadi, Fortunato, 79
SAIIC (South and Meso American Indian Rights Center), 252n9
Salazar Cortez, Tatiana, 225
Salazar Gómez, Eduardo, 58, 115–20, 154, 200, 211–12, 219, 287n38
Sánchez, Jaime, 186
Sancho Jaramillo, Neptalí, 131–32
Sandoval, Bolívar, 143, 157
San Pablo del Lago massacre (1960), 245
Santos, Abelardo, 164
Scotten, Robert, 142
Sebacher, Tom, 253n19
Second World Student Congress (Prague, 1950), 137
Segura, Nelson, 152
Serrano, Colón, 105–6
Shaw, George, 36
Shetterly, Howard, 133–34, 186
Shoulders, Chloe, 253n19
Simbaña, Floresmilo, 4

Simmons, John, 37, 48, 58, 66–67, 96, 131–32, 260n51
Sino-Soviet split, 185, 248–49
Smith, Harold, 111
Smugala, Kelsey, 253n19
Social Christians, 194
social movements: and PCE, 20, 71, 109, 153, 185, 226, 232, 272n1; and political organizing, 11–18, 114; and populism, 110; study of, 2, 4–8. See also *specific organizations*
Sol, El (Quito), 106
Somoza García, Anastasio, 22, 87, 244
Sotomayor y Luna, Manuel, 105
Soviet Union, 249; and China, 185, 248; Khrushchev revelations (1956), 184–85, 210, 226; Moscow gold, 2, 54–55, 57, 59, 63, 68, 180; and PCE, 10, 80, 88, 154–55, 162–63, 215, 225, 248; Russian Revolution (1917), 93, 162
Sowell, Benjamin, 18, 66–67
Spanish names, 254n7
Stalin, Joseph, 135, 162, 184–85
Standard Oil, 230
State Department, 30, 32, 186, 209, 257n9
Stockwell, John, 31
Stroessner, Alfredo, 238, 244
Suárez (Colombian communist), 140
Suárez Veintimilla, Mariano, 194, 256n39
Szulc, Tad, 243–44

Tamayo, José Luis, 21
Tamayo, Oswaldo, 195
Telégrafo, El (Guayaquil), 237
Third World Youth Festival for Peace (Berlin, 1951), 107
TIAR (Tratado Interamericano de Asistencia Recíproca, Inter-American Treaty of Reciprocal Assistance, 1948), 87
Tiempos Nuevos (Moscow), 64
Tierra, La (PSE), 67, 80–81, 107, 133, 214, 223–24
Tigua agrarian cooperative, 56
Toachi River guerrilla uprising (1962), 248
"Towards a Democratic Front for National Liberation" (PCE, 1952), 130
Tribunal de Garantías Constitucionales (tribunal of constitutional guarantees), 72
Trotsky, Leon, 9, 109, 163
Troy, Thomas, 256n1
Trujillo, José Vicente, 126
Trujillo, Rafael, 3, 87, 237, 244
Truman administration, 87, 143
Tucker, Taylor, 253n19

Ubico, Jorge, 22
UDNA (Unión Democrática Nacional Anti-Conservadora, National Democratic Anti-Conservative Union), 246
UDU (Unión Democrática Universitaria, University Democratic Union), 166, 169
Unión Soviética (Moscow), 64
United Fruit Company, 230
United States government: covert action in Cuba, 3; covert action in Ecuador, 16, 187, 204, 211–12. *See also* CIA (Central Intelligence Agency)
Universo, El (Quito), 63, 148
UPR (Unión Popular Republicana, Republican Popular Union), 15
URJE (Unión Revolucionaria de la Juventud Ecuatoriana, Revolutionary Union of the Ecuadorian Youth), 153, 248
URME (Unión Revolucionaria de Mujeres del Ecuador, Revolutionary Union of Ecuadorian Women), 248. *See also* women
USAID (United States Agency for International Development), 32
USIA (United States Information Agency), 32, 187, 192

USIS (United States Information Service), 187, 204
USOM (United States Operations Mission), 32

Vacas Gómez, Humberto, 173
Valdano Raffo, Nicolás, 15
Valencia, Aquiles, 135, 152
Valverde, Cesario, 143–44, 157, 163
Vargas, Getulio, 124
Vargas, Luis, 187
Veintimilla, Mario, 182
Velasco Alvarado, Juan, 252n9
Velasco Ibarra, José María: ARNE and, 15; and Baquero de la Calle, 214; and CFP, 166; government (1944–1947), 44, 119, 121; government (1952–1956), 22, 110, 114–29, 188–89; government (1960–1961), 23, 208, 246–47; and Guevara Moreno, 165–66; and Lasso Plaza, 22; and oligarchy, 22; PCE on, 137, 230; and Peronist government, 123–24; and populism, 14, 192
Velasquista movement, 13, 122, 156, 193
Venceremos Brigade, 253n14
Vera, Alfredo: and 5th PCE congress (1952), 135, 142–45, 148, 150–52, 157, 164; and 1949 coup attempt against Plaza Lasso, 46–47; expulsion from PCE, 158
Vera, Pedro Jorge, 245
Vieira White, Gilberto, 177
Villacreses, José, 152
Villagómez Yepes, Jorge, 126
Villalba, Gonzalo, 127
VM (Vencer o Morir, Win or Die), 248
voting rights, 21, 24, 114, 194, 205, 230
VRSE (Vanguardia Revolucionaria del Socialismo Ecuatoriano, Ecuadorian Revolutionary Socialist Vanguard), 13, 43–44, 107, 115, 117

Walker, Meghan, 253n19
War of the Worlds, The (Wells), 1
War of the Worlds broadcast (Mercury Theatre on the Air, 1938), 1, 49
War of the Worlds broadcast (Radio Quito, 1949), 1–3, 39, 49–52, 260n51
Weatherwax, Robert, 31–32
Weiner, Tim, 29–30
Welles, Orson, 1, 49
Wells, H. G., 1
WFTU (World Federation of Trade Unions), 16, 208, 215
Wheeler, Richard, 31
Wieland, William, 186–87, 193–94
Williams, Albert Rhys, 108
Winkeler, Artemis, 253n19
Witting Shipyard strike (1952), 161–62
women: AFE, 16, 100; in CIA, 31; and communists and socialists, 103, 136, 145–46; gender relations, 66, 136, 190; URME, 248; and voting, 24, 194
World Federation of Democratic Youth (WFDY), 146
World Festival of Youth and Students: 3rd (Berlin, 1951), 59, 146; 6th (Moscow, 1957), 147, 187, 208
World Peace Congress (Beijing, 1952), 170
World Peace Congress (Paris, 1949), 177
World Student News, The, 179
World War II, 21–22
WPC (World Peace Council), 90, 103, 177–78

Ycaza family, 12

Zúñiga, Víctor, 221

www.ingramcontent.com/pod-product-compliance
Lightning Source LLC
Chambersburg PA
CBHW071731270326
41928CB00013B/2631
* 9 7 8 1 4 7 8 0 1 1 3 8 5 *